THE GLOBAL FIGHT AGAINST LGBTI RIGHTS

LGBTQ POLITICS SERIES

General Editors: Susan Burgess and Heath Fogg Davis

LGBTQ Politics: A Critical Reader
Edited by Marla Brettschneider, Susan Burgess, and Christine Keating

Beyond Trans: Does Gender Matter?
Heath Fogg Davis

Disrupting Dignity: Rethinking Power and Progress in LGBTQ Lives
Stephen M. Engel and Timothy S. Lyle

With Honor and Integrity: Transgender Troops in Their Own Words
Edited by Máel Embser-Herbert and Bree Fram

LGBT Inclusion in American Life: Pop Culture, Political Imagination, and Civil Rights
Susan Burgess

The Politics of "Perverts": The Political Attitudes and Actions of Non-Traditional Sexual Minorities
Charles Anthony Smith, Shawn R. Schulenberg, and Connor B. S. Strobel

The Global Fight Against LGBTI Rights: How Transnational Conservative Networks Target Sexual and Gender Minorities
Phillip M. Ayoub and Kristina Stoeckl

The Global Fight Against LGBTI Rights

How Transnational Conservative Networks Target Sexual and Gender Minorities

Phillip M. Ayoub *and* Kristina Stoeckl

NEW YORK UNIVERSITY PRESS
New York

NEW YORK UNIVERSITY PRESS
New York
www.nyupress.org

© 2024 by New York University
All rights reserved

Library of Congress Cataloging-in-Publication Data
Names: Ayoub, Phillip, 1983– author. | Stoeckl, Kristina, author.
Title: The global fight against LGBTI rights : how transnational conservative networks
  target sexual and gender minorities / Phillip M. Ayoub and Kristina Stoeckl.
Description: New York : New York University Press, [2024] | Series: LGBTQ politics |
  Includes bibliographical references and index.
Identifiers: LCCN 2023029944 (print) | LCCN 2023029945 (ebook) | ISBN 9781479824793
  (hardback ; alk. paper) | ISBN 9781479824809 (paperback) | ISBN 9781479824816 (ebook) |
  ISBN 9781479824830 (ebook other)
Subjects: LCSH: Homophobia—Political aspects. | Sexual minorities—Civil rights. |
  Conservatism. | Discrimination.
Classification: LCC HQ76.4 .A96 2024 (print) | LCC HQ76.4 (ebook) |
  DDC 306.76/6—dc23/eng/20230830
LC record available at https://lccn.loc.gov/2023029944
LC ebook record available at https://lccn.loc.gov/2023029945

This book is printed on acid-free paper, and its binding materials are chosen for strength
and durability. We strive to use environmentally responsible suppliers and materials
to the greatest extent possible in publishing our books.

Manufactured in the United States of America

10 9 8 7 6 5 4 3 2 1

Also available as an ebook

CONTENTS

Abbreviations	vii
Introduction: Theorizing LGBTI Rights Resistance	1
PART I: RIVAL NETWORKS	
1. Achievements: The Diffusion of LGBTI Rights	35
2. Resistances: The Opposition to LGBTI Rights	57
PART II: THE ACTORS	
3. Transnational Advocacy Networks: Nodal Organizations	95
4. States and International Organizations: Hungary, Russia, the Vatican, and the Russian Orthodox Church	134
PART III: STRATEGIES, CLAIMS, AND VENUES	
5. Strategies and Claims: The Moral Conservative Narrative	173
6. Venues: The United Nations, Council of Europe, and International Academia	205
PART IV: RESPONSES	
7. Movement Interaction: LGBTI Rejoinders to Global Resistances	233
Conclusion: Gender, Sexuality, and International Politics	257
Acknowledgments	275
Appendix	281
Notes	287
References	301
Index	341
About the Authors	361

ABBREVIATIONS

ADF Alliance Defending Freedom
ASEAN Association of Southeast Asian Nations
CEE Central and Eastern Europe
C-FAM Center for Family and Human Rights
CHE Campaign for Homosexual Equality
CIDH Commission interaméricaine des droits de l'homme, Inter-American Commission on Human Rights
CLGRC Canadian Lesbian and Gay Rights Coalition
COC Cultuur en Ontspanningscentrum, Center for Culture and Leisure
COE Council of Europe
COVID-19 The novel coronavirus disease that spread worldwide beginning in late 2019
CRIN Child Rights International Network
ECTHR European Court of Human Rights
ECLJ European Center for Law and Justice
ECOSOC UN Economic and Social Council
ENAR European Network against Racism
ERC European Research Council
EU European Union
EWL European Women's Lobby
FACH Foundation for African Cultural Heritage
FAGC Front d'alliberament gai de Catalunya, Catalan Front for Gay Liberation
FARC Fuerzas Armadas Revolucionarias de Colombia, Revolutionary Armed Forces of Colombia
FHAR Front homosexuel d'áction révolutionnaire, Homosexual Front for Revolutionary Action
FIFA Federation Internationale de Football Association
FUORI! "OUT!"

viii | ABBREVIATIONS

FWH Federation of Working Groups on Homosexuality
GHEX Global Home Education Exchange
GLF Gay Liberation Front
HOSI Homosexuelle initiative, Homosexual Initiative
HSLDA Homeschool Legal Defense Association
IASD International Agency for Sovereign Development
ICSE International Committee for Sexual Equality
IDAHOBIT International Day against Homo-, Bi-, and Transphobia
IGO International Governmental Organizations
ILGA International Lesbian, Gay, Bisexual, Trans, and Intersex Association
ILGA-EUROPE International Lesbian, Gay, Bisexual, Trans, and Intersex Association of Europe
INGO International Nongovernmental Organization
IO International Organization
IOF International Organization for the Family
IR International Relations
KPH Kampania Przeciw Homofobii, Polish Campaign against Homophobia
LBL/F-48 Landsforeningen for Bøsser og Lesbiske/Forbundet af 1948, Danish National Association of Gays and Lesbians/The Association of 1948
LDS CHURCH Church of Jesus Christ of Latter-day Saints
LGBTI Lesbian, Gay, Bisexual, Transgender, and Intersex
LGBTIQ Lesbian, Gay, Bisexual, Transgender, Intersex, and Queer
LSVD Lesben- und Schwulenverband in Deutschland, Lesbian and Gay Federation in Germany
MCC MATHIAS CORVINUS COLLEGIUM
MEP Member of the European Parliament
MP Member of Parliament
NATO North Atlantic Treaty Organization
NELFA Network of European LGBTIQ* Families Associations
NGO Nongovernmental Organization
NGTF National LGBTQ Task Force
NIGRA Northern Ireland Gay Rights Association

OAS	Organization of American States
OII	Organisation Intersex International
OSCE	Organization for Security and Cooperation in Europe
OSF	Open Society Foundations
PACE	Parliamentary Assembly of the Council of Europe
PIRC	Public Interest Research Center
PMC	Politicized Moral Conservative or Politicized Moral Conservatism
PNV	Political Network for Values
POSEC	Postsecular Conflicts
RFSL	Riksförbundet för sexuellt likaberättigande, Swedish National Organization for Sexual Equality
ROC	Russian Orthodox Church
SHRG	Scottish Homosexual Rights Group
SOGI	Sexual Orientation and Gender Identity
TAN	Transnational Advocacy Network
TERF	Trans-Exclusionary Radical Feminist
TGEU	Transgender Europe
UK	United Kingdom
UN	United Nations
US	United States
WCF	World Congress of Families
WFPC	World Family Policy Center
YP	Yogyakarta Principles

.

Introduction

Theorizing LGBTI Rights Resistance

Holding the floor in a conference room, drenched by the Cyprus afternoon sun, an activist resolutely proclaimed, "*We* are the family values campaign!" Delivered to a room full of organizers nodding heads and scribbling notes, this speech headlined the October 2016 Reclaiming Family Values event in Cyprus's capital of Nicosia. From the conference title, readers might assume the event centered on the "traditional values" politics that gender scholars have become increasingly familiar with and suspicious of in recent years. But it did not. The room was crowded with advocates who work on lesbian, gay, bisexual, transgender, intersex, and queer (LGBTIQ) activism in dozens of countries. The activist speaking was referring to lessons from Ireland's Yes Campaign, which had led to the introduction of marriage equality by a landslide popular vote (62 percent in favor) a year earlier—a once unimaginable success in the small Catholic island nation.

Yet undercutting the jubilation over the movement's landmark achievements was a palpable note of apprehension. The reporters in attendance would write about the week of events using words like "backlash," "retrenchment," and "resistance." The speaker herself identified a precise opposition, arguing for the need to "speak their language to take the wind from their sails." Indeed, using language like "family values," these LGBTIQ activists mimicked the catchphrases of events commonly organized for very different ends. And while leading voices insisted that participants not lose sight of the most important message for the outside world—that "LGBTI rights are making rapid progress"—the hopefulness in the room was imbued with concern. Organizers aimed to address a looming global threat composed of powerful actors—all too familiar in domestic organizing—that increasingly targeted LGBTI rights work at the international venues that had contributed to these actors' successes.

The trepidation that the Cyprus organizers were sensing was justified. One of us (Ayoub) was invited to observe the gathering as a scholar, looking at patterns on the diffusion of LGBTI rights. That same month, he also received an invitation from a colleague to travel to the University of Los Andes in Bogotá, Colombia. The Fuerzas Armadas Revolucionarias de Colombia (FARC) peace deal had just failed passage in a popular vote, a failure driven by an intense opposition from citizens swayed by a discourse of "ideología de género" (gender ideology) that targeted women and LGBTIQ minorities.[1] By the time Ayoub made it to Bogotá, just three weeks after that sunny afternoon in Nicosia, Donald Trump had been elected president of the United States, having pandered to the cultural warriors who had defined the US-based Christian Right and shaped its global counterparts in recent decades.

This same year, the other one of us (Stoeckl) was at a very different conference in Tbilisi, Georgia, organized by the World Congress of Families. There too, one could hear an impassioned discourse around family values, but the goals were wildly different. The congress had been scheduled to coincide with May 17, which many of us know as the International Day against Homo-, Bi-, and Transphobia (IDAHOBIT)—but in Georgia, by decree of the Patriarch Ilia of the Georgian Orthodox Church, it was "Family Day." May 17, 2016, was also the fourth anniversary of the brutal attack by an extremist mob, led by Orthodox priests, against the first Pride parade that local LGBTIQ activists had attempted. As Family Day participants started to arrive at Tbilisi's Radisson Hotel, the international guests—from Russia, Italy, Spain, the United States, and Germany—greeted each other warmly like old acquaintances. Georgian journalists, photographers, and TV crews mingled with the crowd in order to procure interviews and soundbites from the foreign speakers. The first to be interviewed was a Polish participant, who looked into the camera and said that Europe was the source of a militant secularism that sought to destroy religion. He went on to say that Poland was actively resisting this threat, just as it had resisted communism in decades past. The next speaker was a Frenchman, who explained that he was the father of seven children before continuing that his country was an example for how the "gay lobby" was conquering Europe. "Despite the resistance of the majority of our population, the government legalized gay marriage," he exclaimed. "My dear Georgian friends! Resist the gay agenda that wants to destroy your families."

The promotion of family values, religious freedom, and religious conformity dominate contemporary discourses on the world stage. And while LGBTI rights acceptance is on the rise in many states (as evidenced by both legal recognition and societal approval), political resistance to gender- and sexuality-based rights also continues to circulate actively. From Vladimir Putin's commitment to defend states from what he calls a "*Gay*-European" threat (Shevtsova 2020) to the campaign opposing the Colombian FARC peace accord on the basis of its "gender ideology," LGBTIQ advocates have been confronted with a coordinated global opposition. This book focuses on these global resistances to advances in rights for people who are marginalized by their sexual orientation and gender identity (SOGI).[2] It is also, at its core, about how LGBTIQ people have organized and responded to a long history of such resistances at various levels—local, national, and, increasingly, global.

Situating Resistance to SOGI Rights in World Politics

In the last thirty years, the rights of people who are marginalized by their sexual orientation and gender identity have improved rapidly in many countries. The principles of equality and nondiscrimination have led to transformative achievements, like the recognition of same-sex unions in most of the Western world (Kollman and Waites 2009; Paternotte and Kollman 2013), which in many countries follows the decriminalization of homosexuality in earlier decades (Frank, Camp, and Boutcher 2010).[3] Public opinion scholars have also charted previously unimaginable improvements in societal attitudes toward LGBTIQ—though mainly lesbian and gay—populations (Turnbull-Dugarte 2020; Hadler 2012; Adamczyk 2017; Ayoub and Garretson 2017). For the most part, these achievements can be traced back to a "velvet triangle" (Woodward 2004; Lang 2014) involving the transnational mobilization of the SOGI rights movement, the actions of progressive governments in a few pioneering countries, and advances in the human rights frameworks of some international governmental organizations (Ayoub 2016). Much as Kathryn Sikkink suggested in her seminal work on boomerang (Keck and Sikkink 1998) and spiral models (Risse, Ropp, and Sikkink 2013), transnational politics connect the local and the global on SOGI rights (Chase 2016). And this transnational effort has had verifiable effects,

4 | INTRODUCTION

to the extent that scholars refer to developments in SOGI rights as an "example of unexpected and transformative social change on a global scale" (Ayoub 2018, 79), with some going so far as to describe a world "won" for some LGBTIQ people (Weeks 2007).

Yet such successes have not gone unchallenged. The global accomplishments in the field of SOGI rights have been counterbalanced by a growing and, in recent years, increasingly globally connected resistance to such rights. According to Jessica Stern, the US special envoy to Advance the Human Rights of LGBTI Persons, the backlash, "swift [, . . .] violent[, and . . .] far reaching . . . is coming from those who have power and want to hold on to it" (Stern 2022). In 2021, Hungary's parliament passed a ban on so-called gay propaganda[4] following the Russian blueprint of the previous decade, and in Ghana, twenty-one people were arrested for attending a training on SOGI rights organized for paralegals, echoing similar arrests in Egypt following a Marshrou' Leila[5] rock concert some years earlier. While resistance to SOGI rights is well documented in the literature (Fetner 2008; O'Dwyer 2018), its global and networked dimensions are not yet fully understood.[6] Especially in the last decade, this resistance rests predominantly in the hands of transnationally connected social movements—frequently with a conservative religious orientation—and conservative governments, actors that now also attempt to co-opt international human rights law, for example, by rewriting or reinterpreting it (Bob 2019; Burack 2018; de Búrca and Young 2023). We argue that these resistances, which often mirror the boomerang and spiral models of human rights diffusion, employ many of the same transnational tools that have achieved widespread acceptance for LGBTIQ people. In other words, both those who seek the advancement of SOGI rights and those who oppose it use related strategies and instruments for mutually exclusive ends. Theoretically, this means we must take into account contestation at all levels (international and domestic) when theorizing the boomerang and spiral process of norm diffusion. Doing so requires reconceiving that spiral process more as a double helix, with competing Transnational Advocacy Networks (TANs) operating simultaneously. As the double helix metaphor suggests, rival TANs have a reciprocal relationship, having to navigate each other's presence in an interactive space at all levels—not just in the varied domestic contexts of target countries.

Given that SOGI TANs are the subject of extensive work, a second aim is to elucidate processes of organizing on the resisting side. A novelty of our work is also its direct access to key players in the anti-SOGI movement. We show that these resistances are plural, building on a long history of what we call politicized moral conservative (PMC) ideas and institutional infrastructure that unite ideologically incongruent and geographically scattered actors around prevailing perceived threats such as communism, demographic decline, nativist panic, and secularism. All these threats intersect directly with gender, in that they are almost always intertwined with a panic around the destabilization of masculinity and femininity and with challenges to patriarchy and concepts of the nation.[7] Within this broader moral conservative program, gender and sexuality have become lightning rod issues, as they have in many contemporary political debates, with women's and SOGI rights strategically identified as *the* focal political targets. Homo- and transphobia are thus not just an effect of such movements but a tool for constructing and galvanizing political opposition.[8] Transnational moral conservative movements repurpose SOGI rights to create global political divisions—mirroring (while simultaneously complicating) older debates like that over capitalism versus communism or West versus East. For example, many moral conservatives associate anti-"genderism" with anti-capitalism, depicting SOGI rights as the moral agenda of a cosmopolitan and urban elite that threatens local economies, an association with capitalism (especially as it relates to finance) that generates new and weighty consequences for left organizing (Graff and Korolczuk 2022, 12). The central place of sexuality and gender in geopolitics is important for international relations scholarship to recognize. We highlight this pattern of repackaging old fault lines in new ways and emphasize the challenges that this creates for gender justice and SOGI rights movements, which are not free to forge a new political landscape on their own terms but are instead brought into a simplified—and to some extent bygone—terrain of confrontation.

Puzzles

The transformation toward an increasingly globally coordinated resistance to SOGI rights has taken some observers by surprise, despite it being in line with a growing and important literature that has shone a light on the complicated and contested nature of human rights promotion. It is a puzzle for social scientists for many reasons, including four points we highlight here. First, the field of constructivist research achieved its footing in international relations through research that often portrayed transnational organizing as the domain of progressive movements, overshadowing the reality that the same channels are available to all sorts of identity-based movements (Landolt 2004). To be sure, studies of the last decade have complicated that portrayal. International relations scholars, studying a variety of domains from Roma rights to anti-feminism, have introduced a panoply of concepts that recognize this tension, including norm contestation (Deitelhoff and Zimmermann 2019), norm spoiling and proxy wars (Sanders 2018), rhetorical adaptation (Dixon 2017), norm antipreneurship (Bloomfield and Scott 2017), norm evasion (Búzás 2021) and norm polarization (Symons and Altman 2015). Also for SOGI rights, an opposing movement that uses several of the same transnational tools, but for different ends, challenges our conceptual models of rights diffusion and social change.

Second, a general optimism around postmaterial modernity and cosmopolitan secularism (Inglehart and Norris 2003) has clearly been overshadowed by the grip of traditional values around religious and national identities in contemporary politics (Byrnes and Katzenstein 2006). Opponents of secular modernity are well-organized and persistent, to a degree that was overlooked in our fields two decades ago, and that we must understand to fully unpack the polarized (non)spread of SOGI rights (Symons and Altman 2015). While the field has begun to grapple with these the two above puzzles, the ones that follow remain especially important.

Third, recognizing international cooperation in the multiple resistances to SOGI rights has been complicated by the knowledge that *nationalism*—typically antithetical to *transnationalism*—has constituted such a formidable and universal barrier to the advancement of SOGI rights across contexts in the past (Ayoub 2014). Histories of opposition in many states were rooted in nativism, emphasizing the need to maintain local national traditions due to their perceived superiority over those of other nations. In recent years, these self-proclaimed "defenders of the nation" have actively worked across borders to peddle the narrative of a SOGI threat. This is the paradox of the moral conservative movement: it relies on claims of resistance that are rooted in specific contexts around a language of national sovereignty, but it simultaneously deploys globally via transnational cooperation.

Fourth, while moral conservatives consider the secularism of SOGI rights a threat, it is important to remember that not long ago they also saw religious freedom and the idea of equality of faiths as threats. Just like nationalists, religious traditionalists tend to be convinced of the superiority of their own faith and do not easily connect across denominations (FitzGerald 2004, 33). The "conservative ecumenism" (Shishkov 2017) of the religious anti-gender movement, which spans Catholic, Orthodox, Protestant, and Evangelical believers and also can strategically include Muslims and Jewish groups, therefore came as a surprise for many sociologists of religion.[9] It transcends historical doctrinal divides between different faiths by identifying and framing issues such as abortion, divorce, or SOGI rights not in terms of religious injunctions, but as moral, legal, and social problems.

This book addresses these puzzles by exploring how the conservative transnational movement functions, in terms of who composes it and how its agenda is constructed. We seek to explain key actors, claims, and venues of global resistances to SOGI and SOGI-adjacent rights. Furthermore, as moral conservative transnational advocacy networks play an increasingly important role in contemporary world politics, SOGI rights advocates are forced into patterns of action that sometimes mirror their self-described countermobilization. There are rival transnational advocacy networks in world politics, in this case, one championing SOGI rights and a moral conservative one that seeks to undermine the former's accomplishments. Part 1 of this book covers this topic, part 2 sketches the varied actors that compose the transnational moral conservative movement, and part 3 outlines the claims and strategies the moral conservative movement deploys. Part 4 looks at the responses of the SOGI movement to their opposition, and the conclusion summarizes the findings and discusses the project's contributions to international relations and gender studies. We preview each of these parts below.

Rival Transnational Advocacy Networks

The existence and powerful impact of both pro- and anti-SOGI-rights TANs is now established in the literature. Kristopher Velasco (2018, 2023a 2023b) has done the most systematic empirical work in this domain, and his recent body of work justifies our own endeavor in several ways, especially as it concerns tracing the origin stories of, and interaction between, these networks. His large-scale data collection charts both the contraction and expansion of SOGI rights, and the indisputable reality that countries in the international system are influenced by both pro- and anti-SOGI rights TANs. Having established that both movements circulate in world politics, Velasco codes the proliferation and presence of each and uses rigorous quantitative methods to demonstrate their effects on state policies. He compellingly shows that, especially since the mid-2000s, resistances to SOGI rights have emerged and expanded significantly on a global scale, and that their emergence and operation in a state coincides with that state's likelihood of defying the liberal norms of SOGI rights adoption. The reverse is true if a state is more embedded in a pro-SOGI rights TAN, in which case compliance will be more likely (Velasco 2023a, 2023b). The power such conservative resistances wield is considerable.

That said, we know that resistance to SOGI rights does not always lead to success in the long run. For example, Tina Fetner (2008) has shown how lesbian and gay activists in the United States decided they needed marriage equality only *after* the religious right told them they could not have it (see also Dorf and Tarrow 2014). And they accomplished it there eventually (at the federal level in 2015 via *Obergefell v. Hodges*), even if the path there was rocky and uneven. Although the opposition is well-funded and organized, their strategies have often backfired, instead galvanizing and emboldening SOGI rights advocates in various contexts (O'Dwyer 2018; Flores and Barclay 2016; Bishin et al. 2021). In sum, to understand the growing contestation of liberal norms in the world order (Bettiza and Lewis 2020), we must attempt to understand both pro- and anti-SOGI networks and their interaction. In this book, we trace back the historical antecedents of the global resistance's emergence, asking where it came from and how it operates in contemporary world politics.[10] We provide the origin story of its global rise and describe the shifting terrain of maneuver that its presence creates for contemporary SOGI rights movements.

Understanding the interaction between the two networks is also important for theorizing in international relations (IR). Moral conservatives construe SOGI rights as a threat by presenting them as antithetical to traditions of both national and religious identity (Ayoub 2014) and by rooting them in a demographic and gender panic that is said to destabilize masculinity and the moral order (Sauer 2020; Möser, Ramme, and Takács 2022). We trace the norm entrepreneurship and transnational networks through which such arguments have taken hold. To do so, we start from the observation that the movements for and against SOGI rights interact at both international and domestic levels. In a formation that we argue resembles a double helix, the frames and strategies of one TAN are reciprocal to those of the rival TAN. They operate in a shared political space across multiple levels from domestic to international. Interaction and reciprocity (at *multiple* levels) reshape the very claims that TANs make and the demands they place on states. To be clear, we use the double helix metaphor loosely, not as an attempt to bring biology to the socially constructed world we analyze, but rather to illustrate—for IR theory—two side-by-side "spirals" that do not operate in isolation. We do not argue that the two strands hang together for their mutual existence, like those of DNA. Indeed, it is precisely the figure of the geometrical helix (instead of a *double-* or *parallel-spiral*) that is productive because it gives us a third dimension: a helix has depth, illustrating the space for interaction between each spiral, despite the fact that the spirals in our story work against each other.

This has implications for the spiral model of human rights, which scholars use to predict an evolution of positive changes in internationalization and compliance as a result of pressure from a combination of domestic actors, TANs, and other supportive states (Risse and Sikkink 1999; Risse, Ropp, and Sikkink 2013). The presence of two rival TANs complicates the spiral model's five phases, which typically theorize only one TAN in the global space. Furthermore, the notion of international progress and domestic backlash is folded in throughout the model, beginning with the idea that the initial repression toward social change occurs in the domestic sphere. During that phase, the state will dismiss local advocacy groups and subsequently influence responses from allied progressive international groups. A similar pattern follows, including *denial*, in which a state claims sovereignty to throw out the international groups' demands, leading local advocates to seek transnational and international support. *Tactical concessions* come next, when a state makes concessions to local, transnational, or international groups, opening a domestic discourse around the rights in question, followed by *prescriptive status*, in which rights gain standing, with a state "talking the talk" and introducing institutional change. The final phase is *rule consistent behavior*, in which a state's practices conform to the international norms that govern the rights in question, which become taken for granted. The presence of rival networks that share this transnational space—which prompts us to transform the spiral into a double helix—means the original cycle, in which rights are "formalized in the institutions of government and are recognized as habitual practices domestically and internationally" (Shahid and Yerbury 2014, 284; Risse and Sikkink 1999, 32), is at least partly destabilized. Instead, in a double helix model, we should first expect norm polarization with different outcomes in different domestic contexts, given that different TANs may have more or less purchase in any given state. Symons and Altman (2015) predict this, and Velasco (2023a; 2023b) demonstrates it. Second, we should also anticipate that the very content of human rights claims is reshaped in this reciprocal dance of framing and counterframing claims between TANs at the international level. This explains why, for example, the SOGI rights movement relies more on "family values" frames today than it has in the past (chapter 7), as well as why religious conservatism prioritizes resistance to SOGI rights even in contexts where LGBTI achievements are not on the horizon. We develop the double helix model further in chapter 1.

In many ways, moral conservative opposition thus mimics—or "mirrors," to borrow a term from Agnes Chetaille (2015)[11]—the successes of LGBTIQ movements for SOGI rights. For decades, due to shared experiences that defined their minority identity and uniform exclusion from the nation in most states, sexual and gender minorities sought out international venues to influence and diffuse their claims for rights (chapter 1). Moral conservative actors—despite not having a shared experience of their own—have increasingly borrowed[12] these strategies of transnational cooperation and are also forming them anew. The more they have done so, more the spiral model of SOGI rights promotion has shifted into this new double helix process. Deploying a moral conservative background narrative (presented below) to construct an imagined past that binds the people they represent together, moral conservatives are seeking new venues to push their agenda. They also borrow the language of progressive movements, weaponizing the rhetoric of women's rights pioneers, Martin Luther King, or Gandhi to challenge the granting of rights to groups marginalized by their sexuality or gender identity (Kuhar and Paternotte 2017, 2; Bob 2019). Human rights language is used frequently to construct seeming contradictions in this process (Sanders and Jenkins 2022; Cupać and Ebetürk 2022). For example, trans women's rights are often constructed as a threat to cis "biological women" (Bob 2019) and LGBTI rights are framed as infringing on the rights of the child or the right to religious liberty.

Thus, part of the answer to the puzzles driving our work lies in the fact that *national* "politics," "identities," or "traditions" are now increasingly intertwined with transnationally circulating ideas about traditional values and the family that come to play a corresponding role in many states. These networks are often developed around other sets of issues (e.g., migration), despite having increasingly shifted focus to fold in gender, sexuality, and gender identity as tools—rallying cries—for moral conservativism. They thrive in an era of world politics shaped by populist narratives that oppose globalization (Logvinenko and Dichio 2021) and the "ruling global elite" to which SOGI rights are tied (the irony being that the resistance movements are also well-funded by elites and increasingly globalized themselves). Indeed, SOGI rights are often seen as a shared threat to national sovereignty in many states, and they have come to provoke a camaraderie—not only among those keen to "defend" their own nation but those seeking to champion the purity and tradition of an imagined past. Moreover, by taking seriously the fact that transnational organizing is available to all sorts of movements, including ones diametrically opposed to one another, this book deals with the critique that constructivist international relations approaches overemphasize "good" movements in transnational politics. The tools that have propelled the SOGI rights movements to transformational global successes also hold potential for opposing movements, and even movements that often draw on a nationalist ideology have found success in such organizing.

The Disparate Actors That Compose Moral Conservative Resistances

We define the varied and loose conglomeration of actors that compose the resistances against SOGI rights as moral conservatives. The term *politicized moral conservative* (PMC) applies when (*a*) the actors in question construct their program around topics in the field of morality politics, and (*b*) their positions on these issues belong to the conservative normative *denkfigur*, or figure of thought (Mannheim 1995).[13] Such conservatism privileges nationalism over globalism, particularism over universalism, legal sovereignty over international law, patriarchy over equality, hierarchy over democracy, the collective over the individual, religion over the secular, and duties over liberties. Thus, the moral conservative actors we study are not conservative in the dictionary sense of the term, as people inclined to reject new ideas. They are, instead, open to new ideas and strategies, including incorporating a language of human rights (Lewis 2017), if it furthers the development of the moral conservative program. Finally, conservative is also the term these actors most commonly use themselves to describe their own work and agenda (iFamNews 2020). By contrast, we do not use the term "the global right wing" (Bob 2012)—though the actors in question belong to the same spectrum Bob studied—because "right wing" presupposes a global "left wing." Since we want to show how moral conservatives strategically perpetuate a variety of long-standing global political divisions (not just left and right), we try to avoid analytical terms that themselves belong to these entrenched binary divides.

Our inquiry also seeks to identify and understand the various actors that make up the moral conservative advocacy networks. The global resistances to SOGI rights bring together actors that, at a first glance, have little in common: Russia, a series of Muslim states, as well as other states from Central and Eastern Europe and the Global South; Evangelical and Orthodox Christians, Catholics, and Protestants; pro-life civil society groups and anti-migration right-wing populist parties, neoconservative media commentators, small businesses and homeowners, and entrepreneurs in the world of big business and economic consultancy. The analysis explains how these actors cooperate and create thin bridges of commonality that unite them across their persistent divides.

Additionally, the actors that mobilize against SOGI rights frequently come from locales that we might consider as ideologically opposed to one another or that scholarship has tended to view as homogeneous rather than polarized. The clearest example is the EU itself, which is widely considered a forerunner on SOGI rights and has become a motor for these rights in Central and Eastern Europe (Ayoub and Paternotte 2019; Slootmaeckers 2017; Mos 2014). Yet the EU's unequivocal support for SOGI rights in international institutions like the United Nations Human Rights Council has been challenged by some of its own member states (particularly Hungary and Poland in recent years). Civil society mobilization inside EU countries (including in the "old" member states like France or Italy) also remains contested and often rejects the EU's policy line on the matter. Russia, likewise, is widely regarded as a threat for Western democracies and as a source of military aggression and disinformation (Sleptcov 2018; Riabov and Riabova 2014), yet moral conservative groups in the United States and Western Europe have begun to look to Putin's Russia as the last bastion of conservative political power (Kahlina 2022).

Taking account of these transnational actors complicates a simplistic classification of states into "SOGI friendly" and "SOGI unfriendly," in that some of the engaged nodes of moral conservative actors are based in states that are seen as more advanced on SOGI rights. The active involvement of US groups in funding and connecting moral conservative advocacy is all the more fascinating given the United States' increasingly established SOGI foreign policy mandate. The United States moved forward rapidly under the Obama and later the Biden administration in incorporating SOGI rights into its foreign policy (Burack 2018; Carlson-Rainer 2021), all while proliferating and exporting a committed activist base to challenge such rights at home and abroad (Bob 2012).[14] Cynthia Burack has unpacked this tension carefully in her work (2008; 2014; 2018), attributing considerable influence to the American Christian conservative movement's persistent anti-SOGI organizing, both within and (increasingly) outside of the United States—where they are given platforms as "experts" on LGBTI people and the supposed calamitous consequences their existence poses. There is also no clear regional divide, as rival actors challenge the dichotomies of Global North and South, East and West, secular and religious, global and local, or rich and poor

14 | INTRODUCTION

across world regions. Data on the audiences they mobilize also complicate simplified portrayals of certain global regions or international organizations—like the EU—as more or less SOGI friendly (Thiel 2020). In sum, even states and international organizations considered SOGI friendly are in reality more complex, and their position is complicated by powerful actors that firmly bind them to transnational moral conservative advocacy networks.

The complex interplay between state and civil society positions has been analyzed by Stoeckl and Medvedeva (2018). Drawing from United Nations' Human Rights Council data between 2009 and 2016, they compared the voting outcomes of states with submissions by nongovernmental organizations (NGOs) in relation to resolutions on "traditional values" and "protection of the family." While the countries that supported, opposed, abstained, or held mixed positions on questions of traditional values and family roughly showed two blocs—one of European and North American states opposed and a second of African, Asian states, alongside Russia, in favor—the NGOs submissions showed a different pattern. NGOs are often at odds with their state, with conservative NGOs being particularly active in states that took progressive stances, and progressive NGOs also using the opportunities offered by international organizations to push back against their governments in favor of the traditional values resolutions. These NGOs form rival global networks.

As Graff and Korolczuk (2022) explain, there are networks of social movement organizations that tie together these disparate players and diffuse an anti-gender message—organizations which these scholars point out are also connected to right-wing populist political parties that have become a formidable force in contemporary domestic and world politics (on far right parties, see Mudde 2019).[15] These organizations involve groups like the International Organization for the Family (IOF; before 2016, the World Congress of Families), CitizenGo, Agenda Europe, and Tradition Family Property. The IOF connects thousands of actors across borders and at annual summits, and as Stoeckl (2020a) has shown, diffuses Christian right ideas far and wide, for example from the United States to Russia. The online platform CitizenGo was founded in Spain but now spans seventeen countries and specifically targets epistemic communities—artists, academics—and political leaders who champion SOGI rights; they claim twelve million registered users (Graff and Korolczuk 2022, 45). Mimicking many progressive platforms, like MoveOn, CitizenGo is the main moral conservative platform for transnational advocacy in the digital era (Hall 2022). In Europe, Neil Datta's (2018b) work has documented the wide reach of Agenda Europe, an umbrella TAN of more than one hundred organizations in over thirty countries that target SOGI rights by depicting them as an affront to Christian values. In the next section, we argue that these types of actors are intellectually linked by a moral conservative narrative that reserves a disproportionate space for SOGI rights issues.

States and international organizations (like the Catholic and Orthodox churches) have joined with and provided venues for such actors to mobilize and for resistance to SOGI rights to take root. Indeed, scholars such as Meredith Weiss and Mike Bosia (2013) have demonstrated the potential advantages state authorities find in espousing what they call political homophobia, a purposeful state strategy "embedded in the scapegoating of an 'other' . . . as the product of transnational influence peddling and alliances." The concept helps us understand the coming together of relatively varied actors, as well as their deployment of relatively similar and modular discourses around traditional values that institutionalize homo- and transphobia in the state. State actors can use the strategy preemptively to their benefit—they are geared to mobilize supporters—even before a SOGI movement has formed or is on the cusp of any tangible success. It has given states new purpose on the global stage, for example to play a role as defenders of "traditional values" and of the "family." Russia and its Orthodox Church have played an outsized role on this front in the last decade (Stoeckl 2016; Wilkinson 2014; Sleptcov 2018; Cooper-Cunningham 2021). Many other such actors (e.g., Hungary and Uganda) have similarly deployed a rhetoric of resistance to "gender ideology," spread new specifically trans- and homophobic policies, and hosted and supported causes that limit SOGI rights—all under the banner of protecting traditional values, religious liberty, and the family.[16] After the EU sanctioned Hungary for passing legislation that prohibited LGBT "propaganda," various US conservative politicians (including former vice president Mike Pence and former attorney general Jeff Sessions) traveled to Hungary to see "what an actual pro-family, socially conservative government acts like," as conservative writer Rod

16 | INTRODUCTION

Dreher put it (Zerofsky 2021). Budapest hosted the influential Conservative Political Action Conference gathering of US Republican politicians and conservatives in 2022. Furthermore, the US conservative news host Tucker Carlson traveled to Hungary to meet with Hungarian prime minister Victor Orbán and beam his views on "Christian civilization" and family values to Carlson's 3.2 million US viewers (Zerofsky 2021).

In sum, bound by transnational advocacy networks, the opposition creates strange bedfellows and global coalitions that disguise much of the complexity and incoherence within their networks. Their coalitions exist not only between countries but also between groups and individuals across borders, and they lead not only to geopolitical divisions but to conflicts within societies. This book identifies the main actors and processes that have made gender and SOGI rights the new factor causing global political division. It delves into the social and political roots of the resistance to SOGI rights, showing that at times the actors that make up the movement itself are far more multifaceted and complex—spanning varied national backgrounds and religious affiliations—than we might anticipate. We turn now to the language that binds these actors together, which we call the *moral conservative narrative*, and the threat that this narrative attributes to SOGI rights.

Claims, Strategies, and Venues of Resistance

The emergence of a common language of resistance is one of the best indicators that actors are cooperating (Tarrow 2013), and for twenty-first-century moral conservatism, this common language is the resistance to SOGI rights. Moral conservative actors construct their language of resistance around the concept of gender ideology, and opposition to it has mobilized otherwise distinct campaigns, like the French La Manif pour tous campaign and the aforementioned Colombian opposition to the FARC peace deal. In doing so, they have consistently painted SOGI rights as antithetical to traditional values—whatever those may denote in any given context.

The field-defining work on anti-gender campaigns that Roman Kuhar and David Paternotte (2017) and their collaborators conducted has shaped much of our thinking on this phenomenon of gender ideology. The anti-gender movement's campaigns and banners in far-flung contexts use near-identical iconography, these scholars show. For example, multiple demonstrations by Slovenian activists drew inspiration from Italian activists, who themselves were inspired by French activists (Kuhar and Paternotte 2017, 2, 269). While these activists develop their own locally resonant and hybrid versions of resistance to SOGI rights, they actively borrow discourses and repertoires of contention via various modes of diffusion—through both direct network ties and indirect observation and emulation (see also Hodžić and Bijelić 2014; Paternotte 2015; Möser, Ramme, and Takács 2022). While Kuhar and Paternotte's goals differ from ours,[17] their seminal insights demonstrate the diffusion of anti-gender claims and thus help us isolate transnational actors, their claims, and the venues in which they work.

Kuhar and Paternotte trace the terms gender ideology, gender theory, and (anti)genderism to John Paul II's Catholic Church and its insistence on the difference between and complementarity of the sexes. By coining the term gender ideology, the Vatican was responding directly to the rapid changes around gender equality and SOGI rights in the 1990s—especially the United Nation's International Conference on Population and Development in Cairo in 1994 and the World Conference for Women in Beijing in 1995. The church opposed the movements behind these changes and the scholarly community that had spearheaded them by deconstructing essentialist assumptions around both gender and sexuality. Moral conservatives use the term "gender ideology" to refer to an "ideological matrix of a set of abhorred ethical and social reforms, namely sexual and reproductive rights, same-sex marriage and adoption, new reproductive technologies, sex education, gender mainstreaming, protection against gender violence and others[, like trans rights]" (Kuhar and Paternotte 2017, 5).

In this narrative, gender ideology is the central threat to the reproduction of *man*kind and societies in general, not only domestically but across the globe. In their repackaging of the social scientific meaning of gender, moral conservative actors have targeted a wide-ranging umbrella of political movements dealing with women's rights, sexual orientation, and gender identity and expression. Especially in the second decade of the new century, the growing acceptance of marriage equality and gender recognition has put SOGI rights centrally in the purview of the moral conservative movement (Graff and Korolczuk 2022, 5).

18 | INTRODUCTION

SOGI movements and rights are constructed as an authoritative threat, with the potential to dismantle a multitude of core values through the "sexualization of children," the disruption the "natural order," and the rejection of "common sense" (Kuhar and Paternotte 2017, 5; Velasco 2023a). The gender ideology narrative is also deeply entwined with contemporary populist rhetoric that stimulates fear around corrupt elites, decadent intergovernmental organizations (like the United Nations and EU), and Marxism. Take for example this quote from Ryszard Legutko, MEP for the Polish far right Law and Justice (PIS) party: "Gender is an ideological plague. Genderism has become an official doctrine of the European Union. It is put everywhere, in every document, regardless of the subject. Repressive legal regulations and a gigantic censorship apparatus can follow genderism, and often they do" (cited in Adamiak 2021).[18] This rhetorical construction of threat is conspicuously deployed by a variety of state actors and illustrated in a speech Putin gave at a plenary session of the Valdai International Discussion Club:

> Some people in the West believe that an aggressive elimination of entire pages from their own history, "reverse discrimination" against the majority in the interests of a minority, and the demand to give up the traditional notions of mother, father, family and even gender, they believe that all of these are the mileposts on the path towards social renewal. . . . In a number of Western countries, [this] debate over men's and women's rights has turned into a perfect phantasmagoria. . . . Anyone who dares mention that men and women actually exist, which is a biological fact, risk being ostracized. . . . I repeat, this is nothing new; in the 1920s, the so-called Soviet Kulturtraegers also invented some newspeak believing they were creating a new consciousness and changing values that way. (Putin 2021)

Putin's remarks are not unique, and they are also not in response to a looming likelihood of trans rights and gender recognition on the near horizon in Russia. Instead, they are eerily reminiscent of a globally circulating discourse. For instance, US congresswoman Michele Bachman claims "transgender Marxists—transgender Black Marxists—[. . .] are seeking the overthrow of the United States and the dissolution of the traditional family" while the Polish president Andrei Duda called "LGBT ideology" worse than communism in his 2020 election campaign. In doing so, Duda adopted the assertion of the archbishop of Kraków, Marek Jędraszewski, that "LGBT ideology" was, interestingly, both a new Bolshevism and Nazism. In yet another articulation of this shared discourse, Hungarian prime minister Viktor Orbán flattered members of the US Republican Party at the Conservative Political Action Conference (CPAC) in Dallas in July 2022 by comparing their domestic political opponents with the totalitarian rulers who once subjugated his homeland: "The Hungarians defeated communism, which was forced on us by Soviet troops and arms. It took a while. We began our fight in 1956 and won in 1990, but we did it. But communists are tough to beat. They rose from their ashes, came together with the liberals, and come back all around the world stronger than ever. If somebody has doubts whether progressive liberals and communists are the same, just ask us Hungarians. We fought them both, and I can tell you they are the same" (Welch 2022).

In sum, the anti-gender movement paints gender ideology, and by extension SOGI rights, as a Trojan horse that will erase difference between the sexes, ultimately disassemble the social order altogether, and possibly establish a "totalitarian" global order reminiscent of Soviet communism (Carnac 2020).[19] We aim in this book to flesh out the comprehensive conservative content that culminates in this anti-gender message as well as the complex workings of the global moral conservative movement as they pertain to SOGI rights movements. By examining the ties of Catholic anti-gender actors to Orthodox Christianity, Protestantism, and Evangelical Churches, we also move beyond the common empirical focus on Catholics to define the factors beyond religion that generate coherence among moral conservative resistances. Indeed, moral conservative resistances need the issue of SOGI rights to bind them together because the coherence among them is otherwise very loose.[20] As Judith Butler (2021) recently noted, the mobilization by anti-gender actors is rather unprincipled and mobilizes "a range of rhetorical strategies from across the political spectrum to maximize the fear of infiltration and destruction that comes from a diverse set of economic and social forces. It does not strive for consistency, for its incoherence is part of its power." We attempt to zero in on SOGI rights as central building block for transnational moral conservative networks. They provide the thin foundation on which such a loose coherence is established—the issue set which produces agreement among such varied moral conservative actors.

A key component of our argument is that the global motivation and success of today's transnationally connected anti-gender movements lies not only in the fact that they are *against* SOGI rights, but that they stand *for* an alternative to what is perceived as the liberal political mainstream. By misconstructing SOGI rights as the substance of liberal progressivism, the anti-gender movement brands itself as alternative to political, cultural, and even (partly) economic liberalism. In doing so, we argue, resistance to SOGI rights allows moral conservative actors to perpetuate a repackaged twentieth-century ideological antagonism between right and left, from which they draw a political advantage. The conservative worldview generally privileges tradition, religion, patriarchy, and authority over progressivism, secularism, equality, and liberty. This tension is built into modern politics and is therefore not new. What needs explaining, however, is the centrality of SOGI rights for today's articulation of this tension: why the global "backlash" (Faludi 2006; Faludi et al. 2020) against gender and SOGI rights reaches deep into international institutions like the United Nations or Council of Europe, why the populist right in many countries of the world have taken up the anti-SOGI rights cause, or why resistance is high (and felt as urgent) in many countries with no or very limited social mobilization in favor of SOGI rights (Weiss and Bosia 2013; Ayoub and Page 2019). Resistance to SOGI rights is pervasive and global today because these rights are used as a proxy for preexisting ideological divisions that continue to hold power over the political imagination of many people, thus allowing political and state actors to perpetuate politically opportune dichotomies between East and West, North and South, right and left, conservative and progressive.

The Moral Conservative Narrative

The strange bedfellows inside the global moral conservative movement are bound by a narrative that redraws the ideological fault lines of the twentieth century and turns SOGI rights into the vanguard of progressive global liberalism that they seek to withstand. In chapter 5, we reconstruct in detail the moral conservative narrative that gives coherence to the global resistances to SOGI rights. While we use the word coherence with caution, given the major contradictions in logic and inconsistences that narrative holds, it nonetheless serves as a master frame of moral conservative ideology that leads to mobilization. This background narrative is a pillar of our argument, which sees a central purpose of TANs as creating and translating one overarching master "story" to audiences in various linguistic, social, political, cultural, and religious milieus. That story binds a broad range of concerns—regarding religion, family, and life, but also education and economy—into a concrete policy claim: resistance to SOGI rights. Emil Edenborg (2023) has theorized such narratives as discourse coalitions (Hajer 2006), in which stories and metaphors form a condensed statement—stripping the various discourses that make it up of their complexity, before combining them—to produce an ostensibly coherent whole. These narratives work "to conceal complexity, enable communication across differences, and, at times, pave the way for common action and cooperation" (Edenborg 2023, 182). Because SOGI rights are conspicuously central to politicized moral conservative work, Kováts and Põim (2015) have called "gender ideology" a symbolic glue that binds together moral conservative activists' loose claims and long and varied history (see also Grzebalska, Kováts, and Petö 2017; Edenborg 2023). In their rendering, "gender" is an empty signifier that can be filled in different ways, from anti-EU, anti-liberal, anti-communist, and homophobic attitudes to anti-government, anti-Semitic, and anti-immigrant attitudes (Kováts and Põim 2015, 75; Mayer and Sauer 2017).

We agree that this symbolic glue works as they describe when deployed at the *domestic* level, where resistance against "gender" takes on various meanings from context to context. However, we also analyze how this symbolic glue functions at the *global* level, where we see a more structured narrative story. While the symbolic glue concept might suggest that "gender" is just a placeholder for the real topics, at the global level, moral conservative actors have constructed a narrative for which SOGI rights resistance is central. This narrative, no matter how illogical, creates a structure of coherence that functions as a master frame with universal features (Snow and Benford 1992; 2000) from which domestic movements can draw. As a master frame, it is both abstract enough to travel across borders and specific enough to piece together various preexisting ideas—which can then become a symbolic glue at the domestic level, where certain issues may fit more or less well.[21]

At this global master-frame level, we take the role of SOGI rights resistance to be singular and substantive for the moral conservative mobilization we observe today. The narrative of resistance to SOGI rights is so effective as a master frame because it defines potential adherents of moral conservative advocacy as a single coherent group: the group of those who "resist." The various fears and anxieties people experience (from economic insecurity to moral panics) are all presented as conducible to one historical development that rolls forward from the "menace of communism" in the twentieth century to the threat of a "new liberal totalitarianism" in the twenty-first. Politicized moral conservatism folds real grievances into a twisted philosophy of history that draws a straight line from Bolshevism to SOGI rights and, in doing so, scapegoats SOGI people as embodying everything conservatives are meant to reject.

As it relates to the rejection of "liberalism," the moral conservative narrative occupies a complicated space in its position on capitalism and communism. The moral conservative actors' discourse—while entailing a wholesale rejection of communism—does embrace many elements of capitalism and some elements of welfare state socialism. Moral conservatives often nostalgically reflect on a form of "market town" or "Main Street" capitalism—a romanticized capitalism of the past where everyone has an ordered place, typically implying fixed gender roles. They also welcome state welfare subsidies to families as long as these benefit "traditional families" and not single parents or other forms of households.[22] Indeed, the unpaid labor by women in the home was part and parcel of neoconservative ethos that supplemented neoliberal cuts to state spending by shifting labor like carework to the private sphere under the foil of "traditional values" (Cooper 2017; Brown 2019). Moral conservatives are also often resourced by ultraneoliberal organizations and actors, like the Koch brothers (Skocpol and Hertel-Fernandez 2016; we discuss the political economy of moral conservative funding in chapter 3). What is explicitly rejected in the moral conservative master narrative is what we call a *cosmopolitan capitalism*, conceptualized in terms of urbanization, individualization, secularization, and global mobility. Cosmopolitan capitalism is understood as a form of capitalism laced with "decadence" and a departure from norms seen as rooted in history and local culture. SOGI rights stand in as a symbol of this departure that many people, in all countries, are thought to understand. In this book, we intentionally prefer cosmopolitan capitalism over the term neoliberalism (Graff and Korolczuk 2022, 33) to avoid the complications that the diverse usage of the latter term in the North American and European contexts brings with it.[23] In sum, the moral conservative narrative presents itself as social, in that it is about caring for ordinary people, for a silenced majority. It works by creating and translating one overarching story to audiences in various linguistic, social, political, cultural, and religious milieus. This narrative creates effective new political binaries, which, like during the twentieth century, give rise to both divisions and coalitions between countries, groups, and individuals across borders and lead to geopolitical divisions and conflicts within societies.

Scope Conditions

Explicating the study of a complex transnational movement—one that takes on different shapes and forms across varied states and with a multitude of diverse actors—is challenging within the space of a single book. We thus make a set of analytical choices that delineate the scope of the project. First, opposition to movements by those marginalized around their sexual orientation and gender identity is not new. Majorities and groups that hold power have historically been reluctant to grant rights to the marginalized and minoritized. We argue that this opposition now builds on its preexisting foundations, with far-reaching and increasingly *global* ramifications. This shift from the national to the transnational level is unique enough to warrant analysis and explanation.

Second, we purposely avoid terms like war and backlash that commonly appear in popular reporting and activist rhetoric (Faludi 2006), though we do use such language when engaging the claims of particular movement formulations (see Paternotte 2020). The book emphasizes the constant interaction of diverse groups in a plural set of struggles that have made people marginalized by their sexuality and gender identity flagbearers in long-standing ideological debates. While we take some license to parsimoniously model a theory of double helix interaction, we do not argue that the claims for and against SOGI rights operate in binaries. The moral conservative narrative can be deployed even when not in response to SOGI rights claims. Indeed, LGBTIQ people are vilified in some contexts even when they have not mobilized on the ground

24 | INTRODUCTION

domestically, as authorities often cynically target their issues—putting them on the agenda and fueling homo- and transphobia (Weiss and Bosia 2013)—for political purposes.[24]

The plurality and complexity of moral conservative resistances also challenges the binary view—common in popular accounts—of states as pro- or anti-SOGI-rights. The fact that states viewed as SOGI friendly can produce a vigilant civil society on behalf of so-called traditional values (e.g., the United States) and vice versa underlines our point that the complex web of intricacies goes far beyond simplistic dichotomies, including East versus West.[25] Since SOGI norms are often weakly entrenched in the state, many states also take on different identities regarding SOGI rights from one government to the next. Characterizing these movements as two competing ideologies is further complicated by the fact that many LGBTIQ people (and some organizations that represent them) have deeply held religious beliefs that are intrinsic to their identities. Similarly, research on homonationalism shows that some arguments the global SOGI rights resistances make can be alluring to some LGBTIQ people (Puar 2007; Bob 2019). These conflictive identity complexities exist within each individual strand of the double helix.

These complexities, as well as the plurality of the SOGI rights movement and its opposition, form the background of our argument. They inform how we challenge the simplistic binaries—the constructed outputs of both of the overarching movement narratives we chart here—that obscure important variation within. For example, "the SOGI movement" is itself a complicated umbrella representing different groups and interests (Murib 2017), yet their conservative opposition commonly lumps these actors together as a uniform group and simplifies them as a threat to the nation, children, demography, and others (Kuhar 2011). We wish to convey the complexity of each set of actors, while pinpointing how the existence of a transnational network of opposition to SOGI rights alters and influences the work of SOGI rights promotion, given that resistances work in similar ways in otherwise different places.

Third, we focus on key case studies from which we can extrapolate theory, but we do not cover the universe of SOGI and moral conservative mobilization. Indeed, the book does not deal with all resistances to SOGI rights, but with a specific (although very influential) type of prefer cosmopolitan capitalism over the term neoliberalism (Graff and Korolczuk 2022, 33) to avoid the complications that the diverse usage of the latter term in the North American and European contexts brings with it.[23] In sum, the moral conservative narrative presents itself as social, in that it is about caring for ordinary people, for a silenced majority. It works by creating and translating one overarching story to audiences in various linguistic, social, political, cultural, and religious milieus. This narrative creates effective new political binaries, which, like during the twentieth century, give rise to both divisions and coalitions between countries, groups, and individuals across borders and lead to geopolitical divisions and conflicts within societies.

Scope Conditions

Explicating the study of a complex transnational movement—one that takes on different shapes and forms across varied states and with a multitude of diverse actors—is challenging within the space of a single book. We thus make a set of analytical choices that delineate the scope of the project. First, opposition to movements by those marginalized around their sexual orientation and gender identity is not new. Majorities and groups that hold power have historically been reluctant to grant rights to the marginalized and minoritized. We argue that this opposition now builds on its preexisting foundations, with far-reaching and increasingly *global* ramifications. This shift from the national to the transnational level is unique enough to warrant analysis and explanation.

Second, we purposely avoid terms like war and backlash that commonly appear in popular reporting and activist rhetoric (Faludi 2006), though we do use such language when engaging the claims of particular movement formulations (see Paternotte 2020). The book emphasizes the constant interaction of diverse groups in a plural set of struggles that have made people marginalized by their sexuality and gender identity flagbearers in long-standing ideological debates. While we take some license to parsimoniously model a theory of double helix interaction, we do not argue that the claims for and against SOGI rights operate in binaries. The moral conservative narrative can be deployed even when not in response to SOGI rights claims. Indeed, LGBTIQ people are vilified in some contexts even when they have not mobilized on the ground

24 | INTRODUCTION

domestically, as authorities often cynically target their issues—putting them on the agenda and fueling homo- and transphobia (Weiss and Bosia 2013)—for political purposes.[24]

The plurality and complexity of moral conservative resistances also challenges the binary view—common in popular accounts—of states as pro- or anti-SOGI-rights. The fact that states viewed as SOGI friendly can produce a vigilant civil society on behalf of so-called traditional values (e.g., the United States) and vice versa underlines our point that the complex web of intricacies goes far beyond simplistic dichotomies, including East versus West.[25] Since SOGI norms are often weakly entrenched in the state, many states also take on different identities regarding SOGI rights from one government to the next. Characterizing these movements as two competing ideologies is further complicated by the fact that many LGBTIQ people (and some organizations that represent them) have deeply held religious beliefs that are intrinsic to their identities. Similarly, research on homonationalism shows that some arguments the global SOGI rights resistances make can be alluring to some LGBTIQ people (Puar 2007; Bob 2019). These conflictive identity complexities exist within each individual strand of the double helix.

These complexities, as well as the plurality of the SOGI rights movement and its opposition, form the background of our argument. They inform how we challenge the simplistic binaries—the constructed outputs of both of the overarching movement narratives we chart here—that obscure important variation within. For example, "the SOGI movement" is itself a complicated umbrella representing different groups and interests (Murib 2017), yet their conservative opposition commonly lumps these actors together as a uniform group and simplifies them as a threat to the nation, children, demography, and others (Kuhar 2011). We wish to convey the complexity of each set of actors, while pinpointing how the existence of a transnational network of opposition to SOGI rights alters and influences the work of SOGI rights promotion, given that resistances work in similar ways in otherwise different places.

Third, we focus on key case studies from which we can extrapolate theory, but we do not cover the universe of SOGI and moral conservative mobilization. Indeed, the book does not deal with all resistances to SOGI rights, but with a specific (although very influential) type of resistance. For example, we have not analyzed the increasing crackdown on LGBTIQ people by the Chinese State. In a similar vein, we focus on a key network opposing SOGI rights at a global stage, but other (sometimes competing) conservative actors do exist (and are not always fully in sync regarding claims, strategies, and modes of action). While our case of the IOF and its allies arguably constitute the most influential moral conservative network, we focus less on some other socially conservative networks (like the Tradition, Family and Property [TFP] that inspired the ultraconservative Ordo Iuris Institute for Legal Culture in Poland).[26] We also pay more limited attention to the complex and multiple Catholic networks (articulated across ecclesial communities, the Vatican, national churches, and political organizations) and interesting transatlantic and pan-American protestant networks on these issues. Relatedly, organizations like the IOF are more represented in Europe and North America, sparking our initial attention as scholars of these regions. While we analyze the TAN's operation globally (e.g., including its grounding in Latin America with the Political Network for Values), other scholars will chart its impact in many non-European and non-North American regions with greater ability than we do here. In sum, the group and country cases we focus on are globally operative and carefully chosen (based on their outsized impact, see chapters 3 and 4) as ideal types from which we can extrapolate theory. Our focus on transnational moral conservative advocacy and the active involvement of states in Europe and North America is also important for destabilizing the flawed popular perception that the sources of impassioned opposition come purely from the non-Christian world and outside the West—that notion is false.

Our fourth and final scope condition is our homing in on *SOGI rights* as a tool of resistance (used by moral conservative actors to bestow unity to their movement), given the movement's wider net of issues. Indeed, the moral conservative movement targets women's reproductive rights, arguably the original target (Krizsán and Roggeband 2021); gender justice broadly (Piscopo and Walsch 2020); gender studies (Engeli 2020); sex and gender education, justifying a movement for homeschooling; *and* SOGI rights (e.g., same-sex partnership, adoption, surrogacy, and gender recognition). The concurrent battles to roll back abortion rights in many countries (alongside aforementioned targets),

26 | INTRODUCTION

as in the US Supreme Court's June 24, 2022, decision to strike down *Roe v. Wade*, exemplify this broad bundle of targets associated with gender justice.[27]

In short, the opposition to SOGI rights goes hand in hand with broader moral conservative issues that are focused on other gender justice goals (Htun and Weldon 2018). While they do not direct their anti-gender ideology tactic exclusively at SOGI rights, moral conservatives almost always also attribute gender ideology to international LGBTI rights advocates, whose work they reframe in sly ways (Kuhar and Paternotte 2017, 8). For example, given the origins of contemporary LGBTI identities in Western states, opponents of SOGI rights also often dubiously paint SOGI rights as part of neocolonialism, whose decadence should not go unchallenged (Currier 2012). Beyond our own interest in SOGI rights, and the importance of this topic for scholars of LGBTI politics, SOGI rights are conspicuously central to moral conservative work. These movements use SOGI rights to their own ends. For many of the moral conservative actors we spoke with, resistance to SOGI rights is the central tentpole of their wide tent, the point around which their wide tent becomes narrow. This narrowing is the work of transnational actors, and this book is mainly concerned with how and why they accomplish it.

This focus naturally limits our analysis of some of the complex and unique ways the moral conservative agenda is deployed in various domestic contexts (see, e.g., Möser, Ramme, and Takács 2022). By focusing on the implications of the resistances to SOGI rights, we do not diminish the importance of other parts of the movement's wide tent. Indeed, as we trace the history of the movement's presentation of SOGI rights as a threat, we emphasize that it appears alongside a multi-issue platform of a multistate movement network that has roots going back decades, including opposition to communism. This explains why anti-gender actors present themselves as advocates for freedom of speech, thought, religion and conscience, as Kuhar and Paternotte (2017) also note. Gender ideology is deployed as a proxy for opposing a variety of claims around identity, liberalism, democracy, and diversity. We acknowledge these wider connections throughout, and we see our emphasis on SOGI rights for the purposes of this book as a heuristic device that allows us to develop the comparison between SOGI and anti-SOGI-rights mobilization as two rival networks that operate in relation to each other—often deploying related strategies, claims, and venues.

Plan of the Book

Much of seminal work we have charted above has started to explore the actors, claims, and venues of resistance to SOGI and women's rights, usually looking at various domestic responses that employ claims around gender ideology (e.g., Korolczuk and Graff 2018; Kuhar and Paternotte 2017; Kováts and Põim 2015; Möser, Ramme, and Takács 2022; Norocel and Băluță 2021).[28] Our goal is somewhat different here in that we look specifically at patterns that connect these resistances across borders in our interconnected world. As such, we do not dissect how the opposition debate plays out within specific country case studies. Instead, we look at key international forums where the resistance is levied, tracing (*a*) the key transnational actors involved in SOGI rights resistances, (*b*) their primary strategies and claims, (*c*) the venues they use to advocate for those claims, and, finally, (*d*) the transnational LGBTIQ movement's response to their work. We hope that by engaging with this book, readers will gain a handle on who the actors are, their origins, how they operate, what claims they circulate globally, where they promote these claims, and their impact on world politics.

Method

We address these questions using a mixed-method approach— semistructured interviews, participant observation, content analysis, and network analysis—that is attentive to the complex history of anti-SOGI resistance and its global ties. These mixed-methods speak to each other in productive ways, not only for validation, but also to provide a holistic understanding of process (for example, the story of how a network tie came to being). Participant observation gave us an understanding of the key claims and goals, as well as providing access to participants and materials—like conference programs that could be analyzed using network analysis. The interviews offered a wealth of data in substantiating how moral conservatives think of their purpose in the movement and how they strategize and bring people together.

28 | INTRODUCTION

The project draws on our seven years of research funded by the European Research Council (ERC), involving over 120 interviews with transnationally connected moral conservative advocates on issues ranging from traditional values to pro-life, human rights, and religious freedom laws, to homeschooling. Our team conducted these interviews in English (55 percent), Russian (39 percent), German (3 percent), or a combination of those languages (3 percent). The interviews were analyzed in the original languages by Stoeckl, who also translated all the quotes from Russian and German used in this publication. We conducted interviews in person in Russia, the United States, Hungary, Austria, Moldova, and Italy, as well as over electronic media in a few cases. The interviews that are most central to the analysis in this book were sampled on the basis of the interviewees' leadership role in international nongovernmental organizations (INGOs) and NGOs, and their steadfast involvement in the networks studied. In almost all cases, we approached them personally at public events and arranged for interviews to take place at a suitable time on the same day or few days later in order to have time to explain the scope of our research and obtain informed consent. All interviews were anonymized, except in cases when the interviewees explicitly agreed to have their identity disclosed.

Due to these participants' nodal centrality in the moral conservative network (see chapter 3), our analysis naturally devotes particular attention to Russian and American advocates. Our team conducted fieldwork on-site at various moral conservative transnational advocacy gatherings, including the meetings of the World Congress of Families in Tbilisi, Georgia (2016); Budapest, Hungary (2017); Chisinau, Moldova (2018); and Verona, Italy (2019); the meetings of Global Home Education Exchange Conference in Rome, Italy (2017) and Moscow and St. Petersburg, Russia (2018); and the Christmas Readings Pro-life Conference in Moscow, Russia (2017). Our fieldwork in the conservative camp stretched over four years, which meant, in some cases, multiple encounters with key actors, allowing us to assess changes in their roles inside the network. In sum, we exploit a cross-national scope of both key players and target-states in moral conservative activism.

Since our project centers on the idea that global transnational networks for and against SOGI rights function in opposition to each other, we also draw to a lesser degree on our research with the SOGI rights movement (especially in chapters 1 and 7). Part of this research was conducted before the start of the ERC-funded research (cf. Ayoub 2016, 225–45), but it informs our analysis, and we continued to research this network even as we turned our attention to the specific issues this book addresses. Combined, this work includes 125 interviews and focus groups with SOGI activists representing two dozen countries, and a survey of 291 transnationally linked SOGI rights organizations. It also includes eight interviews with dignitaries working on SOGI rights within the governments of the Netherlands, Germany, the United States, and Sweden. Participant observation at strategic activist meetings (including those of ILGA-Europe in 2010, 2011, and 2016; and ILGA World in 2022), the European institutions, and organized protests took place in Belgium, Cyprus, Germany, Italy, the Netherlands, Spain, Poland, and the United States, though we also visited many other countries to conduct the interviews and meet with advocates. The Reclaiming Family Values Conference that the Open Society Foundations organized before an annual ILGA-Europe meeting in Nicosia, Cyprus, in 2016 was especially informative—and symbolic, even in its title—for understanding the mirroring strategies and engagement of these two globally circulating movements.

Structure

We have organized the book as follows. Part I, which includes chapters 1 and 2, centers on the contexts and background stories of these two rival transnational advocacy networks. It seeks to identify key actors, the political history of their involvement, and the process by which they function in a transnational space. Doing so helps set the stage for explaining how they organize and (in chapter 7) how they navigate the tension between them. Chapter 1 focuses on the global diffusion and proliferation of SOGI rights since 1978. We begin by exploring why SOGI rights have spread globally. Our answer draws on existing theories of interaction between social movements and institutional actors, as we demonstrate how the two sets of actors are tied together in a transnational process that has produced tangible outcomes for SOGI rights. We then organize the body of the chapter along these two explanatory dimensions: an overview of transnational organizing around SOGI

30 | INTRODUCTION

rights; and a discussion of international organization (IO) and state action that together have taken up activist claims and contributed to norm formation and proliferation on a global scale. We close with the caveats underpinning this process, and the realization that rival actors increasingly challenge its achievements on the same global plane. This final point introduces our double helix theorization and sets the foundation for the comparison that drives the rest of the book. Chapter 2 follows a similar format to chapter 1 but gives a global overview of the resistance to SOGI rights since the 1990s. We show how the American Christian Right plays a central role in the globalization of the culture wars that target SOGI rights, and we fold them into the broader global resistances we go on to chart in the book. In both chapters of part I, the focus is on the respective groups' origin story, their legal challenges and progress, and their organizing timeline.

Part II turns its attention to the *actors* that make up the politicized moral conservative opposition, analyzing the agents and networks that campaign against SOGI rights as a tool of global political division. Chapter 3 begins by looking at the transnational advocacy networks of moral conservative actors. Here, we trace the history of those TANs that bring the conservative religious right together across borders, namely the World Congress of Families/International Organization for the Family, CitizenGo, the Global Homeschooling Movement, the Alliance Defending Freedom, and Political Network for Values (PNV). We use network analysis to illustrate the reach of their transnational ties as well as the home states that connect them. Interestingly, the locales from which they organize are diverse, representing both states that are sometimes perceived as SOGI friendly and ones that not, with the United States and Russia being two key home bases for such actors. Chapter 4 considers the most supportive states and IOs behind moral conservative organizing. We document these institutional actors—states and IOs—that provide clout to the TANs opposing SOGI rights, namely Russia, Hungary and the Orthodox and Catholic churches, though we also present them in the context of their ties to multiple other states and religious institutions, including the United States and Muslim-majority states (Bettiza 2019).

Part III fleshes out the *strategies* and *claims* of moral conservative activism and addresses the *venues* in which they function. In doing so, chapter 5 is concerned with the construction of a moral conservative narrative, the background story that binds these groups together. This chapter examines the tactics and claims of the movement, showing how it strategizes and frames its demands in a way that the moral conservative actors in various states mimic. It documents how the defense of "the nation," "religion," "children," "women," "family," and "society" more generally are deployed in ways that position the SOGI rights movement as a threat. The illustrative cases of the World Congress of Families' multinational conferences and of CitizenGo's multilanguage universe of online petitions brings these strategies to life. Chapter 6 introduces the international venues in which the resistances to SOGI rights operate. By venues, we mean the spaces where new norms and legal decisions targeting SOGI rights (which often originate in national contexts) are circulated. The focus of our analysis here is on the Council of Europe and its European Court of Human Rights (e.g., the parliamentary assembly and the resolution on internet governance), as well as the European Union and the United Nations Human Rights Council. Moral conservative activists seek out these IOs, which are often harbingers for SOGI rights, as venues for their work. We also include epistemic venues, in the form of (international) academia, as a sphere where resistance to SOGI rights is formulated and circulated. Together the chapters show how rhetoric leads to action in these venues.

Part IV returns the focus to the SOGI rights movement in chapter 7, with an analysis of how it has responded to the global resistance it faces. While the moral conservative resistance has been intense, SOGI rights activists are not complacent, and as with most movements—especially in deeply polarized times—they engage with and counter their opposition in innovative ways (Perreau 2016). As it has in the past, the SOGI rights movement has responded in kind, as the opening vignette from the Reclaiming Family Values conference in Nicosia demonstrates. We use content analysis to demonstrate how the SOGI movement's language has adapted, framing its goals in new ways. Adopting the tactics of and engaging with its resistance—to counter arguments of foreignness—are key strategies of the contemporary movement. They have shaped the introduction of more rooted, national, family-focused, and even religious language in SOGI rights activism (Ayoub and Chetaille 2020).

Beginning with the SOGI rights aspects of the 2022 Russian invasion of Ukraine, the conclusion returns to core pillars of our argument and what they mean for the study of world politics. In particular, our book identifies how the politicized moral conservative narrative centers sexuality and gender in geopolitical conflicts at the heart of international relations theorizing, ranging from war to trade. We also review our contributions to models of human rights diffusion, which we argue are complicated by a double strand, or double helix, of rival networks. This means we must understand a reciprocal relationship between movements that shape how human rights are framed (both for SOGI and anti-SOGI actors) and pushed for in multiple domestic contexts. In general, progressive human rights TANs do not operate alone in the global sphere. Finally, we return to our point that the politicized moral conservative narrative is an important language of resistance that brings disparate actors together across borders. This narrative helps explain various puzzles, from conservative ecumenism to populism, in shaping contemporary struggles in world politics. It is important to grasp it if we are to understand many of the global contestations around progressive politics, as well as the rise of illiberalism and the polarized nature of contemporary normative change.

PART I

Rival Networks

1

Achievements

The Diffusion of LGBTI Rights

In 1978, a group of activists gathered in Coventry in the United Kingdom at an offshoot of a conference headed by the Campaign for Homosexuality Equality (CHE). Representing organizations from multiple states,[1] activists at the meeting discussed strategies for organizing SOGI rights activism on an international level (Paternotte 2012, 2014). As David Paternotte (2012) has carefully traced, activists sought to bolster their effectiveness by placing pressure on the governments and IOs that represented them. For example, a first order of business was to shine a light on anti-homosexual legislation in the Soviet Union and a related law being proposed in Greece. They also sought to influence amendments to the European Convention on Human Rights that would protect against discrimination on the basis of sexual orientation and to pressure the Council of Europe on the issue of decriminalizing consensual same-sex relations.

Targeting IOs like the European Community—an organization that lacked a strong social mandate at the time—was later seen as visionary, but for the activists involved, it followed a straightforward logic. That logic was rooted in the power of numbers, and it allowed them to confront their respective governments as minorities that existed in many states (Ayoub and Paternotte 2014). Since elements of their experience of both marginalization and discrimination overlapped across borders, they could expand their influence by coordinating joint action. In Coventry, the activists would establish a framework for doing just that among themselves and other groups on an international level. This framework resulted in the oldest enduring SOGI rights organization, originally called the International Gay Association. It changed its name in 1986 to include the word lesbian, and in 2008, it became the

International Lesbian, Gay, Bisexual, Trans and Intersex Association (ILGA). Today, ILGA boasts 1,919 member organizations in 169 of the world's 193 states.[2]

This chapter sets the stage for our subsequent analysis by exploring the factors—including the organizing of groups like ILGA—that have affected the global emergence of SOGI rights and recognition. The terrain of social justice around SOGI rights has undoubtedly changed (Magni and Reynolds 2020); lesbian, gay, bisexual, trans, intersex, and queer (LGBTIQ) movements have proliferated such rights with rapidity in recent decades. The once-radical idea of same-sex partnership rights, which existed in no state before 1989, now adorns the legal infrastructure of over three dozen states.[3] The magnitude of this change has been well documented, and accounts often highlight the velvet triangles of movements, states, and IOs that have helped propel a set of domestically sidelined issues into ones of great geopolitical concern (Ayoub 2016; Kollman 2013; Paternotte and Kollman 2013). While the transformation and mainstreaming of this movement has come with serious consequences (discussed below; see also Wilkinson 2015), it is undeniable that SOGI rights—once studied only domestically and relegated to secular and advanced industrialized democracies—have entered human rights frameworks on an international scale.

We argue that transnational politics connect the local and the global on SOGI rights, and they do so in ways that parallel the boomerang (Keck and Sikkink 1998) and spiral models (Risse, Ropp, and Sikkink 2013) that international relations literature has envisioned. This process has diffused SOGI rights around partnership, parenting, antidiscrimination, decriminalization, and gender recognition to all sorts of states, including those we would not have predicted to be likely norm adopters. The fact that the small Catholic island of Malta, which banned divorce until recently, now holds the top global spot in ILGA's rainbow rights index indicates the surprising transformation the world has seen regarding SOGI rights (ILGA 2019).

We trace the history of these advancements, focusing on the factors behind the global proliferation of SOGI rights since roughly the formation of ILGA in 1978. We begin by exploring why they have spread globally. Our answer draws on existing theories of interaction between social movements and institutional actors. The actors we focus on in our simplified model are the activists who function in local, domestic, and international spheres, as well as the leaders of pioneer states and IOs. We demonstrate how these actors are tied together in a transnational process that has produced tangible outcomes for SOGI rights in many countries (even if, as the rest of this book demonstrates, it is resisted by many others). After presenting our theoretical approach, we organize the remainder of the chapter along these two explanatory dimensions: first, an overview of transnational organizing around SOGI rights; and second, a discussion of IO and state action that together have taken up activist claims and contributed to norm formation and proliferation on a global scale. We close with the caveats underpinning this process and the realization that rival actors in world politics—who we define as politicized moral conservative actors—increasingly challenge its achievements globally. This final point introduces our double helix theoretical model and establishes the foundation for the comparison that drives the rest of the book.

Theorizing the Proliferation of SOGI Rights Norms in World Politics

People whose sexuality and gender identity do not conform to normative standards remain largely invisible in much of the world. The rights transformation in some states where they have attained partial recognition has spurred a burgeoning literature in the last decade exploring how such surprising change was possible (Ayoub 2016; Encarnación 2016; Friedman 2012; Kollman 2013; O'Dwyer 2018; Paternotte 2015). Looking at the world around them, scholars were fascinated by the unexpected changes in human rights standards they observed. For example, it is quite remarkable that states like Catholic Ireland and Australia would adopt same-sex marriage by popular vote in 2015 and 2017, respectively. How did groups long thought of as invisible minorities become endowed with this newfound presence and influence in multiple and varied nation states?[4]

The scholarly developments in that domain offered fresh opportunities for the study of sociopolitical change and the diffusion of norms. The most holistic accounts of the process of change argued that we must look at both domestic and international factors (Ayoub 2016; Kollman

2013). The overwhelming focus of the first generation of work was on domestic factors in a few first-mover states, which obscured a fascinating transnational dimension to the contemporary rights transformation (Paternotte 2015). That so many states have, for example, approved same-sex unions "is not a mere coincidence," as Kelly Kollman (2013, 3) observed. It calls on us to take seriously the international dimension of these trends.

Norm Diffusion

In this regard, the literature on the international diffusion of norms provided the easiest link to mainstream political and sociological research. The field had already conceptualized *international norms*, defined as appropriate behavior for a specific set of actors (Katzenstein 1996a, 5), standards that governments or social movement organizations wish to export (Finnemore and Sikkink 1998, 891) or that receiving actors feel they ought to adopt or emulate. By *diffusion*, scholars referred to the spread of an innovation to a state or society, when the decision to adopt the innovation is influenced by some other state or society (Graham, Shipan, and Volden 2013, 676). World polity and constructivist scholars focus on such informal processes of influence, arguing that international norms exert influence on states by defining the contours of appropriate behavior (Finnemore and Sikkink 1998; Ingebritsen 2002; Klotz 1995; Legro 1997; Meyer et al. 1997). For many international relations scholars, rights legislation diffuses to states when those states are convinced of the norm's social appropriateness (socialization) or when they fear the costs of international pressures (political conditionality and economic incentives). These theories—one linked to socialization and the other to material incentives—posit logics of appropriateness and consequences, respectively, both of which play a role in modeling SOGI rights research.

To theorize that the visibility of international norms can lead to social and legal change, researchers commonly draw on evidence from social psychology suggesting that interaction can lead to a reduction in prejudice among individuals. Gordon Allport's (1954) seminal contact hypothesis rested on this idea: interactions among different groups could change intergroup relations by leading to positive perceptions of the other (see also Pettigrew and Tropp 2006). This finding is especially true under conditions of cooperation, common goals, and institutional support, some of which the contemporary global context provides for SOGI rights. Several studies have found that a positive interaction, whether direct or imagined (e.g., via the media), is more likely to reduce prejudice than a neutral one (Stathi and Crisp 2008). The perceived threat associated with new groups is likely to lessen after contact, as new adopters "come to realize they have nothing to fear from such interactions" (Crisp and Turner 2009, 235). Learning through interaction is a central mechanism for change because it reduces the level of threat associated with the out-group.

In the SOGI rights case, such interaction and the resulting norm diffusion is related to the processes by which people work to effect social and political change (i.e., change in society, institutions, or the law) by, for instance, building alliances, exerting pressure, and spreading and adapting knowledge across national borders (Roggeband 2010, 19). Diffusion can also include indirect interactions in which intention is not necessary, such as the transmission of new ideas via the media (Ayoub and Garretson 2017; Garretson 2018). Much of the existing literature on SOGI rights has focused on a combination of social movements and institutional actors to explain this change. A series of transnational actors—such as networked social movements, the EU institutions, the European Court of Human Rights (ECtHR), the UN, and the Inter-American Court of Human Rights—have fostered change by propagating an international norm of SOGI rights and introducing, or at least amplifying, the issue in the domestic discourses of various states (Kollman 2013).

Social Movements

Central to this scholarship are the capabilities of movements and transnational advocacy networks (TANs) (Keck and Sikkink 1998; Roggeband 2010). Contrary to some theoretical expectations (McAdam, Tarrow, and Tilly 2001), LGBTIQ movements have mobilized where domestic political opportunities are most limited, prompting scholars to consider multilevel and transnational opportunities for mobilization. The high risk LGBTIQ activism faces may still prevent mobilization in "culturally closed" contexts (Blumenfeld and Raymond 1988), but activists have responded to roadblocks at home by looking elsewhere. For example, although state and local governments in Poland banned LGBTIQ activists from public assembly in multiple cities, Polish activism nevertheless flourished because of opportunities for organizing in neighboring Germany (Ayoub 2013). Support to Poland also flowed from the EU and ILGA-Europe, both of which drew political attention to the state-sponsored homophobia there. The mobilization of LGBTIQ minorities shows that the multilevel structure of world politics can shift the opportunities described by this approach to new levels, including those outside the nation-state (Sikkink 2005). For instance, when the domestic level is closed and interacting with an open international opportunity structure (at the EU- or UN-level), scholars expect boomerang or spiral patterns, wherein domestic actors sidestep their governments to apply pressure from above (Risse et al. 2013). Risse et al. (2013) also note that activists in an open domestic context can aid those in a closed one. The introduction and diffusion of rights legislation for various minorities, including LGBTIQ groups, has been attributed to the work of such movements (Soule and King 2006; Soule 2004; Htun and Weldon 2018).

Ayoub (2016) refers to the movement actors behind the proliferation of SOGI rights in the last decades as norm brokers. With that concept, he focuses on domestic organizations—that is, groups doing the groundwork in their own local contexts—that are transnationally embedded within external organizations like ILGA and Outright International.[5] Norm brokers help the state and individuals in society give meaning to the issue by framing the SOGI rights norm as a human rights value, which constitutes a new idea in many of the domestic spheres analyzed. Not only do norm brokers help states and societies interpret international information, they also help frame that information in ways that resonate in local contexts (Hafner-Burton 2013, 5). In this conceptualization, brokers connect domestic LGBTIQ organizations to a transnational network of actors and to domestic and international governmental institutions. They are supported by networks of informally organized actors, echoing Alison Woodward's (2004) theory of gender equality policy as driven by a velvet triangle of informally networked epistemic communities. An informal network of multinational and multipositional academics, lawyers, and policy elites have, alongside activists, promoted policies with a shared expertise and commitment to a set of SOGI rights issues (Paternotte and Kollman 2013; van der Vleuten 2014).

Model of Change

The map of where SOGI rights have spread can often be explained by the transnational channels connecting norm brokers, IOs, and states through channels of social information and political rules, as well as by the interpretative work that norm brokers do to help transpose and interpret the norm for various state audiences. Put simply, transnational and international channels provide for the interaction among social actors that leads to a change in ideas. Through mechanisms of norm brokerage and learning, these ideational changes can influence the ways the legal and social structures of the state adopt the norm. The mechanisms most central to this argument are social, and they include norm brokerage and learning.

Norm Brokerage is the process by which actors endowed with local knowledge mediate between often-divergent new international norms and existing domestic norms. Norm brokers aid diffusion by framing the international elements of the norm in a domestically familiar discourse so that it resonates with the local traditions of a given society (Khagram, Riker, and Sikkink 2002, 10; see also Snow and Benford 1992). They also connect disparate actors across contexts in order to politicize and draw external attention to the domestic situations of LGBTIQ people.

Learning is the process by which communities and states reassess their fundamental beliefs, values, and ways of doing things through interaction with new ideas and norms. Learning can refer to the transfer of knowledge between international organizations, governments, societies, and individuals, and it includes both simple learning, which leads to instrumental change, and complex learning, which leads to change in beliefs.[6]

These mechanisms of socialization come together to prime the contexts for diffusion by signaling to society and states that they (as publics and governments) ought to react to the norm. As figure 1.1 shows, SOGI norms circulate in world politics, reaching a variety of states, including resistant ones. Here, State A is a first-mover norm entrepreneur or pioneer state. In the case of SOGI rights, the Netherlands has often been given a State A categorization (Holzhacker 2012; Kollman 2017). State B symbolizes a new adopter target state that finds SOGI rights threatening and thus elicits more active resistance. State B provides no political opportunities for domestic social movements, causing these activists to place pressure on the state from outside its borders, both through horizontal ties to other norm broker groups and vertical ties to TANs and IOs. Poland is often characterized as such a resistant new adopter state, as SOGI rights were perceived there as foreign (incongruent with local values) and thus threatening to state sovereignty and national identity (Ayoub 2013; O'Dwyer 2012). State C is a new adopter state with lower levels of resistance—it still receives attention from all the same channels, but it requires slightly less pressure from activists. Argentina is an example of such a state (Friedman 2012).

The norm brokers that change in these countries depends on are the social movement organizations on the ground (e.g., the Campaign against Homophobia [KPH] in Poland or Háttér Society in Hungary), which are simultaneously connected across borders via INGOs advocating for SOGI rights (e.g., ILGA, Outright International, Transgender Europe [TGEU], Organisation Intersex International [OII]). The IOs, in turn, are supranational organizations like the European Union or the United Nations. The dual arrows indicate the reciprocal and interactive relationships between these actors, who may collaborate and adapt through their engagement. Many times, it is institutional insiders who push adjacently to norm brokers from within IOs and states (Banaszak 2009), such as Claudia Roth, who, in consultation with SOGI rights movements, penned an important report on the status of gays and lesbians while serving as Member of the European Parliament (Mos 2014). The dashed arrows signal the softer pressure mechanisms necessitated in low-threat contexts, where states may also emulate foreign examples and adopt norms voluntarily.

A recent example from Romania illustrates the process figure 1.1 depicts. In 2017, the Court of Justice of the European Union (an IO) reinterpreted the word spouse as it relates to EU freedom of movement laws to include same-sex couples. The case was brought by Adrian Coman of the ACCEPT Association, a transnationally linked Romanian LGBT organization (a norm broker). He and his husband, Clai Hamilton, a United States citizen, were married in Belgium in 2010. Belgium (a first-mover

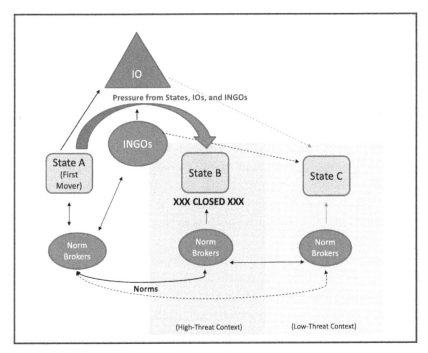

Figure 1.1. A TAN model of SOGI rights diffusion.

or State A) has full marriage equality, but the Coman-Hamilton marriage was not recognized in Coman's home country of Romania (a resistant new adopter or State B). After years of ACCEPT's careful organizing with partners like ILGA-Europe (a TAN), the court ruled that same-sex spouses have equal rights to reside in any EU member state, affecting rights in Poland, Bulgaria, Slovakia, Lithuania, and Latvia. While those states would not be required to grant same-sex unions themselves, they would have to recognize those held elsewhere under their commitments to the EU's principle of freedom of movement. The ruling has also empowered norm brokers in those states to place additional demands on their governments, as well as to further articulate the SOGI rights norm in the domestic discourse of their respective nations.

This model is simplified. Most studies that have contributed to this framework acknowledge that these norms are contested—at the domestic level and, we argue, increasingly at the international level—requiring us to rethink the traditional set of mechanisms that drive diffusion

44 | ACHIEVEMENTS

processes. This leads to our subsequent theorization of a double helix model, which acknowledges the presence of another rival TAN in the space theorized in figure 1.1 (discussed later in this chapter). Theorizing the perceived threat, scholars (Ayoub 2014; Velasco 2023b) show that the effectiveness of these deliberative mechanisms of diffusion becomes complicated when the moral hierarchy between contending norms is difficult for states and societies to establish—a complication which we focus on in subsequent chapters. Previous scholarship has dealt with these shortcomings by bridging cognitive mechanisms (framing, learning, and deliberation) with relational ones (norm brokerage and sociopolitical channels of political pressure) and by theorizing cases of norm rejection and contending norms, as we do in this book on rival movements.

Nonetheless, in many cases, the process depicted in figure 1.1 has compelled states to start complying with the SOGI rights norm by adopting it into their legislative frameworks. Depending on the level of perceived threat domestically, norm promotion can produce social learning in low-threat contexts. It can provoke contestation in high-threat contexts, especially as state actors start to pass laws that anti-LGBTIQ groups then mobilize against. Such resistance leads to heightened public visibility and deliberation. In these high-threat contexts, cautious societal learning and internationalization may ensue on an extended time horizon (O'Dwyer 2018). More positive expectations apply particularly to states embedded in international communities that strengthen the legitimacy of the SOGI norm, such as the EU states. In the remainder of this chapter, we focus on the case history of two key explanatory factors theorized for SOGI rights diffusion: the interactions between social movement organizations (norm brokers) and governmental institutions (states and IOs).

Norm Brokers: Domestic and Transnational Social Movement Organizations

While many of the extensive changes in SOGI rights have only recently come to fruition, there is a long history of domestic and transnational organizing that helps explain them. ILGA was conceived in a decade rich with innovation around SOGI rights. In 1970, eight years before ILGA's Coventry meeting, a diverse group of gay liberation activists, including trans and homeless youth, held the first Pride march in New York City. Commemorating the anniversary of the Stonewall Inn riots of the summer of 1969, this march marked a new era of organizing defined by the formation of the Gay Liberation Front (GLF). The GLF's ethos of public visibility inspired other radical groups, which cropped up in contexts as diverse as Australia, Belgium, Britain, Canada, France, Germany, and the Netherlands (Rimmerman 2014). In Paris, the Front homosexuel d'action révolutionnaire (FHAR) staged a public demonstration in 1971, just a year after the first gay Pride march down the streets of Greenwich Village in Manhattan. In West Germany, gay action groups emerged following Rosa von Praunheim's 1971 film, *Nicht der Homosexuelle ist Pervers, sondern die Situation in der er lebt* (*The Homosexual is Not Perverse, but the Society in which He Lives*), and in 1972, they staged the first "gay demo" in provincial Munster (Griffiths 2021). Gay liberation supported a simple but powerful idea: that sexuality and gender identity must themselves be visible—a matter of public, not just private, concern—before they can serve as a basis for mobilization.

Indeed, the public visibility undergirding the norms that now govern SOGI rights is built on the foundation of a rich history of activism. That history commonly begins with Magnus Hirschfeld, a name synonymous with early transnational SOGI rights. In fact, Dublin's Hirschfeld Centre, along with a financial center in Amsterdam, first hosted ILGA (Paternotte 2012). Hirschfeld was a pioneering German homosexual rights researcher and activist who sought to establish transnational cooperation by founding the Wissenschaftlich-humanitäres Komitee (Scientific Humanitarian Committee, 1897) and the Weltliga für Sexualreform (World League for Sexual Reform, 1928) in Germany (Kollman and Waites 2009). His two organizations were research-based, and they pursued political goals like overturning laws that criminalized sodomy in much of Protestant Europe. A logic parallel to ILGA's appeared then: for ostracized minorities, coordination across borders was a potential pathway to liberation. Before Hirschfeld, homosexual activist Karl Heinrich Ulrichs's writings were translated and diffused across borders in the mid-nineteenth century; they were read as relatable to queer people living in varied societies (Beachy 2014). Once they were received and passed on, Ulrichs's pamphlets spurred mobilization and research around new identities.

While persecution and repression during national socialism eliminated (and quite literally burned) the work of the earliest SOGI organizers—save one small group, *Der Kreis*, in neutral Switzerland—their innovative practices informed subsequent waves of SOGI movement history. A new wave of activism with transnational features, called the homophile (homo love) movement, was to flourish after 1945. The Netherlands replaced Germany as a central node of SOGI organizing in the 1950s, largely due to the active role played by a Dutch organization inconspicuously named the *Cultuur en Ontspanningscentrum* (COC, Center for Culture and Leisure), as well as the annual meetings organized by the International Committee for Sexual Equality (ICSE), which was founded in Amsterdam in 1951. As with ILGA's first Coventry meeting, the ICSE included representatives from nationally diverse organizations, including groups from Denmark, Germany, the United Kingdom, Italy, the Netherlands, and Switzerland (Rupp 2014). Several homophile groups from other states, including prominent emerging organizations in the United States,[7] would also join. Seeing an opening in the postwar period's newfound articulation of human rights and in "mankind's greater awareness of social injustice" in general, the ICSE telegrammed a demand for equal rights to the United Nations (Rupp 2014, 29).

The more clandestine and private activism of the homophile movement would become increasingly public in the late 1960s and 1970s. While targeting the UN was a relatively fruitless tactic in the rights revolution of the time (see below), the homophile movement's efforts maintained the spirit of transnational organizing throughout the 1960s, establishing ties that later spurred multiple Gay Liberation organizations into action following the public-facing activism of the 1970s. Formal transnational networking ties thus started in the 1940s and multiplied with the emergence of ILGA in the 1970s. The early objectives were to advance the human rights agenda and to facilitate networks of solidarity in times of difficulty. As with ILGA's founding in 1978, working across borders opened the door to increased mobilization and the attainment of some SOGI rights gains.

* * *

ILGA's founders were oriented toward international frameworks from the start, recognizing that such frameworks could provide a fertile venue for activism and a pressure point through which to influence reluctant states to address SOGI rights. In many cases, domestic movements for SOGI rights were impotent, even while a handful of European states were paving the way forward in some domains of lesbian and gay rights. This imbalance (as figure 1.1 illustrates) caused great frustration among activists, many of whom identified with each other across borders and saw their situation as shared. In response, these movement actors envisioned a role for the EU, then called the European Community (Ayoub and Paternotte 2014), just as the ICSE had envisioned, initially unsuccessfully, for the UN. For example, ILGA's earliest efforts included supporting decriminalization cases brought by Jeff Dudgeon of NIGRA against the United Kingdom and by David Norris against the Republic of Ireland in the ECtHR (van der Vleuten 2014). ILGA also encouraged Amnesty International to petition for the release of prisoners criminalized under anti-gay legal statutes (Paternotte 2012). The view among ILGA's multinational activists—that supranational institutions could serve as a venue for minority rights politicking—has proven to be both farsighted and revolutionary for SOGI rights politics, especially in Europe and the Americas.

It is through social and political channels (also via insider-outsider coalitions [Banaszak 2009]) across borders that transnational movements play a role in socializing states—by linking SOGI rights norms to membership in contemporary international society, by setting rules of compliance, and by dispensing ideas and images about LGBTIQ people that make them visible.

Institutions: States and International Organizations

For SOGI rights activism to resonate in various states, it has been of paramount importance for the issue to be clearly associated with supportive IOs and made visible within the domestic contexts of the states. In this dimension, states vary in critical ways, and the diffusion of the issue relies both on the extent to which transnational interactions make it visible and on the effectiveness of transnational actors who identify it as one of singular importance to membership in modern international society. Targeting IOs and supportive states—such as the Benelux and Nordic states in the post–Second World War period—did eventually create a space for rights based on sexual orientation and gender identity at the periphery of the broader human rights regime. Over time, the articulations of the norm that LGBTIQ people are entitled to fundamental human rights and deserving of state recognition and protection became increasingly clear in both the rhetoric and the legal framework of IOs—beginning with the Council of Europe (CoE) and EU institutions (Beger 2004). Pioneering or first-mover states like the Netherlands (Kollman 2017) have been swayed by these movements to champion the issue in international forums, tying it to their own values and foreign policy frameworks (Burack 2018; Carlson-Rainer 2021).

Ever since this potential was recognized, the transnational movement for SOGI rights has continued to target international institutions such as the CoE, the EU, the UN, the Organization of American States (OAS), and the Organization for Security and Cooperation in Europe (OSCE). Forums like the Yogyakarta Principles (YP, 2006) have also helped norm brokers articulate a set of normative goals they can advocate for at the UN and elsewhere (Langlois 2015). The original forum established benchmarks for the application of international human rights law, and later, YP + 10 (including the supplement adopted in 2017 to reflect new developments in the field) encompassed the "emerging understanding of violations suffered by persons on grounds of sexual orientation and gender identity and the recognition of the distinct and intersectional grounds of gender expression and sex characteristics" (Yogyakarta Principles 2017). Articulating normative goals has further enhanced the public visibility of SOGI rights and multiplied the presence of SOGI groups across the globe. Viewing, or imagining, the contemporary world as holding norms respecting SOGI people is itself an evolutionary process, built on the interaction between these movements and supranational institutions. It has also led to formal sanctions that have pressured states to change their positions on SOGI rights. For example, the European Parliament, the World Bank, and the United States have sanctioned governments (more or less successfully) including Uganda and Nigeria for laws discriminating against homosexuality (Voss 2018).

While we have seen gains in many world regions in recent decades, the interaction between norm brokers and governmental institutions was originally most pronounced in Europe. SOGI rights have become increasingly related to the idea of European values—symbolized, for example, by activists in many states who take the EU flag with them to protest for SOGI rights and thus frame their struggle in terms of European democratic values and human rights (Ayoub and Paternotte 2014). In turn, European IOs play a central role in this process by legitimatizing the norm and signaling to states and societies how to behave "appropriately" vis-à-vis this issue. The norm that LGBTIQ people are entitled to fundamental human rights and deserving of state recognition and protection is clearly articulated in both the rhetoric and the legal framework of the institutions of the EU and the CoE (Ayoub and Paternotte 2014; Mos 2014; Slootmaeckers, Touquet, and Vermeersch 2017). Article 13 of the 1997 Amsterdam Treaty introduced the first internationally binding law on the issue by prohibiting employment discrimination on the basis of sexual orientation. The 2000 Employment Anti-Discrimination Directive, the European Charter for Fundamental Rights, the 1993 Copenhagen Criteria, various European Parliament resolutions (e.g., the European Parliament Resolution on Homophobia in Europe 2005/2666), European Court of Human Rights decisions (e.g., *Bączkowski and Others v. Poland*, 1543/06), and European Court of Justice decisions (e.g., C-13/94, *P. v. S. and Cornwall County Council*) further institutionalized the norm as part of European human rights values (Ayoub and Paternotte 2019; Kollman 2009; Swiebel 2009; Wilson 2012).

The ECtHR, in particular, has played an activist role on SOGI rights (van der Vleuten 2014), further broadening access points for LGBTIQ norm brokers in the European arena. In this sense, the CoE and the EU have come to play important institutional roles in furthering the publicness of the norm's visibility, and, more recently, have worked to export the norm (Thiel 2020). This is especially true for postcommunist states that wish(ed) to join these IOs, where the "return to Europe" would mean adopting the universal understandings of the LGBTI norm that European institutions now proffer (Ayoub 2013; Chetaille 2013; O'Dwyer 2012; Slootmaeckers, Touquet, and Vermeersch 2017; Swimelar 2017; Szulc 2017). The movement and its complex relationship with EU and CoE institutions explains much about how the SOGI rights norm has diffused and how state institutions have come to adopt it.

In Latin America, too, the courts have played an active role in various states (Lehoucq 2021) and the Inter-American Court of Human Rights has emerged as a vigorous proponent of SOGI rights, often citing examples from European regional courts (Sandholtz and Feldman 2019). In general, the Organization of American States (OAS)—which has passed SOGI resolutions annually since 2008—and the Inter-American Commission on Human Rights—which has had an LGBT unit since 2011—are characterized by an opening political opportunity structure for SOGI NGOs in the Americas in the new century (Kiel and Campbell 2019). Especially when compared to the African Union or Association of South East Asian Nations (ASEAN), IOs in Europe and the Americas have provided a more expansive venue for the pursuit and articulation of SOGI rights (Kiel and Campbell 2019).

The UN has become another important institution for SOGI rights. However, here too, the European supranational institutions also largely preceded the UN in serving as venues for SOGI rights, despite theoretical expectations that the latter would be more likely to uplift NGOs working on social issues (Joachim and Locher 2008). While scholars are right that the EU was historically more hesitant than the UN to deal with ideological issues, as it privileged economic integration, it eventually took on an active leadership role on SOGI rights (Ayoub and Paternotte 2014). By contrast, SOGI organizations had a tumultuous history of access within the UN.[8] With many more dissenting member-state voices, wielding influence has been difficult for norm entrepreneur states and SOGI TANs alike—despite the clout that the UN has with regard to articulating human rights norms in its resolutions and declarations.

ILGA, which had been pushing for UN consultancy status since shortly after its inception, finally received it in 1993 (in the UN Economic and Social Council, ECOSOC). Yet its tenure there was short lived. Almost immediately, the US conservative right targeted it, drawing on moral panic arguments that associated ILGA with pedophilia, and directed particular attention to the US-based group NAMBLA, one of ILGA's many member organizations (Paternotte 2014). Despite ILGA's efforts to explain its stance, and its eventual policing and expulsion of the member groups that had drawn such scrutiny, the UN ejected it in 1994 following US Senator Jesse Helms's threat to cut US funding to the UN should ILGA maintain its status (for a more expansive history, see Paternotte 2014).

More recently, the UN's Human Rights Council has emerged as a key battleground for SOGI rights. According to Voss (2018, 2020), it took a full half century for SOGI rights to make their way into the UN, though they have been much more present since the turn of the century thanks to persistent work by norm broker organizations. It was not until 2003 that Brazil cosponsored a resolution to formally recognize SOGI rights in the UN (at the Commission on Human Rights). In 2005, thirty-two states delivered a joint statement at the commission, attempting to graft SOGI issues into the UN's human rights rhetoric by advocating for protections against violence and discrimination, though they sidestepped the salient issue of marriage equality (Voss 2020). Yet both initiatives faced setbacks: after failing to acquire votes, Brazil withdrew the 2003 resolution, and a vote to end the commission (later replaced with the Human Rights Council) brought "formal SOGI advocacy to a halt until 2011" (Voss 2020). In 2008, a proposed nonbinding declaration for the decriminalization of homosexuality also received about sixty state signatures, but it provoked a counterstatement of comparable size.

Things changed in 2011. Colombia issued a joint statement (this time sponsored by a regionally diverse group of eighty-five states) that revived the goals of the previous ones (McGoldrick 2016), and Brazil and South Africa tabled a resolution on SOGI rights which was adopted by a vote of 23 in favor, 19 against, and 3 abstentions (see Jordaan 2016; cited in Voss 2020). ILGA also regained its consultative status at ECOSOC in 2011, and in 2012, Secretary General Ban Ki-Moon made an impassioned speech saying LGBT people deserved equal rights. As a general rule, though with some exceptions, European, North American, Latin American, and Oceanic states have been the most forceful voices for SOGI rights at the UN, and the international body has produced tangible outcomes legitimizing the work of norm brokers and SOGI rights in some states.

As we will consider in the remainder of the book, other states continue to use the UN—and other IOs—as a forum to limit SOGI rights, for example by articulating claims of state sovereignty and cultural relativity (chapters 5 and 6). As several recent reports by Victor Madrigal-Borloz, an independent expert on protection against violence and discrimination based on sexual orientation and gender identity, make clear, the UN is concerned by the steep rise in "ultraconservative" political leaders, movements, and religious groups that seek to dehumanize and discriminate against LGBTIQ people with the "gender ideology" narrative:[9] "Resistance to the recognition of protection of gender, gender identity and gender expression under international human rights norms is often framed as resistance to the imposition of so-called 'gender ideology,' a linguistic formula used symbolically to refer in an accusatory manner to progressive interpretations of human rights and describe a series of grievances as varied as opposition to equal marriage, gender identity recognition, comprehensive gender and sexuality education and voluntary termination of pregnancy, inter alia." SOGI rights, while making gains in some domains, thus remain hotly contested. For perspective, it is worth highlighting that "SOGI resolutions receive far fewer affirmative votes in the Council than almost any other set of resolutions including highly contentious issues like Syria, Traditional Values, and Protection of the Family. In fact, the only set of resolutions more contentious in Geneva than SOGI are those that focus on Defamation of Religion, which have largely died from the Council's agenda" (Voss 2018, 8).

* * *

It was after the Second World War, then, as part of a rights revolution, that SOGI rights first emerged on the very periphery of the broader human rights regime; in recent decades, they have attained high political salience across many parts of the world. Reacting to unresponsive states that had long prohibited access to sexual and gender minorities, activists sought out new sources of power outside the state. Because people marginalized by their sexual orientation or gender identity and expression exist across all societies, cross-border ties became of paramount importance to political action for the postwar homophile movement, for post–Stonewall Gay Liberation activism, and, later, for the contemporary transnational advocacy networks that groups like ILGA represent. Recognizing that several elements of their situations were shared across borders, many activists found unlikely transformative power by organizing transnationally, and—with a handful of pioneering states that supported their cause—they began targeting international institutions as a venue to challenge the state powers that had previously closed the door to them.

This effort has produced tangible results for some LGBTIQ minorities and for SOGI rights more generally. The transnational channels that activists have brokered, which connect states to each other and to their international communities, make SOGI norms visible both interpersonally to other LGBTIQ people and to the broader public. This visibility leads to heightened mobilization of movement actors, who frame the norm for a local audience and help guide deliberation in the domestic sphere. Such deliberation now exists in many states—including ones that scholars viewed as unlikely or hostile not long ago—and on most continents.

While these achievements are remarkable, they should not overshadow the persistent oppression of LGBTIQ people across societies. SOGI norms continue to provoke resistance, and transnational advocacy is limited in many corners of the globe. To be sure, the mainstreaming of SOGI rights has also come with considerable setbacks that have rightly led scholars to question the notion of far-reaching success. The radicalness of Gay Liberation, which sought to turn on its head the patriarchal and heteronormative, has often been sidelined in favor of mainstream goals like marriage equality that conform to prevailing power structures (Wilkinson 2015).[10] Rights protecting LGBTIQ people also lead to new exclusions and hierarchies. For example, much of the leadership in contemporary transnational organizing (past and present) is made up of the most privileged among LGBTIQ people, overrepresenting the male, white, middle-class, able-bodied, and highly educated (Ayoub 2019a). This naturally affects the types of rights that groups claim to have won, drawing rightful critique from trans, intersex, bi, and lesbian activists, who point out that their specific situations are often sidelined (Balzer and Hutta 2014; Monro 2015; Murib 2015; Schotel and Mügge 2021; von Wahl 2019). This organizing might also privilege certain types of institutions. For example, most of the groups with UN consultative status are from Western states (Voss 2020), and those with the most sway are well-resourced professional organizations (Lang 2013). In Europe too, intersectional analysis shows that transnational activists require a level of language competence in English and a high degree of formal training in grant writing that can exclude more local grassroots organizations (Chetaille 2013). Finally, the association between SOGI rights in some states and IOs is partly a welcome phenomenon but partly a problematic one. It gives fodder to those who wish to use human rights limitations to exclude certain states (like Turkey, which is often deemed not SOGI friendly enough to be European) or certain people, as seen in efforts to paint poor people's movements or immigrants as homophobic, and thus to advocate for their further societal exclusion and the violation of their rights (Mepschen, Duyvendak, and Tonkens 2010). Concepts like homonationalism have emerged in response to such incorporation of SOGI rights by powerful states, who may use the issue to serve other imperial, racist, and exclusionary ends (Puar 2007).[11]

Acknowledging that SOGI rights success means very different things to different communities, and in different states, this chapter has traced important achievements in these rights in many corners of the globe. From this vantage point of tremendous social and political change, with both positive and negative effects, our endeavor begins. Our intention in this book is to chart the global resistances to the SOGI rights revolution we have outlined in this chapter. While such resistance has exhibited fervor in most domestic contexts (Fetner 2008), such as those "high-threat" contexts mentioned above (Ayoub 2014), the last decade has been unique in seeing this resistance expand and proliferate globally in new forms. This expansion complicates the model presented above, in that the transnational ties that bind advocacy groups to states and IOs now coexist next to another TAN that specifically targets SOGI rights in these similar venues.

That means the network arrows depicted in figure 1.1 are metaphorically overlain by the rival TAN we explore in subsequent chapters. Indeed, the fact that they coexist in world politics means that both TANs use IOs as venues of contestation (occasionally even similar ones, like the UN or the EU), and they also mirror each other's claims and strategies. This explains, for example, why SOGI rights activists increasingly speak in terms of "family values" and moral conservative activists often use a "human rights" discourse. Figure 1.2 sets the basis for this idea with a double helix illustration, depicting how states may be met with different TANs, but also that their operation in the same space suggests that their master frames and strategies will influence each other through interaction.

Figure 1.2 illustrates the two movements as strands that operate in reference to each other, pursuing their own goals in awareness of the other, and in which they pull at each other. Depending on the context

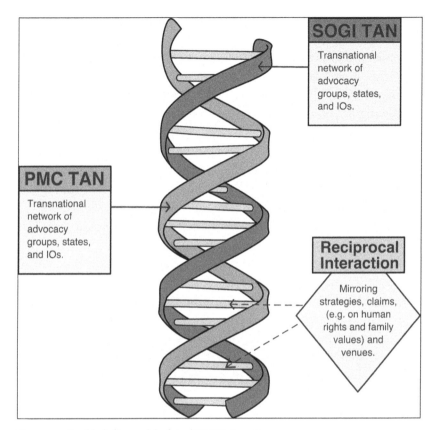

Figure 1.2. Double helix model of rival TAN interaction.

or venue or moment in time, one strand may tug more than the other. Unlike the spiral model, however, which focuses on a lone strand (and often falls into the trap of theorizing resistance only in the domestic space), the double helix metaphor captures the dynamic and tension between two TANs. It thus complicates simplified or static formulations of backlash (e.g., as domestic) and helps us understand variation across time and space, given that one strand may pull harder in Time A than in Time B or in Context A than in Context B. Of course, the strands are not equally important or effective across time and space, which explains the varied outcomes we observe on SOGI rights comparatively. To momentarily draw on the DNA metaphor more directly, an imbalance in the strands in some states may also break the interaction there domestically, clearing the way for one TAN to dominate on its own, as we explain in the conclusion.[12]

Hence, rights protecting LGBTIQ people are met with anti-SOGI resistance at all levels—local, national, and international—and with anti-SOGI laws diffused and spread transnationally through a reverse boomerang or spiral process. We see a concerning trend of norm polarization in this regard, in which rival interpretations of human rights norms emerge and are advocated for. This also means that globally circulating norms become contested—international systems of knowledge do not send unequivocal signals on what the norm is, depending on what state or region one is in (Symons and Altman 2015; Velasco 2023a, 2023b)—and governments in some states conveniently pick and choose from contradictory sets of normative standards. While SOGI rights TANs are dominant in many states that accomplished anchoring a norm like "equality" to LGBTIQ people, a moral conservative TAN may be persuasive in other contexts, such as those where LGBTIQ are invisible or deemed as threatening to the social order, like "State B," ultimately rejecting such an understanding of equality.

The remainder of our book is about this process of resistance, charting the emergence of a politicized moral conservative TAN, describing its functioning, and explaining how it influences the work of the SOGI rights advocates we have presented here. We proceed by looking at the historical foundation of the actors and mechanisms that shape the response to SOGI achievements—the rival moral conservative network strand of the double helix now operating in this transnational space.

2

Resistances

The Opposition to LGBTI Rights

In March 2000, moral conservative activists infiltrated a meeting of the United Nations Preparatory Committee for the UN Special General Assembly. Jennifer Butler (2000, 3) writes, "Scores of lobbyists wearing red buttons emblazoned with the word 'motherhood' swarmed the room where government delegates were gathering . . . conservative lobbyists wore buttons proclaiming 'The Family.' Their physical presence was made more dramatic by a group of cassocked Catholic friars from the Franciscan Friars of the Renewal using 'prayer warfare' to attempt to defeat their feminist opponents. . . . Though still proportionally small in numbers, they were highly visible among the 1,700 NGO representatives."

Nearly five years after the World Conference on Women in Beijing, China, the UN Committee had convened to discuss the gender outcomes and progress made since September 1995. As Butler recognized early on—before most social movement scholars—in her report to the *Public Eye*, Christian Right actors had not only identified international institutions as a place for mobilization, they had also started to imitate the feminist movement's strategies of using slogans, symbols, and performative action to generate a strong visible presence within the venues of international policymaking.

* * *

As we argued in the previous chapter, a long history of movement organizing led to the relatively recent mainstreaming of SOGI rights, including state and court actions to grant civil rights and implement measures against discrimination. While SOGI rights movements have faced extensive local and national opposition since their beginnings, the emergence of transnationally coordinated social movements and civil society actors that mobilize against SOGI rights on the level of international politics is a more recent phenomenon. And while it has become common to identify so-called first-mover or norm entrepreneur countries that have implemented SOGI rights and advocated for them globally, only recently have countries championed an identity as so-called norm resisters of SOGI rights (Nuñez-Mietz and García Iommi 2017). This chapter provides a timeline and an overview of this core focus of our book: transnationally networked social movements and civil society actors that define their goal and purpose as combating SOGI rights and the ideas, tactics, and governments that sustain them. Before we begin that discussion, it is important to point out that if we are to understand today's global polarization on SOGI rights from an international relations perspective, we need to pay attention to how IO and state promotors of SOGI rights (e.g., the EU) are pitted against resisters (e.g., Russia) and how they intersect with the world of social movement organizing and civil society. Like SOGI rights successes, resistance to them also fits the model of norm diffusion outlined in figure 1.1., which also depends on governmental support. States' support for one cause or the other depends on many factors, but it is essentially a sign that SOGI rights have become a key defining element and proxy for preexisting ideological divisions—in national as well as international politics.

This chapter forms a counterpoint to chapter 1, which covered the successes of SOGI rights activism. But while that history can be clearly delineated in terms of key turning points, chronologies, and actors, the history of the resistance to SOGI rights is more diffuse. Paternotte and Kuhar (2017) and Kováts and Põim (2015) have given us a helpful starting point for analyzing this contemporary global resistance by identifying gender ideology as the main focus of the entities that resist SOGI rights; Hark and Villa (2015) and Strube et al. (2020) have done the same in the German context with the term *Anti-Genderismus*. All these studies structure empirical research around the identification of conservative actors and movements that target the notion of gender directly. This has led scholars to focus mainly on those debates and events where conservative actors first opposed gender-based rights using the same terminology as their proponents. In practice, this focus has honed the literature on the gender backlash, typically placing the needle on the record in the mid-1990s with the UN conferences in Beijing and Cairo. Discussion to date has considered these events—a priori—as key moments in the emergence of conservative actors that mobilize transnationally and manifest in anti-gender movements in various domestic spaces.

This focus on gender terminology is a useful way to delimit the daunting scale of the field of politicized moral conservatism, but it also runs the risk of overlooking the deeper historical roots and general scope of the phenomenon. We wish to show that gender has not always been at the center of the mobilization of moral conservative actors, whose goals are almost always much larger than opposing women's and SOGI rights, even if they have a forceful effect on these dimensions. As we have mentioned, Kováts and Põim (2015) have described gender as a symbolic glue that holds various groups of political actors on the political right together today, but politicized moral conservatism has a long and important history that predates the gender terminology and debate. It has also acquired, over time, a noteworthy structure in terms of institutions and strategic networking that explains much about how moral conservative actors took up the battle against gender and SOGI rights in the 1990s.

In a variation on the glue metaphor, we see the way the politicized moral conservative movement uses SOGI rights as comparable to the Japanese art of *kintsugi*, in which a shiny gold filament holds broken ceramic pieces together.[1] Holding together imperfect (or now incongruent) pieces, the gold creates something even stronger than before. While the gold is critically important, its luster should not distract us from the vessel's component parts, the pieces that it holds together. These metaphorical pieces are, in our analysis, the different moral conservative origin stories in various parts of the world, chiefly in the United States and Europe. Christian conservatism has not always necessarily had the same meaning and agenda in different parts of the world. Where topics like abortion, divorce, or school prayer created coherence, denominational difference or nationalism were also factors of separation. SOGI rights can overcome and bind these differences, serving—like the gold in *kintsugi*—to create transnational and cross-denominational coherence between moral conservatives. We cannot, however, overlook the pieces themselves. Without considering the full and varied history of the politicized moral conservative movement, it is harder to understand either the substantive role SOGI rights resistance plays for the anti-gender opposition, or the challenges SOGI rights movements face themselves. In our view, the diffusion of resistances to SOGI rights over the last three decades must be interpreted in the light of a more general history of conservatism during and after the end of the Cold War; we show how this broader history expands upon the existing research on more contemporary manifestations around anti-gender movements.

We interpret the resistance to SOGI rights as the most recent spearhead of a broad and long-standing front of politized moral conservatism and illiberalism, which has allowed moral conservative actors to reach new audiences and to communicate their conservative ideas in novel, successful ways. In order to perceive the contours of this larger picture, this chapter traces the long road to today's resistances to SOGI rights. It starts in the 1970s with a broad sketch of the early origins of moral conservatism in the United States and in Europe (the two key historical nodes of its development). Thereafter, we move to an analysis of the conditions under which the hitherto largely national confrontations between conservatives and progressives globalized during the 1990s, identifying three factors that help explain the transnational diffusion of moral conservative ideas: the Vatican's role at the United Nations, the rise of transnational Christian Right advocacy using a language of human rights, and the end of the Cold War and the subsequent religious turn in formerly communist countries. We end the chapter with an overview of the network today, introducing the central actors, and the claims and strategies of transnational moral conservatism, which we will analyze in greater detail in the rest of the book.

Politicized Moral Conservative Origin Stories

Moral Conservatism in the United States

Moral conservative ideas have deep religious, cultural, and political roots in American society and history. While it is beyond the scope of this chapter to explore all these roots and their ramifications, one source is of particular relevance for our endeavor, as it relates to SOGI rights resistance: American anti-communism and the political ideas and events summed up with the term "Red Scare" (the fear of communism). Erica J. Ryan, in her book *Red War on the Family* (2014), has traced the construction of American anti-communism back to its earliest iteration in the 1920s. At that time, it was expressed primarily in social and moral terms and amplified a marked anxiety over the communist challenge to established views on sexuality, womanhood, manhood, and family life. Communism was perceived both as a foreign threat—due to the rise of the Soviet Union and the crumbling old world order during and after World War I—and as a domestic threat, with ideas judged as radical taking root inside American society. Ryan shows that Americans responded to the threat of communism by strengthening traditional gender and family roles. Subsequently, white, middle-class family life—a heterosexual nuclear family with a working father and a stay-at-home mother living in an upwardly mobile suburban neighborhood—was imposed as a social norm. Indeed, Ryan's articulation of 1920s anti-communist views provides clues to the decades that would follow and has direct implications for the moral conservatism we delineate here. Even if the moral conservative movements that are in the focus of our analysis only started to mobilize domestically in the 1970s, and transnationally even later, the social and cultural anti-communist reaction of the first half of the twentieth century still forms an important reference point for their thinking.[2]

Our fieldwork with transnational moral conservative actors has confirmed the hold that fantasies about supposed early twentieth-century communist sexual and family norms exercise on the conservative imagination. One Russian interviewee explained it as follows:

> When [the] Communist Revolution happened in Russia, you know, Karl Marx, Friedrich Engels, they were against the family, so they said that family is an obsolete social institution, it's oppressive against women, it should be abolished and free love, you know. No private property, no women should belong to anyone, everybody should be making love freely anywhere they want. And that was the ideas that prevailed right after the Bolshevik revolution, so all this radical sex-liberation, and not only this, but also those ideas were tested and implemented in Russia in the twenties. (Interview, Komov 2017)

This narrative has a literary precursor in the works of the Russian émigré-sociologist Pitirim Sorokin, who emigrated to the United States from Russia in the 1920s and claimed, in his book *The American Sex*

Revolution, that changes in sexual morality foreshadow the decline of a society. Sorokin identified such a period of decline in the time of the Russian revolution: "In the first phase of the Revolution, roughly from 1918 to 1926, the institutions of marriage and the family were virtually destroyed within a large portion of the urban population, and greatly weakened throughout the whole Russian nation" (Sorokin 1956, 102). Sorokin's understanding of the perils of sexual freedom had a strong influence on the nascent American conservatism and its early proponents, including the founders of the World Congress of Families (Uzlaner and Stoeckl 2017).

The rise of moral conservatism as a political movement and the formation of the American Christian Right began in the 1970s (Schulman and Zelizer 2008). American society in the 1960s and '70s was changing rapidly. The civil rights movement began to unravel elements of segregation and expanded voting rights for Black Americans; feminist struggles bore fruit, including achieving the Equal Pay Act and the legalization of abortion; pop culture and music targeted and emboldened youth and fueled a vibrant countercultural movement associated with sexual liberation and new ways of living. Matthew Lassiter, in "Inventing Family Values," discusses how, by the middle of the 1970s, the ideal of the middle-class family appeared on the verge of collapse: "Less than half of married two-parent households and under one-fourth of all American households conformed to the nuclear family ideal of a breadwinner father and stay-at-home mother" (Lassiter 2008, 14). Politics were divided over the question of how to address this perceived crisis, or whether it was a crisis at all: the women's movement and progressive groups interpreted the changes primarily in economic terms, advocating for public policies such as funded daycare, family-friendly employment practices, and equal rights protection, while conservative leaders rejected these as a form of government interference and leftist politics. Conservatives blamed what they considered a crisis on a culture of permissiveness and the consequences of the sexual revolution. They felt that they were conducting an uphill battle against the social liberalization and pluralization of the times, which they increasingly blamed on feminists and gay-rights activists (Lassiter 2008, 15).

The 1970s are the period in which the American *culture wars*, a term sociologist James D. Hunter (1991) coined in his book of the same title, began to unfold. Hunter's book starts from the observation that moral debates in American society in the post–World War II period were no longer primarily defined by denominational differences between Protestants, Catholics, and Jews but by ideological differences between moral progressives and moral conservatives (Hunter uses the term orthodoxy to refer to the views of the latter).[3] Importantly, this divide was not between the secular and religious parts of American society—although much of the popular narrative portrays it that way—but ran right through religious communities themselves. The moral progressive and moral conservative divide becomes important for our argument in that a specific intellectual and institutional milieu of moral conservatism was created around it and politicized.

The moral conservatism Hunter and many other scholars describe (Buss and Herman 2003; Dowland 2015; Lewis 2017; Wilcox and Robinson 2011) rested on civic organizations and institutions created to mobilize support for conservative ideas and influence politics. Starting in the 1970s, moral conservative interest groups professionalized and created their own NGOs, think tanks, and foundations composing a network of moral conservatism that would span national borders. Influential leaders such as James Dobson, Phyllis Schlafly, Donald Wildmon, Beverly LaHaye, Anita Bryant, Pat Robertson, and Jerry Falwell founded politically and culturally powerful organizations of the religious Right: Focus on the Family (now called Family Policy Alliance), Family Research Council, the National Federation for Decency (now called American Family Association), Concerned Women for America, Save Our Children, Christian Broadcasting Network, and the Moral Majority, respectively. A catalyzing political moment was the proposed Equal Rights Amendment of 1972, which was designed to add equal legal rights for all American citizens regardless of sex to the United States Constitution. The amendment failed to achieve the necessary ratifications after a sustained movement of conservative organizing against it (Soule and Olzak 2004). Influential pro-life organizations were also created in this period, such as the National Right to Life Committee, the Campaign Life Coalition (responsible for LifeSiteNews, an influential anti-abortion news service active since 1997), and the American Life League. Both the literature and public commentary usually refer to these groups as the Christian Right, an established terminology that we also use in this book when we speak about American groups and organizations. Throughout the book we use the more general concept of politicized moral conservatism (PMC), because it is more inclusive of various Christian groups and those of other religious traditions, such as Islam and Judaism. The moral conservative concept also avoids the connotation that we are always dealing with a dualism, as using the term "right" implies that there is a "left." While this binary correctly described the situation in the United States in the 1970s, the years identified as the birth-moment of the Christian Right, the same cannot be said about moral conservatism in later periods in Europe and in other countries, for example Russia. In these contexts, moral conservative ideas sometimes do not develop at all and sometimes develop not in confrontation with a rival progressive agenda but through the transnational diffusion of the moral conservative narrative.

The movements of the American Christian Right accomplished what Matthew Lassiter summed up as "the invention of family values": a set of claims composing a political agenda, according to which cultural explanations triumph over economic ones in setting the terms of public debate and determining the direction of public policies (Lassiter 2008, 15–16). The institutions and their leaders defined the coordinates of Christian Right conservatism as both an intellectual universe and a style of thinking. The topics conservative thinkers and their organizations addressed ranged from the struggle against abortion, to school education, to traditional family values. They held onto the family model of a breadwinning father and stay-at-home mother, despite the increases in single-parent households, working mothers, and divorce rates. They also targeted homosexuality either by quoting biblical injunctions in the context of a religious agenda or in terms of disease and seduction (Herman 1996), but same-sex marriage and transgender recognition—the topics that motivate much of the moral conservative resistance to SOGI rights today—had yet to enter the discourse.

The 1970s therefore saw the beginning of what is today a comprehensive American moral conservatism complex with its own institutions, key individuals, intellectual networks, publications, and events. Tina Fetner (2008) has demonstrated how the relationship between progressive movements and conservative interest groups unfolded reciprocally in the domestic space of the United States: lesbian and gay activists demanded equal citizenship regardless of sexual orientation and an end to prejudice, and the Christian Right blocked social and political change efforts and organized anti-gay mobilization.

The decade that followed was a period of growth on both sides. During the 1980s, due to the HIV/AIDS pandemic that simultaneously devastated queer communities and invigorated public-facing activism (Fetner 2008, 61–63), gay and lesbian movement organizations responded to the challenges of opposition from the Christian Right with an increasingly higher degree of organization and professionalization. At the same time, the Christian Right increasingly made political inroads in Washington, primarily within the Republican Party. The struggles between lesbian and gay activists and the Christian Right that Fetner describes took place at both local and national level. Both sides operated within the context of state legislatures and US federal law, which was not ready to meet even minimal demands for SOGI rights until well into the 1990s.[4]

In other words, the lesbian and gay movement was on the early articulations of the moral conservative activists' agenda, but primarily in the context of their general lament about what they saw as cultural decay: American society becoming more permissive and liberal. Moral conservatives in that period considered the primary political battlefields to be education, abortion, and the upholding of the father-mother-children family model as a public norm. In addition, the American Christian Right upheld an economic program built around free markets, free trade, and free enterprise, and tried to keep at bay industrial culture and the formation of a working-class identity, which they viewed as urban, modernist, and radical (Moreton 2010).

Moral Conservatism in Europe

Twentieth-century moral conservatism developed differently in Europe than in the United States, primarily due to Europe's experience of fascism. In the aftermath of the First World War, not only did German conservative revolutionaries decry the threat of communism, they launched a wholesale criticism of Western civilization, liberalism, and democracy, and their radical nationalism, racism, antisemitism, and homophobia paved the way for National Socialism. Many conservatives in Germany emerged from the murderous Second World War carrying the weight of guilt and responsibility, and in all other European countries, the shock of the war imposed self-restraint on political forces, giving rise to a general pacifism and anti-nationalism in many corners of the continent. The Catholic and Protestant Churches, too, had discredited themselves by first supporting and later only half-heartedly opposing fascism and National Socialism, and they reentered the political game after the war in a spirit of compromise with the secular and liberal democratic order (Chappel 2018). The very foundation of the European Union, which is today depicted by moral conservatives as an ideological construct based on secularism, materialism, and liberalism, was actually the work of committed Christian Democrats (Driessen 2020). The murderous persecution of people deemed homosexual by the Nazis during the Holocaust likewise moved public debate, despite the fact that European states and their societies took decades to also recognize queer LGBTIQ people as victims of fascism and Nazism (Jensen 2002). In short, unlike the United States, where moral conservatism developed in a continuum from the 1920s onwards, moral conservatism in Europe experienced a pronounced break, a reset in terms of its political agenda. For moral conservative resistances to SOGI rights, this made an important difference—at least initially.

In Western Europe, as in the United States, SOGI rights activists organized with increasing success in the 1970s, using more public coming-out repertoires than previously. Building on the foundations achieved by pioneers like Magnus Hirschfeld (see chapter 1), European activists achieved modest but early domestic policy changes in some states: for example, Denmark introduced same-sex partnership legislation in 1989. While some of the more secular Nordic states moved faster on the path toward SOGI rights recognition in this period, due at least in part to the greater openness of the Protestant churches in these countries, the situation in predominantly Catholic countries like Spain, Portugal, Italy, and Belgium remained restrictive until the 2000s.

Furthermore, in many countries, SOGI rights groups had limited success with finding allies in the secular social democratic parties, which supported feminist social policies—like the right to abortion—but were overall not open to SOGI rights. This is at least partly explained by the reality that the constituents of both left and right parties consistently scored low on the acceptance of homosexuality until recently (Bishin, Freebourn, and Teten 2020; Siegel, Turnbull-Dugarte, and Olinger 2022). Until the 1990s, in Europe, as almost everywhere else, such SOGI activists faced a social and political mainstream that was overwhelmingly socially conservative when it came to issues of sexuality and gender identity, deferring to authoritative churches and party platforms to guide the debate.[5]

Throughout the 1980s, SOGI rights mobilization in Western Europe had some commonalities with its counterpart in the United States, with the important difference that Western Europe had no equivalent to the American Christian Right. The main conservative actors in European morality politics were not NGOs but the two dominant majority Christian churches (Protestant Lutheran and Catholic).[6] Religion was much more institutionally and politically entrenched in Western Europe than in the United States, with its system of religious disestablishment. Many countries, for example, implemented confessional religious education in public schools, and Christian symbols were ubiquitous and uncontroversial in the public sphere. But the public in Western Europe widely accepted the policies of the political left (Studlar 2012). In these countries, the dominant churches sustained mostly conservative positions and could rely on the support of powerful Christian democratic parties and on privileged access to policymakers (Grzymała-Busse 2015). Many controversial policies (for example, on abortion and divorce) were passed as compromise solutions between Christian democratic and social democratic parties, against the will of the reluctant churches (Engeli, Green-Pedersen, and Larsen 2012; Ozzano and Giorgi 2015).

The cooperative models between state and church that remained in place in most European countries, in contrast to the disestablishment model in the United States (Wilson 2012), contributed to descaling moral conflicts (Minkenberg 2003). Abortion, for example, had been decriminalized throughout most Western European states by 1980, but only in the legal terms of exemption from a general law, not as a right. The powerful churches managed to obtain important concessions when it came to legal changes—as can be seen in the case of abortion with the *Fristenlösung* regulation[7] and the significant hurdles in Italian divorce law. Social welfare policies for families were implemented in most

European countries, absent the ideologically charged moral debates characteristic of the United States.

In saying this, we do not mean to downplay or homogenize the conflictual nature of morality policy struggles in Europe before the 1990s. Rather, the social, religious, and political contexts in which these struggles unfolded were different from those in the United States. In social and religious terms, Western European societies were overall more secularized than American society, with church attendance numbers reaching historical lows, and fewer and fewer Europeans identifying as religious (Bruce 2002; Davie 2002; Greeley 2002). In this situation, it was harder for the mainstream churches to convey their message and for the bishops to impose their priorities on politics and the (nominally Christian) conservative parties. The conservative parties that had emerged from the fascist experience were no longer seeking a conservative revolution that would overthrow the secular, liberal, democratic order, and they were ready to move along with a changing society—so long as the changes were sufficiently gradual (for an analysis of German conservatism along these lines, see Biebricher 2018).

The situation in communist Central and Eastern Europe (CEE) and in Russia was different from that in Western Europe. With the churches largely repressed under communism, Christian conservatism was not a public or political phenomenon until much later in this region. Civil society organizing only became a force in the 1980s, when religiously motivated social movements—most famously *Solidarność* in Poland—and secular civil rights movements started to demand political freedoms. While gay and lesbian activist movements were emerging east of the Iron Curtain—for example, in Hungary (Kurimay and Takács 2016) and Slovenia (Greif 2005)—there was a continental divide, with the sexual revolution movements of the 1960–70s and the HIV/AIDs crisis of the 1980s politicizing SOGI rights earlier in Western Europe (Chetaille 2011; Owczarzak 2009). For the most part, the nascent civil societies of CEE during the Cold War were concerned with specific political rights, and the so-called culture war issues of sexual and reproductive rights did not feature centrally in them. In sum, before the 1990s, Europe had no real counterpart to the American Christian Right's intellectual and institutional complex, which (*a*) included powerful NGOs with many members and wealthy foundations that supported them, (*b*) encompassed a whole portfolio of issues—from gun rights to abortion to pornography to school prayer—and (*c*) championed close links with the Republican party.

The Conditions for Globalizing Politicized Moral Conservatism

The American culture wars began to globalize rapidly in the 1990s. We identify three reasons for this new development: debates at the United Nations and the strategies of the Vatican; the creation of international Christian Right advocacy groups as a reaction to the legal successes of transnational progressive human rights movements; and the end of the Cold War, which brought new players to the international scene. Of these three topics, the first two are already well accounted for in the literature on the Christian Right as we summarize below. We argue that the third—the impact of the end of the Cold War—is an important additional source of global moral conservative resistance to SOGI rights today.

The Vatican and the United Nations

Several scholars attribute the global strategy of the American Christian Right to the call to arms issued by Pope John Paul II in the early 1990s (Bob 2012; Marshall 2017; Butler 2000; Kuhar and Paternotte 2017; Chappel 2006). The pope identified secularism and liberalism as the main foes of the church and pushed for a "new evangelization" of Europe in the Special Synod of Bishops in 1991 (O'Riordan 1992). John Paul II's attitude has been defined by James Chappel as "paternal Catholic modernism," according to which the central site of social virtue is the reproductive family. Threats to that family from divorce, abortion, and homosexuality accordingly assumed an outsized significance in the public statements of the church (Chappel 2018, 256).

As the only religious body with the status of non-member-state permanent observer, the Vatican had long been engaged in pushing its moral conservative positions on family and women's issues within the UN framework. Two international forums triggered a particular response from the Vatican: the United Nations International Conference on Population and Development, held in Cairo in 1994, and the Fourth World Conference on Women in Beijing in 1995 (Marshall 2017; Stensvold 2017). The policy vectors identified at these forums established a connection between development, peace, and women's and reproductive rights. This alarmed the Vatican, which saw the use of reproductive and gender rights within the UN human rights framework as an attack on the natural family order and traditional, patriarchal societies. The Vatican's negative reaction to the UN Conferences in Cairo and Beijing fueled the globalization of the American culture wars.

What was so new about these conferences? First, they made it clear that women's rights activists and (to a much lesser degree at the time) SOGI rights activists had been successful in bringing their agenda to the table at the UN. The Holy See, but also Christian Right NGOs that had hitherto focused primarily on domestic struggles, realized that they had overlooked this emerging movement, and they struggled to react. The two UN conferences offered material evidence that transnational and progressive norm entrepreneurship in the language of human rights was having an impact on national legislations. Moral conservative actors, who had thus far not actively considered the international arena their primary playing field, nor made consistent use of human rights arguments to advance their agenda, were increasingly on the defensive (see Buss and Herman 2003).

Second, the politics around the two UN conferences made it clear that support for the Vatican's intransigent position was also wavering among European Catholic nations. The Vatican was forced to confront the fact that its ability to influence Western industrialized countries over reproductive and sexual behavior was substantially weakened (McIntosh and Finkle 1995, 248). No longer able to rely on the political support of the Europeans (and counting mainly on the support of African and Latin American countries), the Holy See under Pope John Paul II turned their attention to the well-organized and resource-rich American conservative NGOs. They did so to counter what they saw as dangerous trends with regard to abortion, reproductive rights, and women's rights (Buss 1998). By opening up to the American Christian Right, the Vatican effectively allied with groups that were not exclusively Catholic, but instead informed by a broad front of Judeo-Christian moral conservatism that included Evangelicals, Protestants, Anglicans, and Jewish groups.

In other words, at a moment when national churches—especially in Western Europe—were no longer able or willing to influence the policy decisions of their governments, alternative players stepped up in the form of conservative civil society organizations of the American Christian Right. Butler (2000) showed considerable foresight in observing the emerging transitional Christian Right coalitions at the UN at the time. Writing from the standpoint of the socially progressive Presbyterian Church of the United States, she recognized early on the novel phenomenon that leaders of different Christian right fringes were finding more in common on certain issues with the conservative leaders of other religions than with their own religion's mainstream (Butler 2000). She observed "increasing strategic cooperation, on key issues, among various Christian denominations and between Christian and non-Christian religions at the international level—such as the cooperation between the Vatican and certain Islamic countries" (Butler 2000, 2). In fact, most of the NGOs that play a central role in the global resistance to SOGI rights today were created in the 1990s for the purpose of forming a pro-family block of NGOs accredited to the United Nations, including the Center for Family and Human Rights (C-Fam), directed by Austin Ruse, who identifies as Catholic; the World Family Policy Center (WFPC), founded by Brigham Young University, a Mormon institution; and the interdenominationally identified World Congress of Families (WCF), which Allan Carlson founded in alliance with Russian partners. In chapter 3, we provide a more detailed look into the background of the WCF. Indeed, the events described here mark the beginning of the dynamic that characterizes our double helix model of mobilization: just as SOGI rights groups and other progressive social movements used international venues to achieve their policy goals, moral conservative NGOs and networks now sought to influence these same venues for opposite ends.

For now, the important takeaway is that the creation of these NGOs with the explicit purpose of fostering transnational moral conservative connections dates back to the mid-1990s, and originates in the context of American Christian Right NGOs mobilizing against women's and gender-based rights at the UN. Once the American Christian Right had mobilized on an international level, the natural next step was to create outposts abroad and establish transnational ties with conservative groups in other countries. The globalization of the American culture wars thus began in the 1990s and reached Europe when the role of Christian churches there appeared to be at a turning point. With numbers of active churchgoers decreasing year by year, the Catholic Church in Europe could no longer rely on a strong base for its conservative agenda. The Protestant Churches were, for the most part, already adopting more progressive policy platforms. Furthermore, SOGI rights had by now become part of the European Union's human rights infrastructure (the 1993 Copenhagen Criteria and the 1997 Amsterdam Treaty both formally incorporated elements of SOGI rights into their legal framework), and even mainstream conservative political parties were—to a large degree—conspicuously silent or (occasionally) supportive of SOGI-friendly policies in many important EU countries and increasingly less likely to be conservative revolutionaries on this front. In this situation, perceived as increasingly threatening to conservative values, the Christian Right NGOs found an open terrain to mobilize the remaining conservative Christians—and eventually even the new conservative revolutionaries: the populist right.

Christian Right Advocacy

Interestingly, the activism of US Christian Right law firms in Europe also helps explain the globalization of the American culture wars. Alliance Defending Freedom International, one of the organizations we study in detail later in the book, is an American faith-based legal advocacy organization that developed a global agenda and has been a steadfast participant in the World Congress of Families. Founded in 1993 as the Alliance Defending Freedom (ADF), it later expanded beyond the United States by establishing an international office in Vienna. Another advocacy group active at the European Court of Human Rights is the European Center for Law and Justice (ECLJ), a branch of the American Center for Law and Justice and a public-interest law firm and political advocacy group founded by Pat Robertson and Jay Sekulow in 1990. It expanded to Europe relatively quickly, with the creation of the European Center for Law and Justice in France (Strasbourg) in 1997 and the Slavic Center for Law and Justice in Russia (Moscow) in 1998. The ECLJ frequently issues amicus briefs on cases before the European Court of

Human Rights and commentary on debates at the Parliamentary Assembly of the Council of Europe, the OSCE, and the EU institutions.

But why have courts become a site of resistance to SOGI rights in the first place? These rights, as chapter 1 pointed out, can be achieved in two ways: through a political process, by which public debate, political party platforms, the parliament, and a government come to endorse SOGI rights and implement them in the law; or through a judicial process, by which a group that has been discriminated against obtains equal recognition of their rights through the courts. The latter process, achieving political goals through strategic litigation, has been a crucial strategy for SOGI rights achievements (e.g., via state, federal district, and supreme courts in the United States, and via international and national courts in Europe and Latin America). It is therefore not surprising, especially from a US perspective, that advocates of politicized moral conservatism would use the same set of tools and strategies to try and block SOGI rights through the courts. It is part of the pattern inherent in the double helix model of mobilization we theorized in chapter 1.

American Christian Right advocates started such legal activism in the 1970s (Den Dulk 2006; Lewis 2017), but for the first twenty years, their efforts in the courts remained largely confined to the national context. Indeed, US courts are notoriously less likely to follow international examples than those of many other states. From the late 1990s, the same groups began to enter the sphere of international human rights politics because conservative actors increasingly realized that international politics and court decisions elsewhere mattered. Elsewhere meant, first and foremost, the European Court of Human Rights (van der Vleuten 2014). From the late 1990s, EU countries were quickly moving ahead on equal rights protection. At around the same time, legal scholars and judges in the United States controversially debated whether US courts should ever cite foreign law and whether, if they did, this might create the conditions for legal changes inside the United States (Brumby 1999). The realization that socially progressive achievements in Europe would likely have an impact on the United States motivated conservative Christian organizations to move above the state level and counter SOGI rights internationally (Bob 2012, 72–90). Preemptive countermobilization has already been studied and theorized for anti-SOGI-rights mobilization inside and outside the United States (Dorf and Tarrow 2014; Weiss 2013).

More recently, legal scholars have also started to empirically document and theorize preemptive legal mobilization by American Christian conservative advocacy groups in other jurisdictions (Annicchino 2018a; McCrudden 2015; Fokas 2018). We build on this literature with our argument that SOGI rights groups and anti-SOGI-rights groups operate in relation to each other, following the double helix model.

When American advocacy groups intervene in European court cases, they do so in two ways: they bring a case to the court as legal representatives for a European claimant, or they file an amicus brief on behalf of one of the parties involved. The Alliance Defending Freedom International acted as legal representative in the case of *Wunderlich v. Germany*, concerning a Christian family that German authorities had prevented from homeschooling their children (ECtHR 2019). The European Center for Law and Justice submitted an amicus brief in the case *Lautsi v. Italy*, which concerned the display of crucifixes in Italian schools (Annicchino 2011).

Moral conservative human rights litigation is underpinned by a zero-sum or competing understanding of human rights, the disputed notion that the expansion of rights in one sphere naturally leads to the reduction of rights in another. This idea, which critical legal scholars have called "the myth of competing rights" (Den Dulk 2006, 200), has been used by conservative advocacy groups to claim that the implementation of SOGI rights—for example the right to same-sex marriage—can limit religious freedom, freedom of speech, or freedom of conscience. High-profile examples making this argument before the courts include the *Masterpiece Cakeshop v. Colorado Human Rights Commission* and *Ladele v. United Kingdom* cases. The former was a US Supreme Court case that involved a baker who had refused to bake a wedding cake for a gay couple due to his religious beliefs. The latter was a case before the European Court of Human Rights that concerned a marriage registrar who eventually lost her job because she had refused to officiate same-sex marriages. The global reach of the legal arguments underpinning these ideas is easy to observe. For example, somewhat similarly to Lillian Ladele, the American Kim Davis refused to issue marriage licenses to same-sex couples in her capacity as a Kentucky municipal clerk—becoming a symbol of religious persecution for the moral conservative movement and eventually winning an audience (alongside many others) with Pope

Francis. According to the competing rights argument, the baker's and the registrar's rights to freedom of conscience were infringed by the nondiscrimination requirement to provide services associated with an event (a same-sex marriage) that they deemed morally wrong.

Following Effie Fokas and Dia Anagnostou, who have studied the "radiating effect" of court judgments, we see that these cases produced not only judgments but discursive logics—the element most important to us in this chapter. Judgments "shape the normative and political frames through which individual and collective actors conceptualize social problems" (Fokas and Anagnostou 2019, 14). The European Court of Human Rights has pronounced authoritative judgments in a variety of areas that encompass how states define and manage religious freedom and diversity. Fokas and Anagnostou argue that the indirect effects of these rulings are even more important than the direct impact, that is, the formal implementation of judgments by state authorities. Indirect effects, according to the authors, "include the ways in which international human rights judgments may influence domestic debates in law, politics, and academia. They may raise public consciousness, change how social actors perceive and articulate their grievances and claims, empower national rights institutions, or prompt mobilization among civil society and other rights advocates" (Fokas and Anagnostou 2019, 9–10). It follows therefore that moral conservative and religious advocacy groups do not only, nor even primarily, go to court to win cases, but to contribute to the public framing of a controversial political question.

For anti-SOGI rights advocacy, the globalization of the American culture wars in the legal sphere has meant, among other things, the globalization of the competing rights framework, which pits SOGI rights and religious freedom against one another. Since we are not legal scholars, we will not discuss the juridical implications of this argument, but from a political sociological perspective, it is plainly evident that the globalization of the competing rights framework glosses over important differences in national politico-religious contexts. The competing rights argument originates in the context of religious disestablishment and a decades-long history of so-called culture war confrontations in the United States. As we have said, the political context in Europe is different; there, the mainstream Catholic and Protestant Churches are bolstered by privileges they have enjoyed for centuries, including legal

76 | RESISTANCES

exemptions and symbolic weight in political decision-making processes. Conservative Christian advocacy groups ignore these differences when they argue that SOGI rights claims inherently threaten religious freedom (we will return to this claim in chapter 5). A globalized understanding of this American notion of zero-sum rights contestation has come to shape politics in multiple locales.

The Christian Right advocacy groups are not alone in their strategy of framing claims in terms of rights. They are, in this case, one of two dueling networks trying to shape this argument in a right-based framework (Velasco 2023a). Indeed, the SOGI rights groups that oppose them also use legal claims and strategic litigation. However, while the conservative network frames the legal debate as a zero-sum game—"if you win, we lose"—SOGI rights advocacy promotes the idea that society as a whole will gain from more pluralism and diversity.

The End of the Cold War and the Religious Revival in Former Communist Countries

The third factor that fueled the globalization of the American culture wars was the end of the Cold War and the ensuing religious revival in countries of the former communist bloc. The 1990s were a period when the Catholic Church set out on a "new evangelization of Europe" (O'Riordan 1992), targeting all historically Catholic countries, including the former communist ones. Other religious groups and organizations in the region, from Orthodox Christians to Protestants, Baptists, and Muslims, also experienced the end of communism as an opportunity to acquire once more a place in the life of ordinary citizens and a public role in society (Ramet 1998). Evangelical and Protestant missionaries from the United States became active in the region; for them, the religious revival in CEE and the former Soviet Union was an opportunity to gain new followers and spread their message (Wanner 2007; Froese 2008). In our reading, the end of the communist regimes in Central and Eastern Europe is the real turning point in terms of global resistances to SOGI rights. The religious revival in the region had two features that are particularly relevant: social ethics and religious nationalism.

In the Catholic parts of Central and Eastern Europe, Pope John Paul II's "paternal modernist Catholicism" (Chappel 2018), which foregrounded the family in its public religious message, became the dominant frame of reference, effectively sidelining alternative Catholic frames, like Catholic socialism or what Chappel has called "fraternal modernist Catholicism." In the Orthodox parts of Eastern Europe and Russia, the search for a dominant frame was more complicated. When the Iron Curtain fell, Orthodox religious institutions were unprepared. Dmitry Uzlaner has compared the 1990s in Russia with the Western world of the 1960s: a period of unprecedented social and political mobility in which diverse lifestyles and ideas proliferated against a backdrop of economic hardship and mass political protests (Uzlaner 2019). Orthodox religious leaders and believers were far from ready to confront all these challenges.

The Orthodox Christian Churches had no social teaching to fall back on, as Orthodox Christianity has traditionally privileged spiritual and liturgical practice over social teaching. In terms of political theology and social ethics, the Orthodox churches had, for most of their history, acquiesced to state policies and did not develop their own body of social teaching to guide believers on contemporary problems. Especially in the early 1990s, with states and governments crumbling and social conditions in flux, the Orthodox churches struggled to define their own stance. The default position was to fall back on traditionalism, anti-modernism, and anti-Westernism. While Orthodox churches were being "epistemically challenged" by social transformations, the influx of American activists and Protestant missionaries had a crucial impact, most notably inside Russia. These actors made a missionary effort to bring conservative moral education to Russia and the former Soviet Union (Wanner 2007; Glanzer 2002). Orthodox clerics and activists were introduced to pro-life activism and the notion of traditional family values by Western Christian conservatives, and they incorporated those moral conservative ideas into Orthodox social teaching. This was particularly the case for Russia, where the ideological influence of Western, especially Evangelical and Protestant Christian conservatism (for which we give ample evidence in chapter 4), has often been overlooked, given the fact that Russia implemented laws that severely restricted the freedom of missionary churches to establish themselves in the country around that time (Stoeckl and Uzlaner 2022).

In chapter 5, we explain in detail the claims of politicized moral conservatism that started to take hold in the context of the religious revival in former communist countries. For now, we point out that the Western Christian Right had always seen itself as engaged in a culture war against the ideas of the political left. The enemy was communism, which the right saw as responsible for the legalization of abortion and the destruction of traditional family structures because communism emancipated women, included them in the workforce, and put children in the care of the state. This narrative rang true for many Christians in the former communist countries and had an immediate public appeal, one that social scientists in the West had not fully anticipated, as they did not foresee the powerful return of religion to politics (cf. Byrnes and Katzenstein 2006). What was certainly new for Christians in the region was the claim, made forcefully by moral conservative activists from Europe and the United States, that Western societies, where SOGI and reproductive rights were moving along the path to liberalization, were also under a "Marxist spell." The efforts of moral conservatives from the West, especially the American Christian Right, helped foment this idea—that Western liberal democracies had lost their way and were somehow being corrupted—to gain currency in the former communist societies. As we discussed above, this narrative spread via the organizations and actors who started to create a transnational moral conservative network in the early 1990s.[8]

Ironically, socially progressive activists approached the former communist countries with a similar missionary zeal, only from the ideologically opposite end, with little or no awareness that they had persuasive rivals on the ground, whose impact they vastly underestimated. Teaching democracy, human rights, equality, and the benefits of an open society were the central aims of numerous human rights NGOs, think tanks, and organizations that established themselves in the region. The bequest of many Western states, including the United States, the European Union became the primary liberalizing and democratizing agent in the region through the implementation of the *acquis communautaire* in view of EU accession.[9]

The fall of the Iron Curtain was also an opportunity for SOGI rights activists. There had been connections among groups across the Iron Curtain—for example, ILGA activists had established an East European Pool in 1981 based on a proposal by the Vienna chapter of the Austrian group Homosexuelle Initiative (HOSI). But the end of the Cold War was an exceptional opportunity to use the expansion of the EU and the desire for a "return to Europe" as a method with which to frame SOGI rights as human rights—originally in discourse common to the US and Western European movements (Ayoub and Paternotte 2014). The preexisting networks and advocacy devoted to CEE expanded after the fall of the Berlin Wall. Indeed, the initial EU grant funding that ILGA received was dedicated to democracy and civil society promotion (through the Phare & Tacis Democracy Programme) in Estonia, Latvia, Lithuania, and Russia. Yet, despite the general optimism, there were signs that liberalism would not be welcomed everywhere (Byrnes and Katzenstein 2006).

In most former communist countries, the religious revival after the end of state-imposed atheism occurred in national terms (Pew Research Center 2017). Many interpreted religious belonging as a way to reconnect to their country's pre-communist history and define anew the society's political and ethnic identity. Byrnes and Katzenstein (2006) provided a rare early warning about the religious factor in the fault lines between a Western-style liberal democracy and the emerging democracies in the formerly communist part of Europe. The tensions they identified in *Religion in an Expanding Europe* (2006) did not concern religious and cultural differences between predominantly Catholic, Protestant, or Orthodox countries, but rather, the tensions between secular pluralism and the conservative religious mainstream.

As a result of these tensions, the drive for national unity articulated in a religious key contrasted sharply with the SOGI rights movement's focus on diversity and pluralism. Especially in contexts where the church was seen as a political authority in the new character of the nation, SOGI rights faced formidable challenges (Ayoub 2014, 2013). This fusion between religion and nationalism was particularly pronounced in Poland. The Polish Catholic Church was remembered as a stalwart of resistance against both fascism and communism, and thus came to hold a disproportionate political role in the newly independent Poland of the 1990s. With the church seen as a champion of liberal democracy, and Catholicism as synonymous with Polishness, the church could vocally articulate positions against SOGI rights and women's reproductive rights. According to Polish SOGI rights advocates: "We [new EU member states] all have the post-Soviet syndrome, a lack of trust in social partners, [and we're] skeptical of NGOs and often homophobic and so-cially conservative. The difference [in processes of change among vari-ous postcommunist states] is the ties between the church and the nation. At any political event [in Poland], there are always ten bishops in the first row" (Ayoub 2016, 164, interview no. 140).

In sum, then, the end of communism and the religious revival in Cen-tral and Eastern Europe and the former Soviet Union amplified the glo-balization of the American culture wars in two ways: first, the religious revival created an enormous echo chamber for American Christian Right ideas and ample opportunities for moral conservative organiza-tions to actively spread their ideas; second, the religious nationalism in many countries in the region made societies ill-disposed to the messages of pluralism, diversity, and nondiscrimination sent out by SOGI rights activists and European institutions. Indeed, our emphasis on the Cold War as a factor in the rise of transnational anti-SOGI rights activism builds on the ways in which the literature on social movements and in-ternational relations has commonly theorized this factor. That literature has isolated the fall of the Berlin Wall as the critical juncture for the pro-liferation of transnational advocacy, arguing that the event compressed time and space via globalization and introduced many independent states into the liberal sphere of nonstate influence (Bandy and Smith 2004; Tarrow 2005). We add to that view by showing another dimension of significance at the end of the Cold War, namely that US-based moral conservative movements reacted by simultaneously perceiving threat and opportunity.

Mobilizing the Moral Conservative TAN

Given that not everybody who holds conservative views becomes an activist, and that not everybody who holds conservative views and actively promotes them uses the language and strategies of trans-national moral conservative movements, we should address how politicized moral conservative networks, specifically, come into exis-tence in the first place. Research on resistances to SOGI rights rarely addresses the question explicitly, as researchers tend to assume that moral conservative actors simply exist, and at some point, come together and mobilize around a certain cause or policy goal. The reality of this institutional growth is much more complex. Stoeckl and Uzlaner (2022) introduce the term conservative *aggiornamento*[10] to highlight the active process of learning and the creation of institutions and terminology that take place when conservative actors join the world of transnational moral norm entrepreneurship. In chapter 5, where we analyze moral conservative claims, we show in detail how transnational moral conservative actors actively propagate a shared language and strategy to draw, if not lure, domestic activists into the movement. Here, however, we begin with a more basic level of analysis and distinguish two reciprocal roads that lead to politicized moral conservative networks: from the national to the transnational, and from the transnational back to the national.

From National to Transnational

The birth of moral conservative networks requires the actors themselves take a leap of imagination—envisioning the ideas they hold as part of a transnational agenda—and then to take substantial strides toward institutionalization, professionalization, and creation of interpersonal networks. A Serbian interviewee, who we met at the WCF in Budapest, expressed the need for internationalization in plain terms:

> If we want to defend traditional values, the values of the family, the importance of Christendom in our history [and] in our culture, . . . we need to cooperate on the international level, on the European stage, because these values are being dismantled [there] by cooperation of these, how to say, anti-family organizations who act on the global scale; while these Christian organizations, parties, Demo-Christian parties, stuff like that, cooperate primarily on local levels and maybe national level. So, the level of organization, cooperation of the organization of this kind is really, really undeveloped. So, that's the thing which we need to work on. All of us. That's it. (Interview, Anonymous 2017e)

International NGOs usually have a different legal form than national NGOs, and their creation requires expertise and management skills that differ from running a national NGO. On the level of interpersonal relations, going international means encountering people from other countries who bring to the cause their own experiences and expectations. Through sustaining transnational networks with their summits, mailing lists, and strategic meetings, moral conservative actors are exposed to new challenges—one being the need to communicate across multiple languages (see a related theoretical process in Doerr 2017). However, social movement research has seen nationalism as an obstacle to transnational networking (Ayoub 2014); indeed, much of the field's foundational work had a statist orientation in that it analyzed movements with the bounds of national borders. But the evidence from our study of SOGI rights resistance movements shows that nationalism and transnationalism can work well side by side in contemporary world politics—an outgrowth of globalization that the scholarly literature did not anticipate.

In our discussion above, we have shown how for many actors on the political right in the United States, the motive behind going transnational was still rooted in national interest: moral conservative advocacy groups devised preventive legal action to forestall any legal challenges in the United States, while moral conservative pro-family groups became active at the UN to prevent human rights from evolving in a direction that would require domestic policy changes.[11] In these cases, a national NGO addressed a primarily national concern and then looked abroad in an attempt to better address that concern. This was the case with Alliance Defending Freedom International and with the creation of the so-called pro-family bloc at the UN in the mid-1990s, which the World Congress of Families largely facilitated. Like the WCF, which was created in 1995 as an international project of the Howard Center (a national NGO), the other organizations discussed above had their roots in national NGOs that existed prior to the transnational entity: Global Home Education Exchange (GHEX), which the US Homeschool Legal Defense Association (HSLDA) created, and the Spanish CitizenGo, which the Spanish anti-abortion NGO called HazteOir ("Make yourself heard") started. In these examples, the national NGOs had existed several years, sometimes decades, before taking the leap to transnationalize their work.

One point to take away from this observation is that transnational moral conservative networks should be analyzed not only ideologically but also institutionally. What institutional material reasons cause a national NGO to operate transnationally? Does it gain a greater visibility, a greater market for potential (fee-paying) members, a greater opportunity for fundraising by attracting new (foreign) donors or by reactivating habitual (national) donors by telling fresh stories? Or do ideological factors play a role, one that is rooted in the resource of moral incentives? In all our examples, the strategy to go transnational appears to have followed not only ideological goals but also, despite the TAN's rhetoric, a material logic of institutional growth.

From the Transnational to the National (NGO-ization)

Transnationalization does not only work from the bottom up. Transnational network activities often catalyze the creation of new organizations on the ground. In Russia, for example, the WCF's networking inspired the creation of at least four NGOs, all founded and directed by the same Russian activists: the Russian Institute for Demographic Research; the Analytical Center for Family Policy Russia; the Saints Peter and Fevronia Foundation for the Support of the Family and Demography; and Klassicheskie Besedy, the Russian partner of the American Classical Conversations homeschooling curriculum (Stoeckl 2020a). Similarly, in Italy, the WCF has played a direct role in the creation of the NGO Pro Vita & Famiglia, the organizer of the WCF Verona in 2019. Formerly two distinct NGOs, Pro Vita, directed by Antonio Brandi, and La Manif pour tous Italia/Generazione Famiglia, directed by Jacob Coghe, merged in the context of the WCF Verona (Pro Vita & Famiglia 2021). The latter already had preexisting transnational ties with La Manif pour tous France. These are just a few examples that demonstrate how local and regional NGOs can proliferate and grow through contact with the transnational network. Akin to the findings of scholars studying NGO-ization on other issues and in other parts of the world (like feminist TANs), moral conservative NGO proliferation via their TANs involves some of the same dynamics of mainstreaming issues and core claims (Lang 2013), which we discuss in chapter 5.

They also generate a sense of community in many places. Participants in transnational moral conservative networks themselves identify as a group, an "us." A good example for this group identification is the website *Volontè Report*, run by the International Organization for the Family, the parent organization of the World Congress of Families. *Volontè*

Report is the resurrection of the conservative *Drudge Report*, a news-aggregation website created by Matt Drudge in 1995 that focused primarily on abortion. After accusations it had taken a leftward turn during Donald Trump's first presidential campaign, the International Organization of the Family launched a new version of the report under the direction of Luca Volontè, an Italian conservative politician and activist whom we discuss more in chapter 3 (Mehta 2020). The report, which has been online since September 2020, collects news around the social conservative agenda (*Volontè Report* 2021a). The most interesting part of the daily *Volontè Report* is the section with long grouping lists: "American Conservative News," "American Conservative Groups," "Canadian Conservative NGO's and News," "Oceanian Conservative Sites," "European Conservative Groups," "Italian Conservative NGO's and News," "Conservative News in Spanish," "Conservative News in German," "Conservative News in French," "Conservative News in Portuguese," and "International Web News and Newspaper Sites." These lists are evidently an effort to create a network of organizations and websites and to self-identify as a coherent group of moral conservatives from different parts of the world. What is further remarkable is the friend-enemy dialectic evident on the website. For example, on the *Volontè Report*'s October 28, 2021, entry, there is a link to an article by Judith Butler, published only a few days earlier in the *Guardian* (Butler 2021). The comment in figure 2.1. misrepresents Butler's argument by claiming that she describes "all" Christians as fascists. It also overgeneralizes in claiming that "all Christians" are "fighting the LGBTI and totalitarian TRANSGENDER ideology," whereas there are in fact Christian movements that endorse SOGI rights (see chapter 7).

In their article, Judith Butler expresses concern about the "electronic networks and . . . extensive rightwing Catholic and evangelical organizations" that make up a global resistance to gendered and sexual minorities. The *Volontè Report* seemingly does not take issue with Butler's characterization of them, but in bad faith goes on to extend that characterization to "all Christians." By employing the dialectic of "us" versus "them [Butler]," the link identifies Butler as part of the antagonist group, a complete list of which is displayed on the website under the unmistakably clear heading "Opposition" (see figure 2.2).[12]

The development of a transnational moral conservative "us" that self-consciously speaks in the name of Christian and traditional values also

Judith Butler describes us and all christians like fascist because we are fighting the LGBTI and TRANSGENDER totalitarian ideology...

Figure 2.1. Screenshot from https://volontereport.com/. Source: *Volontè Report* (2021b).

Opposition

BATORY FOUNDATION

CENTER FOR REPRODUCTIVE RIGHTS

CLINTON FOUNDATION

FORD FOUNDATION

GATES FOUNDATION

GEORGE SOROS

GUTTMACHER INSTITUTE

ILGA EUROPE

ILGA WORLD

INTERNATIONAL PLANNED PARENTHOOD FEDERATION

MARIE STOPES INTERNATIONAL

NARAL PRO-CHOICE AMERICA

OPEN SOCIETY FOUNDATIONS

PINK NEWS

TONY BLAIR INSTITUTE

Figure 2.2. Screenshot from https://volontereport.com.
Source: *Volontè Report* (2021b).

puts the Christian churches under pressure. After decades of bishops defining the public role of their churches as collaborators with political institutions, they are confronted with grassroots movements from within their own ranks that demand a more radical course, often additionally questioning the authority of the clerical hierarchies (see, for example, the French case as analyzed by Lilla 2018).

Transnational Moral Conservative Networks Today

Transnational moral conservative mobilization against gender rights is a phenomenon of the last three decades, with an increasingly explicit and refined focus on SOGI rights in the last decade. What makes the transnational moral conservative mobilization new with respect to the conservative trends of the past—and also with respect to the American Christian Right—is the convergence of different conservative trajectories. In the United States, moral conservatism was articulated as one side in the cultural divide; in Western Europe, it was a domain of the Christian democratic mainstream that usually tried finding compromises between religious sensibilities and societal progress; in the formerly communist countries, it was deeply connected to nationalism. Starting in the 1990s, these three trajectories have come together and intertwined with surprising and paradoxical results.

The contours of present-day global resistances to SOGI rights agglomerate actors of different religious denominations, nationalities, and cultural and social backgrounds. To a considerable extent, the global resistances follow the argumentative pattern, institutional structure, and tried strategies of the American culture wars. Especially since the end of the Cold War, this can be attributed to American cultural hegemony and its pervasiveness on both the conservative and progressive sides of the values spectrum (Brooks and Wohlforth 2008). Activists on both sides of the ideological divide thus too often follow patterns of norm mobilization typically associated with the American cultural blueprint. However, it would be wrong to interpret the global resistances to SOGI rights as only a globalization of the American culture wars, or as the mere extension of a pattern that is well-known and thoroughly researched in its North American context. Instead, transnational moral conservatism is a phenomenon sui generis, with its own dynamics and evolving patterns.

The key to understanding the global resistances to SOGI rights today lies in grasping the development of a productive intertwining of different conservative traditions and the restructuring of the moral conservative field. In Western Europe, the Christian conservative mainstream parties have increasingly accepted some SOGI rights, supporting legal changes that move toward greater inclusion and equality. Against this trend, the populist right parties in many states have discovered anti-SOGI-rights as a new agenda (Graff and Korolczuk 2022)—with populist homonationalism still more the exception than the rule. They have thereby redefined themselves as the true conservatives and defenders of Christian values in Europe, in particular against Muslim immigration, but also against SOGI rights (Bracke 2012). The rejection of Muslim immigrants on the grounds that European Christian culture needs to be safeguarded also motivates the Christian turn of many on the populist right in Europe. Yet it sits uneasily with the global anti-SOGI agenda, given that Islam often upholds the gender norms that moral conservatives endorse. In Russia, in fact, where Islam is considered a "traditional religion," Muslims are included in the moral conservative camp instead of being excluded from it; and in the venues of international institutions, Islamic countries are a part of moral conservative coalitions, even if rarely the main drivers (as chapters 3 and 4 show). A similar mismatch takes place over race. It is undeniable that racism plays a role in moral conservative mobilization in countries where the white Christian autochthonous heterosexual family is presented as the norm over people of color and immigrants. But in the context of *global* moral conservatism, the Global South plays an important role. There are several examples of this in the involvement of groups from Sub-Saharan Africa; for instance, the Black Nigerian activist Teresa Okafor is one of the most committed attendees at the World Congress of Families (see chapter 3). Race, therefore, functions less as a topic of aggregation at this international level than it does domestically, for example, in White Christian nationalism in the United States (Gorski and Perry 2022), because focusing on racial divides would alienate important parts of the moral conservative network. In contrast, resistance to SOGI rights creates a universal coherence for moral conservative networks at this global level in a way that other topics—especially the question of Islam or race—do not. Geva and Santos have used "new globalist illiberal order" (2021) as an umbrella term for this new articulation of the conservative viewpoint. Other authors speak of "illiberalism" (Laruelle 2022), a "new conservatism," or "radicalized conservatism" (Linden 2020; Strobl 2021), "ultraconservatism" (Graff and Korolczuk 2022), or a "fascist trend" (Butler 2021) in an attempt to chart this dynamic restructuring of the conservative field in Europe and beyond. The success of this new political configuration lies not only in the fact that it is *against* SOGI rights, but that it stands *for* an alternative to what is perceived as the liberal political mainstream.

The topics that motivate moral conservative actors in different parts of the world range from abortion and reproductive rights to religious freedom, from education to women's and children's rights, from family values to homosexuality. Most of the organizations and networks studied in this book address more than one of these issues. If we see the politicized moral conservative worldview as a style of thinking and an evolving intellectual space with its own canonical authors, ideas, institutions, and audiences, then it is evident that the policy issues in question change: while abortion was the key issue in the 1970s and remains important today, in the 2000s, the focus has shifted more to SOGI rights. This shift in moral conservative mobilization becomes evident in part II of this book, in which we discuss the case of the World Congress of Families. In 1995, when Allan Carlson, together with the Russian sociologist Anatolij Antonov, decided to create an international organization in support of the natural family, same-sex marriage was not yet a central focus for the organization. Feminism, demographic decline, abortion, and divorce rates were the issues that energized these two activists. Yet it was not difficult later to incorporate same-sex marriage as a key point within their list of grievances. When Brian Brown, the president of the American National Organization for Marriage, took over the leadership of the World Congress of Families from Carlson in 2014, the shift in the WCF's thematic focus was fulfilled, and SOGI rights were directly in the bull's eye.

Understanding how we got there is important. As we have pointed out, many of the arguments against SOGI rights that circulate in transnational social conservative networks today date back to the 1970s and 1980s, and themselves stemmed from the roots of 1920s Red Scare politics in the United States. The claims of the 1970s and 1980s derive from various controversies over public morality, especially over women's right to choose. For example, pro-life arguments were foundational for the Christian Right in the United States, and the movement's encompassing strategies developed around the question of abortion. Initially, a child's right to life was their argument against abortion, symbolizing the "rights-turn" in conservative Christian politics (Lewis 2017). However, the movement extended its pro-life framing to claim that its central aim was also to protect women (McCaffrey and Keys 2000). Another argumentative strategy singled out abortion as a cause of demographic decline that threatens the nation, framing anti-abortion activism as a way to protect society from itself. All these arguments—developed in the pro-life context—connect directly to the claims deployed against SOGI rights, in that the fluidity of the latter is said to threaten the fixity of various aspects of the imagined nation and its society (Ayoub 2014).

In short, the key topic of anti-SOGI rights mobilization is the protection of the nation, society, traditional family, children, women, and religion. In chapter 5, we investigate these topics one by one and disentangle the different argumentative strands. For now, however, we stress that in moral conservative norm mobilization, these arguments are rarely disaggregated. They are used in unison because they form a coherent, evident meaning inside the Christian Right institutional and intellectual complex. We do not insist that anti-SOGI rights mobilization is a latecomer to moral conservative norm mobilization in order to relativize the scope of global resistances to SOGI rights. On the contrary, it is to understand why the opposition to SOGI rights has become a global and pervasive ideology today, that we trace the long history of the moral conservative ideology in which it is rooted. That history did not start with a focus on SOGI rights, even if today it commonly deploys SOGI symbolism to hold it together. Rather, it tapped into a preexisting epistemic community, alongside a wide array of themes to which different people can relate on the basis of increasingly varied experiences. This makes the globalized moral conservative institutional and intellectual complex such a powerful and versatile player.

* * *

The 1990s, then, were the period in which the American culture wars started to globalize, becoming a transnational phenomenon. The global resistances to SOGI rights of today (emerging forcefully around the late 2000s and early 2010s) have roots in this development, which in turn was the result of three factors: the conservative countermobilization at the United Nations; the creation of international Christian Right advocacy groups; and the religious revival with its conservative and nationalist overtones in Central and Eastern Europe and the former Soviet Union. As we show in chapters 3 and 4, most players that we associate with the global resistances to SOGI rights today can be traced back to one of these three developments. The overwhelming majority of NGOs working in the global resistance to SOGI rights are likewise either American, European, or Russian. All hold close ties to the American Christian Right, and their strategies and agenda mirror the work of organizations created in the US domestic context during the Cold War, even if they would potentially seem ill-suited for the varied political contexts they have diffused to. It is for this reason that we put these actors under our microscope in chapters 3 and 4. The Christian Right milieu that produced organizations like Focus on the Family, Concerned Women for America, Human Life International, and the Howard Center for Family, Religion and Society has developed an active international agenda and established ties with conservative groups in other parts of the world in order to convey a vision of society and a model of norm advocacy that is thoroughly rooted in the US culture wars. The Christian Right blueprint also explains the focus on moral choice, religious freedom, and family that we discuss in chapter 5, as well as the relative neglect of economic issues in the moral conservative norm mobilization we observe today. The emphasis on rights, the organizational form of grassroots NGOs, lobbying organizations, and advocacy groups, and the targeting of international organizations and high-level court cases are also evidence of the transnational linkages between the global resistances to SOGI rights and the American Christian culture wars pattern.

Struggles over social mores and values are a feature of every society and every epoch of human history, and controversies between different moral visions and between secular and religious actors are to be expected in modern, pluralistic societies. What we wish to highlight is not the existence of such controversies, but the ways in which they are increasingly becoming a transnational phenomenon and the mechanisms through which this transnational dynamic, in its turn, changes local forms of activism and debate. Having traced the earliest origins of this moral conservative network, explicated the conditions under which it was globalized, and described the lineage of the contemporary transnational network of actors and their claims, we now have the foundation from which to more thoroughly explore the network's various facets.

We begin in the next chapter with a detailed look at the key actors that constitute this network. Where part 1 provided the back stories of two rival transnational advocacy networks, charting the political history of their involvement and the process by which they function in a transnational space, the chapters in part 2 turn our attention to the agents that make up the moral conservative opposition. Chapter 3 covers social movement organizations and their network ties. Chapter 4 documents the institutional actors—states and IOs—that provide clout to the moral conservative TAN.

PART II

The Actors

3

Transnational Advocacy Networks

Nodal Organizations

Father Josiah Trenham, a priest of the Antiochian Orthodox Christian Archdiocese of North America and a native of Southern California, opened his talk at the 2016 World Congress of Families in Tbilisi with a prayer, to which the Georgian audience responded with customary solemnity and the sign of the cross. The talk that followed, however, in which Trenham used the pulpit to address the topic of public toilets, felt starkly different from a prayer. The priest spoke at length about the definition of the term "bathroom cruising," offering his perplexed audience a graphic description of the alleged moral dangers lurking in public toilets. At the heart of this address, Trenham attempted to establish a causal link between the emergence of more inclusive, gender-neutral bathroom facilities in mainstream culture and the homosexual "cruising" culture that preceded them. In doing so, he tapped into the widespread, mostly UK- and US-based, moral hysteria around transgender rights at the time. To a local audience in Tbilisi, however, his talk was a mix of novel, foreign, and bizarre.

* * *

Moral conservative actors have made resistance to SOGI rights a global, pervasive phenomenon by creating a broad, interlocking agenda—a political platform that they present as an alternative to the perceived liberal political mainstream. SOGI rights have become the manifestation of these actors' unifying narrative. The interwoven, networked nature of this phenomenon is evident not only in the consistency with which actors in multiple places focus on these rights, but also in the way that they use institutions, organizations, and strategies previously formed for pro-life or anti-feminist battles to oppose SOGI rights. Likewise, activists have reinvented themselves as leaders on multiple fronts and in multiple institutional settings. In part II of this book, we analyze these actors and organizations and their strategies and venues in detail, to understand the high degree of ideological and institutional interconnection within the networks opposing SOGI rights.

In this chapter, we analyze the features of the moral conservative TANs that oppose SOGI rights through the study of five exemplary INGOs that help compose the moral conservative movement (chapter 4 then turns to state and IO actors). Our task here is made easier by the fact that the literature on moral conservative TANs has been growing rapidly, and new case studies and analyses are constantly being added to this already impressive body of research. The topic of moral conservative norm mobilization has arrived in the scholarly communities of gender studies, international relations, legal studies, political science, sociology, and anthropology. In sociology, Kristopher Velasco's (2023a; 2023b; 2018) careful work has begun to track these networks and their systemic influence on the domestic policies of states in which they function. At this stage however, single country case studies with a focus on Europe are the prevalent form for studying moral conservative actors, as exemplified by the edited volumes *Anti-Gender Campaigns in Europe* (Kuhar and Paternotte 2017), *Anti-Genderismus in Europa* (Strube et al. 2020), and *Religion and Neo-Nationalism in Europe* (Höhne and Meireis 2020). Neil Datta's research and reports for the European Parliamentary Forum for Sexual and Reproductive Rights (Datta 2018b, 2021, 2020), and a wiki-based online encyclopedia entitled *Diskursatlas Antifeminismus*[1] similarly cover the panorama of moral conservative networks in Europe. While our focus is global, Europe plays an outsized role in this chapter because, as explained previously, this region plays the twofold role both as a forerunner in SOGI rights implementation, and as the new battleground for resistance to SOGI rights. The tension over this rights issue has resulted at least partly from the proliferation of transnational advocacy and the religious revival in Central and Eastern Europe.

New actors and networks of contestation around sexual and reproductive rights are also emerging in the Global South, however, as evidenced in the vignette in the introduction on the failed peace deal in Colombia. The contestation around the state's 2016 peace agreement with the *Fuerzas Armadas Revolucionarias de Colombia* (FARC, the Revolutionary Armed Forces of Colombia) took many by surprise, and gender ideology and fears of "homosexual colonization" (Beltrán and Creely 2018) figured centrally into the political discourse of the plebiscite's initial failure:

> Headlines celebrated this "first-ever" peace agreement that emphasized women's rights as a core priority. What was eclipsed by those celebrations, however, was the fact that the public referendum on the agreement failed in part due to inflammatory rhetoric about "gender ideology"—a derisive term used increasingly by conservative religious leaders to stir up a form of moral panic that links gender equality with social deterioration. The original draft of the agreement had a substantial section on gender, women's rights, and LGBTI rights, but it arrived amidst a wave of controversy that had risen to a fever pitch in 2015 over same-sex marriage and LGBTI rights in schools. (Schmidt 2020)

Scholarly bridges are being made to connect these advocacy networks in Europe and Latin America (Corrêa 2020; Corrêa, Paternotte, and Kuhar 2018; Payne, Zulver and Escoffier 2023), as are efforts to look at American moral conservative actors as part of transnational networks (Bob 2012, 2019; Buss and Herman 2003). But, overall, there is still more to do in this domain. Within the scholarly literature, the American Christian Right is still mostly seen as the motor for moral conservative norm mobilization and as a laboratory for new ideological battles, such as the current battle over critical race theory, which US conservatives are framing as a new adversary and adding to the illiberal agenda (Harris 2021).[2] In our analysis, we view the American Christian Right not only as being on the sending end of moral conservative networks and ideas, but also on the receiving end.

Given the daunting scale of this empirical field, the aim of this chapter is not to add more detail on organizations and individual actors in specific regions in the world, but to lay out—using selected organizations as examples—the different functions that various INGOs have within the moral conservative TAN and the ways in which they are connected. Using new data and network analysis to visually illustrate these ties, we offer new insights and elaborate on overarching patterns that help form an interpretation of transnational moral conservative actors and their networks. Furthermore, we ground the broader literature from our colleagues with empirical fieldwork we conducted with these actors. We first introduce five key actors and networks, each of which fulfills a specific function, in order to explicate our analysis. Thereafter, we develop three analytical perspectives on the moral conservative network: how the TAN came into existence, what characteristics the different nodes inside the network share, and what their modes of interaction are. In each of these sections, we identify new insights and summarize key findings on the relationship between the national and transnational and on the status of religion, family, and class inside the moral conservative TAN. We then analyze the varied personal, programmatic, and coordinated modes of interaction these networks foster.

Nodal Organizations

The first step is to introduce the five organizations: the World Congress of Families (WCF, called the International Organization for the Family since 2016); CitizenGo; Global Home Education Exchange (GHEX); Alliance Defending Freedom International (ADF); and the Political Network for Values (PNV). We have selected these five because each of them paradigmatically fulfills one function within the network of global resistances to SOGI rights: the WCF acts as a convenor (comparable to other "network-weaving institutions" [Ingram and Torfason 2010]) for other PMC actors; CitizenGo communicates and creates a shared agenda across different linguistic and cultural contexts; the GHEX provides the educational function of spreading and perpetuating PMC ideas; the ADF practices legal advocacy and strategic litigation; and the PNV represents a political function in which politicians from different national backgrounds are trained in a shared PMC agenda.[3] These organizations are not an exhaustive list of the TAN actors in anti-SOGI mobilization, but they represent the functions these actors may play and the broad moral conservative philosophy underlying the contemporary global resistances to SOGI rights. Our selection necessarily leaves aside other moral conservative organizations and actors, for example the advocacy group Ordo Iuris (Curanović 2021; EFP 2021), the European Center for Law and Justice, and the Agenda Europe initiative, which are also important nodes in the moral conservative TAN. In fact, some of them are connected to the network of the WCF, and we will point out these connections as we move forward. The five organizations exemplify the diversity and reach of transnational ties that carry the conservative discourse forward.

The World Congress of Families (WCF)

The WCF is an INGO inside the moral conservative TAN with the function of convening, at regular intervals, international congresses that bring together moral conservative activists from across the world. It is thus a group node inside the larger moral conservative TAN. It lays claim to the concept of the natural family, by which WCF founder Allan Carlson means a cisgendered, heterosexual, married couple and their biological offspring (Carlson and Mero 2005). Carlson has based his agenda on a narrow reading of Article 16(3) of the Universal Declaration of Human Rights, which defines the family as the "group unit" of society entitled to protection by the state.[4]

In 1999, with significant involvement by Americans, the WCF organized a conference in Geneva.[5] The meeting drew the attention of scholars because it was a moral conservative networking event in the backyard of the world's most expansive intergovernmental organizations. However, that congress in Geneva was only one in a long string of events the WCF organized. Indeed, it has held fourteen international events to date: 1997 Prague; 1999 Geneva; 2004 Mexico City; 2007 Warsaw; 2009 Amsterdam; 2012 Madrid; 2013 Sydney; 2014 Moscow; 2015 Salt Lake City; 2016 Tbilisi; 2017 Budapest; 2018 Chisinau; 2019 Verona; and 2022 again in Mexico City. In addition, the WCF organized smaller regional congresses at irregular intervals between these international summits.[6] Not all WCF congresses captured widespread attention from outside observers, but taken together, they helped the WCF grow and consolidate as a transnational moral conservative network.

For Carlson, the organization's development can only be read as a "success story." When interviewed by us on the history of the WCF, he admitted that he initially did not expect the conference to occur more than once. "I expected the session in Prague would be a sort of a free-standing event. I didn't anticipate having them more frequently or having more of them or certainly not having one every year, which is what we have been doing in the last five years. So, in that sense, it was a success" (Interview, Carlson 2019). The most important change in the WCF's history, according to Carlson, occurred when governments led by conservative parties latched on to the organization and provided increasingly sustained financial support from 2007 onwards: "Early on, we worked on a really tight budget, we did not have government sponsorship officially or even indirectly until the meeting in 2007 in Warsaw where the Law and Justice Party was. This was their first time around, and they helped. At the World Congress of Families in Verona in 2019, we had the support of the League Party. In Moldova in 2018, the Moldovan president was our host. And in Hungary in 2017, the Fidesz Party was our host and cosponsor" (Interview, Carlson 2019). Carlson's comments confirm and exemplify our more general argument about the growth of the moral conservative TAN with the help of states and through access to specific venues (chapter 4), as had also happened with the highly visible congress in Geneva in 2003.

As of today, the WCF is, strictly speaking, not an organization itself, but a label for the international events organized by what is now called the International Organization for the Family (IOF), an NGO based in Washington, DC. The formal organization that supported the creation of the IOF and WCF was the Howard Center for Family, Religion, and Society, founded in 1997 by John A. Howard and Allan Carlson after their split from the Rockford Institute, founded in 1976.[7] With Carlson's retirement, Brian Brown took over the leadership of the IOF in 2016. His previous work as president of the National Organization for Marriage had centered almost exclusively on anti-SOGI mobilization in the context of debates on the legalization of same-sex marriage in the United States. The IOF today unites several different initiatives: the Article 16 Initiative; the journal the *Natural Family*; and—most recently—the *Volontè Report* (see chapter 2).

The WCF has devised a strategy to create regional congresses and summits, advising local partners to reach out to "groups that share your values, as well as organizations and churches of *every denomination*" and to seek "endorsements from prominent political, religious or media figures that can be used in your publicity" (IOF 2020). According to this strategy, the WCF instructs its local partners to "recruit new members," to "train activists and leaders," and to "publicize your positions on crucial issues being debated in your country" (IOF 2020). Indeed, while moral conservative activists often level the empirically false charge that the SOGI rights TAN is practicing "recruitment" and "propaganda," these strategies are routinely used by moral conservative actors themselves. A French participant with connections to the movement La Manif pour tous acknowledged the important role of the WCF as a place for formation and training at the gathering in Budapest: "I am not on the board, I am not a member of WCF, actually, I have just discovered it. This is the first time I come to one of their events, and I must say, I am very impressed by all the associations who are here, by all speakers, their competences, so, I think, that was actually very important. And . . . people, simple citizens, associations, leaders, families are being trained on these issues because they are so essential, and everybody is encouraged to go on, to defend the child and his family" (Interview, Anonymous 2017f). The sentiment of this statement is suggestive of the sense of common purpose we commonly witnessed during our fieldwork at WCF meetings: the WCF plays the central role of convener, providing this networking platform for moral conservative actors and organizations.

CitizenGo

Unlike the WCF, CitizenGo is an international campaigning platform. Inside the global moral conservative TAN, it exemplifies the function of communication and public outreach strategies that actors and organizations use to gather new followers and receive attention. It was created in 2013 by Ignacio Arsuaga, the founder and director of the Spanish ultra-conservative anti-abortion NGO HazteOir. Through HazteOir, Arsuaga, who first participated in the WCF network in 2009 during the congress in Amsterdam, organized the WCF congress in Madrid in 2012. One year later, CitizenGo was registered as an NGO. In 2021, it became the subject of a report by the WikiLeaks platform entitled "The Intolerance Network" (WikiLeaks 2021). The platform released a set of documents relating to HazteOir and CitizenGo from 2001 until 2017.[8] These show that the WCF was instrumental in creating CitizenGo as a transnational and interdenominational NGO, thus significantly expanding the agenda and reach of the hitherto Spanish-only, ultra-Catholic NGO HazteOir.

CitizenGo exists today as multiple websites in different languages: English, Spanish, French, Portuguese, Italian, German, Polish, Croatian, Hungarian, Dutch, and Slovak (the Russian-language site, which existed at the time of writing this study, was taken down in the spring of 2022, presumably to obscure the group's connection with Russian partners in light of the Russian war on Ukraine). It includes two types of articles and petitions: those that are translated and published across all websites; and those that exist only in one language and are geared toward a specific (set of) national context(s). The CitizenGo platform combines both transnational and domestic content, actively grafting domestic content into the transnational sphere (and vice versa) by translating and diffusing its campaign across borders.

As an analytical example, we report here the first seventeen petition topics (out of over several dozens) on the German CitizenGo page on an arbitrarily picked date in 2021. Most of the petitions on the website were repostings (in German translation) of content that was equally available on the other sites. The number of signatures was the same across the different language-sites, meaning that they were being added up cumulatively across all national and linguistic platforms. Among the cross-national moral conservative content, resistance to SOGI rights and SOGI rights awareness was *the most prominent topic*, followed by religious freedom.

TRANSNATIONAL TOPIC: "RESISTANCE TO SOGI RIGHTS"

- A protest against DC Comics, which had announced their intent to portray a bisexual Superman figure
- A protest against the Walt Disney Company for introducing LGBTIQ characters
- A protest against LEGO Toys for "LGBTQ-indoctrination"
- A petition in support of Hungary's law against LGBT-related information in the public sphere
- A protest against the Netflix film *Benedetta* on grounds of the portrayal of the protagonist, a nun, as lesbian
- A petition against FIFA for introducing rainbow symbolism in football
- A petition to the International Olympic Committee to amend existing regulations for transgender athletes

"RELIGIOUS FREEDOM" AND OTHER TRANSNATIONAL TOPICS

- A plea to rescue Christians in Afghanistan
- A petition in support of a Finnish MP who was allegedly persecuted for publishing a Bible verse on her Twitter feed
- A petition opposing the EU's sanctions against Poland for rule of law violations

Only seven out of the seventeen randomly sampled topics were "German only" content; among these, resistance to SOGI rights was again over-represented throughout, but current political debates in Germany at the time (e.g., elections, pandemic) also appeared among the petitions.

"GERMANY-ONLY" TOPICS

- A protest against the German Railways (Deutsche Bahn) for allegedly indoctrinating passengers by displaying a rainbow flag
- A call to buttress more conservative values in German politics
- A protest against a perceived trend of aborting fetuses diagnosed with trisomy
- A petition in favor of school attendance in Germany absent an obligation to wear face masks
- A call for the election of conservative candidates in the regional elections in Mecklenburg-Vorpommern
- A call for the election of conservative candidates in the regional elections in Berlin
- A protest against COVID-19 vaccinations organized and offered inside Vienna's Main Cathedral (posted by an Austrian CitizenGo partner)

The most successful petition (in terms of receiving the most signatures) at the time of our random selection was the one against LEGO toys allegedly leading to "LGBTQ-indoctrination."

CitizenGo has also organized campaigns with billboards and buses that toured cities in North America and Europe. For these activities, the organization relies on a network of NGOs in different national contexts. The strategy of thin diffusion was explained to us by one CitizenGo collaborator:

Figure 3.1. A CitizenGo Germany petition.
Source: CitizenGo Germany (2021).

We have contacts with Poland, and we collaborate with NGOs from the United States and maybe with France, La Manif pour tous. So, I am not sure with whom we are collaborating, but I think it is with some NGOs from France, from Germany, United States, Poland, Italy. One or two months ago, we brought a bus to New York, to the United Nations, to defend freedom of education, of parents, and the freedom of speech. Maybe you have heard about this orange bus which says that boys are boys and girls are girls. For this we had to collaborate with an NGO from the United States, because it is their territory. But mostly we work online. And we need a partner in a country to organize something off-line. (Interview, Anonymous 2017d)[9]

CitizenGo exemplifies how anti-SOGI-rights mobilization communicates across different national and linguistic contexts. Just like the website *Volontè Report*, the campaigns indiscriminately address a range of different topics—from abortion to same-sex marriage to transgender rights to reproductive rights to religious freedom—in the hope that a reader who already agrees with them about one issue, like abortion, will find CitizenGo's views on SOGI rights appealing and will be drawn into the encompassing moral conservative worldview. We analyze that worldview in more detail in chapter 5.

Global Home Education Exchange (GHEX)

We include GHEX, the international branch of the American Home-school Legal Defense Association (HSLDA), among exemplary organizations in the moral conservative TAN, because it fulfills the function of education and (at least theoretically) perpetuation of moral conservative ideas across generations through moral conservative and religious education. GHEX is also connected to the WCF's network through personal ties, as a detailed network analysis by Mourão Permoser and Stoeckl (2020) has shown.

When the homeschooling movement began in the United States in the 1960s and 1970s, it was mostly driven by antiestablishment thinkers who advocated for homeschooling (or "unschooling" or "de-schooling") from a children rights' perspective. Encompassing philosophies from various parts of the political spectrum, the movement criticized the school system for being too coercive and punitive, and for constraining creativity, putting children under pressure, and not taking their individuality into account (Holt and Farenga 2003; Gaither 2008a, 117–21). Even today, a segment of the homeschooling movement is still driven by countercultural, ecological, humanist, and libertarian ideals. However, beginning in the 1980s, conservative Evangelicals in the United States started to exploit the homeschooling agenda (Gaither 2008b; Dwyer and Peters 2019). Since the late 1960s, these conservative Evangelicals had been fighting (and losing) a political battle to instill a Christian worldview into school curricula and ensure the legality of prayer and devotional Bible readings in public schools. From the mid-1980s onwards, the Christian Right changed its tactics and began advocating homeschooling as the ideal model for conservative Christians to educate their children and to combat what they viewed as the perils of secularism, moral relativism, defiance of authority, and libertinism that plagued the public school system (Dowland 2015, 78–108). Another factor that drove Evangelical parents to choose homeschooling was the public schools' science-based curriculum—homeschooling was a way to avoid Darwinian evolutionary theory and sidestep sex education.

Our analysis identifies HSLDA as a key actor among the Christian Right homeschooling network. It is the single most important US organization promoting homeschooling for reasons of moral and religious conservatism, with over eighty thousand members. Based in Purceville, Virginia, HSLDA was founded in 1983 with the aim of promoting the legalization of homeschooling in the United States and offering legal support to homeschooling families facing prosecution (Dwyer and Peters 2019, 63–65). Beginning around 2012, it became a transnational actor as well. Its international activities include accepting international memberships, publishing reports on the homeschooling situation in other countries, helping organize global conferences, offering legal advice and support for homeschoolers facing prosecution at the domestic level, providing support to lobbying initiatives abroad, and helping establish national homeschooling associations outside the United States. Like the other organizations we have discussed, it also has an international branch, GHEX, which describes its goals as "advocacy, outreach, and research." Based in Canada and founded by the chair of the Canadian HSLDA, Gerald Huebner, GHEX primarily organizes international homeschooling events.

GHEX is similar to the WCF inasmuch as it uses global conferences as platforms to promote its worldview and gather new members in different parts of the globe. The choice of locations for GHEX events is strategic, even if these strategies fluctuate between a logic of where they decide they are needed most and where they believe they have the most to gain. For example: "We went to Berlin," Huebner explained, "because Berlin is a . . . very oppressive place, [homeschooling] is prohibited and we wanted to influence that." Rio de Janeiro was chosen due to the "very large growing interest in the country and very large population to reach out to." Russia became a host because of "the interest in the family by both the Russian government and the Russian Orthodox Church" and as "a way to reach not just Russia but also the former Soviet Union countries" (Interview, Huebner 2017). For GHEX, coming to Russia was a logical continuation of their global activities. The 2018 conference in Russia was the biggest international homeschooling event to date. While two hundred people had participated in the previous conferences, over a thousand attended when it was hosted in Russia (Mourão Permoser and Stoeckl 2020). The conference brought international homeschooling parents, organizations, academic experts, and researchers from over thirty countries to St. Petersburg and Moscow. The American co-organizers responded in awe, "predict[ing] Russia would become the second largest homeschooling population after the United States" (HSLDA 2018; GHEX 2018). The conference also had global strategic significance, with the creation of an African subcommittee of GHEX which aimed "to advance, connect, and equip the African home education community in exercising the right to home educate" (GHEX 2019). The biggest-ever event in Moscow thus became a springboard for the expansion of GHEX activities into new countries.[10]

Similar to the WCF, GHEX is made up of a relatively small group of organizations and actors that form a steadfast transnational network, combined with a larger array of local or national one-time attendees. The small group of sustained membership again has an outsized impact on shaping a coherent narrative that reaches a wider membership. One aspect that is unique to the moral conservative homeschooling network is the presence of commercial actors at their events. Homeschooling curriculum providers, like Classical Conversations or the Debra Bell Academy, utilize the network to publicize their merchandise. As a result, Classical Conversations materials now exist, for example, in Russian and Portuguese (for homeschoolers in Brazil). The homeschooling curriculum providers we met explained their global outreach in ideological and missionary-like terms:

> I am from the US. But a lot of countries are new to homeschooling, Kenya or Uganda, or Canada, or Russia. We are giving other countries confidence that they can promote homeschooling, and it's a good thing for families and for their communities and their countries. You know, there [are] a lot of socialists and people who think that children belong to governments and not families. People are trying to stop us, like, maybe, George Soros, because it's easier to control people when you control their education. So anybody who is opposed to freedom is opposed to homeschooling. (Interview, Anonymous 2018c)

The homeschooling movement's wide global reach and its role in engendering key elements of the moral conservative narrative makes it an important—if often overlooked—actor in transnational anti-SOGI mobilization. Homeschooling is essentially an approach to parental authority and family hierarchy, and it forms a cornerstone of the moral conservative philosophy that researchers on SOGI rights have paid too little attention to. Indeed, the proliferation of SOGI rights has led some parents to consider homeschooling as a way to, in their view, shield their children from the worldliness of contemporary society. Given that much research has shown the importance of parasocial contact—via education, social media, and the internet—for both easing the trauma of coming out and for politicizing LGBTIQ people (Garretson 2015; Ayoub and Brzezińska 2015; Alrababa'h et al. 2021), the purposeful shielding of children from exposure to the diversity of the outside world should be of central concern to scholars and advocates of SOGI rights. The transnational networking of the global homeschooling movement is thus important to conceptualize, and it mirrors the activities of the WCF and CitizenGo. We analyze the points of connection between these networks below, showing how they overlap and arguing that a holistic analysis of anti-SOGI-rights activism requires attention to the interaction that occurs through these channels.

Alliance Defending Freedom International (ADF)

The fourth exemplary organization in the moral conservative TAN is the Alliance Defending Freedom (ADF), an American legal advocacy group. The ADF was founded in 1994 and currently has offices in Washington, DC; New York; Mexico City; Delhi; Brussels; Strasbourg; London; and Geneva; with a European headquarters in Vienna that is officially called "ADF International." The ADF describes its work as building "alliances with lawyers and like-minded organizations, providing crucial training, funding and advocacy. In cooperation with these alliances, we develop far-reaching legal strategies that protect religious liberty, the sanctity of life, marriage and family around the world" (cited in Yamin, Datta, and Andión 2018, 546; see also Dick 2021). Indeed, the ADF is deeply intertwined with the world of homeschooling advocacy introduced above. One of HSLDA's founders, Michael Farris, became CEO of the ADF in 2017. Further, homeschooling is part of the ADF's advocacy work, as evidenced when the organization brought the case of a German family— which had, like all other German families, been denied the right to homeschool their children—in front of the European Court of Human Rights (ADF International 2019). In the United States, ADF lawyers have taken cases all the way up to the US Supreme Court for many years. Among such cases is *Masterpiece Cakeshop v. Colorado Civil Rights Commission*, discussed in chapter 2.

We also include the ADF, and ADF International in particular, among the organizations we analyze because it represents the group of moral conservative actors that we called "Christian Right advocacy groups" in chapter 2. However, ADF International is not the only US-based advocacy group with an active transnational agenda. Another is the European Center for Law and Justice (ECLJ)—a branch of the American Center for Law and Justice—with offices in Moscow and Strasbourg. Of these two, ADF has been more actively involved in WCF events than the ECLJ, as our network analysis illustrates. (According to speakers' lists, the ECLJ was only actively present at one WCF summit, while the ADF figures on WCF programs over six times, with multiple representatives taking part in events). Ordo Iuris, a Polish legal organization that has recently expanded to encompass the rest of Europe, is another advocacy group that we do not cover in expansive detail here (Curanović 2021; EFP 2021).[11] Our network analysis suggests that Ordo Iuris does not have personal or institutional ties with the WCF network. This is surprising, given the clear ideological overlap, but an explanation could lie in this particular group's concern with the evident American-Russian composition of the WCF (though we should note that the moral conservative narrative has overcome the common Polish skepticism toward Russian influence for other Polish groups involved in WCF organizing).

Political Network for Values (PNV)

The fifth and last exemplary organization we analyze as part of the global resistance to SOGI rights is the Political Network for Values (PNV). This organization was created in 2014 as a platform for dialogue between politicians (mostly parliamentarians) and conservative NGOs—in particular, the WCF and CitizenGo, whose two leaders (Brian Brown and Ignacio Arsuaga) sit on the PNV board of directors. The founder of PNV was the Spanish politician Jaime Major Oreja, a member of Spain's People's Party and former minister of the interior (1996–2001) during the conservative government of José María Aznar. He created the PNV with a focus on Latin America, but the network has gradually expanded to include countries in other regions. In 2018, Oreja took part prominently in the WCF in Budapest and gave a keynote speech. Subsequently Katalin Novak, at the time, the Hungarian minister for family affairs, became the director of the PNV from 2019 until 2021. Since 2022, José Antonio Knast from Chile has directed it.

The PNV does, in fact, have a distinct Latin American orientation, and most of its members are politicians (acting and former members of national parliaments) from Latin American countries. The PNV claims to promote "a decalogue of shared values among which is the protection of human life, marriage, family or religious freedom and conscience" (PNV 2019b). Similarly to the WCF, the PNV operates through transnational and regional summits, which have also taken place in New York in 2014 (PNV 2014), Brussels in 2017 (EPP 2017), Bogotá in 2019 (PNV 2019a),[12] and (following a pandemic-related delay) in Budapest in 2022 (PNV 2022). However, unlike the WCF, the PNV summits serve to connect politicians and parties, not activists and NGOs. Its function is therefore primarily political.

The PNV specifically targets politicians who "focus on the need for legislative agenda-setting and collaboration among political peers" (EPP 2017). The summit in Brussels, for example, was organized inside the European Parliament. The group of the conservative European People's Party supported it and Laima Andrikiene, a member of the European Parliament from Lithuania, hosted it. "For the very first time, the Transatlantic Summit for Values is taking place in Europe and in the European Parliament," she said during her opening remarks. She added: "It is our honour to host this event. In the turbulent world we live [in] today we need to stay united for our values and our transatlantic cooperation is of crucial importance. Our network of legislators from both sides of the Atlantic, from Africa and other parts of the world should be *spiritus movens* in creating a better society based on Christian values" (EPP 2017).

The PNV summits are networking events that bring together parliamentarians and NGO leaders. On the list of NGOs that have participated in PNV summits are CitizenGo, National Organization for Marriage, Alliance Defending Freedom, the World Congress of Families (later under its name International Organization for Family), the European Center for Law and Justice, Red Familia, and C-Fam. These NGOs are also all part of the WCF network.

TAN Ties among the Organization Nodes

In order to illustrate the wide global reach of these networks, and their truly transnational character, this section provides a series of figures derived from a network analysis of the WCF—which overlaps directly with the other four INGOs introduced above. Up until 2019 (the period included in our network analysis), the WCF had hosted thirteen global summits. We list these summits below with Roman numbers, which corresponds to the numbering the WCF uses:

WCF I 1997 Prague, Czechia
WCF II 1999 Geneva, Switzerland
WCF III 2004 Mexico City, Mexico
WCF IV 2007 Warsaw, Poland
WCF V 2009 Amsterdam, Netherlands
WCF VI 2012 Madrid, Spain
WCF VII 2013 Sydney, Australia
WCF VIII 2014 Moscow, Russia
WCF IX 2015 Salt Lake City, United States
WCF X 2016 Tbilisi, Georgia
WCF XI 2017 Budapest, Hungary
WCF XII 2018 Chisinau, Moldova
WCF XIII 2019 Verona, Italy

The most recent global congress at the time of this writing, WCF XIV, which is not part of our corpus of data, took place in Mexico City in October 2022. We compiled the database for our network analysis from the conference programs, and the data therefore include only speakers, since ordinary participants are not listed on these programs. Figure 3.2 depicts the global network of the WCF, while figure 3.3 zooms in on the European region. As noted above, these conferences have a central function inside the moral conservative TAN. The WCF as convenor connects actors and organizations from around the world for the exchange and diffusion of ideas and strategies—including around resistances to SOGI rights. The organizations that are connected through the WCF promote a moral conservative agenda through communication, education, strategic legal action, and political networking.

The maps in figures 3.2 and 3.3 use shapes to illustrate the WCF conferences worldwide and in Europe, respectively. The circles identify the host cities of the conferences, whereas the triangles show the "sending countries"—those that send participants to the WCF summits. The thickness of the connections between the triangles and the circles is proportional to the logarithm of the number of participants of a country in a congress. The size of the triangles is proportional to the logarithm[13] of the number of participants of a country in a congress, and the size of the circles is proportional to the logarithm of the number of participants in a congress—in other words, the larger the triangle, the more participants that country sent, and the larger the circle, the more participants in the congress. One-time participants of the host country of a conference are excluded, as this would naturally overestimate that country's involvement (the data show that geographic proximity makes attendance much more likely). The geographical coordinates of the congresses correspond to the cities where they took place, whereas the triangles only indicate the country of the participants.[14]

As figure 3.3 shows, much of the WCF activity takes places in Europe, though note the centrality of the United States (in figure 3.2) as a sending country for all the conferences. This partly informs the selection of key actors in this work, given the substantial involvement of some groups like those in the United States, Poland, Italy, and Russia. Again, the size of the triangle is relative to participations, and as is evident from the maps, there is a considerable exchange among countries from around the globe.

Figures 3.4 and 3.5 zoom in on these circles and triangles to focus on the groups and participants themselves to shed light on the key norm entrepreneurs in moral conservative activism. The figures illustrate the frequency of active attendances (speakers), with regular and committed actors likely shaping the modality and narrative of the events consistently over time. Note that these frequency maps show a drop in participation for the WCF VIII summit in Moscow in 2014. This event was scheduled for September 2014, just a few months after Russia annexed Crimea and military conflict erupted in Eastern Ukraine. As a result, Russia faced international sanctions. What was unknown at the time is that one of the main sponsors of the congress in Moscow, Konstantin Malofeev, was financing insurgent Russian fighters in Eastern Ukraine

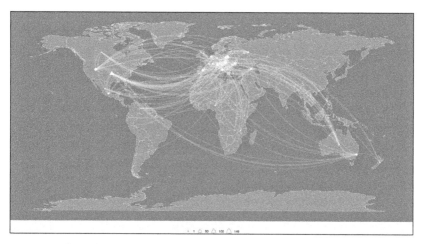

Figure 3.2. The global network of WCF organizing.

Figure 3.3. A spotlight on Europe, a central home of WCF's global organizing.

(see chapter 4). On grounds of these military and international tensions, the WCF suspended the event (Christian News Wire 2014), and it therefore occurred without major international participation, but—as figure 3.5. shows—the WCF "core group" attended nonetheless. (Cf. the NGOs in figure 3.5.)

One insight that can be taken away from the network analysis in figure 3.4. is that the group of central and stable members of the WCF network is not that large. Indeed, relatively few organizations and individuals have been consistent participants in the WCF for over a decade, and even fewer have been present since its founding over twenty years ago. Only around two dozen actors (organizations and individual

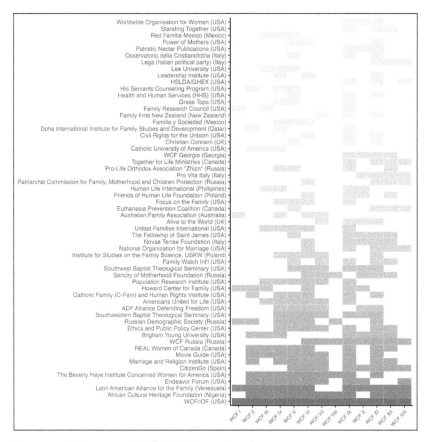

Figure 3.4. NGOs composing the WCF core network.

participants) have attended more than half of the thirteen congresses that the WCF has organized. Among the group of steadfast participants, we count organizations from the United States, Nigeria, Russia, Italy, and Spain. Each of these organizations or their leader is, in turn, a part of a larger regional network of organizations and actors, which makes the entire network geographically complex and multilayered.

Among the most faithful participants in WCF congresses is the Foundation for African Cultural Heritage (FACH), which has been reported as a participant in all but two. This umbrella NGO (not to be confused with the African World Heritage Foundation) has its seat in Nigeria and coordinates a network of organizations and initiatives across the country. FACH is not the only WCF tie to Africa, the congresses have seen representation from Kenya, Cameroon, Malawi, South Africa, Uganda, and Zambia. Our findings on WCF participation from the Global South buttress Rahul Rao's (2020) claim that networks opposing SOGI rights are more complicated than they are sometimes presented to be in critical queer theory, which has often portrayed homophobia in the Global South as solely an import from the West. Viewing them in this way, while it may hold much truth structurally, nonetheless simplifies and erases the agency of actors outside the West (like those from Nigeria, though Rao's cases are Uganda and India) that help propagate this anti-SOGI network. Another finding from figure 3.4 on NGO frequency is that WCF XI in Salt Lake City (2015) reinvigorated the network, with a high number of participating organizations and individuals, many of which subsequently committed to the network and continued to attend future events.

Finally, our analysis of the network in figure 3.5 shows that a small group of committed activists that remain attached to the organization over a long period can have a powerful impact in their local, national, and international contexts. By showing their countries of origin it illustrates the wide global reach of the network. Rather than becoming policy-actors themselves, these activists provide and diffuse a coherent philosophy and worldview to guide concrete policy initiatives on the national level and provide overarching meaning to the activities of existing local and national initiatives and entities. In some ways, like the visionary ILGA activists who understood the need for international SOGI rights promotion, advocacy by the WCF and the other groups studied in this chapter exemplifies the norm brokerage that makes transnational

Figure 3.5. Moral conservative norm entrepreneurs.

connections a central instrument for furthering policy goals and motivating action on the ground. The findings of the network analysis therefore buttress the double helix model of mobilization theorized in chapter 1. Transnational connections propagate the moral conservative narrative and sustain it over time, while modifying it as new challenges emerge from the rival strand of the double helix.

Figure 3.5 also shows the turnover in WCF participation. Above the core group (the first dozen names in the lower section of the graph), the middle range of frequent participants is clustered around the United States. The upper third of the name range indicates that, from around the time of the WCF IX, there is a more diverse national setup and more actors from Europe (Poland, Italy, Georgia, Russia, and the UK) start to attend the WCF annual events regularly. This is certainly not exclusively attributable to the fact that the post-2015 events all took place in Europe (and the former Soviet Union), since earlier WCF summits had also predominantly been organized in European countries, without generating lasting European participation beyond the core group.

Our analysis of the speakers' database also shows that the WCF has diversified over time, notably since 2014. Since the Moscow WCF (2014), participation from countries of the European Union and former Soviet Union has increased. European Union (EU-27) participation rose from 25 percent to 36 percent of the total participants, a 44 percent increase compared to the pre-Moscow phase. For European participation as a whole (fifty-one countries were included for this purpose), the increase is from 32 percent to 50 percent, constituting a 56 percent increase compared to the congresses before Moscow in 2014. The substantial increase, especially with regard to non-EU countries, is due to the congresses organized in Tbilisi (Georgia) and Chisinau (Moldova), which gave advocates connected to the Russian network greater voice in the broader moral conservative network (see appendix). In line with the overall perception developed in the literature, the fact that we see a more diverse European participation after 2015 confirms the increase in the reach of resistances to SOGI rights over the last decade, as well as the globalization of the culture wars beyond the United States. This diversification also confirms that actors from Central and Eastern Europe and the former Soviet Union have begun to play an increasingly important role in moral conservative networks.

Common Features of the Moral Conservative TAN
Interdenominational Characteristics
The transnational moral conservative network includes actors of different religious denominations—mostly Christian, but with some Jewish and Muslim members. The multireligious character of a transnational network like the WCF is not entirely unexpected, given that it spans several continents. However, it is not evident that multiconfessionalism is always an advantage for the growth of the network. From an outside perspective, the unification of resistances against SOGI rights from Catholic, Protestant, and Orthodox actors may appear the natural result of conservative inclinations that exist within each of these confessional traditions. Yet, while it is true that the Christian Churches are often (but not always) conservative, this does not necessarily make them allies in a common cause.

The Orthodox Christian Churches and the Catholic Church split in the eleventh century over theological and political struggles, and the division has continued to deepen over centuries. Notably, the Orthodox Churches do not recognize the authority of the Catholic Pope, and the denominations also disagree on fundamental theological questions. The differences are even bigger in relation to the Protestant and Evangelical Churches, let alone with the Church of Jesus Christ of Latter-day Saints (also called the Mormon Church, the LDS Church). Most Orthodox adherents do not even consider the latter a Christian religion.[15] In the WCF, all these religions are represented, and the Mormon church is an especially central player. Paul Mero, the co-author of the WCF's foundational document, *The Natural Family: A Manifesto*, is a member of the LDS Church (Mero 2017)—his co-author, Allan Carlson, is Lutheran—and LDS hosted the 2015 WCF summit in Salt Lake City, Utah.

This interdenominational composition of the WCF stands in stark contrast to the widespread anti-ecumenism within the Orthodox Churches of Russia and Georgia—the two Orthodox Churches that have thus far most openly expressed support of the WCF. At the May 2016 WCF in Georgia, Tbilisi's Philharmonic Concert Hall was packed—a third of the seats occupied by Patriarch Ilia and his entourage, who honored the WCF with his presence—when Elder Robert Gay from the Church of Jesus Christ of Latter-day Saints walked onto the stage for his speech. Gay began with a personal dedication to his wife (who promptly joined him on stage) and then elaborated the WCF's mission. Listening on their headsets to the simultaneous translation from English, the Georgian clerics politely embraced this cheerful gospel of the family from a man who, in all likelihood, they internally viewed as a heretic. Many years earlier, the Georgian Orthodox Church had deserted the World Council of Churches, one of the institutions aimed at restoring Christian unity, and it only grudgingly welcomed the Pope into the country a few months after the WCF. The Russian Orthodox Church, likewise, has strong anti-ecumenical currents in its ranks (Knorre and Zasyad'ko 2021). Yet both of these Churches have willingly assisted the WCF in hosting congresses in their countries.

What explains this variation? What is it that makes the WCF immune to this anti-ecumenism? Andrey Shishkov (2017) is an Orthodox theologian whose work sheds light on this puzzle. He points out that the insurmountable theological divisions between the Christian churches coexist with overlapping moral agendas. This is why, when it comes to collaboration between Orthodox, Catholic, Protestant, and Evangelical actors, the dogmatic and the moral vector often point in opposite directions: dogmatically they are antipodes, but in morality politics, they can become partners. Shishkov has analyzed the ideological alliances on issues of family, abortion, and gender between Catholic, Protestant, and Orthodox actors as a new form of ecumenism, a "conservative ecumenism" or "ecumenism 2.0" (Shishkov 2017). The distinguishing feature of conservative ecumenism is cooperation by religious actors on issues framed not as religious but as moral or legal. The success of the WCF can in part be explained by this mechanism. The WCF—and in particular Carlson's and Mero's manifesto, *The Natural Family*—provides a confessionally neutral conservative script, to which all Christian religious groups can relate (along with non-Christians, as exemplified by the occasional Jewish and Muslim presence).

Furthermore, apart from ceremonial religious phrases that speakers at WCF events frequently use, none of the events we attended during fieldwork included a religious ceremony as part of the official program. Instead, every congress featured a festive moment (a concert or ballet performance), several included a street march, and in general, the setting was academic and businesslike, with keynote speeches, panels, and PowerPoint presentations.

The strong interdenominational character of the WCF is what distinguishes it from other organizations that researchers have considered key players in the resistances against SOGI rights, such as the Catholic-only organization Tradition Family Property investigated by Neil Datta (Datta 2020). Indeed, interdenominationalism can be an opportunity for actors related to the WCF. For example, the documents WikiLeaks uncovered about CitizenGo revealed that the originally Catholic-only organization faced a crossroads in 2013, when Pope Francis came to office and ultraconservative circles inside the Vatican subsequently became a less reliable source of support (WikiLeaks 2021). According to the leaked papers, the Russian Orthodox benefactor of the WCF, Konstantin Malofeev, stepped in to support this constituency (Datta 2021)—although CitizenGo denied having received "donations of any amount from any Russian 'oligarch', nor from any businessman or corporation connected to Putin or Putin's government" (CitizenGo 2022b).

Catholic cardinals, bishops, and priests, and high-ranking clerics from other denominations have frequently participated in WCF events. Our database of speakers shows that the presence of the official Catholic Church was especially strong at the congresses in Warsaw in 2007 and Madrid in 2013. This is not surprising, given the Catholic dominance in these two countries. Cardinal Alfonso Lopez Trujillo took part in the WCF in Warsaw, and Cardinal Ennio Antonelli took part in the one in Madrid, both in their roles as presidents of the Pontifical Council for the Family. One of the WCF's directors, Christine Vollmer—the Venezuelan founder and president of the Latin American Alliance for the Family—was a member on the same council for many years (see below), and the presence of the cardinals and a number of other bishops attests to the strong "Catholic" connection of the WCF before 2013. Additionally, Cardinal George Pell attended the WCF Sydney (2013). The official presence of the Vatican at WCF events fizzled out after 2013, when Pope Francis made it clear that he was not interested in supporting strategic alliances in the global culture wars. The message was conveyed by the editor of the important Roman Catholic journal *Civiltà Cattolica*, the Jesuit Antonio Spadaro, who called such alliances "an ecumenism of hate" (Spadaro and Figueroa 2017). This shift in the official line notwithstanding, Cardinal Pietro Parolin was present at the WCF in Chisinau, Moldova, in 2018 (Annicchino 2018b; La Stampa 2018). When the WCF took place one year later in Verona, Italy, no official Vatican representative attended, but some Catholic bishops and priests did. Since then, the Moscow patriarchate appears to have become, at least from the perspective of the American collaborators, a key strategic partner of the WCF. Carlson calls Orthodoxy "a global religion" which is taking the place of the Catholic Church on social conservatism, claiming that "under Pope Francis, the Roman Catholic Church is kind of on these social issues pulling back. . . . Francis has decided not to emphasize pro-family and pro-life activities as much as his two predecessors . . . so I think the fact that the Orthodox Church is becoming a public witness internationally on these questions is a huge development" (Interview, Carlson 2018). In chapter 4, in which we analyze the Holy See as a state actor against SOGI rights, we will examine the shifting priorities and alliances of the Vatican in detail.

Catholic Aristocratic Circles and Activist Families

Catholic aristocratic circles and activist families also play an important role inside transnational moral conservative networks, if not necessarily in large numbers, certainly symbolically. For a transnational NGO like the WCF, which may be viewed with skepticism by conservative European Catholics since it is relatively young, American, and multireligious, the presence of Catholic aristocrats bestows legitimacy and reputation.

Catholic aristocrats from Europe or of European descent regularly participate in events of the WCF. For example, the Hungarian ambassador to the Holy See, Archduke Eduard from Habsburg, participated in the WCF Budapest, and Princess Gloria of Thurn und Taxis was seen at the WCF in Verona (2019) and Mexico City (2022). Christine Vollmer also provides an aristocratic and Catholic orientation to the organization. Speaking to us, Carlson was enthusiastic about Vollmer's role and the aristocratic "touch" she bestowed upon the WCF: "Christine comes from a very old European family, I mean, one of the oldest. She's of aristocratic blood just about every way you look. And she knows everybody, I would say, in the Catholic, in the Catholic universe" (Interview, Carlson 2018).

Vollmer was a member of the Pontifical Council for the Family for over fifteen years and a co-founder of the Pontifical Academy for Life

(DoC Research Institute 2021). Vollmer and her team have developed the *Alive to the World* "education in integrity" curriculum, a series of school textbooks devised as an alternative to sexual and civic education in schools. Her husband, Alberto J. Vollmer, served as Venezuela's ambassador to the Vatican, and together they ran the Alberto Vollmer Foundation in Venezuela. One of their seven children, Cristina Vollmer de Burelli, acted as executive director of Alliance for the Family. Christine Vollmer was removed from the Pontifical Academy of Life in 2017, when Pope Francis effectively eliminated its ultraconservative wing, eliciting considerable disapproval from the conservative LifeSiteNews (Bourne 2017). Vollmer herself published an article in the outlet, in which she said that Francis's pontificate had been "hijacked" by a "gay lobby" and that the Vatican was plotting to present homosexuality "as a legitimate use of sexuality" (Vollmer 2018). We will discuss the ultraconservative Catholic attack on Pope Francis via the "gay lobby" accusation in more detail in chapter 4. For now, it is worth noting that the aristocratic members of the WCF represent a Catholic wing that enjoyed leadership and prominence during the pontificates of John Paul II and Benedict XVI but whose fortunes have changed under Pope Francis.

The Vollmer family is also a useful example of a second group that enjoys high visibility inside the WCF, namely activist families. Christine Vollmer is the second-most-frequent participant at WCF events (see figure 3.5.), and the two organizations connected to her—Latin American Alliance for the Family and *Alive to the World*—are among the most consistent partners of the WCF. But the Vollmers are not the only activist family. For instance, Alexey Komov, the director of the Russian chapter of the World Congress of Families, runs a homeschooling curriculum with his wife, Irina Shamolina. In German-speaking and other parts of Central and Eastern Europe, Gabriele Kuby, an author of anti-gender literature which has been translated into many languages, has been succeeded by her daughter, Sophia Kuby, who works at Alliance Defending Freedom International. The homeschooling world is especially known for its family enterprises, such as those of the Bortnis family, who developed the Classical Conversations curriculum.

Personal networks connecting institutions and countries are not unique to the conservative spectrum. Clientelism has also been described as a phenomenon of NGO-ization in general (Lang 1997). However, in most settings, clientelism and parent-child relations in public office are seen as problematic, causing nontransparency and corruption. In contrast, those inside the conservative institutional and intellectual space present their personal networks positively. Since the aspiration within the conservative complex is to create a counterpublic to a perceived liberal hegemony, they consider the cultivation of close personal ties and large familial issue networks an asset. It is also a part of the social conservative's habitus to be visible as husband, wife, daughter, or son. At conservative conventions, it is not uncommon that speakers are announced as "mother of seven children and grandmother to twenty" or "father of five children," nor is it uncommon for parents to travel with their children, who are called to join them on stage at opportune moments. In short, at conservative conventions, it is common to meet several generations of activists. This is indeed an important distinction from SOGI activists, who often have different sexual and gender identities from their parents. They thus break with the common model of political socialization and activist participation as passed down via parents (Ayoub and Garretson 2017)—a pattern common both on the left and the right (Whittier 2010), especially in family-oriented moral conservative activism. The conservative milieu thereby cultivates a narrative which Carlson summed up in an interview with us, referencing Eric Kaufmann's book *Shall the Religious Inherit the Earth* (Kaufmann 2011): "What communities are having more babies, what are having less? Salafi Islam, Mormons, there's certain ultraconservative groups of Lutherans, even in places like Finland, who have big families. The Old Order Amish in the United States, Hasidic Jews have huge families. And his argument is that, you know, if these current trends continue, in about a century and a half the religious vision is the world's future. Secular liberals are just not having children" (Interview, Carlson 2018).

It does not take a lot of effort to uncover the aristocratic and family ties inside transnational moral conservative networks, and scholars before us have pointed them out (Datta 2020; Kemper 2015). Their relevance in the creation and maintenance of a stable Christian Right institutional and intellectual complex must not be underestimated. These ties also account for the innovative potential inside the conservative complex, which continues to grow and exploit new topics and strategies as younger generations follow in the footsteps of their parents. In this case, SOGI rights are also not necessarily the unique and primal focus—rather, they are part of a broad conservative portfolio of targets.

Business-Politics-Activism Linkages

One aspect of transnational moral conservative norm mobilization and global resistances against SOGI rights that preoccupies investigative journalists and the public is the question "Where does the money for all of this come from?" Different investigators have collected information on the money flows inside the moral conservative transnational networks, and the most current findings are gathered in the report *Tip of the Iceberg: Religious Extremist Funders against Sexual and Reproductive Rights* (Datta 2021). This report identified US $700 million that moral conservative sponsors spent between 2009 and 2018. The funding originated from NGOs, foundations, religious organizations, and political parties from the United States, the Russian Federation, and the EU. Data collected by the Global Philanthropy Project (2021), which measures philanthropic, organizational, and governmental sponsorship of gender and anti-gender movements, estimate the funding for moral conservative actors to be even higher, with an uptick in the most recent years. Funding for moral conservative actors "far outpaced funding" to the global SOGI rights moment. One source shows how in the period from 2013 to 2017, the anti-gender movement received more than twice as much as LGBTIQ movements—$3.7 billion compared to $1.2 billion (Global Philanthropy Project 2021, 13). For both movements, much of the global revenue originates in the United States, but—as our spotlight on Russian moral entrepreneurs below shows—a wealth of funding flows from oft-overlooked European (e.g., Spain is especially active) and Russian sources, which also play an important role.[16] The INGOs we discuss in this chapter all figure prominently in the report, especially the WCF, CitizenGo, and Alliance Defending Freedom. We add to this investigative research by providing insights for approaching the business-politics-activism linkages in the key organizations that make up the TAN opposing SOGI rights.

During observation and fieldwork, we learned that for actors in Central and Eastern Europe and the former Soviet Union, conservative norm mobilization is, in some cases, an alternative to professional work. The Russian WCF leaders, Alexey Komov and Irina Shamolina, were frank about this: the financial crisis of 2008 was the reason they abandoned business consultancy and became professional pro-family activists (Interview, Komov 2017). We did not probe further to find out who exactly paid them for working in this capacity, but it was in all likelihood not a single source, at least initially. Shamolina, who is married to Komov, worked inside the Moscow Patriarchate for several years as assistant to the head of the Patriarchal Commission for the Family, and Komov used this platform to launch a fundraising campaign to found his NGO Saints Peter and Fevronia Foundation for the Support of the Family and Demography (Stoeckl 2020a). Their business interests were also evident in their Russian translation of the Classical Conversations curriculum through the GHEX network, since subscribers pay for the teaching material. It is likely that the wealthy Russian oligarchs Konstantin Malofeev and Vladimir Yakunin sponsored this work financially on the Russian side, but their involvement only came about around 2014, when the WCF was already in its second decade of existence, suggesting other initial sources of funding.

In our analysis, a central figure of Russian involvement in the global moral conservative networks is Konstantin Malofeev. A lawyer by training, Malofeev founded an investment fund specializing in telecommunications and a philanthropic fund called St. Basil the Great in 2005. The St. Basil fund, along with his regular contact with the Russian Orthodox Church, became the platform for his involvement with the WCF, CitizenGo, and GHEX. The fund provides assistance to anti-abortion groups, former convicts, single mothers, Orthodox religious education, and churches and monasteries. Malofeev owns a number of moral conservative websites and the online TV channel tsargard.tv, dedicated to Russian nationalism, monarchism, and Orthodox culture. He became known to a wider public in the West in 2014, when he was identified as funding the Donbas insurgency in Eastern Ukraine—an act that was officially described as "humanitarian assistance" per an agreement between his fund and the so-called Donetsk Republic (Laruelle and Limonier 2021, 325). Due to these activities, he has been on the sanctions list of Western countries since 2014. Malofeev was among the most ardent supporters of Russia's war in Ukraine, calling it a holy cause and a fight against "Satanists" (EUvsDisinfo 2022).

Among the central actors in the anti-SOGI TAN, Alexey Komov has created a series of pro-family NGOs inside Russia and currently operates all the international contacts between the WCF, GHEX, and CitizenGo. Malofeev's St. Basil Fund has functioned as official sponsor of events Komov organized. In addition, scholars have managed to trace a series of web IP addresses from the Russian moral conservative digital universe back to Malofeev (Laruelle and Limonier 2021, 326), including the (now discontinued) website of the Russian WCF and other family values related websites[17] and the personal website (now offline) of Elena Mizulina, the chair of the Duma Committee on Family, Women's and Children's Affairs, who was central in passing the anti-"gay-propaganda" law and a law that blocked the adoption of Russian orphans by foreign same-sex couples (*BBC News* 2013).[18]

The third "entrepreneur of influence" worth mentioning, albeit briefly, is Vladimir Yakunin, the former head of Russian Railways. Yakunin runs the Saint Andrew the First-Called Fund, which sponsors pro-life activities, most centrally the NGOs Sanctity of Motherhood and Life. The former is directed by Yakunin's wife, Elena Yakunina, who participates regularly in WCF congresses.[19] All the actors presented in this section have connections to the Russian Orthodox Church and the Kremlin. Their central hub is the Patriarchal Commission for the Family, Protection of Motherhood and Childhood headed by Archpriest Dmitry Smirnov (1951–2020), who participated in several WCF events.

Indeed, the NGOs that make up the moral conservative TAN acquire money through their members, fundraising, philanthropic foundations, and business sponsors on the national level. Some of these NGOs have also become stakeholders on issues of family and sexual and reproductive rights and have gained an expert status that gives them access to governmental funds. One such example is the *Alive to the World* program, which Vollmer initiated and the Hungarian Ministry for Family and Youth Affairs approved as a curriculum provider in 2018—a year after the Budapest WCF summit provided an opportunity to present the program before prominent Hungarian ministers and parliamentarians (Olavarria 2018). While it is known that funders exist for SOGI rights NGOs, others

are also abundantly present for NGOs that mobilize against SOGI rights. The sources of funding also change over time and thus the fortunes of transnational activist networks can fluctuate dramatically.

Money flows in transnational moral conservative networks are not always transparent and, as in the case of Italian politician Luca Volontè, not always legal. Volontè was a parliamentarian at the Council of Europe from 2010 to 2013 and has been convicted and sentenced to four years of imprisonment for money laundering and accepting bribes in this position (La Repubblica 2021).[20] Volontè has reinvented himself as a conservative norm entrepreneur multiple times; he has maintained his position on the board of CitizenGo, has remained operative inside the WCF and IOF as the editor of the *Volontè Report*, and has founded an Italian moral conservative NGO Novae Terrae. He exemplifies the multiple identities—businessperson, politician, and activist—common among the key actors in the networks we study. The fact that important norm entrepreneurs have extensive business connections—a fact seemingly at odds with the anti-global-capitalist philosophy we discuss in chapter 5—is rarely brought to light, and network members rarely mention it, as it sits uneasily with the network's work and goals. It is one of the many contradictions between philosophy and practice that our fieldwork has made apparent—contradictions that are brushed aside via the omnipresent and unifying narrative focus on gender and sexuality.

Modes of Interaction between Moral Conservative Actors

Moral conservative actors in transnational advocacy networks relate to each other and interact in multiple ways. We define three modes of interaction: personal, programmatic, and coordinated. These are not unique to the world of moral conservatism and do not differ, in essence, from the world of progressive norm mobilization (Crossley 2016; Diani and Mische 2015).

Personal

By the personal mode of interaction, we mean that transnational moral conservative activist networks, or at least their leadership structures, depend on people and the personal relations among them. The network analysis of the WCF shows that the core group of activists who have kept the motor of the organization going over the years is actually quite small and stable. New entries into the inner circle of this core group—like Alexey Komov's entry around 2009—took place in the form of discipleship: Komov was writing his PhD dissertation with Anatolij Antonov, the Russian co-founder of the WCF, at the time; it seems that he never finished it (Interview, Komov 2017). Personal also means that functions within the networks we study in this chapter appear to be distributed on the criterium of relational closeness rather than qualifications. Trustworthiness, loyalty, and reliability are clearly the most important criteria for entry, trumping levels of expertise. One could argue that this fact makes these networks rather similar to networks of organized crime or other forms of corruption (Smith and Papachristos 2016). It is certainly different from the staff of SOGI INGOs, which have open and competitive searches, often hiring people with established records in other social movement sectors.

In table 3.1, we have tried to illustrate this point by showing how four key actors in the organizations examined form a small personal network and operational platform. The board of CitizenGo is made up of eight men—it is noteworthy that they are all men. Four are also members of the WCF: Brian Brown, Ignacio Arsuaga, Luca Volontè, and Alexey Komov. Of these four, Komov is also a board member of GHEX, and Brian Brown and Ignacio Arsuaga are directors of the Political Network for Values. In addition, each runs one or more national NGOs.

For social movement researchers, the closely knit personal structure of the network is not entirely surprising. Indeed, personal connections do explain recruitment and participation in activism (Snow and Soule 2009). That said, the centralized nature of the inner group identified in our sample is unique. It is an aspect that is not shared by the networks that promote SOGI rights.

One detail from our analysis is the way in which actors in the moral conservative TAN interact with each other on a personal level. While linguistic, cultural, national, and denominational borders constitute hurdles that could make interaction difficult, during our fieldwork we noticed that key actors related to each other in an informal and personal way. It was while observing the modes of interaction at WCF events in the former Soviet Union (Tbilisi and Chisinau) that this phenomenon

TABLE 3.1: Key networkers of CitizenGo, GHEX, PNV, and national NGOs, 2021

Name	IOF	CitizenGo	GHEX	PNV	National NGOs	
Brian Brown	President	Member, Board of Trustees		Member, Board of Directors	Co-Founder, National Organization for Marriage	
Ignacio Arsuaga	Organizer, WCF Madrid 2012	Member, Board of Trustees		Member, Board of Directors	President, Spanish anti-abortion NGO HazteOir	
Luca Volontè	Editor, *Volontè Report*	Member, Board of Trustees			Founder, Italian NGO Novae Terrae	
Alexey Komov	Main representative, Russian component of the WCF | Organizer, WCF Moscow 2014	Member, Board of Trustees	Director, CitizenGo Russia	Board Member		President, Russian NGO Fond Podderszhki Sem'i i Demografii [Fond for the Support of the Family and Demography]	President, Russian NGO Family Policy.ru Advocacy Group

Note: Table 3.1 is based on information in the public domain, namely on the lists of the respective directing boards on the organizations' websites (accessed November 6, 2021). The last column, which lists the national NGOs directed or founded by the four individuals we have identified as key networkers, is based on our own research. By July 2022, Komov was no longer mentioned as a board member on several of CitizenGo's different language websites, but his name still appears on the English-language sites.

struck us most. (For an acutely observed report in this regard, see also Gessen 2017.) Particularly noticeable was the mixture of American-style and local modes of personal interaction. Operating mainly in English, all the WCF gatherings we observed had an egalitarian ethos that everyone was on a first-name basis. But that approach immediately disappeared when participants reverted back into a native language, like Russian, German, or Italian, in which the formal "you" is typically obligatory. Second, many of the inner-circle actors had clearly known each other for many years and thus interacted informally—patting shoulders, joking across the room, sharing news about family over the breaks. In ways that are comparable to business networks (Inkpen and Tsang 2005), moral conservative actors in these networks build up social capital that helps them perform better in their role as moral conservative activists in an international context. Fieldwork observation and interviews revealed the following elements useful for building such social capital: being accompanied by one's children; personal storytelling about one's individual path to the pro-family cause; and the sharing of strong emotions—usually negative emotions like outrage and disgust. During the WCF in Tbilisi, the Italian speaker Antonio Brandi talked himself into a tearful rage over the question of surrogate motherhood, moving his audience emotionally. As we left the auditorium, we could overhear approving comments about his "performance," which turned out to be a regular feature of the other WCF events we observed in later years.

Programmatic

The programmatic mode of interaction differs from the personal one insofar as it does not require closeness. This is more characteristic of all issue networks: an NGO or a social movement articulates a grievance and formulates a set of goals, and those who identify with them are welcome to become members of the NGO or to feel involved in the social movement. For this to work, the program must be clear (involving prognostic and diagnostic framing) and made public. The organizations we have studied have been successful in making their program explicit in this fashion. Both the WCF and GHEX have passed declarations and principles in which they stake a claim on a certain topic (e.g., the family or homeschooling) and embrace a certain argumentative strategy that often depends upon human rights frames (WCF 1997; GHEX 2016, 2012). Just as the WCF has done with Article 16 of the Universal Declaration of Human Rights, GHEX has championed a human rights article: Article 26(3), which addresses the "right of parents to choose the kind of education that shall be given to their children." Through these declarations, the activists remap the discursive space of international human rights law, locate their claims in relation to specific articles in human rights documents and treaties, and develop a relatively consistent strategy and terminology through which to present these claims. This observation follows research that shows the normative power of human rights (Sikkink 2017) and reveals that even those who challenge human rights as they are often understood nonetheless simultaneously seek to use their language (Bob 2019).

The programmatic nature of the WCF and GHEX may not seem particularly noteworthy, but if we contrast it with another widely reported transnational anti-SOGI-rights initiative, the relevance becomes clearer. This initiative is Agenda Europe, which was a thematic platform born around 2013 (Datta 2018b). First appearing publicly that year in the form of an anonymous blog, the Agenda Europe manifesto covered news and developments in European politics by critiquing legal and political advances in human rights in relation to sexuality and reproduction. Agenda Europe quickly became a go-to source for traditionalist perspectives on sexual and reproductive rights, and in the year that followed, various religious advocates heralded it as a promising new initiative for the movement to preserve religious authority in the battle for sexual and reproductive rights (Datta 2018b, 5). In 2017, a production of the Franco-German ARTE Television network published a number of documents that shed light on the people behind Agenda Europe. These documents included programs for a founding meeting in 2013 and subsequent annual Agenda Europe summits, a social media master list with participants' names, as well as the common manifesto for the Agenda Europe network, entitled "Restoring the Natural Order: an Agenda for Europe" (Datta 2018b, 5). The actors behind Agenda Europe were conservative, mostly Catholic politicians and members of parliament from different European countries. Datta retrieved the programs and speakers' lists from the Agenda Europe summits, and from these sources, we see that Agenda Europe overlapped with the TAN actors studied here. His report includes an extensive list of anti-SOGI-rights initiatives that he believes are the work of the Agenda Europe network, including the referendum for constitutional revision for Marriage and Family Protection in Romania (Datta 2018b, 43). The Agenda Europe summit programs he retrieved also include some of the individuals we mentioned above.

This example shows how anti-SOGI mobilization can also work behind closed doors—differently from the public face of many of the TAN actors we analyze in this chapter—secretively and hidden from the public. Once the information mentioned above about Agenda Europe became public (via ARTE's program and the Datta report), the people behind the agenda (who continued to remain anonymous) were forced to release a statement disavowing the whole initiative. While the initial blog is now discontinued, a new website was created solely for the purpose of denying all charges regarding the existence of an organization or manifesto. It claims that the Datta report "incorrectly 'identifies' and links three distinct entities as components of Agenda Europe: The Agenda Europe Blog, the yearly Summits, and the manifesto 'Restoring the Natural Order.' The Agenda Europe network has no links to or control over the Agenda Europe blog (and the Twitter Account), despite use of the same name. The document 'Restoring the Natural Order' is not an Agenda Europe publication. It is a paper drafted by an individual person without any involvement of Agenda Europe" (Agenda Europe Network 2018). There have not been any visible Agenda Europe activities since 2018, which suggests that the network was either short lived or has become more adept at keeping its activities away from the critical public gaze.

Coordinated Actions

The third mode of interaction that is relevant for understanding moral conservative transnational networks is coordinated actions. This is not peculiar to moral conservative organizations, but it is part of the social movement repertoires of all the organizations presented in this chapter. CitizenGo relies primarily on coordinated action, describing its goals as "using online petitions and action alerts as a resource, to defend and promote life, family, and liberty" (CitizenGo 2022a). For example, the organization launches petitions in multiple languages, generating coordinated debates and initiatives across multiple countries. Back in 2017, during an interview with us, the Russian WCF leader Alexey Komov prided himself on his transnational connections. He offered this example about the coordination of Moscow protests against an initiative to amend the constitution to legalize same-sex marriage in Mexico:[21] "When our Mexican friends . . . I think it was this fall [2016] . . . when their president tried to introduce same-sex marriage on the federal level in Mexico . . . our Mexican friends they asked to make a big lobbying rally near the Mexican embassy in Moscow and we did it. With some posters. And we arranged it in Washington, in Madrid, in many countries around the world" (Interview, Komov 2017).

This form of coordinated action mirrors that of SOGI rights activists. They too commonly protest in front of embassies that pass homo- and transphobic legalization, for example, staging protests in front of Russian embassies in Berlin and many other cities in 2012 after Russia's so-called anti-gay-propaganda law (Ayoub 2016). And the SOGI TAN and important funders in that network (e.g., Mama Cash and Open Society Foundation) also help coordinate and fund groups doing these local manifestations. Many SOGI groups mobilized to protest the WCF's meeting in Verona, and, as we discuss in chapters 1 and 7, they too were supported by a global network of allies.

* * *

The INGOs analyzed here—the World Congress of Families, CitizenGo, Global Home Education Exchange, Alliance Defending Freedom International, and the Political Network of Values—are central nodes of an increasingly coordinated moral conservative TAN that concentrates more and more on resisting SOGI rights. In this chapter, we have tried to shed light on the inner workings of this complex TAN by analyzing its origins, the ties that bind actors in the network together, and the modes of interaction that they pursue to mobilize people in many corners of the globe. We now turn our attention to the key states and IOs (often religious institutions) that support the work of this TAN and together make moral conservativism a defining feature of contemporary world politics.

4

States and International Organizations

*Hungary, Russia, the Vatican, and
the Russian Orthodox Church*

In June 2020, Russian President Vladimir Putin mocked the US embassy in Moscow for flying a rainbow flag during Pride month, making a petty and vitriolic comment about the flag reflecting the sexual orientation of the diplomats who worked there (*Moscow Times* 2020). Indeed, United States embassies regularly display symbols supportive of SOGI rights in a variety of countries; while in some countries the practice is not encouraged, a rainbow flag is no longer an unusual occurrence. The gesture dates back to US State Department guidelines President Barack Obama set up, and it even continued at select embassies during the time of President Donald Trump—though in a much more limited fashion, since the Trump administration officially put a halt on SOGI symbols (Morello 2019). Embassies of many other countries also lend such support in places where SOGI rights are under pressure. At the height of protests against Hungary's contested anti-LGBTIQ bill in July 2021, the British Embassy in Budapest distributed little "Love is Great Britain" flags emblazoned with a rainbow version of half the Union Jack. Rainbow flag diplomacy is just a minor symbolic example[1] of how states and international organizations (IOs) show support for SOGI rights, but it complements the broader incorporation of such issues into governmental bodies, sometimes in a form that lends tangible support to local activists and transnational advocacy networks (TANs) mobilizing for such rights.

In chapter 1, we distinguished between pioneering or first-mover states that have become forerunners of SOGI rights and the many states whose governments are compelled to take initial steps to incorporate SOGI rights as these rights become part of a set of international human rights norms. Most of the LGBTIQ politics research on states that then take action to resist these norms has focused on resistance in the national realm. But this state-led opposition to SOGI rights is also increasingly leveraged internationally. This chapter introduces a selection of key states and international organizations that play a central role in supporting transnational moral conservative activism. Naturally, states are not uniform entities that act by themselves, and their positions also depend largely on specific governmental action, which varies on the basis of domestic constituencies and electoral outcomes. In short, states as actors for or against SOGI rights are neither permanent nor impermeable; governments change and political constellations inside a country shift in light of domestic and transnational political dynamics, shifts that explain strategic attitudes vis-à-vis SOGI rights. Consider the United States, whose role as either a facilitator or a blocker of SOGI rights internationally depends on which domestic political constellations control foreign policy, with more recent Democratic administrations (especially post-Obama) acting as global facilitators of SOGI rights and Republican administrations rolling them back (Huckerby and Knuckey 2023; Langlois 2020; Burack 2017).

In talking about states as actors in the global resistance to SOGI rights, we take a parsimonious approach and identify only states that have played an outsized role as leaders of the global resistance to SOGI rights today while recognizing that this role is not determined or fixed. We do this by tracing the complicated history of interaction of state and IO authorities with moral conservative actors (including some that readers will recognize from chapter 3). These authorities have done much work to promote an image of their states and IOs as an alternative to a secular, liberal democratic model of politics. Through the lens of constructivist international relations (IR) theory, we explain how this process also builds state identity around issues like so-called traditional values and specific moral conservative claims, which we then analyze in more detail in chapter 5. The state and IO actors we select as ideal types in this chapter currently play an active role as blockers of SOGI rights in world politics and at various international governmental organization (IGO) venues, in ways that we describe in chapter 6.

This chapter analyzes two states that exemplify resistances to SOGI rights in recent years: Russia and Hungary. These are certainly not the only two states whose governments actively oppose SOGI rights in the international sphere, but they are among the most vocal candidates in

136 | STATES AND INTERNATIONAL ORGANIZATIONS

this domain and the most familiar to us and our interviewees, making them ripe for analysis. They are also two countries that have hosted a WCF event.

Hungary has in recent years been especially vocal in opposing and questioning the SOGI rights policies the EU has advanced, though this is often also true of Poland under Law and Justice (PIS) governments (Ayoub 2013; Juhász and Petö 2021). It is also no surprise that Russia has been in the purview of gender politics scholars for almost a decade, given its prominent role in blocking SOGI rights advancements in both domestic and international institutions (Stoeckl 2016; Wilkinson 2014; Sleptcov 2018; Nuñez-Mietz 2019; Carlson-Rainer and Dufalla 2016). We argue that, despite differences between them, the resistance to SOGI rights plays a similar role to the governments' positions in Russia and Hungary: it creates domestic consensus by scapegoating LGBTIQ groups, and it lays the groundwork for transnational alliances in defiance of liberalism.

Like states, international organizations can either facilitate or block SOGI rights. For example, the EU Commission, and more recently the UN agencies, are typically viewed as facilitators of SOGI rights, whereas faith-based IOs often oppose them. The IOs we focus on in this chapter are the Vatican and the Russian Orthodox Church, which exemplify global resistance to SOGI rights.[2] While much of the book thus far has analyzed the social movement organizations and INGOs that make up the moral conservative transnational advocacy network, the IOs and state actors we explore here actively facilitate the reach and impact of moral conservative ideas and networks.

While Hungary, Russia, the Vatican, and the Russian Orthodox Church are all worthy candidates when studying resistances to SOGI rights, less obvious—and somewhat less explored—are the common facets that bring them together in an alliance. Indeed, at first sight, there is much more that divides them: Hungary is a member of the EU and NATO, which Russia considers as geopolitical antagonists. In Hungary, Russia—the successor of the Soviet Union—was long viewed as the historical oppressor. Russia and Hungary are also different cases as Russia cannot be considered a democracy; it is an authoritarian regime and has used a discourse of traditional values (including resistance to SOGI rights), illiberalism, and anti-Western exceptionalism to garner domestic and international support. Hungary has used some of the same rhetoric, but it is instead a (fragile) democracy, despite the fact that the ruling party, Fidesz, has put in place legal mechanisms that restrict fair elections (Transparency International 2022). A similar record of differences is true for the two IOs. The Catholic Church and the Russian Orthodox Church are historically divided by a millennium of theological and ecclesiastical rivalry and disagreements, which no shared suspicion of SOGI rights could easily gloss over. What needs to be explained, therefore, is how resistance to SOGI rights can form a bond between states and IOs that remain simultaneously divided in terms of doctrine, political alliances, and geopolitical interests.

Movements for SOGI rights have developed a set of symbols—such as the rainbow flag—that have become powerful identifiers for their cause with global reach.[3] Resistances to SOGI rights have been attempting to catch up in terms of symbolism, for example, with the creation of a pink (sometimes blue) "natural family" flag with a stylized heterosexual couple and two (sometimes three) children, often displayed at pro-family rallies. For the most part, however, state agencies and IOs have instead developed a shared language and terminology. States and IOs identify each other as part of a global resistance to SOGI rights by invoking the term traditional values. Moral conservatives define these values roughly as follows: insistence on a unique and homogeneous character of the nation based on religion, culture, and history, often by cultivating one authoritative understanding of past processes and events; emphasis on the visibility of religious or national symbols in the public sphere; defense of the rights of believers or autochthonous citizens at the expense of the rights of religious and sexual minorities or foreigners; opposition to all forms of SOGI rights; and restrictions on women's and reproductive rights. The term traditional values suggests continuity with the past and rootedness in established practice, but as a political ideology for international alliance-making, it is actually relatively new.[4] It is a label given to practices and ideas which conservative actors dramatize as politically and normatively relevant in response to the liberal and egalitarian evolution of the international human rights system and its impact on domestic politics. (In chapter 5, on claims, we explore in more detail the meaning and emergence of so-called traditional values as a moral conservative anti-SOGI ideology.)

Figure 4.1. The so-called natural families flag. Source: Monaghan (2015).

The states we discuss in this chapter have taken on identities as defenders and mouthpieces of the traditional values agenda, actively lending support to the moral conservative actors and IOs that mobilize in the name of those values. We first trace the development of Russia and Hungary and then of the Russian Orthodox Church and the Vatican as SOGI rights resisters. Subsequently, we address their motivation, asking why states and IOs actually invest political and institutional resources in prolonged efforts to oppose SOGI rights.

Russia

Russia launched a military attack and large-scale territorial war against neighboring Ukraine in February 2022. Russian leaders and commentators advanced many arguments to justify the war: security concerns over NATO moving closer to the Russian border; the safety of the population living in the separatist regions of Donbas and Luhansk allegedly threatened by an imminent Ukrainian counteroffensive; the "ingratitude" of the Ukrainian nation vis-à-vis its "generous" Russian neighbor; the "illegitimacy" of the elected Ukrainian government; and the threat of nuclear weapons that Ukraine was allegedly developing. Among these claims, one stuck out: the defense of Orthodox Christians against Western values and gay Pride parades (Riccardi-Swartz 2022). The Russian President Vladimir Putin likewise used resistance to SOGI rights to justify Russia's conflict with the West, calling the sanctions which Western states were imposing on Russia an example of "cancel culture" and comparing them with the reaction to J. K. Rowling's exclusionary statements on transgender rights (*Guardian* 2022). Such arguments were not new, given the vehemence with which the Russian state and the Russian Orthodox Church had criminalized expressions of gay and trans identity and condemned the West as a destructive force over the past two decades. But, however unsurprising, it remains alarming to observe anti-SOGI speech employed to justify a war. How did we get to this point?

With the dissolution of the Soviet Union, the Russian Federation became its legal successor state and thereby a signatory of the Universal Declaration of Human Rights and the Helsinki Accords. In 1996, the country also entered the Council of Europe and, through the ratification of the European Convention of Human Rights, fell under the jurisdiction of the European Court of Human Rights (ECtHR) in 1998. Russia was objectively not ready for membership because it failed to meet several criteria, but it was admitted to the Council of Europe nonetheless, in the hope that membership would produce the positive Strasbourg effect and bring the country closer to Western liberal democracies (Mälksoo and Benedek 2017, 4). This was wishful thinking in many respects, not only with regard to SOGI rights. But it was the issue of SOGI rights that made it immediately clear that Russia had no intention of integrating into the liberal international system of human rights. While few IOs had clearly articulated rules and norms on SOGI rights in the mid-1990s, Russia would stand out as a resister to these rights as they became more incorporated in Strasbourg. The ECtHR rulings in this area, including *Bączkowski and Others v. Poland* in 2007, ruled that public assembly for LGBTIQ people had to be respected.[5] Despite this, in 2013, the Russian Duma passed a law that banned "the propaganda of non-traditional sexual relations to minors." "Propaganda," the Russian law specified, was the "distribution of information directed at creation of non-traditional sexual arrangements, attractiveness of non-traditional sexual relationships, a perverted image of the social equality of traditional and non-traditional sexual relationships, or the imposition of information about non-traditional sexual relationships and creation of interest in such relationships among minors" (Russian Federation 2013). Several Russian cities had already passed similar legislative amendments. The one enacted by St. Petersburg in 2012 used especially explicit language and redeployed a homophobic trope that links homosexuality to pedophilia: "Public actions directed at propaganda of homosexuality, lesbianism, bisexuality, transgenderism among minors will be subject to application of an administrative fine. . . . Public actions directed at propaganda of pedophilia will be subject to application of an administrative fine" (St. Petersburg Law 2012)

Among other things, these laws were intended to prohibit Pride parades, which had started to take place with some regularity in Russia after 2006 (Wilkinson 2014). At a time when Russian LGBTIQ activists were slowly starting to demand more visibility and rights, the state was using a heavy hand to quash such hope. Meanwhile, the Council of Europe and the European Court of Human Rights responded as they did in Poland, but with a far less potent effect: in 2010, the European Court of Human Rights ruled that repeated bans of Pride marches by the city of Moscow had been discriminatory and violated the European Convention of Human Rights; in 2017, the European Court of Human Rights found that the 2013 law banning "propaganda of nontraditional sexual relations" was discriminatory; and in 2021, the Council of Europe once more "expressed concern" over the fact that Russia never implemented the recommendations to repeal the law (Council of Europe 2021b). These efforts were to no avail; in 2022, in the wake of the invasion of Ukraine, the federal law against "LGBT-propaganda aimed at minors" was extended to include "LGBT-propaganda to adults," de facto criminalizing any act or public display of same-sex relationships (Sauer 2022), and in 2023, the Kremlin introduced another law banning gender reassignment surgery and changes to gender identity markers (*Guardian* 2023).

* * *

We spotlight Russia's crackdown on LGBTIQ people, and the limits of the European human rights regime for a specific reason: more than twenty years after Russia joined the Council of Europe, it exhibited no identifiably positive Strasbourg effect but rather a human rights backlash. By

2022, it had effectively severed its ties with the Council of Europe over the war in Ukraine, thus putting an end to this period of aspirations and frustrations (European Parliament 2022). What becomes evident, looking back on the last two decades, is that SOGI rights had become the chief battlefield on which Russia demonstrated its disdain for the international human rights regime and Europe's supranational institutions. It is the first country inside the Council of Europe to have rebuked the nature and authority of the European Court of Human Rights in such a direct manner—exemplified in 2015 when it implemented the idea that its domestic institutions had national constitutional primacy over international human rights law. Hungary has tried to do the same within the EU, as we discuss below. What is more, by willfully ignoring rulings and recommendations from the Council of Europe, the Russian authorities consistently demonstrated to Russian citizens that they could not count on support from European institutions. The extent of that disdain for these institutions was on display when, as frictions arose with the Council of Europe over the war in Ukraine, Russian prime minister Medvedev announced that ending Russia's membership would allow the country to reintroduce the death penalty (*Moscow Times* 2022b).

Russia has built its image as defender of traditional values and resister of the liberal human rights regime in great part on the exclusion and scapegoating of the Russian LGBTIQ community. Russian authorities have taken little risk in doing so, as the Russian public holds overwhelmingly negative attitudes vis-à-vis homosexuality—and elite cues of political homo- and transphobia have worsened those attitudes. According to the Pew Research Center, only 14 percent of Russians said in 2019 that society should accept homosexuality, marking a drastic decline from 22 percent in 2002 (Laruelle 2023; Pew Research Center 2020). Homosexuality was only decriminalized in Russia in 1993 and removed from the list of psychiatric illnesses in 1999. Consequently, the practice of coming out, as well as LGBTIQ activism, are somewhat recent phenomena in Russia—though that is also true for many other countries in the world, and several have not decriminalized homosexuality at all. The constant pressure by the government and the official policy of enforcing traditional values has emboldened extremist hate-groups to attack the LGBTIQ community, meaning that very often, becoming visible is dangerous and potentially life-threatening (Buyantueva 2018, 474–75; Feyh 2015).

A considerable body of research now explores and explains the widespread homophobia in the light of Russia's history and recent political developments (for starters, see Healey 2017; Moss 2017). Several authors have pointed out that homophobia—and sexuality in general—have become tools of political legitimation for the Russian regime (Sperling 2015; Essig 2014). Indeed, the scapegoating of the LGBTIQ community links sexuality and gender to broader geopolitics, as queer people are externalized through being branded as foreign agents (Kollek and Rasputin 2023). In 2012, one year before the anti-gay-propaganda law, the Russian Duma passed a law that made it obligatory for politically active NGOs that receive financial support from abroad to self-register as foreign agents—an approach related to the one the United States used during McCarthyism in the 1950s. The foreign agent law has undermined the strength of SOGI rights organizations, as they cannot receive funding from the domestic government and thus have historically depended on international funding sources (Pakhnyuk 2019, 489). In its actions, Russia exposes the full range of what Weiss and Bosia have called "political homophobia," a purposeful state strategy of scapegoating sexual and gender minorities for political purposes.

Our analysis up to this point may seem overly simplified: the Russian state capitalizes on societal prejudice against the LGBTIQ community for political gain and in order to snub Western governments and human rights institutions. However, the complete story has additional layers, one of which is the agency of politicized moral conservative actors.

With the end of the Soviet Union and the difficult economic transition of the 1990s, Russia plunged into a crisis of national purpose. By the early 2000s—during the first presidency of Vladimir Putin— the creation of a state ideology thus became a central objective of the Kremlin. By 2005, the new ideology promoted by the presidential administration was labeled as "conservatism," representing a centrist position between liberalism and communism (Laruelle 2017). By stimulating the general demand for an ideology of conservatism, the Kremlin opened a space for a diversity of conservative narratives to flourish. According to Marlene Laruelle these doctrinal products were elaborated "by different groups of ideological entrepreneurs who have room to act, to determine their preferences, and to cultivate their own networks. Their fragile entrepreneurship must work in permanent negotiation and tension with competing groups and the presidential administration itself" (2017). The Russian participants in the transnational networks of anti-SOGI-rights activism that we mentioned in the previous chapter—the oligarchs Konstantin Malofeev and Vladimir Yakunin, and Russian WCF leader Alexey Komov—represent one camp in this internal struggle for the Kremlin's attention. They were instrumental in connecting the Kremlin's strategic preference for conservatism with Christianity, morality politics, and traditional values (for a more comprehensive assessment, see Stoeckl and Uzlaner 2022; see also the following investigative reports: Datta 2021; Dornblüth 2019; Southern Poverty Law Center 2018). Ultimately, all these actors, organizations, and networks, including the Moscow Patriarchate, which we write more about below, should be interpreted as crafting a coherent moral conservative agenda which is attractive to the Kremlin: they create the agenda of traditional values, in the name of which the government can restrict liberal freedoms back home, and they create a global network of moral conservative allies who sympathize with Russian positions (even against those of their own governments) when it comes to questions of geopolitics.

In the intricate world of Russian conservatism (see Suslov and Uzlaner 2019), different ideological concepts rallied for political prominence: patriotism, monarchism, nationalism, imperialism, and traditional values. A look at the evolution of Russia's national security doctrine shows that "traditional values" largely prevailed (Stoeckl 2022). We argue that three factors are decisive in explaining why these traditional values became so prominently linked to opposing SOGI rights: the Kremlin's search for a conservative content that would stand out as anti-Western, illiberal, and defiant of international human rights; moral conservative actors, including the Russian Orthodox Church, that formulate and provide this content using the resistance to SOGI rights as a central marker and as a topic that creates coherence with moral conservative actors elsewhere; and a Russian mainstream society that holds largely negative and exploitable views on LGBTIQ issues, and therefore a mainstream seldom motivated to question official discourse and policy in that domain. Each of these three levels plays a part in Russia's transition from a hopeful new member of the Council of Europe in 1996 to a proud resister of SOGI rights today.

The resistance to SOGI rights that we often associate with Russia today has evolved over more than two decades. Around 2000, as manifest in the publication of its Social Doctrine, the Russian Orthodox Church became alert to SOGI rights as a "problem" and responded by formulating arguments around traditional values and demanding preventive action (Social Doctrine 2000). Around 2005, the Kremlin settled on conservatism as a national ideology, giving a green light to all sorts of actors (think tanks, religious actors, politicians in parliament and in the regions) to begin to elaborate conservative agendas. In 2009, the Moscow Patriarchate got the opportunity to test its traditional values idea at the United Nations Human Rights Council (see chapter 6). By then, the actors, think tanks, and groups clustered around Malofeev and Yakunin had entered the scene, forcefully representing Russia inside moral conservative TANs like the WCF or CitizenGo (see chapter 3). By 2012, the traditional values machinery was fully operating both domestically and internationally: a World Congress of Families was held in Moscow in 2014, two more Congresses were held with Russian participation in Tbilisi (Georgia) in 2016 and Chisinau (Moldova) in 2018, the GHEX took place in St. Petersburg in 2018, the Moscow Patriarchate coorganized the World Summit in Defense of Persecuted Christians with the Billy Graham Evangelical Association in 2017, and the Russian branch of CitizenGo set up their own website. The constitutional amendment of 2020 incorporated "traditional values" and "marriage between man and woman" into the Russian Constitution.

All these developments have made Russia a global player against SOGI rights, and they are met with widespread recognition inside the moral conservative TAN. One participant interviewed at the WCF summit in Budapest stated: "There are congresses every year, well, almost every year. And they are all special, and they have their own merit. But I have to say up to that point, Russia absolutely shone out like a beacon" (Interview, Anonymous 2017b). This feeling was also shared by other long-standing WCF members: "Russia is standing out. President Putin is very much admired by so many people. The press tends to be so against him that many people perhaps mute their admiration because they are afraid of what people will say, but everybody admires what he is doing. He is a real leader, he is looking out for the good of his country, and many people in Western Europe and in America are envious" (Interview, Vollmer 2017).

With hindsight, this timeline may look as if there were a carefully designed plan to turn traditional values and resistance to SOGI rights into a tool of Russian soft power. But in our view, these developments are better described as the outcome of a series of loosely coordinated initiatives and policies, all of which, in one way or the other, responded to the Kremlin's idea to make conservatism the ideological foundation of the Russian state. Malofeev and those like him were successful in turning moral conservatism and resistance to SOGI rights into one of the most productive chapters in the Kremlin's "conservative playbook" (Laruelle 2020)—indeed, so productive that it would be used to justify the war against Ukraine in 2022.

Hungary

Inside the European Union, Hungary and Poland are the two countries that have most openly challenged the EU's anti-discrimination and pro-SOGI policies, though many other member states also have a troubled record when it comes to the ratification of the EU's equality directives (Ramet 2006). We focus here on Hungary, which has emerged more visibly in the transnational moral conservative network reaching out to Russia and to the United States, in contrast to Poland, where anti-gender and anti-feminist politics have largely remained geared to a domestic audience and to Brussels.

In 2017, Hungary hosted the WCF. It was a three-day event, complete with a street fair and "family day" in the center of Budapest. Hungarian prime minister Viktor Orbán and his then-minister for family affairs, Katalin Novak, gave the WCF delegates a warm welcome. Novak subsequently played a leadership role in the PNV, as we mentioned in chapter 3, serving as board director of the network that was otherwise almost exclusively composed of Spanish and Latin American politicians. Like those in Russia, Hungarian businessmen are among the funders of moral conservative activities. Datta has identified several wealthy Hungarian entrepreneurs as sponsors of anti-gender activities (Datta 2021), and Hungary has been involved as financial sponsor and host of the WCF, CitizenGo, and the PNV. Among these and other actors in the moral conservative TAN that we studied and analyzed in detail in chapter 3, Orbán enjoyed a high reputation as a defender of family values and was often named in one breath with Vladimir Putin. As one regular WCF participant put it, while praising the hospitality received in Hungary, lashing out against homosexuality was more welcome in Central and Eastern Europe.

> Each of the events that I've been to has had a little bit different character. The one in Amsterdam, for example, well, this is Western European country, quite liberal, and they were kind of reluctant to have anyone even talk about homosexuality . . . they were afraid that the authorities would shut it down, or they would get too much negative publicity, and so we could talk about the family in general, promoting, you know, family structure. But they didn't want me to hand out publicity about homosexuality. Now that, here in Eastern Europe, that's not a problem at all. (Interview, Anonymous 2018e)

Moral conservative actors regularly considered the model of Putin's Russia and Orbán's Hungary as a reliable axis in their universe—one to emulate. Christine Vollmer said, "I think that Russia and Hungary are giving an example which I hope many countries will have the courage to follow" (Interview, Vollmer 2017).

In 2021, the Hungarian government passed a law that banned information about SOGI topics and simultaneously imposed new penalties for pedophilia. What has been referred to as both an anti-gay-propaganda law and the Hungarian Anti-Pedophilia Law calculatedly conflated homosexuality and pedophilia in an example of state-sponsored homophobia. The so-called anti-gay-propaganda measure prohibits educators and television broadcasters from offering information about LGBTI people to children under the age of eighteen—effectively limiting LGBTI rights discourse and advocacy in the public sphere. The bill is inspired by infamous legislation the Russian parliament passed in 2013 (Verseck 2021), which Human Rights Watch says has imperiled LGBTIQ youth there since (Human Rights Watch 2018).

Orbán himself set the tone for this constructed conflation of issues when he stated: "Hungary is a tolerant, patient country with regard to homosexuality, but there is a red line that must not be crossed: Leave our children alone!" (quoted in Verseck 2021). Many civil society organizations, including Amnesty International, protested against the move, and a petition opposing the legislation reached more than a hundred thousand signatures (Verseck 2021). About ten thousand people demonstrated on the streets of Budapest, and the UK government displayed the "Love is Great Britain" banners that we mentioned earlier.

The law served two purposes: it was a calculated affront to EU legislation, by which Orbán wanted to demonstrate that Hungary should be free to disregard EU regulations, and it also helped elevate Hungary's reputation inside the transnational moral conservative universe. Inside the EU, much outrage was directed at the new Hungarian legislation. Political leaders like EU Commission president Ursula von der Leyen—who called it a "shame"—and German chancellor Angela Merkel spoke out against the Hungarian government's breach of the rights and values associated with EU membership (Siebold 2021). But several of the leaders of former communist Eastern Europe refused to sign a letter of condemnation, highlighting a wider rift across the continent on positions regarding the rule of law, human rights, media rights, and LGBTI rights (Wesolowsky 2021; Furedi 2018).

Unsurprisingly, Hungary received praise from the American Christian Right, where some public figures openly wished that the Hungarian move would be emulated in their country: "What the Hungarians banned, or at least restricted, was advertising and other forms of information aimed at propagandizing children and minors for a permissive, left-wing take on LGBT. . . . Given what US parents are learning about how teachers and school officials systematically deceive them on how they propagandize children to accept genderfluid identities, a lot of us would love it if our local representatives passed a similar law" (Dreher 2022a). While related laws have a long history in the United States as a result of the Christian Right mobilization in the 1970s—making it somewhat unclear who is emulating whom—moral conservative activists got their wish in Florida, which passed its own, more limited, anti-gay law, which activists refer as the Don't Say Gay Bill, in 2022 (Mazzei 2022). Hungary's reputation as a stronghold of conservative values in Europe has indeed grown steadily among conservative Christians in the West, with its steadfast supporters providing flashy headlines. Conservative writer Rod Dreher's remarks that "Orbán defends Euro Christianity better than the Pope" (Dreher 2021) appeared alongside similar endorsements from Fox News and Donald Trump (Zerofsky 2021). After February 2022, when Putin

148 | STATES AND INTERNATIONAL ORGANIZATIONS

and Russia became a less appealing partner inside the moral conservative transnational advocacy network, due to Russia's invasion of Ukraine,
many conservative actors, especially in the United States, appear to divert
their praise and hopes to Orbán's Hungary. The American Conservative
Political Action Conference (CPAC) was organized in Hungary in both
2022 and 2023 (cf. Sanders and Jenkins 2023). The American Conservative
Union described the conferences as "a flagship project for conservatives
building their international alliance, and this year's CPAC Hungary will
concentrate on the liberals' nightmare: the international convergence of
national forces" (CPAC Hungary 2023). At the conference, visitors could
have their picture taken under a banner proclaiming a "No Woke Zone"
and speakers repeated common talking points against liberal media, immigration, and gender and sexuality.

Hungary's record on SOGI rights is mixed. It decriminalized homosexuality in 1961, making it something of an outlier in the former communist bloc though also not unique, as Poland had decriminalized it
in the 1930s (Szulc 2017). Hungary's first SOGI rights organization was
formed in 1988, and lesbians and gays were included in domestic partnership legislation as early as the mid-1990s. Unregistered cohabitation
was passed in 1996 and registered partnership was passed in 2007. The
notorious paragraph of the Hungarian Criminal Code that mandated
different ages of consent for homosexual and heterosexual relations was
revoked in 2002 (Renkin 2007, 269).

At the same time, however, SOGI rights awareness in the country
remained low and the gender mainstreaming measures the European
Union enforced in its accession requirements were not widely welcomed
(Kováts 2020; Fodor 2021, 13). In fact, after its landslide victory in 2010
(followed by successive electoral victories in 2014, 2018, and 2022), one
of the first pieces of legislation Viktor Orbán's Fidesz government rolled
back were gender mainstreaming measures, ending the requirement to
eliminate gender stereotypes in the national curriculum for kindergar-
tens. Subsequently, the parliament refused to ratify the Istanbul Convention by claiming offense at the word gender in the document. The Fidesz
government also stopped funding NGOs that addressed gender equality
(Fodor 2021, 2). A constitutional amendment in 2012 enshrined the requirement that marriage consist of a man and a woman, albeit leaving
untouched earlier legislation on registered same-sex partnerships.

In 2018, Hungary changed its law on higher education institutions and banned gender studies from universities (Engeli 2020). Gender studies were harmful, useless, and ideological, according to one politician's statement. The statement represents much of the debate: "You don't have to be a specialist or an expert to see that the demand for gender studies on the job market is pretty low. It is no secret that we want to build a Christian democratic country in Hungary that protects normality and life based on Christian values. Well, the fact of the matter is that the idea of gender is not a science but an ideology, moreover closely related to the liberal ideologies, and therefore, I think, cannot fit in" (cited in Perintfalvi 2020, 176). The gender studies ban was only the beginning of more systematic political attacks on institutions of higher education such as the Central European University and NGOs like the Open Society Foundation (Geva and Santos 2021) (see chapter 6 for academia as a venue of SOGI rights resistance).

Fidesz's anti-SOGI-rights agenda has largely been determined by what we describe in the next chapter as the "nationalist" moral conservative claim (Forest 2018). The party emphasizes the nation over the individual and collective, communal values over individual human rights. Buzogány and Varga (2018) have traced the root of this ideological agenda to conservative epistemic communities inside and outside Hungary that were inspired by the classical European conservatism of Leo Strauss and Eric Voegelin. They come to the conclusion that it is not, or not primarily, a reaction to neoliberalism (centering the negative consequences of the minimalist state from a welfare perspective) that motivated Hungary's conservative identity under Orbán, but a more general conservative critique of the state's failure to define, pursue, and promote national interests (Buzogány and Varga 2018). Orbán's conception of "illiberal democracy" was explicitly directed against the liberal democratic project, focusing on international human rights law and anti-discrimination directives (Orbán 2021).

* * *

Eszter Kováts and Andrea Pető (2017) have emphasized that the anti-gender mobilization in Hungary happened almost exclusively from the top down. They speak about "anti-gender discourse without a movement" and show that, unlike in countries like Poland or Russia, it has been not strong Christian churches that guide the government's line on sexual and reproductive policies, but the majority party. Christianity does play a role in the conservatism of Fidesz, but mostly as a Christian identity marker against Islam (Perintfalvi 2020). This leading role for the majority party is something that Hungary shares with Russia—and it distinguishes the mobilization around traditional Christian values in these two countries from that in Poland, where the influence of the Catholic Church is key and the population is strongly influenced by the teachings of conservative Polish clerics. In Hungary and Russia, the state has led on anti-gender campaigning, not activist groups. In those states, the resistance to SOGI rights is a political tool for attacking international human rights and the international political system, which both Putin and Orbán reject (Nuñez-Mietz 2019). Both countries thus follow the logic of Meredith Weiss and Mike Bosia's (2013) understanding of political homophobia, which state authorities can implement preemptively for political gain—with or without movements demanding action for or against SOGI rights.

The Russian Orthodox Church

> Since [US secretary of state] Hillary Clinton has announced that gay rights are human rights . . . and all the Sodomites of the planet are under the protection of the USA, there is one thing left for us to do: take all the children on Earth under our protection, and stand up for their right to grow up and be raised in normal families . . . the Church, until the end of its days, will defend the rights of every little one to not be dragged into sin. (Hieromonk Dmitry [Pershin] quoted in Hill 2016, 31)

The priest of the Russian Orthodox Church who made this statement, Hieromonk Dmitry, had participated in hearings at the Saint Petersburg court in February 2012, prior to the adoption of the law "On Administrative Violations in St. Petersburg" that put a ban on "propaganda of homosexuality." The Russian Orthodox Church, or more specifically the Moscow Patriarchate as its ecclesiastical leadership and strategic center, played a key role in the adoption of this regional law, as it did in the adoption of the federal law approved by the Russian State Duma less than a year later.

Scholars have frequently viewed the Russian Orthodox Church (ROC) as an instrument of Russian soft power and foreign policy, treating the Moscow Patriarchate not as an independent actor but as a kind of ideological arm of the Kremlin (Curanović 2012). Here, we argue rather that in the context of the global resistances to SOGI rights, the Moscow Patriarchate has acted as agenda-setter for the Russian state, and in doing so, compliments the more-studied role of the Catholic Church in transnational moral conservative activism (see below). The earlier section on Russia explained how the Moscow Patriarchate interacted with other moral conservative actors in order to influence the Kremlin's strategies against SOGI rights. In this section, we focus on the ROC as an international organization and moral norm entrepreneur in its own right.

To start with, it is important to recognize that for the Russian Orthodox Church, the post-Soviet decades brought not only freedom but also enormous internal and external challenges. The church experienced an undisputed revival: the state restituted thousands of church buildings and religious artifacts; monasteries reopened; a large number of Russians (re)discovered the Orthodox faith; and the church restored its role as the public religion in the eyes of Russian citizens (Burgess 2017; Stoeckl 2020b). During the first ten years after the collapse of the Soviet Union, the church focused on itself—its place in society, religious education in schools and the military, church entitlements and privileges, and restitution of the property and religious artifacts taken away during Communism. The church's rapid growth in wealth and influence was accompanied by highly symbolic and visible signaling, such as the reconstruction of the Christ-Savior Cathedral in the center of Moscow.

In terms of religious teaching, however, the church was poorly prepared to address modern life challenges. It needed to catch up in almost all areas of pastoral work and social teaching. The publication of *Bases of the Social Concept of the Russian Orthodox Church* (the Social Doctrine) in 2000 was a first step in this direction. In this document, the church laid out its position on a number of issues: church-state relations, law, family, society, biotechnology, globalization, and homosexuality. Overall, the Social Doctrine showed the Russian Orthodox Church to be dyed-in-the-wool, dogmatically conservative. It addressed the twenty-first century through the writings of the church fathers of the first millennium, largely ignoring alternative or reformist currents that also exist inside Orthodoxy.[6] The document was also explicit in its position toward homosexuality:

> The Holy Scriptures and the teaching of the Church unequivocally deplore homosexual relations, seeing in them a vicious distortion of the God-created human nature. . . . The debate on the status of the so-called sexual minorities in contemporary society tends to recognise homosexuality not as a sexual perversion but only one of the "sexual orientations" which have the equal right to public manifestation and respect. It is also argued that the homosexual drive is caused by the individual inborn predisposition. The Orthodox Church proceeds from the invariable conviction that the divinely established marital union of man and woman cannot be compared to the perverted manifestations of sexuality. She believes homosexuality to be a sinful distortion of human nature, which is overcome by spiritual effort leading to the healing and personal growth of the individual. Homosexual desires, just as other passions torturing fallen man, are healed by the Sacraments, prayer, fasting, repentance, reading of Holy Scriptures and patristic writings, as well as Christian fellowship with believers who are ready to give spiritual support. (Social Doctrine 2000)

The ROC is unequivocal in its rejection of SOGI rights in the Social Doctrine, turning resistance against them into a central feature of the church's teaching and agenda. The Doctrine uses language like "propaganda for homosexuality" that is a forebearer of the terminology that the legal amendments enacted throughout Russian regions in the years to come employed:

> While treating people with homosexual inclinations with pastoral responsibility, the Church is resolutely against the attempts to present this sinful tendency as a "norm" and even something to be proud of and emulate. This is why the Church denounces any propaganda of homosexuality. Without denying anybody the fundamental rights to life, respect for personal dignity and participation in public affairs, the Church, however, believes that those who propagate the homosexual way of life should not be admitted to educational and other work with children and youth, nor to occupy superior posts in the army and reformatories. (Social Doctrine 2000)

The Social Doctrine also included a direct and distorted condemnation of transgender identities as a form of "perverted human sexuality," as "rebellion against the Creator," and as "sin." Curiously, the drafters of the Social Doctrine gave precise instructions on how to treat transgender members of the church: "If 'a change of sex' happened in a person before his or her Baptism, he or she can be admitted to this Sacrament as any other sinner, but the Church will baptise him or her as belonging to his or her sex by birth. The ordination of such a person and his or her marriage in church are inadmissible" (Social Doctrine 2000).[7]

Unmistakably, the Russian Orthodox Church's clearly expressed position toward LGBT people in the Social Doctrine is one of profound intolerance and rejection. Just like the Catholic Church and other conservative Christian churches, the Russian Orthodox Church expresses an attitude aptly summarized as "love the sinner, hate the sin" (Lynch 2005). In practice, at least as it relates to sexuality, this means that lesbian, gay, and bi believers are welcome inside the church as long as they live celibately, but they are unwelcome and ostracized when they embrace their sexuality. In Christian circles in the United States, this distinction is sometimes discussed as "side A" and "side B"—the latter referring to lesbian, gay, and bi Christians who espouse to a celibate or ex-gay lifestyle, the former to Christians who actively endorse their sexuality and seek accommodation by their churches, for example through the celebration and blessing of same-sex marriages (Mason 2021). The Moscow Patriarchate's teaching on homosexuality seems influenced by this distinction, placing the focus almost exclusively on it as an issue of public (and ecclesiastical) policy and public morality.

The Russian Orthodox Church's teaching on homosexuality combines a long tradition of Russian homophobia (Healey 2017), patristic doctrine (Zorgdrager 2013), and a global anti-SOGI-rights agenda that has its origins outside Russia, in the global culture wars. This last aspect interests us most here. The church's contacts with the American Christian Right date back to the early 1990s, and its pro-family positions, which have become the central tenets of Russian domestic and foreign politics today, were deeply influenced by cooperation with American pro-family and pro-life activists. American Christian Right groups actively promoted conservative family values and traditional gender roles in the early years after Perestroika (Glanzer 2002, Essig 2014). They helped create the first

Russian anti-abortion groups and pro-family groups that determine the church's anti-SOGI stance today. The Patriarchal Commission for the Family, Protection of Motherhood and Childhood, which we previously mentioned as part of the orbit of the moral conservative norm entrepreneur Malofeev, was particularly instrumental in integrating Christian Right ideas into the official teaching of the Russian Orthodox Church (Stoeckl 2020a; Uzlaner and Stoeckl 2017; Mancini and Stoeckl 2018). Other ideas and practices more commonly associated with the American Christian Right—like homeschooling—have also been imported into the Russian Orthodox milieu (Mourão Permoser and Stoeckl 2020). All this is evidence for our argument that the role of the Moscow Patriarchate as a force against SOGI rights is not simply rooted in a conservative church's prejudice against homosexuality and transgender identities but is instead the result of a learning process in which Orthodox religious actors came to see themselves as part of a global resistance to SOGI rights.

This vision of participation in a global battle over SOGI rights is visible in the priest's statement quoted at the beginning of this section, combining as it does references to US secretary of state Hillary Clinton, human rights, the protection of children, and the "sodomites of the planet." It is, of course, deeply ironic that the construction of "the homosexual" as a foreign agent in the service of an external power (the United States) that has to be resisted in the name of innocent children is also a foreign import—it follows the global moral conservative narrative against SOGI rights discussed in more detail in chapter 5.

The Russian Orthodox Church has been instrumental in promoting the laws that discriminate against LGBTIQ people inside Russia, but it has also acted as a force against SOGI rights in the international sphere. The Moscow Patriarchate has interrupted ecumenical relations with several Western Christian churches over divergent attitudes on homosexuality: in 2003, the Russian Orthodox Church broke off all relations with the Episcopal Church of the United States because of the latter's consecration of an openly gay priest, Gene Robinson, as bishop of New Hampshire; in 2005, the church cut ties with the Lutheran Church of Sweden for blessing same-sex marriages; and in December 2012, it declared that it would no longer recognize baptisms carried out by the Evangelical Lutheran Church of Denmark as valid because of its decision to bless same-sex marriages (Zorgdrager 2013, 215–16).[8] For the world of SOGI activism, these ecclesiastical skirmishes may not seem important, but in the context of Christian ecumenical relations, the actions of the Russian Orthodox Church have a profound impact. The Moscow Patriarchate is effectively pressuring other Christian churches to reject SOGI rights or to stay silent in the face of discrimination and violence (Kelaidis 2017).

The Russian Orthodox Church has also tried to partner with the Catholic Church in the name of traditional values. Conservative values were at the heart of the idea of a "Holy Alliance" between the Russian Orthodox Church and the Roman Catholic Church, born around 2010. In 2009, Kirill had just become the new patriarch of Moscow. For years, he had been the motor behind the traditionalist tendencies inside the Russian Orthodox Church in terms of social teaching: he had overseen the crafting of the church's Social Doctrine, he had consistently repeated the traditional morality argument against individual human rights in his speeches, and he had founded the church's formal representative office at the European institutions in Strasbourg. Together with Metropolitan Hilarion (Alfeyev), his successor as the head of the Department for External Church Relations, he had great plans for the church in relation to Europe. Hilarion set forth his vision as follows:

> The Russian Orthodox Church, with its unique experience of surviving the harshest persecutions, struggling against militant atheism, reemerging from the ghetto when the political situation changed, recovering its place in society and redefining its social responsibilities, can . . . be of help to Europe. The totalitarian dictatorship of the past cannot be replaced with a new dictatorship of pan-European government mechanisms. . . . The countries of Orthodox tradition, for example, do not accept laws that legalize euthanasia, homosexual marriage, drug trafficking, the maintenance of brothels, pornography, and so on. (cited in Moynihan 2010)

The invitation came just around the time when conservative Christian leaders in the United States issued the Manhattan Declaration (2009) "pledging renewed zeal in defending the unborn, defining marriage as a union between a man and a woman, and protecting religious freedom" (cited in Moynihan 2010). The announcement of a Holy Alliance—a term apparently coined by the Italian journalist Sandro Magister

(2010)—sounded like a call to arms against secularism and progressivism, but the Moscow Patriarchate undertook few concrete initiatives to intensify the collaboration between the Russian Orthodox Church and the Catholic Church.

Since around 2008, the Moscow Patriarchate has actively promoted a conservative discourse on human rights. To this end, it maintains an office in Strasbourg that follows debates at the Council of Europe and European Court of Human Rights. The Patriarchate was particularly alarmed by the fact that the European Court of Human Rights was, in the eyes of the church, interfering with its inner workings. Several cases that came before the ECtHR concerned cases of parishes that wanted to move away from the jurisdiction of the Moscow Patriarchate (Rimestad 2015, 40–42). In the case of *Alekseyev v. Russia* (2011), over the right to hold a Pride parade in Moscow, the Russian Orthodox Church was cited as being responsible for human rights violations. The Interreligious Council of Russia, an organization that represents the four traditional religions of the Russian Federation (Orthodoxy, Islam, Judaism, and Buddhism), criticized the pro-LGBTI stance of the Council of Europe, arguing that the ECtHR "does not and cannot determine the moral conceptions of our society. This is beyond the force of international law. We reject therefore the lawless attempt to export to Russia any amoral behaviour standards wrapped in legal form" (cited in Rimestad 2015, 44).

In order to counter the perceived threat of the European Court of Human Rights, the Moscow Patriarchate has collaborated with Russian lawyers who have repeatedly published legal opinions on cases before the ECtHR (cf. Ryabykh and Ponkin 2012). In 2011, Church-associated Russian lawyers published a manifesto in which they argued that it was a human right to assess homosexual relations (and the laws permitting them) as a deviation from the norm (Ponkin, Kuznetsov, and Mikhaileva 2011, cited in Rimestad 2015, 52). From our fieldwork and interviews, it has become evident that these Russian lawyers and the church's representative in Strasbourg had regular contact with the European Center for Law and Justice (see chapter 3).[9]

In 2009, Russia launched a set of resolutions at the United Nations Human Rights Council on "promoting human rights and fundamental freedoms through a better understanding of traditional values of humankind." We address this episode in chapter 6 as the most striking example of the church's international norm entrepreneurship and of the coordination between the Kremlin and the church in Russia's anti-SOGI politics.

Vatican

The role of the Vatican as an anti-SOGI-rights actor has been widely covered in the literature, most recently in the volume edited by Roman Kuhar and David Paternotte, *Anti-Gender Campaigns in Europe* (Kuhar and Paternotte 2017), and the German edited volume *Anti-Genderismus in Europa* (Strube et al. 2020). The main motor of the anti-gender campaigns studied by these authors is the Catholic Church. It was the Vatican that spearheaded the elaboration of a counterstrategy after the 1994 UN conference on Population and Development in Cairo and the 1995 Beijing conference on Women (Buss and Herman 2003; Case 2016). In terms of religious anti-SOGI mobilization, the Vatican was involved first (at least ten years before the Russian Orthodox Church), and the Catholic Church elaborated anti-gender ideas that—by way of the TAN we discussed in chapter 3—have come to define the global resistance to SOGI rights. Our assessment of the Vatican as key actor in the global resistance to SOGI rights builds on this earlier research as we update the analysis and relate the Catholic position to that of its emerging counterpart in the field—the Russian Orthodox Church.

The Holy See's anti-gender campaign and long-standing Catholic opposition to advances in family law and sexual and reproductive rights constitute the wider tent of anti-SOGI-rights mobilization. All the Catholic arguments against gender theory are, in some way or the other, used by the anti-SOGI-rights actors studied in this book. The Vatican's resistance to SOGI rights is rooted in "paternal Catholic modernism" (Chappel 2018, 256) according to which the central site of social virtue is the reproductive family. This basic stance in social and ethical teaching goes back a long time and antedates the terminology of "gender" (Kuhar and Paternotte 2017, 8; Paternotte, Case, and Bracke 2016). The most important milestones for the development of the Catholic Church's agenda against SOGI rights—already much earlier than the mobilization around the UN conferences in Cairo in 1994 and Beijing in 1995—included the *Declaration on Certain Questions Concerning Sexual Ethics* of 1975

(Congregation for the Doctrine of Faith 1975), the *Letter on the Pastoral Care of Homosexual Persons* of 1986 (Congregation for the Doctrine of Faith 1986), the document *Considerations Regarding Proposals to Give Legal Recognition to Unions Between Homosexual Persons* of 2003 (Congregation for the Doctrine of Faith 2003), and the Synod on the Family of 2014. The Catholic Church's highest authority in terms of doctrine and teaching, the Congregation of Faith, has elaborated statements on homosexuality at roughly ten-year intervals for the past five decades, but the main positions have remained unchanged since the 1970s. Pope Francis has indeed not substantially altered the Catholic Church's position on homosexuality and SOGI rights from the conservative stance of his two predecessors (Kuhar and Paternotte 2017, 8).

In comparison to the Russian Orthodox Church's teaching on homosexuality, the Catholic statements since 1975 have been longer and more detailed. The document of 1975 called homosexuality "intrinsically disordered," a phrase used once more in 1986. The document of 2003 called homosexuality "a troubling moral and social phenomenon" and aimed to "give direction to Catholic politicians by indicating the approaches to proposed legislation in this area which would be consistent with Christian conscience." In terms of resistance to SOGI rights (and not more generally to homosexuality), the document of 2003 is the most important. In it, the Catholic Church rejects the idea of same-sex marriage, proclaiming it inadmissible and illegitimate. The legalization of same-sex marriage is also called "the approval and legalization of evil," and the document goes on to exhort believers to exercise the right to conscientious objection in order to avoid cooperation with the enactment of "unjust laws." The Vatican's statement gives reasons against SOGI rights in a context where—as the drafters are fully aware—these rights are already in place in many countries. The tone is that of a rearguard action, where believers are encouraged to retreat and resist. This somewhat defensive tone in the Catholic document is different from the social teaching of the Russian Orthodox Church, which—inside Russia—is the leader of public policy debate.

The Congregation of Faith determines the Vatican's line of argumentation against SOGI rights. In this task, it relies on other bodies of the Vatican and individual experts. One institution which is important in this context—not least because some of its members are connected to the network we analyzed in chapter 3—is the Pontifical Council for the Family. This council published, in 2003, a document entitled *Lexicon: Ambiguous and Debatable Terms Regarding Family Life and Ethical Questions*. Translated into numerous languages, including German, French, English, Spanish, Portuguese, Russian, and Arabic, the document claimed to inform its readers "about the true content of words, about the true reality which must inform their usage" (Lopez Trujillo, cited in Kuhar and Paternotte 2017, 11). Unsurprisingly, this cryptic formulation targeted "gender." According to the interpretation of a longtime insider familiar with the workings of the Congregation of Faith, bodies like the Pontifical Council for the Family have considerable power over the agenda of the Vatican, since they act as experts—without being, in reality, experts on the subject (Paternotte, Case, and Bracke 2016, 229).

The Vatican's anti-SOGI-rights policies proceeded to become a mobilizing tool for massive social movements, such as La Manif pour tous in France. Between 2013 and 2018 referenda for the definition of marriage "as being between a man and a woman" took place in Croatia, Slovakia, and Romania, all to prevent same-sex marriage legislation from being introduced (Norocel and Băluță 2021). A similar referendum took place in Slovenia over abrogating existing same-sex partnership legislation (Juroš, Dobrotić, and Flego 2020; Slootmaeckers and Sircar 2018; Kuhar and Čeplak 2016; Guasti and Bustikova 2020). Slovenia, Croatia, and Slovakia are Catholic-majority countries and in all of them, the Catholic bishops supported the referendum.

This mobilization against SOGI rights in the name of religious freedom and traditional social policy continued from the 1990s until well beyond the election of Pope Francis in 2013. Pope Francis to some degree reshuffled the cards in the Vatican's resistance to SOGI rights. His actions quickly indicated that the fate of the radical anti-gay groups and the Christian Right inside the Catholic Church was about to change. His appointment also ended all plans for a Holy Alliance between the Vatican and the Russian Orthodox Church. At the same time, he continued to draw on key concepts regarding life, gender, and sexuality that the Congregation of Faith had developed in documents since the 1970s.

Considerable media attention followed when, in July 2013, on a return flight to Italy from Brazil, the Pope answered a journalist's question about gay priests with the phrase "Who am I to judge?" (Donadio

2013). On subsequent occasions, he sent messages that could be interpreted as communicating a greater tolerance for gay people and SOGI rights within the church. The papal encyclical *The Joy of Love* (2016), although negative about same-sex unions, was nonetheless interpreted as potentially welcoming to some gay people (Salzman and Lawler 2016), and on one occasion, Francis even expressed support for same-sex civil unions (Elie 2020). In 2017, he reorganized the Pontifical Academy of Life and did not renominate most of the members chosen by his predecessors John Paul II and Benedict XVI. As noted previously, Christine Vollmer—one of the WCF's most regular participants—lost her position, and she responded with a vitriolic opinion piece stating that the pontificate had been "hijacked" by the "gay lobby" (Vollmer 2018). In 2023, Francis eventually called for the decriminalization of homosexuality and encouraged bishops in countries where homosexuality is illegal to work to repeal laws that persecute LGBTIQ people. Observers considered the timing of this remark, just weeks before the Pope's visit to Africa, important, since several African countries still criminalize consensual same-sex relations (Lamb 2023). In the same breath, however, Francis confirmed the church teaching according to which homosexual acts "are a sin, as is any sexual act outside marriage" (Outreach 2023).

Let us disentangle the question of Francis's positioning on SOGI rights over his tenure step-by-step. The first point to make is that Francis did not change the official teaching of the Catholic Church on gender and SOGI rights and has even confirmed earlier statements which considered same-sex marriages or second-best rituals like blessings of same-sex unions as inadmissible inside the church. Indeed, he also pursued different strategies in different contexts; his face adorned billboards opposing same-sex marriage in Slovakia, for example. At the same time, however, Francis has used a more open and appreciative language when talking about LGBTI people. Liberals inside the Catholic Church have felt encouraged by this change in style, seeing it as the initial step in an incremental strategy toward more inclusion of LGBTI—especially lesbian and gay—believers in the church (O'Connell 2021).

The Pope's more open discourse has not translated into concrete action, however. The case of the priest Krzysztof Charamsa, who came out with his partner before the Synod on the Family only to be fired from his job and excluded from priesthood, generated global headlines (Paternotte, Case, and Bracke 2016). Five years later, SOGI rights again created a stir in the church when the Congregation of Doctrine of the Faith issued a "responsum regarding the blessing of the unions of persons of the same sex." This document, published in spring 2021, gave a negative answer to the question whether the church should bless unions of persons of the same sex. Using an argument that evoked the 1975 description of homosexuality as a "disordered" nature, the document insisted that the church can only bless "positively ordered" (read: heterosexual) relationships. Bishops and priests of the German Catholic Church, who had hoped for a more progressive and inclusive line of argument, criticized the statement and organized a protest action, ostentatiously blessing same-sex couples in their churches (Strack 2021). The view that Francis was not interested in changing the position of the Catholic Church on SOGI rights was confirmed when the Vatican issued a protest note to the Italian government in response to plans to implement a bill that would have included LGBTI provisions in a law against discrimination (Horowitz 2021). Charamsa's case, the response to blessings of same-sex marriages, and the protest note all exemplified how many progressive theologians saw Francis as failing them by not changing the official church teaching on the matter.

Despite the Pope's resistance to making any official changes to Catholic doctrine on homosexuality and SOGI rights, the conservative right wing of the Catholic Church has nonetheless adopted the view that Francis is a "liberal" and "leftist" pope who has abandoned them as well as the moral rigor of his two predecessors. The sentiment Christine Vollmer expressed is overwhelmingly shared among Francis's conservative detractors, namely that he is "queering the Catholic Church" (Dreher 2022b). By this, conservatives may mean that the feeble examples of inclusive language are a slippery slope toward full endorsement of SOGI rights, which would, in their view, amount to the end of the Catholic Church. Or they may mean something more conspiratorial and complicated: that the Catholic Church is itself a queer institution run by a "gay lobby," which in their view would also amount to the end of the church. We briefly consider this last view below because it is relevant for understanding the role of the Catholic Church—and conservative Catholics—in the global resistances to SOGI rights.

The conservative right wing inside the Vatican, led from the United States by Archbishop Carlo Maria Viganò has accused Pope Francis of being connected to a "gay lobby" inside the Vatican created with the intention of elaborating pro-gay Catholic teachings in order to cover up the church's sexual abuse scandals (Senèze 2020, 88). The accusation rests on the ungrounded idea that homosexuality and pedophilia are linked, and is all the more implausible given that, according to most recent accounts, many of the most criminal sexual abusers inside the Catholic Church were also the greatest champions of conservative family and pro-life values. The "gay lobby" accusation is evidently driven by the desire to find a scapegoat for the sexual abuse scandals inside the church and to readjust the Vatican to a conservative hard line (Senèze 2020; Cloutier 2019). As long as this does not happen, the Catholic Church has a stalwart conservative competitor: the Russian Orthodox Church. The latter only stands to gain from a situation where ultraconservative Christians flock to Orthodoxy, as is already happening in the United States (Riccardi-Swartz 2021).

In sum then, the Vatican was the first global activist IO working against SOGI rights, and conservative Catholics indeed continue to pursue this policy line through TANs, like the moral conservative TAN described in chapter 3, and through collaboration with governments like Hungary's and Poland's. When it comes to official policies, however, the pontificate of Francis has downsized the role of the Vatican in the global resistance to SOGI rights, even if SOGI activists rightly view that downsizing as far from sufficient. As a result, the Catholic Church has sent out confusing and contradictory messages to important leaders within its establishment, as well as to the public as a whole.

Discussion

Having given this overview of states and IOs that serve as examples of the global resistance to SOGI rights, it needs to be asked why such states and international organizations choose to resist SOGI rights instead of following or acquiescing to new norms governing SOGI rights. We do not suggest here that there is one causal explanation. Rather, we identify a set of reasons why some states and IOs may find it advantageous to resist SOGI rights, including the benefits it affords them in terms of status, identity, and alliances in world politics.

Status

Status issues are primary for those states, especially small, medium-sized, and declining powers in world politics, whose "insecurity [compared to established great powers] . . . makes the status game even more important to them" (Wohlforth et al. 2018, 528). The international relations (IR) idea that such states—with more limited options in terms of power resources—are likely to aim for status "by being conspicuously good or moral actors" is compelling, even if it has rarely been applied to SOGI rights. Indeed, the states we have discussed as buttressing the moral conservative TAN do use morality in this way. However, the idea that striving for status motivates states' positions on SOGI rights would also explain why small states like the Netherlands are pioneers in those rights (Kollman 2017). According to Wohlforth, de Carvalho, Leira, and Neumann (2018, 527, 542), states are guided by status considerations "in their social dealings with other states in the everyday life of international politics," and the field of international relations has often overlooked the fact that "status seeking permeates the international system." While this is not wrong, there is also a theoretical blind spot in their assumption that status is affirmed by a unitary understanding of what is moral or good. An analysis of contested norms—like SOGI rights—underscores that there are different understandings of what is moral or good, with rival networks aiming to define this affirmation for states. Indeed, in this chapter we have shown that the notion of tradition has a lot of currency as something both moral and good in many parts of the world in which states like Russia are seeking to promote their status.

There can be no doubt that the traditional values agenda has allowed some states to gain new purpose and to play a role on the global political stage. Russia, having suffered a status loss with the fall of the Soviet Union, has seized the opportunity to again become an ideological leader of a global alliance supporting so-called traditional values. While it remains to be seen what will become of its leadership status in the morality domain following the war against Ukraine, it is also evident from the anti-SOGI justifications given for the war that Russia is determined to hold onto its role as a traditionalist power. For Hungary, the traditional values agenda has also been a tool to carve out a strong identity, in this case regionally among the EU-27, instead of being relegated to the relatively unimportant status of a middle-sized member state.

Whereas Russia's most recent affirmation of status through military aggression comes with considerable costs in the form of sanctions imposed by Western states, for Hungary, the soft power demonstration of promoting traditional values and opposing SOGI rights has been a tool to carve out a strong identity vis-à-vis the liberal democratic political mainstream. It goes without saying that this same position would carry steeper audience costs in many states whose citizens have more favorable views of both SOGI rights and a liberal democratic world order (Cooley and Nexon 2020).

For the Vatican and the Russian Orthodox Church, status has also become closely intertwined with SOGI rights. As discussed above, under Pope Francis, the Vatican has—at least in some states—downplayed the controversy around SOGI rights without taking any real steps to mitigate it. The contradictions in the Vatican's position across states and its failed efforts in mitigation have left the field open to ultraconservative Christian groups and to the more conservative Evangelical and Orthodox Christian Churches. The latter have seized the opportunity to boost their status as "authentic" conservative churches through their radical anti-SOGI-rights stance. Bridging IR theory with religious market theory—which has shown that unwaveringly conservative churches can attract more believers than liberal churches (Iannacone 1994)—may help explain why this positioning on SOGI rights has become common for religious organizations that are competing with each other on the global stage.

Identity

For the states and IOs that endorse it, the traditional values agenda carries with it not just potential geopolitical status, but the advantages of identity politics. While religious beliefs or coming out as LGBTI are often considered individual experiences, Alexander Wendt's (1999) formative argument that states have malleable identities of their own suggests that they too can develop identities. Indeed, states and IOs have an "ability to shape conceptions of 'normal' in international relations" through a set of values (Manners 2002, 238). For the European Union, for example, this covers a broad range of core issues from environmentalism to inalienable human rights. Adopting a constructivist approach to identity that recognizes that agents and structures interact and are mutually constituted (Katzenstein 1996b), we make the case that the moral conservative actors we have analyzed, whether advocacy groups, state authorities, or IOs, help shape state identities in an environment that is also imagined and socially constructed (Anderson 1983).

Along these lines, Ayoub (2016) has argued that states can do important signaling work by recognizing certain groups as part of their human rights frameworks. Take, for example, the Swedish Peace and Arbitration Society's creative campaign to mark the country's territorial waters. In response both to broader Swedish opposition to Russian anti-LGBTI propaganda laws and to reports of rogue Russian submarines in Swedish waters, the Society transmitted from the territorial boundaries a message in Morse code that proclaimed, "Sweden, gay since 1944" (Taylor 2015). The act illustrates that SOGI rights can merge with state identities, whether real or imagined, and can play a role in contemporary world politics. The Russian fixation on an alleged (and inaccurate) identity of Ukraine as "gay-friendly" (Riccardi-Swartz 2022), simply because Ukrainians voted for a pro-European, Western-oriented political leadership, is another example of how an imagined and projected state identity can have real political consequences.

The same is true of state identities constructed as rooted in opposition to SOGI rights. These states typically construct their identity as in continuity with a pure and imagined past rooted in religious tradition (Hayes 2000). Resistance to SOGI rights has become a shortcut to signal and affirm a state identity as "Christian" or—in light of low levels of active church participation—"still Christian" (Anderson 2015). This is exemplified by the statement of Patriarch Kirill of the Russian Orthodox Church, who legitimized the war in Ukraine as a form of resistance to SOGI rights (Riccardi-Swartz 2022; Moscow Times 2022a). The global public considered his take egregious, but moral conservatives abroad identified the underlying message. The reaction of Rob Dreher, the conservative writer, indicates how Russia and the Russian Orthodox Church have acquired status as leading moral conservative champions in the last decade or so, in ways that outlast even blatant warmongering:

> Patriarch Kirill was wrong (in my view) to invoke this in a sermon addressing the war in Ukraine, a nation that is every bit as culturally conservative on LGBT matters as Russia. But in terms of contrasting the West and Russia, he's got it right. . . . The post-Christian West is increasingly godless and the enemy of the natural family. Russia, for all its sins and failings, including its unjust warmongering against Ukraine, is not. This is why I warn that everything being done to Russia . . . is eventually going to be turned against traditional Christians and other social conservatives in our country. (Dreher 2022c)

What we see in this statement is an identification of conservative Christians in the West with Russia on the sole ground of shared resistance to SOGI rights. The return to Christianity as a form of national identity is not only related to morality politics, however. It is, as we have seen in the case of Hungary, also a question of nativist opposition to immigration, especially from Muslim countries. The Christian turn in right-wing populism in Italy, Austria, or Hungary was originally related to anti-immigration politics, pitting "Christian Europe against Islam" (Marzouki, McDonnell, and Roy 2015). For states and governments, the projection of national identity as Christian may carry domestic and international advantages, in terms of both electoral success and international alliance building.

Alliances

The identity and status politics we have described also produce tangible outcomes for states and IOs in the form of alliances in world politics. After Hungary was sanctioned by the EU for passing the anti-LGBTI-"propaganda" legislation, various US conservative politicians (including former vice president Mike Pence and former attorney general Jeff Sessions) traveled to Hungary to—as Dreher put it—see "what an actual pro-family, socially conservative government acts like" (Zerofsky 2021). The desire to create alliances can motivate states and IOs to invest resources in the moral conservative TAN. The fact that Christian conservatives in the West identify (or identified) with Putin's Russia on grounds of opposition to SOGI rights could have worked in Russia's interest when it came to easing the sanctions-regime imposed after the annexation of Crimea in 2014. While the lifting of sanctions has become out of the question since February 2022, Hungary nonetheless demonstrated a certain degree of closeness and alliance with Russia when it announced that it would not allow weapons to be transported across Hungarian territory into Ukraine.

Alliance building is not just a central element in the workings of the global resistances to SOGI rights but also one of the main factors explaining why acting against SOGI rights may been seen as beneficial to some governments and IOs. Through resistance to SOGI rights, alliances can be forged or broken. For the Russian Orthodox Church, the breaking of ecumenical relations with several Protestant and Anglican Churches over the issue of SOGI rights, for example, was a relatively minor loss compared to its gains in status as a stronghold of global conservatism. Inside the Commonwealth of Orthodox Churches, the Moscow Patriarchate thereby affirmed its position as a hardliner and became a potentially more attractive partner for interorthodox alliances than the Ecumenical Patriarchate of Constantinople, which has a more liberal reputation.

Another concrete example of alliance building that emerges from our fieldwork is Russia's soft diplomacy on pro-family values in countries of the former Soviet Union. After the WCF's 2014 summit in Moscow, the WCF organized two more congresses in the former Soviet Union in quick succession. In 2016, the network convened in Tbilisi in Georgia, and in 2018, in Chisinau in the Republic of Moldova. Both Georgia and Moldova were in frozen military conflicts with Russia over disputed territories (South Ossetia and Transnistria), but the politicians who welcomed the WCF and the Russian participants were open about their pro-Russian agenda. The hosts in Tbilisi (Levan Vasadze) and Moldova (Igor Dodon) pitched their pro-Russian orientation as a political agenda for the benefit of families allegedly threatened by a SOGI-friendly European Union.

Among the participants in these congresses were activists from Belarus and Ukraine. Brian Brown, from the WCF, and Gerald Huebner, the director of GHEX, toured both countries in what appeared

168 | STATES AND INTERNATIONAL ORGANIZATIONS

at the time to be preparations for another possible congress in one of them. Huebner explained his itinerary of spring 2017: "I am going to be speaking in two weeks in Kyiv, and doing a home school conference there, myself and my daughter, and then will be going to two cities in Belarus, Minsk and Gomel, where we will be also reaching out and developing contacts there" (Interview, Huebner 2017). Brian Brown's Twitter account at the time contained evidence of meetings and travels in Belarus and Ukraine (Feder 2017; Barthélemy 2018). Intentionally or not, these trips created a pro-Russian consensus built around moral conservative values among politicians and civil society in those countries. In a long article and video Komov produced in 2017 (Komov and Smirnov 2017; Komov 2017), several American conservatives are quizzed on the importance of Christian education. Their statements are put in the context of education in Ukraine: "For example, in Ukraine for the past twenty-five years, many school textbooks have been written by the team of George Soros and printed with his money in Canada. The result is quite concrete and hardly reversible" (Komov 2017). Russia, the article claims, can bring "proper" education to Ukraine with the help of American moral conservative friends. The claim to political influence over the region has, however, taken a calamitous turn since the Russian attack on Ukraine in February 2022.

* * *

States and international organizations use resistance to SOGI rights as a tool for raising status, defining identity, and forging transnational alliances. Our four examples—Russia, Hungary, the Russian Orthodox Church, and the Vatican—could each serve as a complete case study of how resistance to SOGI rights serves these purposes. While the four cases are comparable, the ways each of these states or IOs arrives at defining identity and status by resisting SOGI rights and creating alliances with other moral conservative actors are unique. Our analysis here offers only a brief overview of these different trajectories. Yet it supports the view that, after two decades of SOGI rights successes, the rise of mobilization against these rights is not simply the result of a backlash.

Instead, it appears that actors may draw concrete benefits from being part of the global resistances to SOGI rights—benefits in regard to domestic politics and electoral success as well as in terms of status, identity, and alliances. The felt strategic benefits actors like these enjoy in some contexts contribute amply to the reason SOGI rights rank high on the international political agenda. This process is not wholly different from the way other countries and IOs gain benefits from alliance-making around other topics more welcome in liberal states. IR and social movement theory can therefore encompass and explain the moral conservative mobilization without much trouble if it widens its focus by taking the double helix model into consideration. In fact, detailed comparative analyses of state norm entrepreneurship would be highly desirable to pinpoint more clearly what benefits states and IOs draw from supporting or resisting SOGI rights. This chapter has sought to take a first step in this direction.

PART III

Strategies, Claims, and Venues

5

Strategies and Claims

The Moral Conservative Narrative

"Homintern" was the name Connolly, Auden and others [like Jocelyn Brooke and Maurice Bowra] jokingly gave the sprawling, informal network of friendships that Cold War conspiracy theorists would later come to think of as "the international homosexual conspiracy."
—Woods 2017

In part II, we showed how the moral conservative TAN has cohered over a long stretch of time despite a considerable degree of difference—and even contradiction—among its individual components. In this chapter, we dig deeper into the claims and narratives that unite this global resistance to SOGI rights. On the most general level, one could argue that moral conservative actors are held together by their resistance to the SOGI rights movement. It would be more accurate, however, to say that they are held together by their resistance to *their own construction of* the SOGI rights movement. This is a key point of distinction, which we will develop further in relation to scholarly work on conspiracy theories (Radnitz 2021). Moral conservatives *construct* their adversary by willfully misrepresenting the SOGI rights movement and transforming it into a symbol of everything else they reject: communism, global capitalism, liberalism, and international institutions. As moral conservatives link these disparate topics into one coherent narrative—coherent from their perspective—they come to identify as victims of the SOGI movement, but also as the privileged few who have special knowledge about the mechanisms that drive this movement and its role in global politics. The moral conservative narrative thus functions in a similar way to conspiracy theories, creating among its adherents an intense sense of identification with a shared cause.

Moral conservatives motivate their resistance to SOGI rights with a series of claims, namely that their resistance will protect the nation, society, children, women, the family, or religion from the effects of growing diversity, pluralism, gender equality, and liberalism. This list reiterates a series of claims identified by earlier researchers (Kuhar and Paternotte 2017; Graff and Korolczuk 2022). However, we reconstruct and flesh out this list using material developed by moral conservative networks themselves, taken in part from a set of interviews and publications gathered around the World Congress of Families summits in Tbilisi in 2016 and in Budapest in 2017. After outlining our theoretical linkage to scholarship on conspiracy and identifying the moral conservative movement's claims, we present a section on strategies reconstructing the multicomponent narrative that moral conservative actors use to affirm their identity as a group and to legitimize their claims and actions.

Conspiracy

The word "homintern" from the epigraph humorously brings to life the idea of an international homosexual culture, "meaning the life experiences and innate personality traits that connect gays more closely with gays from other countries than with the heterosexual citizens of their own country, or even their own family" (Allen 1996; cited in Binnie 2004, 37). While scholars of intersectionality remind us that individual experiences of SOGI-based marginalization are still unique, creating varied outcomes from individual to individual even within the same country (Murib 2017), what unites most SOGI rights advocates and motivates their collective transnational mobilization is a lived experience of discrimination and difference in relation to their everyday surroundings. Ignoring or downplaying the reality of this process of mobilization and action in response to constant and visible discrimination, detractors of SOGI rights often insinuate that SOGI activism is really about something else, and that activists are motivated by a hidden agenda that pursues different goals: gaining power over entire countries by causing demographic decline, confusing people in their sexual orientation so they will be easier to manipulate politically, disrupting local communities and family networks, turning people into malleable consumers, eradicating religion, and the like. We encountered all these claims during fieldwork and will highlight them in the text as we proceed.

The idea that a specific group is attempting to usurp political or economic power, violate rights, infringe upon established agreements, or alter bedrock institutions is typical of a conspiracy theory. Conspiracy theories are attempts to explain the true causes of significant social and political events and circumstances using claims of secretive plots by a few powerful actors (Douglas et al. 2019, 4). In this era of populist rhetoric, with theories like QAnon taking root in many states, the conspiratorial language used to shape the moral conservative narrative rings familiar. In our sample, the "powerful actors" that moral conservative actors identified were "the gay lobby" or "the EU." Interviewees also claimed that influential business networks with financial interests were in reality driven by SOGI activism. This is apparent in the following example, in which Alexey Komov claims that the "surrogacy industry" was responsible for starting the 2014 war between Russia and Ukraine, as well as for the sanctions imposed on Russia: "They are people of influence and you know how influential, for example, the gay lobby is in Europe. The Russian Olympics in Sochi were boycotted before any crisis in Ukraine started, and they were boycotted because we'd passed this anti-gay-propaganda law to children . . . only after this Ukraine was organized or happened. And then the sanctions were introduced. But actually this campaign started because of the gay issues before, half a year before" (Interview, Komov 2017). Conspiracy theories like this are not unusual, especially in Russia and the former Soviet Union (Radnitz 2021), where they allow political actors to divert attention from their own decisions and blame actions or events on foreign powers. Scholars of conspiracy theories have found that people have a deep desire, if not a need, to feel warmly about the groups to which they belong and that the conviction that some other is conspiring against one's group can boost self-esteem (Douglas et al. 2019, 6).

Many moral conservative actors believe that their religious beliefs are threatened by secular culture, or feel that certain life-choices they make, based on their understanding of authority, tradition, and hierarchy, are cast into question by the more *laissez-fare* majority society that surrounds them. It is this mentality of the besieged that makes moral conservatives especially prone to conspiracy theories, although it should be stressed that moral conservatism per se is *not* a conspiracy theory. Instead, the narrative embeds certain claims inside the moral conservative universe that amount to conspiracy theories (like the explanation offered for the 2014 war in the quote above). In the case of the moral conservative narrative, it is therefore most accurate to speak of a "conspiratorial mindset" (Douglas et al. 2019, 5)—a tendency for some people to prefer conspiracy explanations because of a bias against a disliked group.

The idea that SOGI rights are the fruit of a global conspiracy occupies an important role in moral conservative mobilization. From our fieldwork with moral conservative actors, it becomes clear that resistance to SOGI rights is frequently not the first step in moral conservative norm mobilization, but it is what actors eventually arrive at through a process of framing their personal issues of concern in a specific way. Indeed, some actors who attach the highest ethical value to issues like abortion or religious freedom may not actually think of themselves as intolerant vis-à-vis LGBTIQ people. However, inasmuch as their ethical choices become interlocked with a conspiratorial worldview that positions them both as victims of a dominant secularist and liberal culture and as chosen to resist, they assimilate into the anti-SOGI-rights universe.

We argue that transnational moral conservative actors and their organizations play an essential role in this process of framing or packaging a set of ideas in such a conspiratorial key. A frame is "an interpretive schema that simplifies and condenses the world out there by selectively punctuating and encoding objects, situations, events, experiences and sequences of actions within one's present or past environments" (Snow and Benford 1992, 137). Concrete acts of resistance to SOGI rights may still take place mostly on the national level, be it through lawmaking or social mobilization. However, behind the various referenda and policy initiatives geared toward preempting or limiting the diffusion of SOGI rights into the domestic space, a coherent moral conservative worldview now exists that drives such actions on the ground. This moral conservative worldview, which travels between languages, societies, cultures, and religious denominations, is the work of transnational networks of actors who contribute to framing policy issues in a way that engenders resistances to SOGI rights.

As we know by now, a central actor for the construction of the transnational moral conservative narrative is the World Congress of Families

(WCF). Their guideline "How to Organize a World Congress of Families Regional Event, Regional Conference, or Summit" contains the building blocks of what we call the *moral conservative narrative* in a pithy nutshell: "Focus on issues relevant to your country/region—those currently discussed/debated or the basis of legislation or judicial action. This might include marriage and (efforts to redefine) abortion and other life issues, declining birth rates (Demographic Winter), parental rights, sex education, home schooling, pornography, drugs, attacks on faith, the 'gay rights' movement and attempts by international organizations (e.g. United Nations, European Union) to promote a radical sexual agenda" (IOF 2020). The WCF can be seen to be a central player of SOGI rights resistance not (only) because it advocates against these issues, but because it interlaces all these topics. It combines them into one tight narrative perceived as coherent by many in its vast membership. The quote above from guideline is not just a list of issues, but a program, and insofar as each congress is encouraged to include the *entire program*, the WCF contributes to the diffusion of this global moral conservative narrative. The moral conservative activists that drive the global resistance to SOGI rights are guided by a strategic political rhetoric built on the conviction that these issues all coalesce and relate to each other. It is this perceived knowledge, a shared moral conservative conspiracy theory about the alleged goals and consequences of the SOGI rights movement, that creates a faux coherence among a broad range of actors, countries, and organizations.

Claims

Many of the claims against SOGI rights have circulated in transnational moral conservative networks since the 1970s and 1980s. They derive from different controversies over public morality, particularly the issue of abortion. The pro-life topic was foundational for the Christian Right in the United States, and abortion galvanized the Christian Right's argumentative strategies—often rooted in a spin on human rights discourses. As we flesh out the most common claims against SOGI rights below—regarding the nation, religion, women, children, and family—it is important to stress that in moral conservative norm mobilization, these claims are rarely disaggregated. They are wielded in unison—often quite literally within a single sentence—because they take on a coherent meaning *inside* the moral conservative institutional and intellectual complex.

"Protect the Nation"

Moral conservatism is often part of the repertoire of nationalism. Belief in the superiority of the nation, its strength, durability, and privileged history leads moral conservatives to reject the message of pluralism, diversity, and transnational solidarity inherent in the SOGI rights movement. A key argument used against the proliferation of SOGI rights is that gender and sexuality, in their fluidity, threaten the fixity of various aspects of the nation (Ayoub 2014). In the WCF, which brings together actors of different nationalities, a common identification with so-called traditional values is exploited as a bond, as an interviewee from the WCF summit in Budapest expresses:

> In the world between nations, traditional values are what strengthen individuals, homes, families, communities, nations, and the world. They are like cornerstones. And they provide a foundation upon which communities, individuals, and nations can build great things, and become great societies. If they, well, make sure that those cornerstones are firm and in place, and then build upon them. They are what links us together in a common bond of things that are integral and basic, and important to life, to the future, to generations, and to the success of nations. Nations who have abandoned traditional values, have abandoned their citizens and their culture. And they do not thrive. (Interview, Vollmer 2017)

This line of thinking is leveraged in different ways, for example, by associating SOGI rights with foreign imposition from the West that tramples domestic sovereignty and leads to moral decay and demographic decline (Weiss and Bosia 2013; Kaoma 2013). For example, in transnational moral conservative advocacy, outside influence on a nation's legal sovereignty is often linked to colonialism, mirroring nationalist discourses that paint SOGI rights as imposed (Ayoub and Chetaille 2020). By elevating opposition to SOGI rights to a global level, the moral conservative movement can thereby gain traction in many non-Western contexts (Currier 2012; Rao 2020).[1]

For example, during the WCF summit in Tbilisi in the former Soviet Republic of Georgia, the host, Levan Vazadse, was trying to keep a delicate balance. Speaking to a large local audience, Vazadse urged the need to resist SOGI rights in order to protect the nation from Western influences—the nationalist note being visually underpinned by his donning of Georgian national costume. The effect was somewhat comical, given that Vazadse was sharing the stage with Larry Jacobs and Allan Carlson from the WCF and therefore was clearly engaging in cooperation with the West. Partners of the WCF from Eastern Europe and the Global South have internalized a split perception of the West, with conservative actors representing what they perceive as the good West, while SOGI rights activists, the EU, liberal NGOs, and the like represent the bad West. The former are dissociated from any neocolonial associations, while the latter are explicitly depicted as modern-day colonizers. This is particularly evident in Russia, where liberal actors run the risk of being branded as foreign agents when they have Western contacts, while the Russian partners of the WCF have not yet been subject to this treatment.

* * *

The same is true in countries of the Global South like Namibia and South Africa (Currier 2010) and India and Uganda (Rao 2020), where moral conservatives (local and transnational) often frame SOGI rights as a colonial imposition, sidestepping the European origins of colonial laws that proscribed and criminalized SOGI behavior and expression. In many cases, moral conservatives are building on that colonial heritage. A notorious articulation of such moral conservative national-transnational collaboration is that of Massachusetts-based Evangelical pastor Scott Lively, who influenced the Ugandan "Kill the Gays" Bill in 2009 (Bob 2012). His targeted anti-SOGI organization, Watchmen on the Walls, focused more on Central and Eastern Europe and Africa than on the United States. In statements documented by the Southern Poverty Law Center (2021), he has focused on various countries in those regions, including Uganda and Russia:

The gay movement is an evil institution [whose] goal is to defeat the marriage-based society and replace it with a culture of sexual promiscuity in which there's no restrictions on sexual conduct except the principle of mutual choice. (Conference in Kampala, Uganda, March 2009 [Southern Poverty Law Center 2021])

Homosexuality is a personality disorder that involves various, often dangerous sexual addictions and aggressive, anti-social impulses. ("Letter to the Russian People," 2007 [Southern Poverty Law Center 2021])

Lively's framing of SOGI rights as a dire threat—as seen from the above quotes—was mixed with a local framing that linked that threat to the trauma of colonialism in Uganda and several other Global South countries. Relatedly, in Russia and several CEE countries, that threat was mixed with broader narratives surrounding foreign and Western intrusion on domestic sovereignty.

The postcolonial argument against SOGI rights mimics related claims against abortion. Moral conservatives from the Global South frequently point to the United States as the main culprit of global birth control policies that were allegedly designed to keep low-income countries both weak and subordinate. Reproductive control is associated with Western colonial imposition, as this interviewee from Africa at the WCF in Budapest explained to us: "The big problem in Africa is that the Western NGOs are trying to impose a culture of death on us. You know, like promoting abortion, which they claim is safe motherhood. And it isn't safe at all. Even if it's in a legal context, it's not safe . . . and, you know, the Western donors, the one who, ones who are trying to impose their agenda on us, don't fully understand the cultural context and the current political and social context" (Interview, Anonymous 2017a). The conspiratorial logic is evident in accounts like this. Actors—in this case the Western donors who are investing in health care aid—are said to, in reality, be plotting an agenda of death. When the Obama administration made US aid conditional on the recipient country's respect for both equal rights and religious freedom, conservatives from the Global South—supported by allies from the Global North—saw this as yet another neocolonial state strategy to reach the same goal: keeping Global South countries poor, dependent, and small (limited in population).

Nationalism also plays a role in legal claims against SOGI rights. Through transnational norm entrepreneurship, the use of international governance venues, and international human rights law, SOGI rights activists have obtained policy goals that would have been harder to reach in the domestic context alone (see chapter 1). The international human rights system has revealed itself as a powerful tool to interfere with national legal sovereignty, and many moral conservative nationalists resent this deeply. They consider the SOGI rights movement, the European Union, and the United Nations as agents of infringement of national sovereignty. Hungarian prime minister Victor Orbán—who opened the 2017 WCF in Budapest with a speech that accused the EU and George Soros of wanting to weaken and destroy the Hungarian nation by incentivizing "mass immigration of Muslims" instead of incentivizing native births (IOF 2017)—has himself devoted ample attention to SOGI rights. The Hungarian Child Protection Act of June 2021 (also referred to as the Anti-Pedophilia Law), which banned information about SOGI topics, was a calculated affront to EU legislation strategically employed by Orbán to demonstrate that Hungary should be free to disregard EU regulations (Orbán 2021).

Migration and SOGI rights are, of course, not the only policy fields where supranational legal standards impact national legislations, but moral conservatives single them out as primary examples of this legal dynamic. In particular, the salience of marriage equality has ruffled feathers the world over, even where the issue itself was not being introduced in a country. Something as seemingly mundane as anti-discrimination in employment or housing could be seen as a slippery slope to erosion of the nation-state. For sure, concerns about nationalism and foreign imposition are also of central concern within feminist and LGBTIQ communities, who have indeed seen their issues weaponized to justify imperialist state politics—for example when the 2003 invasion of Iraq by a US-led coalition was justified in the name of women's rights (Farris 2017; Puar 2007). Yet the moral conservative construction of the threat to the nation takes on a very different meaning and is deployed for very different—if not incomparable—goals.

"Protect Religion"

This American participant at the Homeschooling congress in St. Petersburg was convinced that SOGI rights were a threat to religion: "LGBTQ rights supersede the right of free speech and the right of religion. Which is, in our Bill of Rights, that is the number one right in our Bill of Rights, is freedom of speech and freedom of religion. LGBTQ outranks that now. Although it's not stated anywhere in any of our legal [documents], it is treated by the court system as a superior right even to free speech and freedom of religion" (Interview, Anonymous 2018f).

Moral conservative critics of SOGI rights depict the language of equal rights as part of a totalitarian project intended to restrict or extinguish religious freedom. "The new times, the new world order," wrote the Spanish conservative politician Jaime Major Oreja for the Budapest World Congress of Families, "has a sick, pathological obsession to destroy Christian values in terms of civilization, and replace them with nothing" (Major Oreja 2017, 8). Moral conservatives understand religious freedom as the right to affirm their conservative religious convictions, like the rejection of homosexuality or same-sex marriage, in the public sphere. However, from the perspective of SOGI rights activists, agreeing to this demand would exclude SOGI-identifying people from the public space and justify discrimination and the expression of hateful speech.

The moral conservative narrative makes frequent use of the zero-sum competing rights claims (see chapter 2), according to which gains in SOGI rights lead to a loss of religious freedom. For Cynthia Burack (2022), "SOGI human rights versus religious freedom" is the central frame for understanding Christian conservative opposition to US involvement in international SOGI issues, and moral conservatives used it to unravel SOGI programs and policies during the Trump administration. In chapter 2, we outlined how the competing rights framework originates in the context of religious disestablishment and culture wars in the United States. A debate about an anti-hate-crimes law to protect against homophobia and transphobia in Italy in 2021 showcases how the concept also travels to contexts with a dominant majority religion and a church-state concordat. When the proposal for the law was brought before the two chambers of the Italian parliament, the Vatican intervened and urged the Italian government to stop the initiative due to concerns it would infringe upon the Catholic Church's freedom of thought (Tondo 2021). The ensuing scenes of politicians cheering and celebrating in parliament when the initiative was blocked were reminiscent of football fans watching a victory goal—a surprising reaction to rejecting a hate-crimes provision and yet another indicator that SOGI rights hold symbolic weight in contemporary politics.

The claim about protecting religion is so ubiquitous in moral conservative mobilization that one can easily overlook the fact that SOGI rights are also contested within religious communities themselves. There are numerous examples of religious and theological discourses that endorse and affirm SOGI rights that do not see such rights as incongruent with or detracting to religion (for Orthodoxy, see Chryssavgis 2022; Gallaher 2018; Papanikolaou 2017; for Catholicism, see Marschütz 2014; Strube et al. 2020). Further evidence that the narrative about protecting religion from SOGI rights is partial is the fact that many religious people with LGBTIQ identities come out in their churches and demand an end to discrimination—for example, members of the European Forum of LGBT Christian Groups or of Salaam, which represents LGBTIQ Muslims in Canada. Yet moral conservative advocates either ignore or directly attack theologians and groups engaged in such bridge-building reconciliation projects.

"Protect Children"

Moral conservatives often claim that SOGI rights are a threat to children. They argue that sexual education (for example, in schools) exposes children to nontraditional relationships and early sexualization. One source for this far-reaching claim is *The Global Sexual Revolution* by Gabriele Kuby (2012), which has been translated into fifteen languages, including Hungarian, Bulgarian, Ukrainian, and Polish—and which builds on centuries-old stereotypes. Often, the claim is paired with the wrongful insinuation that homosexuality is connected with pedophilia, and that society has to protect children from potentially predatory homosexuals (Jacobs 2017, 18). During our fieldwork it became apparent that for most participants, opposing abortion went hand in hand with opposing SOGI rights and LGBTIQ-inclusive sexual education. The remarks of an American pro-life activist at the Chisinau World Congress of Families showcase the narrative thread of this argument: "I tell you what really bothers me besides abortion is this comprehensive sexuality education. I discovered that when I was at the UN a few years ago, when I first started

184 | STRATEGIES AND CLAIMS

hearing about it. And I thought, "What the heck is comprehensive sexuality education?" And I did my own research and I started digging [and] digging. Guess where it [comes] from. You know who came up with the curriculum? International Planned Parenthood Federation" (Interview, Anonymous 2018b).

Opponents of SOGI rights have claimed in the most varied domestic spaces that they are protecting children. Notoriously, the Russian government made this claim when it passed a law in 2012 against so-called gay propaganda (Wilkinson 2013), and Victor Orbán made it in Hungary when he attempted the same in 2021. In the mid-2000s, some Polish parliamentarians unsuccessfully floated the idea of banning LGBT people from teaching in primary schools (Ayoub 2013). This frame is also placed centrally in debates around education on transgender rights: in the United States, most conservative airwaves (and increasingly political campaigns as well) are filled with allegations that gender identity, like critical race theory, is a looming threat to children and American families. Florida's Don't Say Gay Bill from March 2022 demonstrates this (Mazzei 2022). As in many other contexts (e.g., concurrent proposals in Paraguay, Mexico, and New South Wales, Australia), moral conservatives in Florida and other US states present gender identity as a powerful plot intended to confuse children and eventually unravel the fabric of the family, though only the rarest of schools has an inclusive educational framework that teaches about transgender people and the rights they are due.

Claims against SOGI rights in the name of protecting children primarily aim to manipulate and create fear. Much like populist right-wing discourse, the moral conservative narrative operates through a process of constructing negative emotions and moral panic (Wodak 2015). Especially when it comes to the claim of protecting children, moral conservative activists use vivid visual images and even objects. For example, in 2018, the Italian moral conservative NGO Pro Vita Generazione Familia raised billboards that showed a gay couple shopping for a baby (Lepore 2018). While surrogacy is already banned in Italy, in 2023 Prime Minister Giorgia Meloni's government is proposing to criminalize Italians seeking such services in countries where it is legal, even though most Italian couples who use surrogacy abroad are actually heterosexual (Tebano 2023). The government has also pushed to remove "non-biological" parents from their children's birth certificates. At the WCF in Verona, in 2019, at which Meloni was a speaker, activists distributed little plastic fetuses, a tactile object regularly used for pro-life campaigning. Just as anti-abortion activists claim to protect the lives of unborn children, the detractors of SOGI rights present themselves as defending children from adoption by same-sex couples or from surrogate motherhood and other practices of assisted procreation.

"Protect Women"

The claim that moral conservative values protect women has already been widely used in anti-abortion arguments, which valorize concepts like natural motherhood, bodily integrity, and health. More recently, the claim is being deployed in new ways in the resistance to SOGI rights, namely as the so-called protection of cis women from the expansion of transgender rights. Moral conservatives—in an unexpected alliance with gender-critical or trans-exclusionary radical feminists (TERFs)—have come to argue that equality for transgender people amounts to the cancellation of biological (cis) women and that cis women have to be protected in various societal domains (Bassi and LaFleur 2022). For example, moral conservatives give undue attention to normative questions about trans women in sports or the use of school bathrooms that match one's gender identity (claims that often overlap with the "protect-the-children" and "threat-to-nation" frames), even though study after study shows that no actual societal threats derive from the inclusion of transgender people in society. This construction is a key example of the competing rights language, with cis women's rights being weaponized against those of transgender women (Bob 2019, 175–81).

The disproportionate attention moral conservatives bestow on the transgender bathroom question was evident at the WCF in Tbilisi. A full third of the congress hall was filled with clerics of the Georgian Orthodox Church, who attended the event as part of the entourage of Patriarch Ilia. The fact that the Patriarch was personally present for more than an hour is remarkable, considering that half a year later, during the visit of Pope Francis to Georgia in October 2016, he only agreed to meet the Pope at the airport. As noted in chapter 3, the whole WCF audience rose to their feet when Father Ternhan, an Orthodox priest from the United States, began his speech with a prayer—only to then swiftly sit down when he moved on to a graphic description about alleged gay encounters in public bathrooms in California and the so-called threats posed by transgender people using public bathrooms. The stark contrast between the talk's beginning, with his black-cloaked appearance and solemn opening prayer, and its closing, which we can only describe as between vile and voyeuristic, could not have been greater.

One more aspect to the moral conservative claim about protecting women deserves mention, though only indirectly related to SOGI rights. This is the claim that moral conservatism makes life easier for women because it disciplines men, turning them (as the thinking goes) into gentlemen. As one long-term participant of the WCF put it, referring to "parts of our society where there are no fathers, or fathers and mothers don't live together," it is only with proper Christian education that "these kids become gentleman. It's amazing. From being, you know, killers, thieves, they become good men because that is what every human being wants to be is a good man or a good woman" (Interview, Vollmer 2017). This philosophy implies that rainbow (same-sex-parented or trans-parented) families could not produce good men or good women.

Moral conservatives indeed claim that traditional moral values protect women better than measures by state or civil services, using this extended claim to reject legislation on domestic violence. Paradoxically, they blame advances in domestic violence legislation on SOGI activism. In 2019, the Moscow Patriarchate's Commission for Family, Defense of Motherhood and Childhood published a statement sharply condemning a proposed Russian legislative bill on domestic violence protections, calling it "unacceptable" and highlighting that it was "actively supported by organizations associated with radical anti-family ideologies ('LGBT' ideology, feminism), as well as a significant number of organizations officially receiving foreign funding" (Patriarchal Commission for Family Affairs 2019). The Patriarchal Commission's statement includes a reference to an expert report entitled "Legal Analysis of the Draft Federal Law 'On the Prevention of Domestic Violence in the Russian Federation'" (FamilyPolicy.ru 2019), which the Russian Center for Family Policy had prepared in close collaboration with the World Congress of Families.[2] It is, of course, ironic that the Russian Orthodox Church opposed the law on domestic violence and blamed it on foreign organizations, while itself relying on a transnational foreign organization to formulate arguments against the law (Stoeckl and Uzlaner 2022, 2).

"Protect the Family"

The claim that moral conservative values protect families is ubiquitous in global resistances to SOGI rights activism and often subsumes all the other claims pertaining to threats to children, cis women, and the nation. Some of the claims regarding the protection of the family remain specific, however, and concern the institution of and the term family. First, for moral conservatives, heterosexual cisgender couples and their offspring represent the only legitimate form of family life. Due to this specialness and superiority, they argue, this unit should not under any circumstance be made equal—neither before the law nor semantically—with same-sex marriages or partnerships, or (for some) even single-parent families. In the context of human rights debates at the UN, moral conservative activists regularly and vehemently condemn the notion that families exist in different forms. When the so-called pro-family bloc of states (see chapter 6) at the United Nations Human Rights Council launched a resolution on "the protection of family," Russia blocked an initiative by the EU to insert the phrase "different forms of family exist" with a no-action motion (Stoeckl and Medvedeva 2018). This narrow understanding of family determines a whole set of policy claims that regard family life, such as taxation and divorce law.

Second, moral conservatives claim that families are a singular unit and building block of society and that the state should treat them as such. They reject child welfare protection laws and domestic violence legislation because such laws grant state authorities direct access to the black box of the family—which they consider off limits and uninfringeable. Indeed, at the 2017 World Congress of Families in Budapest, Katalin Novak, a member of the Hungarian Parliament and vice president of the Fidesz party—at the time also the Minister for Family and Youth Affairs—gave a speech entitled "A Strong Nation is Built on Intact and Happy Families." In it, she distinguished "an approach emphasizing only individual rights and individual needs" from a broader "support for communities" as she announced Hungary's commitment to this community (Novak 2017). The reference to an "individual approach" in this

188 | STRATEGIES AND CLAIMS

sentence must be read as an allusion to SOGI rights, as well as reproductive and sexual rights for women, which conservatives view as problematic for the nation and for demographic growth.

"Protect Society"

Claims geared at protecting society from SOGI rights are also commonplace. These regard people who are often not directly concerned with SOGI policies at all but who can supposedly be affected by them. The claim that societies require protection from SOGI rights is usually built around the right to conscientious objection, which we mentioned earlier in connection to the abortion case. For example, a couple of legal initiatives discussed in Russia around 2014–15 decreed illegal advertisements for abortions and sought to exclude abortions from the public health service in order to "liberate" believers from being forced to comply with the murdering of children by contributing to the state-imposed social security tax (Mancini and Stoeckl 2018, 247). Conservative activists used that same argument to oppose the Obamacare health scheme in the United States, claiming that that taxpayers would become complicit in abortions if those were included in the healthcare scheme (cf. Burwell v. Hobby Lobby Stores, Inc., NeJaime and Siegel 2015). While research (Mancini and Stoeckl 2018) has not identified a direct relational connection between the Russian and American discussions of conscientious objection among taxpayers, the parallel policy initiatives and the timing (possibly facilitated through indirect channels and emulation) is nonetheless striking. It serves as a further example of why moral conservative claims and strategies must be studied from a transnational perspective.

As pointed out above, many SOGI rights opponents have invoked the same notion of rights, claiming that marriage registrars or service providers at weddings have the right to refuse their involvement in any event, typically a same-sex marriage celebration, that they feel violates their belief system (NeJaime and Siegel 2018). In Europe and North America, where SOGI rights have increasingly been established, conservative Christian law firms have taken several such cases to the US Supreme Court and the European Court of Human Rights.

Another aspect of the "protect society" claim is related to demography around population growth and development. At WCF events, demographic decline is regularly depicted as a major threat for societies the world over (the terms demographic winter and demographic implosion are frequently deployed). The issue crops up at all congresses, each of which features sections and speeches on the topic of demography.[3] Low birthrates in Western societies are blamed on the decline of the family, along with what is perceived as insufficient state policies to support the natural model of the family. In Western Europe, the demographic frame resonates with concerns about aging populations and immigration.[4] In the posttransition countries of Central and Eastern Europe, the demographic frame addresses the concrete experience of drastic population decline through emigration and lowering birthrates and living standards.

This demographic anxiety links smoothly with other claims around the nation, children, women, and the family. Reproductive rights and abortion were the first international battle for Christian conservatives during the UN Conferences at Beijing and Cairo, and the WCF's pro-family agenda continues to prioritize them. Moral conservatives view reproductive rights for women as interfering with the natural family model, and they see abortion in particular as a direct threat. Many of the long-standing member organizations of the WCF are single-issue pro-life groups, for example, the Italian Pro Vita or the Russian Sanctity of Motherhood. At the congresses we attended, the pro-life theme was always centrally represented and vocal. For example, at the WCF in Tbilisi in 2016, speakers elaborated the alleged harmful effects of abortion on women and used scientifically dubious evidence to push the argument that abortion causes breast cancer. The association between demography and anti-abortion activism is easily extended to SOGI rights issues, for example through the idea that homosexuality—seen as individualistically frivolous and childless—directly lowers birthrates. Recent scholarly research shows a direct relationship between the discourse on perceived demographic threats and public resistance to SOGI rights (O'Dwyer and Jung 2018).

* * *

The claims presented in this section—framed as aiming to protect the nation, religion, children, women, family, and society—cover a wide range of policy fields. At first glance, it is not immediately obvious why all these claims would translate into an anti-SOGI-rights agenda: after all, the struggle of SOGI rights activists to obtain the right to form a legally recognized family or to conceive, adopt, and raise children are also direct efforts to strengthen family life. Indeed, during various more politically radical phases of the SOGI rights movement, queer activists rejected claims about the right to build normative families (and some still do) because such claims had clear conservative roots (Jackson 2015; Weeks 2015). The choice by same-sex couples to get married with a religious ritual likewise endorses, not undermines, the persistent value attached to religion (Bahgat 2021). Identifying claims as morally conservative is therefore not sufficient to understand why they translate into the rejection of SOGI rights.

The claims moral conservative actors articulate hang together by way of an encompassing philosophy of transnational moral conservatism. Scholars of contentious politics have determined that underlying values shape how movements operate; for example, the strategy of nonviolence used by the Reverend Martin Luther King, Jr., became a root value that shaped how the civil rights movement articulated its claims and led to innovative tactics like the sit-in (Snow and Soule 2009). Similarly, a transnational moral conservative philosophy serves to justify moral conservative claims. For moral conservative advocacy networks, an encompassing worldview is increasingly perceived as persuasive in conservative, traditionalist, and religious contexts that were hitherto more parochial and local. This is a finding not only from our own fieldwork but confirmed by other sociologists of religion (for Italian Catholicism, see Prearo 2020; for Russian Orthodoxy, see Shishkov 2017). It is therefore necessary to elucidate and reconstruct the strategy and justification that underpins these claims and bundles them together into one coherent agenda and transnational moral conservative philosophy.

The Strategic Deployment of the Moral Conservative Narrative

The strategic deployment of moral conservative claims outlined above follows a comprehensive philosophy or logic that is implicit in the moral conservative narrative. In what follows, we reconstruct this narrative from the perspective and through the articulations of moral conservative actors. We show how they use this narrative to justify the anti-SOGI-rights claims that this transnational network deploys. The narrative entails a full rewriting of twentieth-century political history and a reassignment of roles (of Russia, the West, human rights, and the like) that is hard to grasp at first. Taking this moral conservative narrative seriously does not mean taking it at face value; rather we reconstruct it in order to understand how the movement articulates the claims that generate a sense of belonging and purpose for moral conservative actors. We compare the moral conservative narrative with the conspiracy theories it in many ways resembles (Radnitz 2021). Like conspiracy theories, which create a sense of belonging among those who believe in them, the moral conservative narrative creates unity among the actors across the multireligious, multilingual, and multinational moral conservative TAN that we analyzed in chapters 3 and 4.

Local attendees at WCF gatherings we observed during fieldwork, especially in Central and Eastern Europe and the former Soviet Union, were frequently encountering a clearly defined philosophy of transnational moral conservatism for the first time. Many of them did not speak foreign languages, and the simultaneous translation offered during WCF summits offered them access to completely new ideas that they may or may not have had the capacity to filter or contextualize. At the congresses we witnessed, there were very few opportunities for questions from the public, debate, or discussion. Instead, the same set of speakers usually delivered the staple topics in a hierarchical fashion. These speakers composed the core group of frequent attendees at WCF gatherings (see figure 3.4 in chapter 3), and their politically infused speeches were orated like sermons.[5] Drawing on our WCF case studies, we disentangle the building blocks of the philosophy of transnational moral conservatism the speakers presented, the philosophy that created the focus on SOGI rights that we see today. It includes several threads: the rejection of communism, the critique of capitalism, the refutation of liberalism, and the placement of blame on international institutions.

Rejection of Communism

As mentioned earlier, the central focus of the WCF, and, by extension, the many groups that attend their international gatherings, is the promotion of a traditional family model, as summarized in the book *The Natural Family: A Manifesto* by Allan Carlson and Paul Mero (Carlson and Mero 2005). Built around a narrow reading of Article 16(3) of the Universal Declaration of Human Rights—"The family is the natural and fundamental group unit of society and is entitled to protection by society and the State"—the pro-family agenda of the WCF is extremely simple and straightforward. It rests on two key points.

First, that the family is a unit and should be treated as such. Therefore, rights and policies that aim to strengthen the position of individuals within the family or that open the closed space of the family to society and the potential interference of the state (for example, through child protection services) are rejected. Moral conservatives also reject various rights issues—children's rights, women's rights, policies against domestic violence, compulsory public schooling, public childcare—because these rights and policies address individuals and situations *inside* the family, and do not treat the family as a *unit*. The strategy is contradictory here, because on other occasions (as pointed out above) moral conservatives do use rights language that centers a moral conservative version of women's and children's rights if they are entrenched in the broader family unit. The *Natural Family* manifesto brushes aside possible inconsistencies and centers on a very narrow reading of rights and the family as a group unit.

Second, the family consists of a married, heterosexual couple and their children. This family model is called "natural" in the manifesto in order to match the legal language of the Universal Declaration and to amend the term "traditional family," which the authors decided was not appealing enough. Based on this definition, the pro-family agenda rejects the idea that diverse forms of family—single-parent or rainbow families—should be treated in the same way as cisgender heterosexual families. Rights and policies that aim to treat as equal all forms of family life—single-parent allowances or tax benefits for single parents, same-sex marriage and partnerships, adoption for same-sex or trans parents—are viewed with suspicion by moral conservatives because they do not privilege a normative cisgender heterosexual, married-with-children family model.

While the WCF's so-called pro-family agenda is simple, it has several implications for state policies. Of interest here is that the WCF's founder,

Carlson, articulates his pro-family agenda in social and economic—
rather than religious or moral—terms. One major reference point for
Carlson's ideas is the Swedish welfare state model of the 1950s (Carlson
2005; Carlson 1990). To Carlson, Sweden appears to be a kind of model
state (both positive and negative), and one that he believes conservatives the world over can learn from. The choice of Sweden was likely
not random. Carlson himself is Protestant Lutheran and claims Swedish
descent. When he was a doctoral student of modern European history
at Ohio University, his dissertation research was on Swedish family policy (Carlson 2015). His interest in and understanding of the European
situation set him apart from the economic libertarianism dominant in
the American Christian Right. In our interviews, Carlson idealizes the
Swedish state of the 1940s to 1950s—a period, it should be remembered,
when it navigated between the two antagonistic forces of Soviet communism and Nazism, in stark contrast with the politics we associate with
Sweden today. His interest in two Swedish social democratic reformers
of the 1940s, Anna and Gunnar Myrdal, deserves to be quoted at length,
because it demonstrates his preoccupation with a relatively rare political
condition in which extreme right and extreme left options are equally
viable:

> I learned to think about family policy from the Myrdals, Alva and Gun-
> nar Myrdal in Sweden. There was a tension in their work. . . . Alva Myrdal
> started off as a socialist feminist and atheist and internationalist. Gun-
> nar Myrdal, there was always a conservative tug to him, which I didn't
> fully understand, even when I met him and interviewed him a number of
> times. But ten years after his death, they released papers. A box of his ear-
> liest papers. Which showed that as a young man—and I'm talking about
> somebody at age 18 or 19—he was not a social democrat. In fact, he was
> an extreme right-wing young man. God, soil, country, pro-aristocracy,
> he opposed women's suffrage, he was a strong Swedish nationalist
> Christian. . . . Their program for pronatalist, pro-marriage policies re-
> flects a kind of moderate Swedish nationalism. . . . In fact, I have no real
> quarrel with what the Swedes were doing in the 1940s and 1950s. Tech-
> nically a socialist country, their textbooks on marriage and family and
> sexuality could have been published by any Christian organization at the
> time. So, things there could have stayed that way. And I am planning one

of these days to write a defense of the Swedish welfare state, but the welfare state of 1955—not what it is today. (Interview, Carlson 2019)

Sweden subsequently becomes Carlson's negative model for the social democratic welfare state. He frequently cites Sweden to denounce the effect of so-called leftist reforms on family politics and to make the point that the social democratic models of welfare state capitalism (Esping-Andersen 1990) in Western Europe were in fact purely socialist societies:

As launched by the Myrdals seventy-five years ago, the strategy was to achieve a socialist society through the revolutionary transformation of private life, rather than through the hitherto conventional socialist method of state ownership of the means of production. Marriage and private life would be deconstructed, to be replaced by the universal dependency of all adults and children on the central state. Women, men, and children alike would be separated from each other and from their homes for the better part of the day. The tasks of the housewife (child care, basic health care, early education, food preparation, elder care, cleaning) and of the breadwinner (economic support for a woman and her children) would be socialized, with the same women now paid to perform their traditional tasks as state specialists, using industrial techniques. Same-sex partnerships and adoption were, in some respects, afterthoughts to this much larger social reconstruction project. (Carlson 2007, 169)

The Swedish case allows Carlson to construct a narrative according to which post–World War II Western European politics were "centrist" (and therefore, in his view, positive) but were gradually taken over by what he calls a "radical leftism," beginning in the 1960s. This, he argues, led to an abolition of the strong nation-state (which he also blames on the creation of the EU) and the disintegration of the traditional social and moral fabric of the society (with SOGI rights, as expressed in the above quote, as a logical consequence of that disintegration). Carlson's analytical takeaway is that during the Cold War, Western countries (not just the state-socialist countries of Central and Eastern Europe) were also under a "Marxist spell." The extension of that idea—namely, that post-communist countries overcame communism after 1989, while Western countries still have not—has gained considerable traction among critics of the EU in new member states in Central and Eastern Europe.

Critique of Cosmopolitan Capitalism

In much of the literature on the Christian Right, moral conservatism is linked to neoliberalism. Melinda Cooper, for example, connects the birth of the neoconservative ethos—with its insistence on traditional gender roles and the unpaid care work attributed to women—to neoliberal cuts to state spending (Cooper 2017). Moral conservatives and their causes are also often funded by ultraneoliberal actors and groups (Skocpol and Hertel-Fernandez 2016; Wuest and Last forthcoming). Our own findings confirm this picture yet also complicate it. The view that Western Europe and the EU are "quasi-socialist" states is relatively mainstream among American conservatives (Fieschi 2019), but a sizable contingent of the moral conservative universe we studied, especially those coming from Europe, are actually in favor of the welfare state—as long as it clearly benefits "traditional families" and not single parents or other forms of households. What American and European conservatives share is a nostalgia for a "market town" or "main street" capitalism—a romanticized capitalism of the past where everyone has an ordered place, typically implying fixed gender roles.

Carlson's argument on the economy, for example, advocates not a wholesale rejection of capitalism but a targeted excision of cosmopolitan capitalism, which for him appears to imply urbanization, individualization, secularization, global mobility and detachment from local cultures and traditional modes of production. He repeatedly writes that families should rely (at least in part) on working their own land for their subsistence (Carlson 2000, 1993; Groves 2020). From the earliest WCF congresses onward, the programs contained speeches on the topics of the home economy and social policies. The congresses depicted these themes in their earliest titles, such as "The Power of the Home Economy," "The Family—Economy and Insurance for the Future," and "Family, Economy and Development," (WCF Warsaw 2007, WCF Mexico City 2004, and WCF Geneva 1999, respectively) and they have remained central and relevant during all subsequent WCF gatherings (Jacobs 2017).

Uzlaner and Stoeckl (2017) have traced the origins of the logic of home economy to writings from the 1930s and 1940s by the American sociologists Pitirim Sorokin (1898–1968) and Carl Zimmerman (1897–1983). This entire agenda has gained a renewed attractiveness today, with moral conservatives drawing on the primary social concerns of sustainability and ecology. Moral conservative ideas about nature, agrarianism, and the economy thus have the potential to occupy some of the organic trade and ecological farming sector. Viewed from this vantage point, the natural family that Carlson advocates gains a concrete and modern veneer that may appeal to those who come to this agenda not from religious or moral conservatism but from a critical detachment from consumerism and global capitalism. Carlson addresses precisely this potential clientele with sentences like, "The family, particularly the family that feeds itself in its garden or does some home production and does things is not a good consumer . . . it limits the potential of the consumer market, so capitalism, in the abstract, has no real place for strong families, either, they really don't want them" (Interview, Carlson 2018).

For those familiar with US politics, this take on capitalism may come as a surprise, given that ecology, alternative lifestyles, and rediscovering old trades and traditions in order to resist the forces of global capitalism are normally associated with the political left and not, prima facie, with the Christian Right. The Christian Right has the political home of the US Republican Party, which is usually associated with a libertarian, pro-capitalist orientation. In fact, Carlson describes himself and his ideas as "untypical" for an American conservative: "I favor broader property ownership. I'm in favor of things that shock people in America. We should limit the size and the number of Walmarts or we shouldn't even allow a Walmart to exist. And there's a way to do that—again, using tax policy. You do progressive taxation on corporate income" (Interview, Carlson 2019). The more universally shared elements of Carlson's critique, however, is his home economy agenda, which criticizes a capitalist system in which global modes of production reduce livelihoods for families or require women (read: mothers) to work for the family income due to rising living costs. It is not hard to see how Carlson's antisocialism, paired with a critique of global finance capitalism, could be quite attractive to certain audiences. In fact, our reconstruction of moral conservativism's capitalism critique here goes hand in hand with Graff and Korolczuk's argument that the persuasiveness of anti-gender politics rests in people's disaffection with neoliberalism (Graff and Korolczuk 2022). What our analysis of the narrative adds, however, is that the moral conservative critique of capitalism is not merely a reaction to an economic order characterized as neoliberal. It offers, on the contrary, a positive counterproposal built around what could be called a main street capitalism and self-reliant agrarianism.

What is new is that, seen through the unique lens of family—that is, motivated by the question of what type of economy is best for families— moral conservatives arrive at a striking, unexpected equation: global cosmopolitan capitalism and communism are equally bad because they both have detrimental effects on families. While communism interfered with the natural family by including women in the labor force, legalizing abortion, and providing state care for children, institutions of social welfare in liberal democratic states likewise interfere with the natural family in the name of equal rights and social justice, and capitalism, especially finance capitalism, destroys the livelihoods of families by creating unemployment and pushing up living and housing costs. The founding declaration of the WCF contains a passage that makes this conflation of communism, welfare states, and capitalism explicit: "Those policies of Marxism, neo-Marxian, totalitarian welfare states and economic consumer capitalism which have forced mothers into the workforce, have thereby deprived children of the proper benefits of full and continuous maternal care" (WCF 1997).

This equation of communism to capitalism as equally bad appeared in several of our interviews with moral conservative actors. Prompted to explain their worldviews, more than one tried to give an explanation based on a history and economic philosophy of their ideological choice. The statement by an Italian participant of the WCF in Chisinau is representative: "Marxism and capitalism are the two faces of the same coin. We have seen that in the way in which big capital has collaborated with the Soviet Union and how it is now collaborating with the communist regime in China. Both Marxism and capitalism, [and also] liberalism, are based on a material instinct that is individual and egoistic. [They all] teach that man has to be liberated from moral and religious pressure in order to be truly free" (Interview, Anonymous 2018d).

The narrative that communism equals capitalism has considerable pervasiveness in former communist societies, especially Russia, where people have still not processed the tremor and hardship of the postcommunist transition. From the vantage point of the natural family agenda, moral conservatives tell the history of transition from communism to capitalism not as a rupture, but as continuity. (Here, the natural family agenda, as Carlson devised it, is an ideally discursive entry point for a larger story that has come to shape contemporary moral conservativism and SOGI rights opposition today.) The real rupture, they argue, lies ahead, in the form of a conservative revolution against liberalism.

The Refutation of Liberalism

Behind the moral conservative claims that shape almost every aspect of anti-SOGI-rights framing—protecting the nation, society, family, and children—there is a refutation of liberalism. Moral conservatives blame liberalism, or more precisely liberals, for most everything they resent. For one homeschooling mother, the GHEX-organized seminar in Rome where we interviewed her was her first encounter with the complete moral conservative narrative, and it became what she described as a learning experience:

> There are many people that want to teach values that are not traditional moral values in the education system. And so, of course, that's why a lot of people homeschool: because they do not want their children to have anti-values, they want them to have true values, right. And in the international context, there [are] governments that do not support values and they do not support the value of the parent in the family. And so they want to separate kids from the parents. One thing that I learn[ed] today was how a liberal government is similar to an authoritarian government. The outcome is still the same: they separate the parents from the kids. (Interview, Anonymous 2017g)

Liberalism as a political philosophy is identified as the root of the problem, due to its emphasis on the individual. Liberalism is also connected with secularism and the rejection or decline of religion. The idea that "liberalism has failed," as expressed in the extensively discussed book by the American political scientist Patrick Deneen (2018), is widely accepted as a truism among moral conservatives. On a less sophisticated level, the word liberal comes to signify, in conservative usage, everything associated with progressive or—in the context of Russian conservatism—Western ideas. In this sense, the concept also differs from its proper definition in political theory. Moral conservatives use liberalism as a synonym for leftism and cultural Marxism, which, from the standpoint of political philosophy makes little sense; Marxism was born as a reaction to liberalism and critical theorists, like Foucault or Butler, are themselves critics of liberalism.

Moral conservatives regularly blame societal decline on Western consumer culture, the cultural revolution of the 1960s, and cultural Marxism, by which they mean leftist, feminist, and pro-SOGI politics.[6] Just like the equation of capitalism with communism, the one of liberalism with cultural Marxism is deeply paradoxical, but from the moral conservative standpoint, it becomes a logical construction. SOGI rights activists become, in this worldview, the quintessential embodiment of the meaning of "liberal," and are therefore singled out as focal culprits.

Blaming International Organizations

The moral conservative narrative singles out international organizations (IOs)—particularly intergovernmental organizations like the United Nations or European Union—as culprits for the advancement of reproductive and SOGI rights policies. Indeed, in many parts of the world, advances in the field of sexual and reproductive rights are the fruit of IO transnational norm mobilization and human rights advocates. Transnational moral conservatism has emerged partly in response to this phenomenon, and moral conservatives are explicit about its motivating effect on them. Speaking about the International Planned Parenthood Federation, a participant at the WCF in Chisinau said, "They want to indoctrinate innocent children, get them thinking sexually way before their time and introduce them to homosexuality and all this junk, which is not natural" (Interview, Anonymous 2018b).

The WCF's founding declaration states that "the United Nations, its N.G.O.s and agents, have pursued dangerous philosophies and policies that require population control, limitation of family size, abortion on

200 | STRATEGIES AND CLAIMS

demand, sterilization of men and women and have sought to persuade Third World countries to adopt such policies" (WCF 1997). Gabriele Kuby echoes this idea in her book *The Global Sexual Revolution* (Kuby 2012) and in a piece on her blog:

> The United Nations, founded to proclaim and protect human dignity and freedom after World War II, has become an organization dedicated to the destruction of human identity. When state authorities undermine a society's identity through mind manipulation, legislation, sanctioning political incorrectness, and undermining parental rights, they establish a new, "soft" form of totalitarianism. The UN work in cooperation with other "global players": business enterprises, billion-euro foundations, NGOs. This is what the UN is all about: The creation of the new human beings who freely choose their gender, practice sexuality as hedonistic pleasure with any number of partners of any gender. The UN wants to throw marriage and family on the scrap heap of history. (Kuby 2018)

The equation of communism, capitalism, and liberalism is thus enlarged to include international organizations, namely the UN and, subsequently, the EU. The UN is singled out in the above quote as an agent of demographic decline. Similar arguments are made in the Global South, where the UN is portrayed as an instrument of imperial or colonial control over countries in Africa, Asia, and Latin America, which are "persuaded" to follow the liberal agenda (for this argument, see Rao 2020).

Revolutionaries and Counterrevolutionaries

In the complete moral conservative narrative that equates communism, capitalism, liberalism, and international organizations, SOGI rights activists are assigned the role of the new revolutionaries; they are depicted as a group that is planning a revolution—just like the Bolsheviks a century ago. The moral conservative narrative, in fact, develops a rather circular view of history, according to which the world at the beginning of the twenty-first century faces precisely the same totalitarian challenge as it did at the beginning of the twentieth century. Alexey Komov, the leader of the Russian section of the World Congress of Families, has become an ambassador for this circular narrative. He repeats versions of it on various public occasions, and we therefore reconstruct it here to exemplify the logic of the equation between communism, capitalism, liberalism, and international organizations.[7]

Bolshevism—the narrative goes—was a Western imposition on the Russian people aimed at destroying family values and national unity by introducing feminism and the right to abortion. The Russian people were saved by Stalin, who repressed the progressive Trotskyists and re-installed both patriarchal authority and patriotic values. "Stalin," Komov says, "brought down a destructive revolutionary wave. For this reason, the ideologists of Marxism moved to the West" (AVA 2014).[8] In the West, the narrative continues, the Trotskyists embraced the political program of Antonio Gramsci, which consisted of a "long march through the institutions" (by which Gramsci meant the institutions of the democratic state, as opposed to a revolutionary approach). The "heirs of Trotsky," in Komov's terms, are now attempting to destroy the traditional family through popular culture and the dissemination of progressive ideas, in particular the idea of gender. "This happened," Komov explains, "largely due to the activities of the so-called Frankfurt School of Neo-Marxism, which operated in the 1920s–1940s. The theorists of this school (Marcuse, Adorno, Horkheimer, Fromm) combined the ideas of Marx with Freudianism and gave rise to the concept of the sexual revolution of the 1960s" (AVA 2014). Komov cites Western democracies, international bodies like the United Nations or the European Union, and philanthropists such as George Soros and Bill and Melinda Gates as the agents of this strategy. Yet he warns his audience not to homogenize the West as an ideological monolith: "In the West, there are liberals and conservatives. Western liberals are socialists and atheists, while conservatives advocate private initiative and Christian and family values" (AVA 2014). Komov repeated this account in our interview, with a full conspiracy-theory spin that is worth quoting at length:

> In the West, you know, there was after the French Revolution, there was a lot of efforts to destroy any religious identity, then in the recent one hundred years to destroy any national identity; so globalism, citizens of the world. Now, they are destroying gender identities, and I think the ultimate battle will be transhumanism, posthumanism. So, to get rid of

your human identity. Experiments, make a genetic fusion with animals, with robots, with a computer, drugs, enhancing memory, physical ability, people connected to, you know, supercomputers or microchips, etc. They already have these movements of transhumans. (Interview, Komov 2017)

In all likelihood, Komov is not the original author of this narrative. We find it—in more or less camouflaged language—throughout the writings of Allan Carlson, Larry Jacobs, and other regular WCF speakers. In fact, in the moral conservative universe, the historical circularity of equating communism, cosmopolitan capitalism, liberalism, and international organizations is viewed as self-evident, staple knowledge (see also Paternotte and Verloo 2021). The 2012 WCF Congress in Madrid featured sections on "the revolution against the family" and "the homosexual lobby" (WCF Madrid 2012). Similarly, the 2018 WCF Congress in Chisinau included a section entitled "Against the Family—The International Networks Undermining Family and Faith" and "Gender Ideology—The Latest Attack on the Family and the Legal Challenges It Poses" (WCF Chisinau 2018). These are just examples that depict a broader trend: in the moral conservative worldview, rights for sexual and gender minorities come to epitomize what is seen as bad about communism, cosmopolitan capitalism, liberalism, and international organizations, and the activists behind these rights become their main adversaries.

We underscore here that moral conservatives depict SOGI activists as communist revolutionaries. They do so not just metaphorically, but quite literally, as in this quote, where the red communist flag is likened to the rainbow flag: "The 1960s, 1970s [were] the continuation of this revolutionary trend that we experienced in Russia in a more straight forward violent, brutal, red form. And now it has this rainbow flag" (Interview, Komov 2017). Thus, moral conservatives see international organizations that support SOGI rights as communist institutions. When moral conservative politicians in Central and Eastern Europe criticize Brussels as being like the Moscow of the Soviet Union, what they mean is that they see the European Union as a communist project of sorts. This is a wild stretch of the imagination for most, but amid the crowd at WCF congresses, it becomes hard to separate this all-encompassing narrative from reality. When moral conservative actors in the United

States criticize social justice activism as a new kind of totalitarianism, they see themselves—also quite literally—in the role of anti-communist dissidents (Dreher 2020).

Our purpose in reconstructing here the moral conservative narrative is to show how it is used to justify the claims—including anti-SOGI-rights claims—that this transnational network deploys. The whole narrative has the timbre of a conspiracy theory: it offers so-called new knowledge about historical developments that mainstream (academic) culture presents in a completely different light. It interprets evidence against the grain of what is normally understood to be (or to have been) the case and creates links between topics that are usually seen as opposites. It identifies a group of people as perpetrators, and those who hold conservative views as victims. For those who are initiated into this narrative, the new knowledge becomes a marker of belonging. Readers may wonder why the "SOGI-revolutionaries" are seen to want to pursue all the destructive strategies that the moral conservative narrative claims to have uncovered. Like all conspiracy theories, the moral conservative narrative answers that the motivation behind all these strategies is the quest for power. In the face of what they view as a struggle for domination of one group over another, moral conservatives see themselves simultaneously as victims and as empowered, because they can claim to have seen the truth and to have taken up the challenge of leading the counterrevolution.

Our analytical takeaway from this reconstruction of the moral conservative narrative, and from the claims that derive from it, is that the transnational moral conservative network's strategic goal is to diffuse and perpetuate its own structure and agenda of a conservative counterrevolution of sorts. This may sound tautological at first; yet it is important to recognize that the moral conservative narrative presented here is not only new and baffling for researchers interested in the phenomenon; it is also new for many of the activists who are drawn into the networks of transnational moral conservatives. Most activists who attend WCF events listen to speeches by Allan Carlson and other regular attendees or pick up some translations from the book fairs and encounter this narrative for the first time. The fact that the WCF perpetuates this narrative each time and in all locales where a WCF summit takes place is significant. It incorporates the range of topics covered, for example, by CitzenGo, and it is the reason why WCF, AFD, GHEX, and the PNV—despite their different organizational structures and aims—make up one coherent moral conservative TAN. In the last decades, moral conservatives have built up this narrative to identify and construct SOGI rights—and the institutions that support them—as the main focal point of twenty-first century ideological struggles. In conjuring up a vision of a SOGI-revolution, moral conservatives can become the counterrevolutionaries.

All other strategic goals follow from this overarching narrative. The self-proclaimed counterrevolutionaries do have the strategic goal of blocking SOGI rights. However, according to the moral conservative agenda, a win on the abortion front, the homeschooling front, or on religious freedom is de facto also a step toward blocking SOGI rights. For moral conservatives, all these claims hang together. For a deeper understanding, as scholars or human rights practitioners, it is important to recognize that in the global resistances against SOGI rights, all the above arguments flow into each other smoothly. Naturally, for those who are not members of this audience, the narrative will be read as departing from "standards of consistency or coherence" (Butler 2021). For the moral conservative audience, however, it makes up one global, coherent narrative.

6

Venues

The United Nations, Council of Europe, and International Academia

Anti-gender narratives defend a world of absolutes that must be challenged if human rights are to be enjoyed universally.
—Victor Madrigal-Borloz, UN Independent Expert

Historically excluded sexual and gender minorities have sought out international venues to advance and diffuse their claims for rights at home, as we showed in chapter 1. Politicized moral conservative (PMC) actors have increasingly borrowed these same strategies, targeting SOGI rights work at the very venues that have contributed to the movement's successes: the United Nations (UN), the European Union (EU), the European Court of Human Rights (ECtHR), and the Council of Europe, as well as in international academia. Indeed, as the words of Madrigal-Borloz, UN Independent Expert on protection against violence and discrimination based on sexual orientation and gender identity, make clear, their work in these spaces is of central concern to many at international organizations like the UN. In this chapter, we look at the international venues where moral conservative networks pursue and articulate resistances against SOGI rights. We show how political majorities that both support and oppose SOGI rights form and are tested in this transnational space and operate there in line with our double helix model. Today pro- and anti-SOGI political stances translate roughly into geopolitical blocks that mirror the common divisions in world politics: with exceptions, the transatlantic West—including the United States and the European Union—takes an increasingly pro-SOGI stance; Russia, China, and African countries oppose SOGI rights; and Latin America navigates in between (Stoeckl and Medvedeva 2018).[1]

206 | VENUES

The venues we discuss in this chapter are spaces where new norms and legal decisions regarding SOGI rights are developed and circulated—both in ways that promote SOGI rights and in ways that target, roll back, and restrict them. Venues also provide the space and opportunity for encounter and contestation between SOGI activists and moral conservative activists. Thus, the clash of agendas over SOGI rights takes place not only at state level but also in the realm of social movements. Most of the time, this encounter and contestation is not as visible and immediate as in the scene with which we opened chapter 2: in that instance, moral conservative lobbyists used slogans and symbols to visually take over a room in which government delegates were gathering to discuss women's rights. More commonly, states allied with the anti-SOGI cause (see chapter 4) prepare the venues for moral conservative actors to mobilize—as in the example below, where Russia's resolution on traditional values at the UN Human Rights Council gave scores of moral conservative NGOs registered with the UN Economic and Social Council the opportunity to submit their opinions.

We will examine three venues for the contestation of SOGI rights: the UN Human Rights Council (UNHRC); the Council of Europe's Parliamentary Assembly and its European Court of Human Rights; and the epistemic venue of international academia. The first two are relatively well accounted for in the literature, whereas the third is not usually considered a venue in itself. However, our research in moral conservative milieus reveals the importance of epistemic communities as sites of knowledge production and diffusion for mobilization against SOGI rights.

United Nations

SOGI rights promoters and opponents alike recognize the UN as a central venue to push their respective agendas (Bob 2012, 2019; Butler 2000; Buss and Herman 2003). Starting with the mobilization around women's and reproductive rights in the UN conferences in Cairo and Beijing (chapter 2), the UN has become a key site of moral conservative movement organizing. Two of the moral conservative actors analyzed in chapter 3—the World Congress for Families (WCF) and the Political Network for Values (PNV)—were created with the explicit aim of influencing policies at the UN. Russian WCF websites list Alexey Komov, the Russian leader of the World Congress of Families, as, among other things, ambassador of the World Congress of Families to the United Nations (TVSOYUZ 2015), though that title is absent on the International Organization for the Family (IOF) website. This notable designation caused considerable confusion on at least one occasion, when Komov spoke at the 2013 party congress of the Italian right-wing party Lega and was erroneously introduced as the Russian ambassador to the United Nations (Lega Salvini Premier Channel 2013). According to official UN documentation, the WCF is not registered as an NGO at the UN ECOSOC Council, nor is the IOF or the PNV; but the Howard Center for Family, Religion and Society, founded by Allan Carlson, has been registered there since 2003 (UN ECOSOC 2021). Nevertheless, the United Nations occupies a central position in the workings of the WCF, also founded by Allan Carlson, the original goal of which was to defend Article 16(3) of the Universal Declaration of Human Rights and the family as a fundamental unit of society (IOF 2022).

In venues like the UNHRC, resistance to SOGI rights manifests itself not only in debates centered on SOGI but in an extended list of topical issues, including family, traditional values, education, and religious freedom.[2] Every resolution at the UNHRC generates a series of gatherings or seminars, in which NGOs and experts exchange drafts, amendments, and working papers and issue recommendations and opinions. Every resolution, in other words, creates small semantic universes, in which participants formulate and contest the meanings of terms, argumentative strategies, and policy goals. For social scientists, these arenas of meaning construction provide rich data for understanding how ideas spread, as well as a baseline for the mechanisms of the promotion of contested policy areas (Acharya 2004; Benford and Snow 1999; Finnemore and Sikkink 2001).

Table 6.1 lists the adopted resolutions that were instrumental either for advancing SOGI rights or for framing the resistance to SOGI rights at the UNHRC.[3] The resolutions that signaled resistance did not include SOGI (sexual orientation and gender identity) in the wording of the resolution, but they targeted SOGI rights indirectly—through the back door—with a language of family and traditional values.[4]

TABLE 6.1: Adopted resolutions at UNHRC for/against SOGI rights

Title	Year (resolution)
Full list of pro-SOGI resolutions	
Human rights and sexual orientation	2003 (not adopted)
Human rights, sexual orientation, and gender identity	2011 (A/HRC/RES/17/19) 2014 (A/HRC/RES/27/32)
Protection against violence and discrimination based on sexual orientation and gender identity	2016 (A/HRC/RES/32/2)
Mandate of the independent expert on protection against violence and discrimination based on sexual orientation and gender identity	2019 (A/HRC/RES/41/18)
Examples of anti-SOGI resolutions	
Promoting human rights and fundamental freedoms through a better understanding of traditional values of humankind	2009 (A/HRC/RES/12/21) 2011 (A/HRC/RES/16/3) 2012 (A/HRC/RES/21/3)
Protection of the family	2014 (A/HRC/RES/26/11) 2015 (A/HRC/RES/29/22) 2016 (A/HRC/RES/32/23) 2017 (A/HRC/RES/35/13)

Note: All the resolutions are accessible through the United Nations Electronic Archive: https://documents.un.org/prod/ods.nsf/home.xsp

SOGI rights had a difficult start in the UNHRC. As table 6.1 shows, in 2003, EU countries tabled a draft resolution, "Promotion and protection of human rights: Human Rights and Sexual Orientation" (gender identity was missing from the wording at the time), but it was neither adopted nor followed through. It was not until 2011 that the first resolution to mention SOGI rights was adopted, followed by a second in 2014. In the working schedule of the UNHRC, three years of silence on a particular topic is unusual (Voss 2018, 7). In fact, compared to the annual rhythm of the Traditional Values and Protection of the Family resolutions, the advances on SOGI were more intermittent. With Resolution 32/2 in 2014, the UNHRC created the position of an independent expert on sexual orientation and gender identity, which fundamentally changed the nature of the resolutions in Geneva by adding significantly more legitimacy and power to the movement to protect LGBTIQ individuals from discrimination and violence (Voss 2018, 3).

Unlike pro-SOGI initiatives, resistance to SOGI rights in the UN framework commonly works through amendments, whereby member states try to extinguish gender-sensitive language from UN resolutions. A recent example, included here because it involved the Russian Federation, was the debate around the resolution "Rights of the child: realizing the rights of the child and family reunification," adopted on April 8, 2022 (A/HRC/RES/49/20). This resolution was proposed by a broad coalition of countries and aimed specifically at family reunification in the context of migration. Russia submitted a list of twelve amendments to the draft resolution, most of which sought to eliminate gender-inclusive language. For example, the amendments demanded "gender" be replaced with "sex" and "gender-responsive" with "gender-sensitive" throughout the resolution (analysis based on documents A/HRC/49/L.39–50). Russia tabled these amendments at the UNHRC on March 31, 2022, in the middle of its war against Ukraine. A week later, on April 7, the UN General Assembly suspended Russia from the HRC by majority vote (UN Affairs 2022).

Our observations on resistance to SOGI rights at the UN rest on analysis of the activities around the resolutions on Traditional Values and Protection of the Family, along with existing research about the pro-SOGI resolutions by Voss (2018). From both analytical angles—pro-SOGI and anti-SOGI—our observations suggest that advocates for SOGI rights and the stakeholders who oppose them are in a standoff: each presents their own position in line with prior international human rights law and accuses their opponents of being revisionist and relativist.

Let us briefly disentangle this argumentative standoff. Since the UNHRC's foundation, its workings have been characterized by a struggle between actors who have promoted the implementation of transversally valid, universal human rights standards and those who have argued that human rights have to be realized—and thus relativized—according to specific religious, cultural, and political contexts (Alston and Goodman 2012; Lenzerini 2014). The contextualist, cultural-relativist, and rights-skeptical positions on human rights were first formulated in a 1947 statement by the executive board of the American Anthropological Association, which argued that rights must be integrated in different cultures by "the only right and proper way of life that can be known to them, the institutions, sanctions and goals that make up the culture of their particular society" (McCrudden 2014, 4). Often the human-rights-skeptical view has been associated with African, Asian, and Middle

Eastern countries (the Global South), but Western scholars have also taken a critical view by drawing attention to the exclusivist nature of human rights (Moyn 2015). The universalist position is prima facie associated with Western liberal democratic countries—though this rendering has also been challenged by those who trace important origins of human rights to the Global South during decolonization in the 1960s (Jensen 2017).[5] However, the struggle over SOGI rights has restructured the debate, with both sides now claiming to speak for the universal position on human rights.

The Russian Federation promoted a series of Traditional Values resolutions in the UNHRC between 2009 and 2013, which Stoeckl and Medvedeva (2018) identify as the starting point for a consistent framing of resistance to SOGI rights as a universalist human rights stance. The Traditional Values resolutions originated in the programmatic work of the Russian Orthodox Church to define (and limit) individual human rights in terms of religiously and culturally defined norms and values (Stoeckl 2014). In this process, the Russian Orthodox Church reiterated time and again the argument that Article 29 of the Universal Declaration of Human Rights legitimized contextual parameters as guiding norms for the interpretation of human rights (see chapter 4). The church thereby interpreted human rights not in an individual light, but in a social and public one. The focus was not on how human rights protect individuals, but on how they enable them to do certain things, for example change one's religion or use freedom of speech in what the church called a "blasphemous" way. It wanted to limit this enabling side of human rights, and it defined this limit in terms of "traditional morality." However, Article 29 of the Universal Declaration, which church officials cited as the source for this idea, does not contain the term "traditional morality"; it speaks instead of "just requirement of morality . . . in a democratic society." In other words, the Universal Declaration articulates limits for human rights, but it portrays these limits as the fruit of a democratic process. The Moscow Patriarchate twisted the meaning of Article 29, using "traditional morality" to seal off public morality from change through democratic deliberation, instead privileging past practice and traditional mores as sources of legitimacy.

Church documents not only provided ideas for the Traditional Values resolutions, they also became the textual reference for Russian diplomats working on the resolution inside the UNHRC. In 2009, these diplomats tabled the resolution "Promoting human rights and fundamental freedoms through a better understanding of traditional values of humankind," which requested convening a 2010 workshop "for an exchange of views on how a better understanding of traditional values of humankind underpinning international human rights norms and standards can contribute to the promotion and protection of human rights and fundamental freedoms" (A/HRC/RES/12/21). It was adopted despite the opposing votes of several Western countries and, one year later, on October 4, 2010, the envisioned international workshop entitled "Traditional Values and Human Rights" took place at the UNHCR in Geneva. The press service of the Moscow Patriarchate reported extensively on the workshop and the preceding resolution, presenting it as the outcome of Kirill's address to the United Nations General Assembly in March 2008 (Stoeckl 2016, 138).

In 2011, Resolution A/HRC/RES/16/3 requested that the Human Rights Council Advisory Committee prepare a study on how a better understanding and appreciation of traditional values could contribute to the promotion and protection of human rights and present that study to the council at its twenty-first session (Stoeckl 2016, 139). By the time the twenty-first UNHRC session was convened in September 2012, the study had not been finished, but the Russian rapporteur Vladimir Kartashkin presented a "preliminary study" (UNHRC 2012; Stoeckl 2016, 139). Throughout the entirety of this process, cooperation between the Russian UN diplomats and the Russian Orthodox Church was evident: a representative of the Moscow Patriarchate participated in a seminar organized at the UN headquarters in Geneva in 2010 (Ryabykh 2010), and one Russian diplomat received an award from the Patriarch for "service" to the church (Russian Orthodox Church 2010). In sum, the Traditional Values resolutions offer a clear example of norm entrepreneurship at work: a nonstate actor (the Russian Orthodox Church) relies on the support of a state (Russian state diplomacy) to utilize a venue (the United Nations Human Rights Council) to construct a restrictive definition of human rights that it can test by having NGOs submit responses to it and UNHRC members vote on it.

The UNHRC Advisory Board studied the Traditional Values resolutions and essentially dismissed the idea of using the traditional values of humankind to set limits on the expansion of human rights. However, the resolutions had already sent a powerful signal to conservative actors across the globe, giving a new universalist twist to the rights-restrictive approach of conservative, religious, and traditionalist actors inside the UN. Horsfjord concludes that, from the point of view of the moral conservative actors, the UNHRC Advisory Board's dismissive study was "the hegemonic international human rights discourse reasserting its power. It is the voice of 'these fellows' who reflect 'the opinion of a narrow circle of experts, functionaries, or noisy but well-organized minorities'" (Horsfjord 2017). From the vantage point of the moral conservative supporters of the Traditional Values resolutions, the main takeaway was that the international human rights regime was (still) in the hands of a progressive elite, but the traditionalist position more accurately represented the will of the majority. This traditionalist universalism is expressed in the following statement by the American Center for Family and Human Rights (C-Fam): "Only a few developed countries have changed their laws to recognize a special status for homosexual relationships, yet they argue this requires a change to the universal, longstanding understanding of family for all UN member states and UN policy" (C-Fam 2015). C-Fam here depicts the pro-SOGI position as elitist and sectarian ("few developed countries") and the traditionalist position as truly universal ("all UN member states"). The same pattern was used in 2016 debates around pro-SOGI resolutions, as Voss has analyzed (2018). Saudi Arabia, for example, attempted to halt Resolution 32/2 on SOGI rights with a no-action motion that stated that "the universality of human rights does not mean the imposition of certain so-called human rights concepts or ideas that are imposed from the point of view of another party; especially when these concepts run counter to our own beliefs, culture and specificities" (cited in Voss 2018, 11).

In concomitance with the debate on the pro-SOGI resolution "Protection against violence and discrimination based on sexual orientation and gender identity" in 2014, Egypt launched another draft resolution entitled "Protection of the Family." The similarity between the titles is hardly a coincidence. In the wake of this resolution, a new group was created within the UNHRC in early 2015—the "group of the friends of the family," made up of Bangladesh, Belarus, Egypt, Indonesia, Iran, Iraq, Kuwait, Libya, Malaysia, Nicaragua, Nigeria, Oman,

Pakistan, Qatar, the Russian Federation, Saudi Arabia, Somalia, Sudan, Tajikistan, Turkmenistan, Yemen, Uganda, and Zimbabwe. Belarus announced the creation of the group (Belarus 2015); however, a background interview confirmed that Russia had initiated it (Interview, Anonymous 2017c).[6] Belarus—it should be noted—is an Orthodox-majority country, and the Moscow Patriarchate is the head of the Orthodox Church in Belarus. However, from the available documents, it is not evident that the Russian Orthodox Church was as centrally involved with the resolutions on Protection of the Family as it was with those on Traditional Values. What we did find is an active involvement of individuals and groups associated with the World Congress of Families. The Howard Center for Family, Religion and Society took part in a panel discussion, which was held on September 15, 2014, during the twenty-seventh session of the UNHRC (a report on this discussion was published on December 22, 2014) (UNHRC 2014), and the Russian CitizenGo website (another one of the numerous projects of Alexey Komov) published a call on its website to support the Group of Friends of the Family (CitizenGo 2015).

What is remarkable about the resolutions on Traditional Values and Protection of the Family is that they mobilized a stable coalition among the UNHRC member states which included Russia and the post-Soviet states, the countries of the Organization of Islamic Cooperation, and other countries from the Global South (McCrudden 2014). This coalition was met with consistent opposition from Western European countries, the United States, and a few others. Coalition-making over moral conservative content is not a novelty inside the UN—conservative mobilization against topics of sexual orientation and gender identity in the human rights context dates back to 1994, when the Vatican, together with religious and nondenominational conservative NGOs and Muslim-majority states, raised arguments about the "natural" and "traditional family" at the Cairo Conference on Population and Development (see chapter 2). What was new about the resolutions detailed here is that Russia maintained leadership of these debates, supported by its close ally Belarus and a variety of Muslim-majority and other Global South countries. Heiner Bielefeldt, former UN special rapporteur on freedom of religion, confirmed to us that Russia has become the leader in a discussion which, ten years ago, was primarily associated with Muslim-majority states (Interview, Bielefeldt 2017). Its central role was corroborated by two interviewees from the NGO sector, one of whom said, "Russia is taking over. This is quite clear" (Interview, Anonymous 2018a). Given the fact that the UNHRC voted Russia out in 2022 on grounds of the war in Ukraine, the country's leadership role in the promotion of a traditionalist agenda in the UNHRC has an uncertain future.

In sum, there are clear indicators that beginning around 2012 to 2014, the moral conservative camp began a new phase in moral conservative norm protagonism at the UN. This new phase is characterized not by new topics but by a new argumentative strategy. The moral conservative agenda now presents itself as universalist; it redraws the conceptual boundaries between the universalist and contextualist positions in the human rights discourse by calling into question the previous characterization of the universalist position as liberal, egalitarian, and progressive, and of the contextualist position as illiberal, restrictive, and relativist. Instead, the moral conservative agenda presents itself as just as universal as the liberal position that Western states and, indeed, the UN bureaucracy itself promotes. This change in strategy also has an impact on how SOGI rights are promoted inside the UN. For example, transnational SOGI rights movements, which operate in the same spaces as transnational moral conservative movements, have shifted their framing strategy by embracing the frames of family, faith, and religion (see chapter 7). We have in mind the effects of this relational interaction—between SOGI rights and moral conservative movements and their respective supporting states—when we theorize the double helix model of norm promotion.

Council of Europe

The promotion and contestation of SOGI rights in the context of European institutions differs from that which occurs at the UN. In the European context, we do not generally find a comparably strong polarization between two mutually exclusive universalist positions as we find in the UN. Instead, the situation is multifaceted. European institutions like the Council of Europe and the European Union incorporated SOGI rights early on, and Europe hosted and inspired activism on the continent and transnationally. At the same time, the image of Europe as SOGI friendly has paradoxically become a tool of exclusion—as countries like Russia construct SOGI rights as a threat from without and right-wing populists and European moral conservative activists construct them as a threat from within (Ayoub and Paternotte 2019). The latter have used the issue to help exclude certain groups, especially Muslim migrants, from membership in European society, or states such as Turkey from political membership. The multifaceted relationship of Europeans, European institutions, and SOGI rights produces outcomes that move in choppy fashion two steps forward and one step back. But this does not necessarily lead to the stand-offs and stalemates we observe at the UN. In this section, we analyze SOGI rights contestation in two arms of the Council of Europe, the European Court of Human Rights (ECtHR) and the Parliamentary Assembly of the Council of Europe (PACE). The ECtHR examines violations of human rights in its member countries and produces case law based on the European Convention of Human Rights, while PACE publishes resolutions and recommendations.

The ECtHR

The ECtHR has done more than any other institutional venue to advance SOGI rights (van der Vleuten 2014). The court's factsheet on LGBTI Persons' Rights lists thirty-three cases in which the ECtHR has broken new ground in combating discrimination on the basis of sexual orientation and gender identity (Council of Europe 2021a). The ECtHR has tackled discrimination of LGBTI+ persons on all levels of private and professional life, including decriminalizing homosexual relations, combating hate crimes, and legally recognizing gender identity to access social rights and succession-of-tenancy agreements. In this way, the court has created a consistent body of case law that guides the EU's anti-discrimination policy and has earned the EU the reputation of a "champion" of SOGI rights (van der Vleuten, 2014; Johnson 2013).

However, the ECtHR has also become a central site of contestation of SOGI rights. Chapter 2 explained how Christian Right advocacy moved from the United States to Europe precisely to target the proliferation of SOGI rights within the international human rights system and to prevent a spillover of European progressive legal achievements to the United States (Bob 2012, 72–90). US Christian Right law firms have been involved in cases—either by bringing a case before the court, or by filing amicus curiae briefs—that revolve around moral conservative issues, including religious freedom, homeschooling, free speech, abortion, or euthanasia (Annicchino 2018a; Fokas 2018). In chapter 2, we briefly discussed *Ladele v. United Kingdom*, a case concerning a marriage registrar who lost her job because she refused to officiate same-sex marriages. The Christian Right advocacy group Alliance Defending Freedom (ADF), which represented the registrar, lost this case, as the judges at the court did not find a violation of the European Convention of Human Rights. In other high-profile cases, however, the ADF has been more successful, specifically on abortion in Ireland, freedom of religion and church autonomy in the UK and Hungary, and the display of the crucifix in Italian schools (ADF International 2022b). However, among the "legacy cases" that the ADF has brought before the ECtHR, none has yet restricted SOGI rights directly.[7]

Legal contestation of SOGI rights operates principally through claims to freedom of speech, freedom of expression, and freedom of religion, along with more specific rights, like the rights of parents to choose the education of their children. All these cases apply a zero-sum logic of rights, arguing that more SOGI rights lead to fewer rights for religious conservatives ("if you win, we lose"), whereas SOGI rights advocacy promotes the idea that society as a whole will gain from more pluralism and diversity. The second claim behind the legal contestation of SOGI rights at the ECtHR is that of defending national sovereignty against international human rights standards. In *Lautsi v. Italy*, which concerned whether Italian public schools could display crucifixes, the ADF won the appeal when the court ruled that Italy had a "margin of appreciation" to decide the matter itself, deeming it outside of the court's competences (Annicchino 2011). *Not* obtaining a judgment from the ECtHR can also be a goal of strategic litigation by moral conservative activists.

How does moral conservative litigation at the ECtHR work? The court only presides when all previous levels of jurisdiction in national legal systems have been exhausted. The ADF therefore strategically picks cases *before* they reach the ECtHR, with the intention of winning or losing a case in national contexts and moving it forward all the way to the ECtHR. The case law of the court is cumulative: new judgments usually rely on previous ones, but there are sometimes changes in the legal assessment of a claim. Stakeholders can thus choose to repropose similar cases to the ECtHR, hoping to achieve a win where past cases have been lost. For example, in 2012, the court was asked to rule on the case of *Vejdeland and Others v. Sweden*, which involved four Swedish citizens (not represented by the ADF) who were prosecuted for going to a secondary school and distributing leaflets containing statements against homosexuality. In Sweden, they had been sentenced to fines for hate speech. The ECtHR confirmed the Swedish judgment and stated that limiting freedom of speech was justified in cases where speech was "incompatible with democracy and human rights," "infringe(d) the rights of others," and "constitute(d) a serious threat to public order" (Interights n.d.). Less than ten years later, the ADF represented Finnish parliamentarian and former minister Päivi Räsänen, who had been charged with hate speech for expressing the view that homosexuality was sinful. The ADF won this case in the Finnish court, and all charges against Räsänen were dismissed (ADF International 2022a). Though it never reached Strasbourg, the ADF saw this case—which was very similar to the earlier Swedish SOGI rights hate-speech case—as a legacy case. The high-profile nature of the trial is indicative of the moral conservative strategy of contestation.[8]

The ECtHR is and will continue to be a central venue for the contestation of SOGI rights. The court is the main reason why Christian Right advocacy groups like the ADF or the European Center for Law and Justice (ECLJ) became active in Europe in the first place—it is the main motor for SOGI achievements, and it has, thus far, been a force that holds SOGI contestation at bay.

PACE

The political function of the Parliamentary Assembly of the Council of Europe is particularly relevant for understanding the contestation of SOGI rights at the Council of Europe (CoE), since political majorities are formed at PACE. Additionally, like the UNHRC, new ideas can be formulated and tested there. PACE's resolutions and recommendations mostly have a declaratory character, in that they express an opinion by the assembly. They are not binding on member states, but they are suggestive of the normative stances PACE takes on issues.

It is easier to identify the resolutions, recommendations, reports, and debates in favor of SOGI rights than those against. The Council of Europe became concerned with discrimination on the grounds of sexuality early on, with debates on homosexuality starting in the 1980s (Dunne 2020; P. Johnson 2022). Since 2010, CoE documents have used the terms "homosexual" people, "transgender" people (previously sometimes referred to as "transsexual" people in these documents), and "gay and lesbian" people in identifying stakeholders. The council itself has a website dedicated to SOGI rights (Council of Europe 2014). In comparison, it is much less evident what the anti-SOGI agenda inside PACE consists of. However, utilizing our argument about the double helix and the broad moral conservative narrative, it is nonetheless possible to identify claims against SOGI rights that moral conservative actors strategically employ within PACE. These claims include the protection of the nation, religion, children, women, the family, and society, in line with the analysis in chapter 5. In the context of PACE, this broad umbrella of claims translates into resolutions which do not target SOGI rights directly but contribute to creating a political perspective in which SOGI rights are unimportant or even detrimental to reaching certain desirable policy outcomes.

Table 6.2 provides a list of pro-SOGI and anti-SOGI resolutions and documents issued in PACE. The list of anti-SOGI debates is incomplete, but we have selected exemplary topics that demonstrate the mechanisms of resistance to SOGI rights within PACE.

Debates within PACE commonly start when a member of the parliamentary assembly raises a motion for a recommendation; what follows can include a report and recommendation, amendments, and a resolution. Occasionally, NGOs and stakeholders organize offshoot events surrounding a report or resolution. The process of debate between a motion and the final resolution usually takes more than a year and leads to a watering down of the original claim, turning controversial motions into diplomatic resolutions that are almost always unanimously approved. Motions of resolutions within PACE often start as partisan and end up being supported by a majority of members of parliament. This makes the dynamics in PACE different from those inside the UNHRC, where resolutions often produce polarized outcomes.

The contestation of SOGI rights inside PACE takes two forms: submission of amendments to pro-SOGI resolutions that alter their meaning or

TABLE 6.2: Adopted resolutions at PACE for/against SOGI rights

Title	Resolution (Year)
Full list of pro-SOGI resolutions	
Discrimination against homosexuals	Recommendation 924 (1981)
The conditions of transsexuals	Recommendation 1117 (1989)
Situation of gays and lesbians in Council of Europe member states	Resolution 1474 (2000)
Discrimination on the basis of sexual orientation and gender identity	Resolution 1728 (2010)
Tackling discrimination on the grounds of sexual orientation and gender identity	Resolution 2021 (2013)
Discrimination against transgender people in Europe	Resolution 2048 (2015)
Promoting the human rights of and eliminating discrimination against intersex people	Resolution 2191 (2017)
Private and family life: achieving equality regardless of sexual orientation	Resolution 2239 (2018)
Combating rising hate against LGBTI people in Europe	Resolution 2417 (2022)
Examples of anti-SOGI resolutions	
The protection of the rights of parents and children belonging to religious minorities	Motion for a resolution 13333 (2013) by Valeriu Ghiletchi (Republic of Moldova)
Result: The protection of the rights of parents and children belonging to religious minorities	*Resolution 2163 (2017)–adopted after amendments*
Coordinated strategies for effective internet governance	Motion for a recommendation 13280 (2013) by Robert Shlegel (Russian Federation)
Result: Internet governance and human rights	*Resolution 2256 (2019)–adopted after amendments*
Fighting the over-sexualization of children	Motion for a resolution 13777 (2015)
Fighting the over-sexualization of children	Report 14080 (2016) by Valeriu Ghiletchi (Republic of Moldova)
Result: Fighting the over-sexualization of children	*Resolution 2119 (2016)–adopted after amendments*

implications and submissions of resolutions that create political perspectives and modes of justification which marginalize, downplay, or limit SOGI rights as a relevant area of policy. We will demonstrate these two forms of contestation with regard to the resolutions listed in table 6.2.

To examine the impact of an amendment submitted to a pro-SOGI resolution, we looked at resolution Nr. 2417, "Combating rising hate against LGBT people in Europe." This resolution was approved by a wide margin (72 in favor, 12 against, 8 abstentions), but only after a series of amendments that clearly aimed to alter its implications. One amendment, for example, unsuccessfully demanded deleting the following paragraph: "The Assembly condemns the highly prejudicial anti-gender, gender-critical and anti-trans narratives which reduce the fight for the equality of LGBTI people to what these movements deliberately mischaracterise as 'gender ideology' or 'LGBTI ideology'. Such narratives deny the very existence of LGBTI people, dehumanise them, and often falsely portray their rights as being in conflict with women's and children's rights, or societal and family values in general. All of these are deeply damaging to LGBTI people, while also harming women's and children's rights and social cohesion" (PACE 2022). Other (unsuccessful) amendments requested inserting the word "sex" (after "based on their") in sentences such as this: "based on their sexual orientation, gender identity, gender expression and sex characteristics" (PACE 2022). The verbatim insistence on "sex" before the expressions "sexual orientation, gender identity, gender expression and sex characteristics" is a way by which conservative actors stress the primacy of anatomical sex over sexuality and gender as an orientation, identity, expression, or characteristics. In the debates we analyzed, it represents a typical pattern of proposing amendments to contest SOGI rights.[9]

The contestation of SOGI rights through the promotion of resolutions on items on the moral conservative agenda similarly follow a standard pattern. The motion for Resolution Nr. 13333 (2013), "The protection of the rights of parents and children belonging to religious minorities," was presented by Valeriu Ghiletchi from the Republic of Moldova.[10] Discrimination against Christians is frequently used to contest SOGI rights, and Datta (2018b, 33) identifies at least two additional motions within PACE prior to 2013 (promoted by Luca Volontè) that sought to limit SOGI rights through this frame. In the case of the motion for Resolution 13333, the phrase "unnecessary restrictions" leaves room for interpretation regarding whether parents can refuse sex education for their children and whether the principle of gender equality must be included in teaching materials: "The Assembly has expressed concern regarding discrimination that may arise from unnecessary restrictions on the rights of parents to raise and educate their children in conformity with their own religious and philosophical convictions" (PACE 2013). Ghiletchi's report and draft resolution present his agenda more directly, arguing that a state is not entitled to regulate beliefs and worldviews. That sounds plausible, but in fact, it opens a back door to demands not to implement principles like gender equality in public school curricula, since such teaching could be interpreted as regulation of beliefs. "The Assembly considers that it is not the role of member States to regulate or validate the beliefs and world views of its population, but to accommodate different perspectives and convictions, and allow individuals to thrive together within the boundaries of public order, health and morals. It considers that the genuine recognition of, and respect for, diversity and the dynamics of cultural traditions and identities and religious convictions are essential in order to achieve social cohesion" (PACE 2017).[11]

The presentation of the report and draft resolution was accompanied by a side-event the ECLJ and the European Christian Political Movement organized (ECLJ 2016). PACE approved the final resolution with 38 votes in favor, 19 against, and 9 abstentions—a relatively close margin that mirrored the divide between conservative-right and progressive-left political groups inside PACE. The resolution is a glaring example of how moral conservative actors claim to protect religion as part of their strategy to oppose SOGI rights, even as its text references positive values like respect, diversity, social cohesion, and the acceptance of cultural and religious traditions and identities. Without naming SOGI, the resolution connects these positive values to a focus on "boundaries of public order, health and morals," implying that SOGI rights transgress these boundaries.

A second example concerns a motion for a Recommendation Nr. 13280 entitled "Coordinated strategies for effective Internet governance," submitted by the Russian delegate to PACE, Robert Shlegel.[12] The motion stated a goal that appeared to invite broad consensus: "Growth of cyber-crime, theft of money and personal data, fraud, unpunished defamation, threats, dissemination of extremist information, child pornography and malicious software have led to a slowdown in the use of the Internet compared with the rate of its expansion. . . . The task of creating legislation in this area should be systematic and international, and should be accomplished by concerted action of all member States of the Council of Europe" (PACE 2012). Shlegel was subsequently nominated rapporteur on "Coordinated strategies for effective Internet governance," and in this function, he participated in the UN Internet Governance Forum (IGF) held in Bali, Indonesia, in October 2013 (PACE 2014). He did not end up writing a report on the subject, however, because in 2014, the work of the Russian delegation at the Council of Europe was suspended. In 2016, the topic was transferred to an Estonian member of parliament, Andres Herkel, who completed the report by 2019 (PACE 2019a). Herkel announced that "the emphasis of the report, laid by Shlegel, would have to be changed," and he raised the accusation that "this topic has been seen as a hidden attempt to probe the possibilities for restoring Russia's rights [inside the Council of Europe]" (Riigikogu 2016). The news flooded Russian websites, where Herkel was promptly accused of being an Estonian nationalist hostile to Russia (Regnum 2016).

Around 2012 and 2013, Shlegel played a key role in the Kremlin's ideological turn to traditional values,[13] particularly as the founder of the youth organization Nashi (Ours). He also crossed paths with actors from the Russian Christian Right. In February 2013, he participated in a conference organized by the League for Safe Internet (*Liga Besopasnogo Interneta, LBI*), an organization founded in 2011 which belongs to the conservative enterprise Konstantin Malofeev set up around his Saint Basil Foundation. Since 2018, it has been directed by Ekaterina Mizulina, the daughter of conservative Duma-member Elena Mizulina (see chapter 5). Members of the League have spoken out in favor of Russia's "anti-gay-propaganda law," claiming that the internet has to be made safe for children lest they access online information about SOGI rights and topics. In the context of Russia's traditional values discourse, internet governance to prevent the dissemination of extremist information constitutes a limitation of freedom of expression more generally. PACE's final recommendation based on Herkel's report expressed awareness of this "hidden agenda" behind the topic of internet governance when it demanded that Council of Europe regulations should "prevent user protection and security requirements from becoming pretexts for silencing dissenting views and undermining media freedom" (PACE 2019b).

Our final example of the unfolding of an anti-SOGI semantic universe within PACE is the resolution "Fighting the over-sexualization of children," again proposed by Valeriu Ghiletchi (PACE 2015). The resolution concerned the dangers of inappropriate exposure of children to sexual content and sexual representation of girls and women on the internet and in the media. The wording of the motion for the resolution itself did not convey an openly anti-SOGI position, but the references to the gender identity of cis men and women that were included in the explanatory memorandum Ghiletchi prepared in support of the draft resolution illuminated the actual target:

> The way in which we perceive ourselves as men and women is defined by biology and gender-specific characteristics conveyed through family values, education and the social environment. In this social environment, different kinds of media are strong players for all of us, including for our children. The sexualisation of children happens in everyday life, in the media, in advertising campaigns, through industrial and consumer products, and often in a manner which is not age appropriate, thus as "over-sexualisation". Following this understanding, the notions of sexualisation and over-sexualisation may sometimes be used in a synonymous manner in the present report. (PACE 2016)

The report was again accompanied by a side-event the European Christian Political Movement organized; the members of PACE approved the resolution based on the recommendation by a wide margin of 69 votes in favor, 8 against, and 5 abstentions.

The three examples discussed here show that it is not always immediately evident which topics within PACE amount to an anti-SOGI agenda. Topics that are framed as being raised with the best of intentions are often also directly weaponized for an anti-SOGI purpose. The anti-SOGI agenda draws on the broad moral conservative narrative analyzed in chapter 5, through which the rights of religious minorities, internet governance, and the oversexualization of children become interconnected concerns. These resolutions do not directly target or deny SOGI rights, but they nonetheless succeed in building a semantic and political context in which SOGI rights can be seen as detrimental for reaching certain desirable policy outcomes.

Finally, PACE is an assembly of political deliberation, where transnational political party groups form and define their agenda. Inside PACE, these groups are the Group of the European People's Party; the European Conservatives Group and Democratic Alliance; the Socialists,

Democrats and Greens Group; the Group of the Unified European Left; and the Alliance of Liberals and Democrats for Europe. Of these five, the first two are commonly associated with the moral conservative program. Luca Volontè, the moral conservative activist we highlighted as a key networker in chapter 3, exemplifies the ideological work of the PACE party groups. He was a member of PACE, first as substitute member and then as representative, for a relatively short period (2008–13), but during this time, he submitted a lengthy list of written declarations that anchor the moral conservative agenda.[14] A written declaration is an expression of opinion, first by the politician who proposes it, and then by the signatories who adhere. It does not have legal effect, but it indicates the overall agenda and ideological orientation of the signatories. Written declarations are used by all party groups, and we list here examples of those proposed by Volontè:[15]

- "The right to the family as the fundamental unit of society" (2013)
- "Obligatory deconstruction of 'gender stereotypes' and violation of parents' rights" (2013)
- "The autonomy of churches and religious communities" (2012)
- "Surrogate Motherhood" (2012)
- "Natural Human Rights" (2011)
- "Personhood, Sexuality and Reproduction" (2011)
- "Investing in family cohesion as a development factor in times of crisis" (2008)

This list echoes the agenda of the World Congress of Families, of which Volontè was a long-standing participating member, along with the overarching moral conservative claims outlined throughout this book.

Researchers interested in mobilization against SOGI rights have so far largely overlooked PACE, but this body of the Council of Europe plays a central role in the creation of moral conservative networks and agendas. While the nonbinding nature of PACE resolutions, recommendations, and declarations makes this institutional body seem less important for policy analysis, our sketch of pro-SOGI and anti-SOGI mobilization shows that PACE is the place where political ideas can be tested, where likeminded politicians meet, and from where politicians bring such issues back to their countries for discussion.

Academia

Knowledge production and diffusion have historically played a key role in fostering broader social acceptance for the claims of marginalized groups. The institutionalization of women's and gender studies departments at universities from the 1970s onwards often came hand in hand with activism—activism and academia acting as mutual catalyzers (Ergas et al. 2022, 123–24). But knowledge production can also work against SOGI rights. While to a lesser degree, it is also a venue of SOGI contestation because academic activities include the publication and translation of books that diffuse anti-SOGI claims, the circulation of speakers with an anti-SOGI agenda at conferences and public venues, and the restriction or closure of gender studies programs in public universities and educational programs. All three are related: the global resistance to SOGI rights, albeit often motivated by conservative religious convictions, uses the epistemic language of social science, history, philosophy, natural sciences, and medicine to bolster claims that SOGI rights harm society and should be curtailed as much as possible. Academic detractors of SOGI rights, who present themselves as a besieged academic minority that resists the powerful progressive-left mainstream, reframe for their purposes the postmodern argument that knowledge cannot be separated from the power arrangements that produce it and sometimes also postcolonial claims against "powerful Western academic elites." In the United States and increasingly also in Europe, debate over these issues is in full swing under the headlines of "cancel culture" and "wokeness" (Geva 2019; Norris 2021).

Not all the books that circulate in the anti-SOGI intellectual universe qualify as academic literature; in fact, for the most part, their authors are highly contested within the academic world and fail to meet scientific standards. However, intra-academic struggles over what counts as good scholarship have not stopped gender-critical academic literature from being accepted in the public domain. Indeed, moral conservative activists often take such works at face value and cite them as scientific proof for an anti-SOGI agenda. We give just two examples, which, although fifty years apart, convey a similar dynamic and demonstrate the intellectual lineage of such thought.

226 | VENUES

Pitirim A. Sorokin, the Russian émigré Harvard sociologist (1889–1968), has now been relegated to the margins of his discipline, but his legacy as a conservative intellectual persists in the public domain in the United States, and has soared in Russia over the last two decades. (For a detailed analysis, see Uzlaner and Stoeckl 2017.) Sorokin's reputation among moral conservatives is largely based on his book *The American Sex Revolution* (Sorokin 1956). Billy Graham, the American evangelist and founder of the Billy Graham Evangelical Association, quoted it, calling Sorokin "one of the most astute observers of America's sex scene" in his *World Aflame* (Graham 1965). The book also became a major reference for a 1965 documentary movie, *Perversion for Profit*, which warned against the negative consequences of sexual liberation (Perversion 1965). Despite the long time that has passed since the publication of the book, moral conservative activists and writers repeat claims Sorokin made to argue against the legalization of same-sex marriage (Mohler 2004, 2005, 2015). Other writers have concentrated on Sorokin's theory of the sensate culture—the notion that contemporary Western culture is doomed to decline because it is overly individualistic—to decry the effects of secularization and call for a reconversion to Christian faith (Dreher 2013, 2015; Berman 2012; Benne 2015). For Carlson's WCF, Sorokin is among the "must-reads" for pro-family activists (Brown 1996; Calvinist International 2013). His influence on American Christian pro-family circles became evident on the highest political levels when, in 2006, then congressman Mike Pence quoted him in a Marriage Protection amendment at the peak of US debates about same-sex marriage: "Marriage matters according to the researchers. Harvard sociologist Pitirim Sorokin found that throughout history, societal collapse was always brought about following an advent of the deterioration of marriage and family" (Pence 2006). Likewise, Sorokin became a leading academic reference in Russia's conservative turn (Uzlaner and Stoeckl 2017) and the translation and study of Sorokin was instrumental in the forging of ties between Western and Russian conservative academics (Stoeckl 2020a).

A more recent example that conveys a similar dynamic of transnational epistemic communities is the work of American sociologist Mark Regnerus, whose sociological studies on sexuality and marriage in the United States have been at the center of academic controversy, sparking debates about scholarship and Christian faith (Oppenheimer 2012).

In 2012, Regnerus published an analysis based on data from the New Family Structures Study in which he concluded that adults who had grown up with a parent in a same-sex relationship had a greater risk of experiencing adverse life conditions such as unemployment or poor educational attainment (Regnerus 2012). The study was widely criticized by US social scientists, who disputed the validity of the data, as well as the methods used and the conclusions Regnerus drew (Stambolis-Ruhstorfer 2020).

While the controversy shows that intra-academic mechanisms of peer review and debate can work as regulators in the social sciences, the wider impact of faulty academic works like this is often more difficult to tamp down. Despite the unwelcome reception of his study in the United States, Regnerus's book was picked up by theologians in the Vatican (Paternotte, Case, and Bracke 2016) and he was invited to Russia (Ruskline 2018). The transnational research ties between Regnerus, the Vatican and Russian academia are just one more indicator of how epistemic communities create venues for ideas to spread. Academia connects ideas and actors transnationally, and our research provides ample evidence that academia as a venue plays an important role in building global resistances to SOGI rights: from the works of Sorokin to the founding moment of the WCF through the encounter of Allan Carlson and the sociologist Anatolij Antonov (chapter 2) to the most recent example of Regnerus's teaching on Christian marriage in Russia.

The importance of academia for the spreading of the moral conservative agenda has increasingly attracted the attention of scholars in recent years (Fassin 2016; Eslen-Ziya and Giorgi 2022). Some have emphasized the anti-elitism of right-wing political leaders, which is usually paired with the denigration of academic knowledge (Read 2018). Moral conservative actors, in contrast, understand their agenda as one of extensive sociopolitical transformation and it is therefore quite natural for them to work through domains of action that extend beyond party politics, movement organizing, and advocacy. Moral conservative epistemic communities are logical venues for resistance to SOGI rights because academia and education create vectors of change in a society (Geva and de Santos 2021, 1402). Gender studies programs were also such vectors of change, and they actually came first in bringing together academia, education, and activism for an emancipatory project of gender equality and SOGI rights (Ergas et al. 2022, 123). In line with our analytical model of the double helix, the emergence of a globalist illiberal knowledge base that includes (but is not exclusively about) the resistance to SOGI rights is therefore not completely surprising (see also Paternotte and Verloo 2021, who describe the process as "isomorphism").

"Knowledge politics matter immensely to educated conservatives," writes Geva, who studied the moral epistemics of French conservative mobilization against same-sex marriage (2019, 415). She points out how much this intellectualized European moral conservatism actually differs from American evangelicalism, which largely dismisses universities and university-produced knowledge. Indeed, in Hungary, the right-wing government has gone so far as to deregister universities' gender studies degree programs—courses were not simply canceled, but in some universities, they were replaced by "family studies" (Ergas et al. 2022; Petö 2020). The Hungarian government also created a new educational institution, the Mathias Corvinus Collegium (MCC), to promote "a patriotic mindset and a realistic approach to the world" (MCC Vision 2023). Among the many international guests hosted by MCC are active members of the moral conservative TAN analyzed in this book, such as Luca Volontè, Grégor Puppinck (head of the ECLJ), and Jaime Mayor Oreja, but also well-known figures on the American Christian Right, such as Rod Dreher and Tucker Carlson (MCC International Guests 2023). In the United States, the unaccredited University of Austin was proposed as a counter to perceived liberalism in academia. Its founding faculty included Kathleen Stock, who achieved notoriety in the United Kingdom for her transphobic views (Kelleher 2021). Today, the Austin Institute for the Study of Family and Culture serves a similar function to the MCC.

The publishing outlet of MCC has published Hungarian translations of numerous programmatic anti-SOGI rights titles, such as Ryan T. Anderson's *When Harry Became Sally: Responding to the Transgender Movement*, Joanna Williams's *Women vs. Feminism: Why we all need Liberating from the Gender Wars*, Abigail Schrier's *Irreversible Damage: The Transgender Craze Seducing Our Daughters*, Maria Keffler's *Desist, Detrans & Detox: Getting Your Child Out of the Gender Cult*, and the book *GenderGaga: Wie eine absurd Ideologie unseren Alltag erobern will* by the German author Birgit Keller (MCC Press Catalogue 2023). It is not hard to see a connection between the legislative attempts of the

Hungarian government to curb SOGI rights (see chapter 4) and the diffusion of such works. Paternotte and Verloo (2021) have demonstrated how, in creating alternative epistemic institutions, moral conservative actors pursue a conservative politics of knowledge to build their particular understanding of what counts as true. Academia, in short, is a venue where the double helix model of pro-SOGI and anti-SOGI mobilization applies—epistemic communities matter for the diffusion of SOGI rights *and* for the global resistance to SOGI rights.

Among the epistemic communities that matter for the global resistance to SOGI rights are also conservative pundits and public commentators. While not academics, they portray themselves as public intellectuals and play an important role in the proliferation of moral conservative ideas. Among the most widespread and widely read publications directed against SOGI rights that fit this classification is the book *The Global Sexual Revolution* by the German Gabriele Kuby (2012), which has been translated into fifteen languages. Much like the books published by MCC, Kuby's work is not directed at an academic audience but rather at a general one. Nonetheless, the books are billed as research (Kuby identifies herself as a sociologist) and they frequently include an academic apparatus. The title *The Global Sexual Revolution* is a clear allusion to Sorokin's *American Sex Revolution*, and the book strives to be part of the same genre. Rod Dreher's book *The Benedict Option* is likewise a transnational moral conservative bestseller (Dreher 2017), as is his *Live Not by Lies* (Dreher 2020); both have been translated into several languages. Apart from speaking to the Christian Right community in the United States through his blog on the *American Conservative* website, Dreher is also popular in Europe. A long-term visiting fellow at MCC and frequent traveler between Europe and the United States, Dreher explains the US culture wars to a European audience, for whom the standard moral conservative talking points and vitriolic attacks on "woke culture," LGBTIQ persons, and SOGI rights that he mixes into his political and theological commentaries are actually quite new. Authors like Kuby and Dreher also have a record as public speakers, either at venues created by local NGOs interested in hosting distinguished international guests, or as part of international events like the World Congress of Families. Usually, these contexts are not organized by universities and do not draw an academic audience, but the speakers are nonetheless almost always presented as academic authorities on the subject. The effect of books and writings by intellectuals on the global moral conservative movement should not be underestimated. Frequently, this content is reposted and disseminated in other languages on social media accounts, blogs, and websites. In this way, the culture wars are becoming transnational and the moral conservative agenda becomes available across languages and countries.

* * *

The venues we have described in this chapter are important for two reasons: first, they are where policies are prepared and formulated by way of political and legal decision-making processes; and second, they connect ideas and actors transnationally. NGOs registered at the UN as well as diplomats and delegates active inside the UNHRC or PACE work with or against each other for political goals that are rooted in rival normative projects, much in the way our double helix model of norm promotion predicts. Pro-SOGI and anti-SOGI mobilization inside the venues we have described mirror each other, again, much like our model predicts. Academic venues as a platform for mobilization against SOGI rights are frequently overlooked, but our brief sketch of the transnational connections demonstrates how central they are for giving a concrete shape and agenda to the moral conservative narrative that we discussed in chapter 5. Given their coexistence in these spaces, SOGI rights advocates grapple with the narrative and efforts of moral conservative activists frequently, which also leads to a shift in their own ways of working, which we discuss next.

PART IV

Responses

7

Movement Interaction

LGBTI Rejoinders to Global Resistances

We are the family values campaign!
—SOGI activist, 2016

The remarkable accomplishments of the SOGI movement's long transnational history have no doubt galvanized—even inspired—the politicized moral conservative movement that opposes it. The two movements can be seen as operating next to one another at various levels of international politics, with the actions of one inciting the reactions of the other, the actions and reactions neither equal nor fully opposite, but relational and referential. As noted earlier, while these rival transnational advocacy networks in some ways adhere to the spiral and boomerang models of norm diffusion, they also both deploy structured networks of transnational advocacy organizations, draw on supportive authorities representing states and IOs, and use comparable movement strategies and instruments—if for mutually exclusive ends.[1]

It is largely because of these similarities that we envisage norm diffusion for and against gender and SOGI rights as a double helix rather than a boomerang or spiral. This image provokes the book's final imperative question. If the rival movements operate next to each other—from the chambers of the UN to the streets of Cairo—and are also reciprocally shaped by each other in a double helix model of interaction, then how has the transnational organizing of the politicized moral conservative movement in turn impacted that of SOGI rights activism? This final chapter will explore SOGI movement responses to seeing their cause—and in many cases their communities—denigrated and weaponized to advance moral conservative politics.

We focus on a case of responses from one type of highly professionalized SOGI movement actor (drawing largely from initiatives by activists affiliated with ILGA, ILGA-Europe, OSF). Indeed, there are many other movement initiatives against moral conservative actors that compliment this case that we do not fully explore here—these include actions focused on demonstration, knowledge production, media exposure, intelligence sharing, and legal training.[2] Furthermore, temporality matters, as responses will continue to evolve and change over time as double helix interactions persist (Ayoub and Chetaille 2020). The first part of the chapter draws on both secondary literature and original data from focus groups and interviews carried out at international SOGI-activist summits and conferences, including the 2016 Reclaiming Family Values conference in Nicosia, Cyprus. The second section uses a content analysis of European SOGI rights movement documents from 2004 to 2016 to track how the movement reframed the notion of family values and traditional values, including the proliferation of proactive SOGI responses in the later years of this period.

SOGI Movement Responses

In 2016, activists in the Polish Campaign against Homophobia (KPH) began to embrace the frames of faith and religion, which they had not directly foregrounded in the past. One activist described this by saying, "We realized that if we want to reach people [including society at large], we have to talk the values of Christian faith." The poster in figure 7.1 depicts a key element of their campaign, *Przekażmy Sobie Znak Pokoju* ("Let us offer each other a sign of peace"), showing shaking hands, one wrist adorned with a rosary and the other with a silicon rainbow bracelet (*Przekażmy Sobie Znak Pokoju* 2016). The phrase resonates in Poland both because it captures the common greeting across pews during a Catholic mass and because it refers to a reconciliatory letter that Polish Bishops sent German Bishops in 1965—the twentieth anniversary of the end of the Second World War—to say "we forgive."

KPH worked strategically with a faith-based Polish SOGI group called Wiara i Tęcza (Faith and Rainbow) to launch the campaign because, as one activist put it, "They had contacts and they had the heart. I have no heart for the Church." The campaign also included a display of four hundred posters (the largest of which were eight meters high)

Figure 7.1. Poster for the *Przekażmy Sobie Znak Pokoju* campaign.
Source: Przekażmy Sobie Znak Pokoju (2016).

across ten Polish cities, along with a compilation of twelve short videos of Catholic allies—across varying ages and walks of life—discussing the extension of their faith, love, and understanding to LGBTIQ people.[3] Activists perceived the reaction to the campaign as positive from the beginning. According to one KPH activist, the "media coverage was a huge success," with the campaign mentioned in over 4,400 publications in the months after its inception in 2016. The Bishop of Kraków did condemn the campaign a day after its launch, but that inadvertently created a dialogue in which the media—and even a variety of priests and nuns—spoke out largely in support of LGBTIQ people. For example, in a quote used by the campaign, Archbishop Józef Kowalczyk, the retired primate of Poland, said, "Homosexuals are people and full members of the Church. Let us not despise them, let us not disqualify them on the basis of preferences, nor exclude them from the community of the Church." Developments like these, focused on building new coalitions and reframing the claims of the countermovement, have shaped much SOGI rights activism in the last decade.

* * *

In large part a response to the politicized moral conservative movement, KPH's campaign illustrates new frontiers of survival and resilience that may influence how societies understand the family and so-called traditional values. That campaign also demonstrates how social movements always address multiple audiences and operate in interactive, and never static, environments, helping us understand and theorize their strategies and frames more holistically (Benford 1997; Meyer and Staggenborg 1996). SOGI rights movements, like women's rights movements (Korolczuk 2020), often assume that perseverance will be required in the face of contestation, as counter movements brand them as externally imposed threats to the nation, the family, and tradition (see chapter 5; Ayoub and Chetaille 2020). Increasingly, the frames that SOGI rights activists have made universal—like the idea that love underpins the right to have a partnership recognized—are challenged in coordinated ways at the international level, as this book has shown (see also Ayoub 2018). Applying the double helix metaphor, one would anticipate that SOGI movements—which are now increasingly bound to the coordinated moral conservative movements that resist them in an interactive environment at the international level—would have to actively update and reshape their universal master frames at this higher level. This would occur alongside the more commonly theorized grafting work that domestic activists have to do to broker resonance in their politically and culturally varied domestic spheres (Ayoub 2016).

Innovations

It should thus come as no surprise that SOGI rights activists have refocused their strategies and frames in response to the increasingly international mobilization of politicized moral conservative activists, especially in the last decade. The KPH in Poland is only one example. In a 2017 publication by ILGA-Europe and the Public Interest Research Center (PIRC), activists generated a framework guide—intended for implementation in multiple national contexts—to respond to the moral conservative movement and its narrative (Blackmore and Sanderson 2017, 12). Indeed, the moral conservative presence has been a focus of the SOGI rights movement in recent years; Blackmore and Sanderson wrote in the guide that movement actors recognize that this period "requires deep shifts in thinking: changes in how we define ourselves and those around us, and how we view our relationships with the natural world and our economic systems" (Blackmore and Sanderson 2017, 12). These shifts pose a new challenge for activists, for whom "it has become more urgent than ever to answer the question: how can the LGBTI movement respond to this reality?" (Blackmore and Sanderson 2017, 10).

The 2017 guide places much emphasis on new SOGI rights framing that connects emotionally with the audience, avoids condescension and reactive discourses, creates a common ground, and shares personal stories instead of focusing on rationality and fact. It recommends this approach to disarming the moral panic arguments that the traditional values narrative utilizes. This new framing encompasses various tactics, such as finding shared identities with which to build bridges, connecting personally with people, asking people to consider new perspectives, and using messengers who the audience trusts—including cis and straight allies who can speak without the label of biased self-interest (Blackmore and Sanderson 2017, 34; the strategy relates to academic literature, e.g., Harrison and Michelson 2017). Clearly informed by the rising populism of the era, activists offered ways to do this through movement messaging that makes people feel good and boosts their self-esteem (e.g., "We're a good country . . . a kind of country that respects all its people"), as opposed to appealing to people's fears and worst selves (e.g., "We are unkind to queer people"). One of the activists presenting the guide was from the United Kingdom and referred to positive campaigns like Ireland's Yes campaign (discussed below), contrasting it directly with negative campaigns like Brexit: "Facts don't change people's mindset, people are more emotional than rational." Many of these themes were also apparent in the Polish *Przekażmy Sobie Znak Pokoju* campaign, which integrated religion and family values.

New best practices in this vein have proliferated in recent years. For example, the aptly titled guide "Using Family as a Frame in Social Justice Activism" (Coffin et al. 2017) has its roots in the Reclaiming Family Values conference discussed on the first page of this book's introduction;[4] the guide's authors represent multiple rights organizations, including INGOs like TransgenderEurope and the Open Society Initiative for Europe. In the webinar that accompanied its launch, Bruno Selun, said: "It's important [to reclaim family values] . . . for a simple reason: we progressives have left the field of family and family values almost entirely to conservatives and neoconservatives over the last few years. As a result, when you talk about family values to anyone, they would usually think mother, father, child, marriage. Because conservatives and neoconservatives have successfully claimed that for themselves, and we've let them do it . . . it is important to reclaim family values and the family itself, from our perspective" (Reclaiming Family Values 2017).

For many SOGI activists, taking back the family values frame was a way to reach people who felt left behind by societal changes—communities swayed by the contemporary populist arguments the moral conservative movement exploited. Dozens of comparable resources illustrate attempts to influence these communities and demarcate this shift in SOGI activism. Many such guides can be found in the online archive of the Network of European LGBTIQ* Families Associations (NELFA), for example, which includes reports, webinars, and podcasts on issues such as rainbow family rights, a strategy on the rights of the child, a compendium of inclusive family law, information on trans parenting, the results of theological research (e.g., by the Wijngaards Institute) on the misinterpretations and mistranslations of same-sex families in contemporary Catholic theology, and attempts to enhance coordination between lay and faith-based SOGI rights organizations (NELFA 2022).

SOGI Activist Discourses

While discourse on family values is certainly not new in SOGI rights politics, transnational groups are increasingly using focused language to react to and proactively reframe so-called traditional family values. Beyond our decade-plus of interviews with SOGI rights activists, we track this phenomenon in two different ways: participant observation at SOGI activists' meetings and discourse analysis of SOGI movement materials. The first participant observation component highlights some of the on-the-ground work that activists are pursuing to reframe and reclaim societal understandings of the family and traditional values and the important place of LGBTIQ people in them.

Our participant observation at strategic international activists' meetings provides a qualitative narrative to buttress the trends we chart in the content analysis below. At these meetings, many activists recognized that their strategies had to adapt to the moral conservative actors' globalized family values narrative. For example, a Slovenian activist noted their initial hesitance in dealing with the topic of the family, given its firm rootedness in the conservative milieu, saying, "We didn't want to touch it." But they too have begun to switch emphasis, focusing not just on the rights of adults, but centering children and their well-being. Emphasizing that rainbow families exist and talking about the safety of the children in them proved to resonate with wide audiences, and doing so felt increasingly necessary for activists given the double helix nature of their human rights advocacy in the last decade. This reframing work has taken on several dimensions, redefining the family and challenging the politicized moral conservative narrative in various ways.

Redefining the Family

Activists from various countries discussed what "the family" means to the SOGI rights movement at their meetings. Given that so many LGB-TIQ people become estranged from their biological families, and many political barriers exist for partnership or parenting rights, they have a long history of building new unconventional families—so-called chosen families—of their own (Hull and Ortyl 2019). For example, a group of friends can replace and even surpass the functions (e.g., care work) of traditional support networks based on biological relations within cis and heterosexual family units. According to Hull and Ortyl (2019), such chosen families continue to prevail in the self-understanding of SOGI people, even if legal recognition of the rainbow family is beginning to appear in some countries. SOGI rights activists are trying to put into words these lived realities of many LGBTIQ people, with a holistic understanding of families *as spaces where individuals experience care, support, respect, protection, and affection, as well as give back those invaluable qualities to others.*[5]

Activists discussed at length, and not with full agreement, definitions of the family that could be understood as liberating for LGBTIQ people. Conversations stressed the individual need for recognition and support, as well as the privileges and responsibilities that becoming a family may offer. That privilege often is understood in the form of rights from the state and wider societal acceptance. A concern for SOGI activists was that if one does not follow the narrow models of the family provided, one is seen to be selfish and uninterested in the societal good. The state-society discourse that would emerge around the COVID-19 pandemic in many states exemplified this, almost universally centering the traditional heteronormative family—the well-being of children and working parents, access to family holidays, the ability for limited numbers of households to meet, and so on—while media and politicians often vilified (even the low-risk) meeting spaces that queer people made for themselves to avoid constant isolation. For example, open-air gatherings and parties in Berlin's city parks were frequently cast as frivolous and unsocial on the news cycle, even if LGBTIQ people—presumably because of their activism and closer proximity to the HIV/AIDS epidemic—were the more likely to accept public health measures for the social good (Marks 2021; P. Johnson 2022). Furthermore, state policies overlooked various elements of rainbow families' lives; for example, the fact they are less likely to live in the same household (so a policy stipulating that only two households are allowed to meet may mean that only two members of a rainbow family can gather). Activists consistently stressed that any new and inclusive definitions of the family—which they sought to help construct—be broad enough that diverse family units were eligible for protection and recognition from the state.

Of course, there remain prevailing misconceptions and counter-frames that activists were required to grapple with and overcome when discussing the family. Many lamented entrenched—but debunked (Gartrell, Bos, and Koh 2018)—societal misconceptions, for example, that it is irresponsible for LGBTIQ people, especially two gay men, to raise children. They also discussed the major challenges presented by politicized moral conservative actors' deployments of the family that we outlined in chapter 5. Finally, there were also concerns among a few SOGI rights activists in some countries that it was irresponsible to bring children into a homophobic world.

Groups stressed both domestic and international solutions to counter the logic of moral conservative conceptions of the family, including the idea of "coming into existence" via various ideas and images (some of them international) that stand apart from traditional conceptions. For example, if a court like the European Court of Human Rights comes to recognize a rainbow family as real, then it becomes more difficult for moral conservative arguments to delegitimize that family within state institutions. Other mediums for broadening the concept of the family are social: "If your children have smart phones, they know about LGBTIQ people and know they have families," an activist said. Indeed, a SOGI rights funder pointed out that moral conservatives are "losing [relative to SOGI rights activists] at the policy level, which is why they are hitting so hard at the soft level of public opinion and referenda." The funder was keen to fund legislative campaigns seen as low-hanging fruit, like in Montenegro, where, in 2016, the possibility to pass SOGI rights legislation was considered high, even if public support was still low. As they explained, "Why not go for it if we have a pink-washing government. Fund it, and see what activists do with it."[6]

Alliances

In order for inclusive understandings of the family to travel, activists stressed the need to identify productive alliances with groups that work on family issues. This coalitional work helps fill the sizable gap in knowledge about LGBTIQ people among family-focused organizations, shifting the frame to creating a loving environment for the child. SOGI rights groups' educational outreach as it pertains to rainbow families can be limited, but if partnered with groups that are working on family issues, it reaches a wider audience and makes the message appear more credible.

For example, in Italy, service providers are lacking in general, both for rainbow families and for traditional families, creating a common ground for collaboration. Italian SOGI rights activists also worked in coalition with feminists, who were countering traditional family frames around the idea that a woman's place is in the home. In Croatia, a parents' association organized a campaign on women's experiences during birth, and SOGI rights groups worked with them on that initiative. According to one SOGI activist, "Since the opposition made it about children, we made a coalition with parental organization for legitimacy."

At the international level, there are several organizations that SOGI-right activists have partnered with or identified as potential partners, including the European Family Support Network, Eurochild, Child Rights International Network (CRIN), European Women's Lobby (EWL), and European Network against Racism (ENAR). One example of a coalition at this level is ILGA-Europe's work with the European Commission and other partners on the 2021 "EU Strategy on the Rights of the Child" (ILGA-Europe 2021). Under the slogan "Children's rights are human rights," the commission's communication also addressed SOGI imperatives, including intersex genital mutilation, the cyber harassment of LGBTI children, and freedom of movement for rainbow families. Activists say that international coalitions like this, with partners working on family issues, might help shape the discourse domestically and challenge the interventions of moral conservative groups' narrative, as well as influence positive collaboration on the ground (Ayoub 2019a; Irvine, Lang, and Montoya 2019).

Reframing in Practice

"Family First"

Much of the SOGI rights movement's attention has been given to reframing an understanding of the family in their own work, and there are plentiful examples of this practice. In fact, the family, faith, and children have increasingly played a central role in SOGI campaigns of the last decade. In Italy, activists focused on the parents of LGBTIQ people to advocate for marriage equality. A similar strategy was deployed in Washington State ahead of a marriage equality referendum in 2012. Irish activists also did something similar in their successful Yes Campaign for marriage equality in 2015, centering elderly Catholics with children in their campaigns to generate resonance. For example, a television ad featured then ninety-year-old Madeline Connolly, who, wearing a large cross and looking lovingly at a picture of her multi-generational family (including fourteen living children and thirteen grandchildren), spoke in favor of saying yes to marriage equality: "I'm very disappointed with the pope. I was sure he was going to be on our side. I'm a Catholic. I go to church. I know that everybody is going to heaven. God made everybody. They will all be in heaven. I don't like this whole 'No' thing. I say: 'Keep saying Yes and include everybody'" (McTeirnan 2015).

The American SOGI rights movement, whose activists also advised their colleagues in Ireland, actively reframed marriage equality as a children's rights issue, partly in response to the opposition's "threat to children" and "parental rights" frames, which featured centrally in the National Organization for Marriage, Protect Marriage, and the Mormon Church's successful 2008 campaign to oppose marriage rights in California's Proposition 8 (Murray 2009; McKinley and Johnson 2008).[7] American activists spoke of their learning process after losing on marriage equality in California—a comparatively socially progressive US state—on the same night the country ushered in a historic victory for social change, electing Barack Obama as its first black president.

"Love Is a Family Value"

In recent years, the successful SOGI movement frame of "love" or "love is love" has also been tied to family, through the notion that *love is a family value*. For example, a campaign by the SOGI rights group All-Out capitalized on this strategy by making reference to homophobic politicians—including Brazilian president Jair Bolsonaro, who had commented that he would "rather have a dead son than a gay son"—and focused on mothers expressing love for their sons. In Slovakia, activists deployed the frame "love is the traditional value" to headline the 2014

Bratislava Pride. In Malta, the Drachma Parents' Group and the Malta LGBTIQ Rights Movement worked together to highlight *families*—rather than just two partners—in the SOGI campaign framed as "love and rights." Showing images of rainbow families in a public campaign would have made them vulnerable in a small country of about five hundred thousand people (where they are more easily identifiable), but the Maltese activists did show pictures of the families to the politicians in meetings behind closed doors. In many countries, like Germany and Poland, activists encouraged religious leaders themselves to serve as mouthpieces, proclaiming that rainbow families deserve their love and respect. Indeed, the gay publication the *Advocate* controversially selected Pope Francis as Person of the Year in its 2013 cover story, which included an image of the pope's face donning a photoshopped "NoHate" insignia commonly worn by supporters of SOGI rights (Grindley 2013). The extent of Pope Francis's actual support for LGBTIQ people—beyond tepid statements like "Who am I to judge?"—was less important to the publication, which seemed content to confuse Catholics around the world about his actual stance on SOGI rights—even if that meant overlooking powerful LGBTIQ advocates like Edie Windsor, the lead plaintiff in the landmark 2013 Supreme Court civil rights case *United States v. Windsor*,[8] for its cover.[9]

* * *

Activists felt reframing was necessary (given who holds the societal power to articulate who belongs in many spaces), as was exploring how family and faith can be a positive and transformational force in their own work. While some spoke with conviction of wanting reconciliation among faith, family, and SOGI identities, others saw the effort toward such reconciliation more strategically. Several activists argued that "the family" should amount to nothing more than a campaigning and framing tactic, given their hesitance to present it as the primary model of fulfillment or happiness in queer life. "Make no mistake," a SOGI activist noted, "our opposition use it in that way too, and in their case, it is to wield patriarchy, misogyny, and bigotry."

The strategic element was a factor for some SOGI groups who had already deployed traditional values frames but disagreed on principle with centering notions of the family in their own lives. For example, an activist pointed out her group's imperative to use the family in its direct response to the impassioned mobilization La Manif pour tous against marriage equality in France: "As a lesbian feminist activist, in my group [redacted], of course we're never going to get married, of course we don't want children, but we fought for marriage and reproductive rights, because it's an important tool . . . You can't ever say you're opposed to 'the family'; so we have to deal with it . . . We can use 'family values' to win allies. Faith is important."

Irish activists explained that they purposefully declared themselves, saying, "We are the family values campaign," to take wind out of the sails of the opposition. There too, at least one central activist noted, "I led the marriage campaign, but there is no way I'm getting married to my partner of twenty years." A Polish activist, when reflecting on their faith-based campaign, asked: "Do we want to support a patriarchal institution defined by the religious institutions that oppose us? It's stifling to even think about supporting this institution [and the Catholic Church] with compromise. But at the end of the day, we want our rights, everyone can relate to the family, for better or worse." Across the board, activists acknowledged how uneasily some elements of the new discourse sat with the earlier liberation politics the movement had espoused, but they also articulated a pragmatic awareness of the potential of mirroring their moral conservative rivals' messaging, as well as the hetero- and cis-normative world they operate in more generally.

There were also concerns about how available strategies such as using personal narratives to combat populism were to activists in countries where it was difficult to come out. For this reason, the solution of centering the parents or grandparents of LGBTIQ people—even if it may be seen as invisibilizing LGBTIQ people themselves—emerged in some cases. Activists also noted the costs of this work to the emotional well-being of their communities. One said, "The cost of this campaign, is that it's not an academic exercise. It gets personal." By this, they mean that rainbow families are also hurt in the process, seeing their lives made painfully visible and contested in the public sphere; "They have to explain the world to their children, who see posters saying they are not valid." Australian activists lamented the pain of this debate when marriage was put before the public in a drawn-out plebiscite (Altman 2017).

That said, the activists of the Yes Campaign noted that the canvassers who experienced the most trauma (those who needed counseling)

Figure 7.2. The deployment of the family in the Irish No and Yes Campaigns. Source: Murtagh (2015).

during the Irish referenda were the straight ones: "[Unlike us], being exposed to such bigotry was not something they were accustomed to." Straight allies played a unique role in the Irish movement, when, in an interesting twist of fate, Yes campaigners won the support of the people who had been the face of their countermovement. The better-funded opponents of the Yes Campaign had used a stock image of a family for their posters (shown on the left side of figure 7.2) to insinuate that marriage equality was a threat to children. However, when the family in the photo discovered how the image was being used, they offered to model for the Yes Campaign posters (depicted on the right side of figure 7.2), flipping the narrative of what was best for their child.

In sum, these framing adjustments did not occur without debate. There was a palpable tension between (*a*) concerns surrounding the embrace of the term family in SOGI rights activism—because it is widely seen to be within the contemporary domain of the moral conservative resistance—and (*b*) the strategic potential in doing so, to reclaim it from the moral conservative narrative and depoliticize it as such. Others remained concerned that the framing moves—including a focus on children—could exclude nonparent families and nontraditional families and could diminish the issues with long histories in that space, including misogyny and domestic violence. "Some of us have families from hell," an activist noted, concerned that frames could elevate biological conceptions of the family. Thus, a broad, inclusive, coalitional (especially with feminist groups[10]) and holistic conception of family became an essential prerequisite for the redefinition and deployment of the term in SOGI rights discourse. The compromise that was compelling to most was being strategic while simultaneously deconstructing the moral conservative movement's frames—for example, focusing on the children of LGBTIQ people, who suffer from having their families unrecognized. Undisputed by all was that a formidable opposition was circulating in international venues, voicing a transnationally resonant narrative that needed challenging.

Content Analysis

We turn now to a content analysis that triangulates the qualitative data described above, one that will also show an increasing pattern in which the SOGI rights movement proactively engages with traditional and family values narratives in their discourse. We argue that in many ways this is an outcome of the parallel nature of these double helix rival networks, in which master frames must adapt to respond to human rights contestation at the international level. To conduct a discourse analysis around the SOGI rights movements' use of family values, we coded organizational documents from the one of largest transnational LGBTI organizations, ILGA-Europe, which represents over six hundred SOGI organizations across fifty-four countries in Europe and Central Asia. We home in on this INGO due to its centrality in SOGI rights activism, and we use ILGA-Europe documents for their transnational scope, breadth of membership, regional leadership on LGBTIQ issues, and the accessibility of organizational documentation.[11] Finally, our access to these materials made them invaluable for our research. Several different types of organization documents were coded, including annual reports, organization newsletters (*Euro-Letter*), and, most importantly, the annual conference delegate packets made available to us. (Document types are described in the book's appendix.)

We concentrate the analysis on the shift toward the incorporation of traditional or family values into the LGBTIQ movement's discourse; however, because there was so little conversation around family *values* until the idea began gaining traction around 2011, we also opted to code different categories of family issues alongside family values. Discourse was coded not by each appearance of "family" (which was our main search term), but instead by the number of articulations of themes, in the form of fully developed action (such as organizing a workshop on the issue). This helped us in tracking themes versus tracking raw counts of terms. For example, in the delegate packets, if a single workshop dealt with reclaiming family values, it would be coded only once; we would not code each mention of family values in the various presenters' titles.

Categories of Analysis

The family has been a central issue within ILGA-Europe's organizing since its inception in 1996, even if not always in response to the moral conservative movement. The ways this movement talks about the family and issues surrounding the family, however, has shifted over time and even year by year. Broadly speaking, "family issues" captures those topics that are central to the formation of the family and what constitutes family (e.g., same-sex partnership and the children of same-sex partners), as well as issues that centrally concern family members (e.g., the freedom of movement and ability to claim asylum for LGBTIQ family members). Much of this discourse has happened regardless of moral conservative organizing. To capture the diversity of family-centric issues, we divided family issues into three subcategories—immigration, children, and partnership—in the first part of the analysis. Family issues that did not specifically fit into these subcategories were coded as the core category (family issues) and included more general mentions around LGBTI family diversity, non-specific mentions of LGBTI family rights and movement organizing (e.g., "Secondly, there is exploration of how to build up or strengthen LGBT-Family movements in the countries of the workshop attendants" [Delegate Packet 2012, 24]), or other related LGBTI family issues that were not specifically coded (e.g., societal acceptance of LGBTI families, LGBTI-family-friendly workspaces).

Next, and most importantly for the purposes of our book, the phrase "family values" was central to the discourse analysis. We take a relatively conservative approach to what we code as family values, looking for explicit mentions, such as "family values," "traditional values/families," or "attacks on the family." In order to better understand why family values were brought up, we also divided this category into two subcategories of SOGI responses, as show in table 7.1. First, the subcategory *reactionary* was used when family values were only brought up in reference to an event that has happened—for example, if country X has targeted SOGI rights activists, depicting them as being against family/traditional values. This subcategory shows instances when others utilize family values as a frame, but it does not necessarily denote that the SOGI rights movement or ILGA-Europe deployed the frame themselves. By contrast, text was coded under the *proactive* sub-category when SOGI activists directly assess and utilize the family values frames for their own work.

We created these two subcategories to highlight the distinction between how ILGA-Europe (and the broader movement it represents) has come to highlight and deal with the backlash from the traditional family values movement. While the reactionary subcategory shows the recognition by ILGA-Europe that countermovements are using a family/traditional values frame, it may not necessarily imply that activists are organizing to respond. The proactive subcategory, on the other hand,

---

TABLE 7.1: Examples of reactionary and proactive responses to SOGI rights

Reactionary	Proactive
a. "In April 2003, the lower house of the Polish parliament focused once again on the matter, spelling out clearly that the "moral order of the social life, family dignity, marriage and education" must not be challenged by international regulations." (2002–2003 Annual Report, 7)	a. "We want to make sure our members and allies are equipped to deal with this trend [of mobilizing around family values] and respond confidently in public debates." (Annual Report 2015–2016, 11)
b. "A spokesman for the nation's Catholic hierarchy called the measure 'an attack against . . . marriage and the family.'" (*Euro-Letter* 96, March 2002, 8)	b. "Voices of parents help challenge and positively reframe the language of 'traditional family values' and 'protection of children.'" (Delegate Packet 2015, 30)
c. "You will come to a city and a country full of contrasts . . . open and friendly people as well as homophobic church leaders, the so called 'family movement' and politicians." (Delegate Packet 2014, 2)	c. "This workshop outlines past and current opportunities, challenges and backlash in the European political landscape with regards to rainbow families and poses the question of how to respond to these, for instance by reclaiming the (conservative) notion of family values." (Delegate Packet 2016, 40)

250 | MOVEMENT INTERACTION

shows instances where ILGA-Europe is addressing the frame head on and discussing ways to counter such a frame, or even co-opt it, changing it to celebrate family diversity.

As within the family issues category and subcategories, a text is always coded in the family node (core category) and can have none, one, or both child nodes (subcategory). Having both is rare, but it does occur occasionally. This means for the raw counts, the sum of the subcategories will not necessarily be a total of the core categories. The subcategories are useful to understand why the frame is used. For the family issues category, the subcategories help us understand the types of conversations around the family that are common within ILGA-Europe. The family issues categories also help situate us within the broader conversation of family issues as they relate to the LGBTI movement—since issues of the family have clearly been of concern for the movement for decades. The family values categories, as discussed above, make it easier to identify why ILGA-Europe would start discussing this framing tactic. While it may have begun as a mere reaction to the countermovement, the organization shifted to directly address the frame later.

Results and Discussion

Table 7.2 presents the raw counts of the family issues and family values discourse analysis. While we will discuss the results of all the different document formats, the greatest weight should be given to the delegate packets in table 7.3. Due to the many changes in the layouts of both the annual reports and the *Euro-Letter* newsletters, it is difficult to make conclusive comments on their relative coverage of the family frames. In addition, since the main concern of this analysis is the usage of the family/ traditional values frame, we focus on that side of the discourse analysis.

There are, however, a few general trends related to the coverage of specific family issues (left side of table 7.2). On the subcategory *immigration*, the freedom of movement directive for the EU that came into force in 2004 was the main point of conversation. ILGA-Europe advocated for LGBTI people and their families to be considered in this directive, which would help explain the level of discussion around and before 2004, and well as the relative dip in some of those document types after 2011. That said, conversation continued around the Free Movement Directive, as

TABLE 7.2: Raw counts for family issues and family values in combined document types. Source: Data compiled from ILGA-Europe annual conference delegate packets and the Euro-Letter newsletters, 2004–2015

Year*	Family issues	Immigration	Children	Partnership	Family values	Reactionary	Proactive
2004	15	5	1	4	5	5	0
2005	23	4	4	2	3	2	0
2006	22	2	1	4	3	3	0
2007	24	1	3	0	3	2	1
2008	34	7	11	5	1	0	1
2009	38	8	8	6	0	0	0
2010	20	2	4	8	3	2	1
2011	25	2	8	7	1	1	0
2012	17	2	5	3	1	0	1
2013	16	1	6	3	1	0	1
2014	10	0	2	2	6	5	2
2015	11	0	2	1	5	1	4

*Raw counts only presented for years in which all three document types were coded.

ILGA-Europe pushed for full implementation of the directive and advocated for LGBTIQ families facing difficulties exercising their freedom of movement rights. Other common conversations surrounded ILGA-Europe responding to council directives on asylum and on family reunification (especially in the early 2000s). Next, the discussion of *children* typically centered on issues of adoption by LGBTI parents and of the rights and legal status of children of LGBTI families, often made in relation to the issue of same-sex partnership. Just as same-sex union policy was (and is) a popular conversation in political discourse, the related issue of adoption was often discussed in national and transnational (EU) policy debates and in legal cases (often highlighted in the *Euro-Letter*). Other common mentions of children's issues came from the discussion of published research related to children of LGBTI parents. Finally, the main issue discussed in the ILGA-Europe documents in relation to partnership was of same-sex unions, whether in the form of legal recognition of marriage or domestic partnership of same-sex couples. The number of mentions typically followed domestic conversations on the passage or rejection of same-sex union policies.

While it is hard to decipher clear patterns in this combined analysis given the varied and large focus of these document types, we do see an increase and more steady deployment of proactive framing in the movement. For example, in the annual reports, the last mentions of family values frames in the data set—one reactionary and one proactive—occurred in the 2015 report.[12] Qualitatively, they illustrate a clear recognition of the countermovement's co-optation of family values, of "mobilization around the family, understood to exclude diverse rainbow families." It is difficult to make any conclusive comments from the annual reports (see appendix). There are many references to family values frames across the *Euro-Letter* newsletters, with the vast majority coded as reactionary and only a few coded as proactive. Family values frames were mentioned as early as 2000, though the first family values framing reference coded as proactive did not appear until 2007 and 2008.[13] The mention from 2007 states that "four social NGOs are reminding the EU that any definition of families should reflect the diversity of families which exist in European societies. Increasingly the traditional concept of family is challenged by the evolution of society" (*Euro-Letter* 142, May 2007, 7). The 2008 mention identifies how "populism has historically exploited the 'family values' argument to justify repressive policies on issues as diverse as interracial marriage, slavery and women's rights and have been at the root of much incitement to hatred in the past" (*Euro-Letter* 150, January 2008, 8). A significant conclusion from this is that the framing of family values by the countermovement has a long history. How the family values frame is levied, to what degree of intensity, and at what venues, has changed. The delegate packets, which are the organizing programs of actual activist gatherings, are the most informative sources and provide a clearer picture of these frames.

Table 7.3 zooms in on the delegate packets from 2004 to 2016, with the family values frame first appearing in 2011. After 2011, there was a very slow increase in the number of references to family values per delegate. In comparison to the other document types, there was a relatively larger proportion of texts (seven) coded as proactive, compared with four texts coded as reactionary. This shift toward relatively more proactive texts makes sense considering these conference programs are meant to directly address issues within the LGBTI community. Also depicted in figure 7.3, the timing of the family values frame also matches with the

TABLE 7.3: Delegate packet raw counts for family issues and family values. Source: Data compiled from ILGA-Europe annual conference delegate packets, 2004–2016.

Year	Family issues	Immigration	Children	Partnership	Family values	Reactionary	Proactive
2004	0	0	0	0	0	0	0
2005	5	2	1	0	0	0	0
2006	1	0	1	0	0	0	0
2007	1	0	1	0	0	0	0
2008	1	0	1	1	0	0	0
2009	1	0	0	0	0	0	0
2010	1	0	0	0	0	0	0
2011	2	0	2	0	1	1	0
2012	8	0	3	2	1	0	1
2013	8	0	5	3	1	0	1
2014	2	0	2	0	2	1	1
2015	2	0	1	0	3	1	2
2016	3	1	1	2	3	1	2

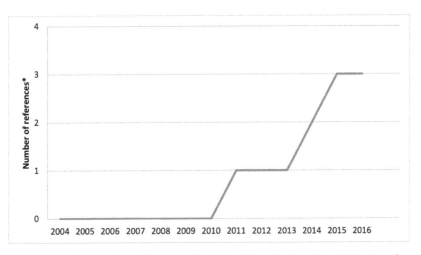

Figure 7.3. Delegate packet references to family/traditional values. Note: *Number of references includes both reactionary and proactive coded texts.

intensification of moral conservative activism at the international level, especially when compared to other kinds of family issues.

What differentiates much of the language in the delegate packets is the directness in addressing family values. Some of the workshops, even in their names, mentioned "reclaiming" family/traditional values (for example, see Workshop 6 from Delegate Packet 2013, 9; and Workshop 19 from Delegate Packet 2016, 28). While less explicit, many workshops took on the issue of how to reframe and celebrate family diversity and discuss family values in relation to LGBTI parenting (see Workshop 27 and Workshop 39 from Delegate Packet 2015, 30, 36)—much as our qualitative analysis of movement discourse in the last section showed. As with the analyses from the other document types, it seems clear that the embrace and direct response to the right-wing claim toward family values (i.e., the proactive coded text) is a more recent phenomenon, surfacing only within the past five to ten years.

* * *

SOGI rights activists are carrying on untiring work in response to the increasingly globalized resistance levied against their movement. For example, the ILGA World Conference in 2022 included a workshop called "Building our Collective Strength to Counter the Anti-gender Opposition," which was intended as a space to innovate in response to moral conservative activism. That workshop followed an earlier "strategic dialogue" on "Countering Anti-gender Actors and Narratives" that had been cosponsored by several important SOGI rights groups (e.g., TGEU) and involved 120 experts from across the globe, bringing together representatives of donors, IOs, states and movements working SOGI rights, women's rights, sex workers' rights, youth and sexual and reproductive health rights. Similarly, SOGI rights groups have begun to organize to build a network of LGBTIQ counter disinformation experts who are tasked with developing strategies and sharing information to challenge homo- and transphobic campaigns. Finally, as we noted at the outset of the chapter, we have focused on the work of highly professionalized SOGI rights actors working in transnational advocacy networks. As we have discussed, this specific type of work is not accepted uniformly and uncritically by the movement, nor is it exhaustive of all SOGI responses, which include a wide repertoire of tactics.

Of course, in some post-marriage-equality countries, SOGI rights are taken for granted or seen as inevitable, but the continued struggle for them is a forewarning. The innovations generated by SOGI rights activism speak of the maneuver and adaptation required for the movement's perseverance. For scholars, these shifts in the SOGI movement's master frames—to include religion and family values—make all the more sense if we theorize contestation between rival movements at the international level. For this reason, we propose the double helix metaphor to reorient our thinking, given that the SOGI movement operates in parallel to its opposition at all levels of politics. The growing focus on SOGI rights by the moral conservative movement in transnational spaces has led to a shift in SOGI frames themselves, and this is a reflexive reaction. Indeed, the moral conservative movement's mirroring strategies and their use of rights frames indicates how they themselves are shaped by this contested field.

Conclusion

Gender, Sexuality, and International Politics

If humanity accepts that sin is not a violation of God's law, if
humanity accepts that sin is a variation of human behavior,
then human civilization will end there.
—Russian Orthodox Patriarch Kirill, 2022

In his sermon just two Sundays into the war reignited by Russia's 2022
invasion of Ukraine, the Russian Orthodox patriarch Kirill zeroed in on
SOGI people to justify both Putin's attack and his geopolitical worldview.
Much in line with the moral conservative movement we have dissected
in this book, for the patriarch, the tremendous tragedy of the war in
Ukraine is "far more important than politics" (*Moscow Times* 2022b).
It boils down to a rejection of SOGI rights as "Western values" and a
contest between the governments that support or oppose those rights
(Cooper 2022). For Kirill, the Russian incursion was justifiable—and
even on the side of humanity and of God—because those "Pride parades
[in the West] are designed to demonstrate that sin is one variation of
human behavior. That's why in order to join the club of those countries,
you have to have a gay Pride parade" (Kirill, cited in Cooper 2022).[1]
Framing SOGI rights as a "loyalty test" to "the West," Kirill argued in his
sermon that the people of Ukraine (specifically in the separatist region
of Donbas) had stood up for what was morally right:

> For eight years there have been attempts to destroy what exists in Donbas.
> And in Donbas there is a rejection, a fundamental rejection of the so-
> called values that are offered today by those who claim world power. We
> know that if people or countries reject these demands, they are not part
> of that world, they become strangers to it. . . . Therefore, what is happen-
> ing today in international relations does not only have political meaning.

258 | CONCLUSION

It is about something different and much more important than politics. It is about human salvation, about on which side of God the Savior of humankind will end up. (*Moscow Times* 2022b)

As he commonly does, Putin himself used a similar line of moral conservative argumentation in his February 24, 2022, speech announcing a "special military operation" in Donbas dedicating a whole paragraph, as Emil Edenborg (2022) put it, to lamenting the existential threat of the West's effort to erode "traditional values": "Properly speaking, the attempts to use us in their own interests never ceased until quite recently: they sought to destroy our traditional values and force on us their false values that would erode us, our people from within, the attitudes they have been aggressively imposing on their countries, attitudes that are directly leading to degradation and degeneration, because they are contrary to human nature. This is not going to happen. No one has ever succeeded in doing this, nor will they succeed now" (Putin, cited in Edenborg 2022).

It may come as less of a surprise, then, that in the midst of the war in Ukraine, J.K. Rowling—the British children's author who has provoked astonishment among fans due to her repeated trans-exclusionary positions in recent years (Taub 2022)—woke up one morning in March 2022 to an endorsement by Vladimir Putin. In a speech to the Presidential Young Artists that month, Putin again moved seamlessly from nationalism to globalism with rhetoric typical of the moral conservative narrative. "Patriotic culture has always defended Russia's uniqueness," he quipped, and this culture "is keeping the Russian nation safe today . . . when seemingly *age-old norms* are being undermined in *various countries*, where history is distorted and the laws of nature are being smashed" (cited in and translated by Garner 2022, emphasis ours). This notion of history and nature being defiled led him to Rowling, whom he presented as a martyr fighting against the Western SOGI culture that destroys the innocence of children and, ultimately, the Russian nation itself. As one observer summed it up, according to Putin's narrative, "Russia is under attack at home and abroad; only a culture, commerce, and mindset that are sufficiently patriotic and Russian in nature can save you" (cited in Garner 2022).[2] While the reasons that Russia invaded Ukraine are complex, misguided, and plentiful, it is important to note that gender and sexuality—as articulated in the moral conservative narrative—factor centrally in them. For Putin, the war is about a contest between a rule-guided liberal democratic global order and, in his view, determined spheres of political, cultural, and religious influence. In line with the moral conservative narrative, he turns SOGI rights into the essence of the former, and traditional values into the symbol of the latter. In these gendered justifications for war, SOGI rights are weaponized as "new norms" that defy "common sense" and push against the old norms that he sees as rooted in nature and history. The moral conservative narrative symbolizes this divide and offers a return to a desirable (if imagined) past.

Gender, Sexuality, and International Politics

Putin's and Kirill's rhetoric illustrates several takeaways that we wish to emphasize as we conclude. The first, most general point is that sexuality and gender are intricately embedded in international relations. However, scholars of international relations have overlooked the powerful centrality of gender and SOGI rights in the geopolitics they study. For example, they often dismiss as peripheral to the high politics of war and peace these decades-old ideas—carefully articulated by the well-networked moral conservative transnational movement we chart—that shape many of the ideological and political contests of our times. By studying the transnational advocacy network of groups, IOs, and states that make up the politicized moral conservative movement, we are better able to understand the peculiar placement of sexuality and gender at the heart of the biggest European war of the new century. Certainly, as Edenborg (2022) points out, "it is not necessary to dig deep or read between the lines to make the argument that national security in Putin's Russia is a gender and sexuality issue," given that the words "traditional values" appear over twenty times in Russia's *Federal National Security Strategy* (2021). Our analysis helps trace the origins of this narrative, as well as the consequences it has for national and human security. And while wars like the one in Ukraine garner much attention, what happens on the ground due to moral conservative politics, like the uptick in hate crimes and health emergencies following Russia's 2013 so-called anti-gay-propaganda bill, Florida's 2022 Don't Say Gay bill, or Uganda's most

260 | CONCLUSION

recent Anti-Homosexuality Act is also intricately connected to security and our understanding of it (Clark 2023; Tickner 2014; Cohn 2018; Enloe 2007).

The placement of SOGI rights at the heart of the war in Ukraine—the illustrative example we choose to focus on in this conclusion—should not have come as a surprise for the international relations field. Indeed, the centrality of the issue has been in plain sight for many years, and a clearer understanding of the moral conservative narrative and network helps explain that. Geographically close to both Russia and the EU, Ukraine has not gone unnoticed by feminist and queer scholars as an example of SOGI rights contestation—even if many IR security scholars made this link for the first time in the weeks following Russia's 2022 invasion.[3] Since SOGI rights efforts are often portrayed as the attempt by a foreign power to control the domestic sphere, moral conservative state authorities, representatives of international organizations, and movement advocates have always problematically conflated them with secular or Western imposition.[4] In the mid-2010s, in exchange for liberalized travel visas, the EU compelled Ukraine to adopt measures with protections against employment discrimination on the basis of sexual orientation. After two failed attempts to pass such a bill in early November 2015, Ukrainian parliamentarians were obliged to make the third time the charm, begrudgingly introducing the bill after pressure from state leaders and EU officials. Yet the bill's passage was accompanied by a simultaneous politics that refused such norms (Elsner 2021). Political leaders across Ukrainian parties initially assured their citizens that Ukraine would not introduce any additional rights for SOGI minorities and that tolerance toward LGBTIQ people would not be internalized as part of Ukrainian national values. Then president Petro Poroshenko declared that "family values will remain inviolable," while the "speaker of parliament assured deputies that the law would not threaten 'family values', saying: 'I hear some fake information which says that there may be same-sex marriages in Ukraine. God forbid this will ever happen. We will never support this'" (*BBC News* 2015). In 2016, a Pride march in Lviv that the state said it would not protect was called off after right-wing groups came to the planned meeting point shouting "kill, kill, kill," prompting the SOGI organizers to flee the city (Bateson 2016). Societal backlash also ensued, including an arson attack on a cinema during a screening of a gay-themed film in October 2014, as well as targeted attacks on activists (Kenarov 2015). Amid safety concerns spurred by increased repression, as we noted in chapter 4, Ukrainian LGBTIQ activists opted to protest outside Parliament without the symbolic rainbow flag. Indeed, this refusal of typical SOGI symbols—largely because they buttressed the Russian Duma's claims that pro-EU Maidan protestors were all "gay"—was so evident that an LGBTIQ organization attributed a flash mob of protestors using the rainbow flag to a fabricated provocation organized by pro-Russian groups and the Ukrainian Security Service (Kenarov 2015).

In 2022, several months into the newest war, Ukrainian SOGI rights activists petitioned President Volodymyr Zelensky to reconsider the constitutional ban on same-sex marriage, drawing attention to the sacrifices LGBTIQ-identified soldiers were making. Activists hoped that Ukraine's hitherto reluctant and opposing politicians would finally endorse SOGI rights as a way to burnish the country's liberal credentials as it seeks to join the European Union and draw closer to the West (Levenson 2022). In December of that same year, Russia expanded and sharpened the former (2013) anti-gay-propaganda law to limit SOGI content from anyone, including adults. The Russian crackdown continued in 2023 with new legislation banning gender reassignment surgery and changes to official identity markers, as well as annulling marriages where one partner's gender identity has "changed" (*Guardian* 2023). The intensification of state violence toward people living in "non-traditional lifestyles" also includes support for sexologists to help "convert" LGBTIQ people, a practice banned in many states.

For the last decades, Ukraine has stood between two gateways leading toward Russia and the EU, which were constructed to represent the two antipodes on SOGI rights. The Russian Orthodox Church and Putin have used traditional values rhetoric to present Russia as the international protectorate of conservative morality politics, justifying the passage and diffusion of so-called anti-gay-propaganda laws that classify sexual difference as decadent and deviant (Wilkinson 2014). This politics of traditional values has been used as a geopolitical tool with which to distance Russia from Western power. However, when, as Ian Bateson (2016) described, the Ukrainian "pro-Kremlin media was attempting to portray the pro-EU [Maidan] protests two years ago as a tantrum by

LGBT people yearning to join 'Gayropa,'" the response of Ukrainian society was clear: people continued to support the pro-European course of the government, albeit without endorsing SOGI rights. The Ukrainain example shows the effects of the Russian dichotomization of traditional values and SOGI rights as representative of two rival visions of political order (see chapter 6).

Russia's adoption of the paradigm of politicized moral conservatism—alongside many other states and influenced by ideas from a wide tent of activists—has fueled contestations around SOGI rights at the international level more broadly. Its appeal is attractive to various actors, including several in the West, and it has polarized the field of human rights. Instead of advancing an increasingly strengthened international norm, the SOGI rights movement grapples with norm polarization (Wilkinson and Langlois 2014). This international polarization involves one group of state governments refusing the values deemed to be native to another group, making SOGI rights part of a geopolitics in which governments co-opt the values that align with what they see as their side (Symons and Altman 2015).

Emil Edenborg's (2022) article on the invasion of Ukraine in the *Boston Review* encapsulates how many of the themes we lay out are important for international relations. His analysis dovetails with our understanding of the far-reaching transnational scale of the moral conservative network and its narrative in contemporary world politics:

> There is nothing uniquely Russian about imagining collective identity or national security in gendered terms. Associating the geopolitical foe with sexual or gender perversity is part of a queer-phobic state repertoire known from many contexts. The 1950s gay panic in the United States, when accusations of homosexuality became a smear tactic in Joseph McCarthy's anti-Communist crusade and homosexuals were barred from serving in the federal administration as they were seen as potential Soviet spies, has obvious similarities to how LGBT movements in today's Russia are described as a fifth column planted by the West. In several countries in Sub-Saharan Africa, including Uganda and Zimbabwe, political and religious leaders talk of homosexuals and LGBT activists as pawns of Western attempts to re-colonize Africa. A somewhat similar pattern can be noted in the Chinese government's recent regulation banning "sissy

men," referring mainly to male celebrities inspired by South Korean and Japanese androgynous fashion trends, from appearing on television and streaming sites. (Edenborg 2022, 6)

Gender, sexuality, and gender identity are central to world politics. By establishing a bridge between scholarship on contentious politics, international relations, and the sociology of religion, this book helps make sense of these connected realities—linked across various decades and from the United States to Russia to Uganda—and the contested nature of social politics in international relations. We hope that it advances our understanding of progressive change in world politics, as well as the limits of such change and the persistently hard-fought struggles that underpin it.

Puzzles and Takeaways

We began this book with four puzzles, and the answers to them tell us much about the direction of contemporary struggles around gender and sexuality politics and their embeddedness in international relations. First, conventional explanations for transnational organizing in many fields have underestimated the grip of traditional values around religious and national identities that drive anti-SOGI mobilization. There is too much evidence of contestation—not only at the domestic, but also at the transnational level—for us to continue to theorize progressive movements that operate in an enlightened transnational space and overcome the "backward" politics of various states' domestic spheres. The multiple countervailing pressures at play in this domain matter, as Kristopher Velasco's (2018, 2023a, 2023b) work compellingly demonstrates and theorizes, alongside the rich scholarship of many other works in sexuality and gender politics (Kuhar and Paternotte 2017; Corrêa, Paternotte, and Kuhar 2018; Graff and Korolczuk 2022; Verloo 2018). Indeed, the politicized moral conservative movement resists the progressive change of SOGI rights TANs at all levels of politics (local, domestic, and international) and in the process often learns from and mirrors the transnational strategies utilized by their SOGI counterparts. These resistances often resemble the boomerang and spiral models of human rights diffusion and employ many of the same transnational tools that have won LGBTIQ people widespread recognition in some parts of the world. That acknowledgment means rethinking our models as less of a spiral and more of a double helix. Doing so will help account for the relatively different ways TANs operate in different states—because usually more than one network is at play.

A second and related puzzle is informed by the relative persistence of religious and traditional values movements, even those deriving from economically prosperous and secularizing states, and the ongoing pushback against human rights norms governing sexuality and gender. Indeed, the field of politics previously held an optimism around post-material modernity and cosmopolitan secularism (Inglehart and Norris 2003) that has been complicated by the transnational emergence of politicized moral conservative networks and ideas. While some states have progressed rapidly on SOGI rights—drastically transforming life for LGBTIQ people over the course of twenty years—others have retrenched their rights, and violence and precarity are on the rise in many places (Symons and Altman 2015; Hadler and Symons 2018). This retrenchment especially holds true for trans communities, whose recent and hard-fought progress has been challenged with increasingly exclusionary policies and targeted violence the world over. By tracing the moral conservative movement and identifying the main actors and processes that are responsible for the extensive pushback against SOGI rights, such contestation becomes less surprising. Shining a light on the rival movements both for and against vulnerable SOGI rights—instead of holding a blind belief in inevitable progress—offers scholars and practitioners the insights and tools that may contribute to furthering more inclusive and progressive goals in world politics.

Finally, in the third and fourth puzzles, scholars theorized nationalism and the distinctiveness of varied faiths as impediments to cross-border organizing and the ecumenism of the politicized moral conservative movement. But we have shown that the moral conservative narrative has helped overcome both these impediments. Nationalist moral conservative actors are happy to work in concert globally, in defense of multiple nationalisms. Similarly, though convinced of their own faith's superiority and suspicious of religious freedom and the equality of the faiths, contemporary religious actors are content to collaborate around what the moral conservative narrative puts forward as greater goods (at this global level). They can come together in this domain even if they have different positions in other issue areas; for example, on immigration, the Catholic Church and Evangelicals in the United States take different positions, with the latter strongly opposed (Whitehead and Perry 2020; Zepeda-Millán 2017). These moral conservative actors use SOGI rights as a proxy for (and thus perpetuate) ideologically resonant and politically opportune dichotomies—such as East versus West, North versus South, right versus left, religious versus secular, and conservative versus progressive—that have captured some peoples' imaginations in decades past. In their construction of a moral conservative narrative, homo- and transphobia become important tools for galvanizing political support and uniting ideologically incongruent and geographically disparate movement actors around various perceived threats—including communism, demographic decline, nativist panic, and secularism. This newfound global perspective is driven not simply by their opposition to SOGI rights, but their conviction *for* an alternative to the liberal political mainstream in which resistance to SOGI rights is an important pole supporting a wide tent of moral conservative issues. Understanding this narrative and its origins exposes both its strengths and weaknesses as they relate to the pushback against SOGI rights progress.

In sum, this book addressed these puzzles by exploring how the politicized moral conservative transnational movement functions, who composes it, and how its agenda is constructed. We have charted and described the key actors, claims, and venues of global resistances to SOGI and SOGI-adjacent rights. Drawing on over a decade of fieldwork and over 240 interviews with SOGI, anti-SOGI, and various state and IO actors, this book has provided the origin story of this unexpected movement's global rise and describes the challenges that its presence poses for present-day human rights movements. We show that these resistances are plural and build off a long history of what we call the politicized moral conservative narratives—the institutional infrastructure that unites ideologically incongruent and geographically scattered actors. All these perceived threats intersect directly with gender in that they are almost always intertwined with a panic around the destabilization of masculinity and femininity and challenges to patriarchy.

* * *

There are two broader takeaways for the various fields we speak to—beyond the overarching point above that gender matters to international

266 | CONCLUSION

relations, a point that should be clear but needs constant repeating—that deserve highlighting in conclusion.

First, the double helix metaphor is helpful for thinking about human rights in the current era. We live in a multilevel world where TANs compete at all levels; the specific time periods and domestic contexts they interact with help us to understand the varied outcomes we observe on SOGI rights comparatively. Unlike the boomerang or spiral models, our metaphor captures the dynamic and relational tension between *plural* TANs. It complicates static formulations of domestic backlash, which exists at multiple levels in world politics. Furthermore, the double helix metaphor also helps us to understand the reflexive nature of the two TANs' engagement with each other, and how that shapes their claims and strategies in unexpected but important ways. Moral conservative transnational advocacy networks play an increasingly important role in contemporary world politics, cornering SOGI rights advocates into patterns of action and countermobilization. The vignette from 2016 that opened the book—one scene in Cyprus at the SOGI TAN's Reclaiming Family Values meeting and one in Georgia at the moral conservative TAN's World Congress of Families summit to honor "Family Day"— can only be understood by theorizing such rival contestation. The same is true for how this contest plays out within countries. For example, the Singaporean government's 2022 decision to repeal Paragraph 377a,[5] a British-era law that criminalizes same-sex relations between men, was followed by the announcement that it also intends to amend the constitution to "protect" opposite-sex marriage and the family.[6]

While this book has zeroed in on the illustrative example of gender and SOGI rights, the double helix metaphor has currency for human rights research and activism more generally. This model may be applicable to a variety of contested issue areas in world politics, especially those that are prone to unfold with rival networks organizing around competing interpretations of basic human rights claims. For example, there are similarities in the rival organizing around racial equality and racism, with various groups, primarily in Western countries, advocating for the racial equality of historically marginalized minorities, while an emerging TAN of white nationalists has begun to organize against racial equality using the rhetoric of "colorblindness" or "reverse racism"—that is, appropriating the language of discrimination to claim that white people are on the receiving end of discrimination (Búzás 2021, 455–56). While *white* nationalism is surely the greatest threat to the liberal international order in this example, future research will have to monitor if advocates of white nationalism make strange bedfellows with other opponents to racial equality, like groups advocating for racial nationalism that have sprung up in India and China (Búzás 2021).

Other double helix examples abound.[7] Going back to the early twentieth century, a TAN in support of temperance and abolition clashed with groups advocating for liquor rights and colonial-imperial interests, interacting in fascinating ways that led first to the widespread legitimacy of prohibition laws, before a sharp and uniform reversal (Schrad 2010). The debate between those advocating the universality of human rights and those focusing on cultural relativism (e.g., the female genital mutilation case) also exhibits some double helix dynamics. Similarly, those advocating for environmental and animal rights clash with cultural relativists, for example, in favor of whaling in Norway and Japan (Ingebritsen 2002). The issue of misinformation provides a further example, where one strand has mobilized around a free speech position, while groups in another strand (some of which embrace a "right to truth" frame) worry about the harm misinformation causes to democracy and human rights. The contestation between Israel and the United States and the Palestinians and Non-Aligned Movement at the UN Security Council over the issuing of declarative resolutions and their meanings also plays out at multiple levels (Graubart and Jimenez-Barcardi 2016), as do the clashes between the United States and human rights communities over the legal meaning of the laws governing extra-judicial killings (Brunstetter and Jimenez-Bacardi 2015). The mobilization of father's or men's rights movements operates transnationally and also deploys the rights language of gender equality and children's rights in their contest with feminist TANs (Wojnicka 2022). Certainly, and returning to mobilizations we have studied, transnational advocacy in relation to contraception and abortion plays out in this dynamic, with moral conservatives opposing it while transnational women's rights and health groups advocate in favor.

The growing use of similar human rights languages, even if for opposite ends, challenges the existing international system of human rights protection and advancement.[8] The institutions that states built to advance a global consensus on human rights after the tragedy of the Second World War (first and foremost, the UN) are likely to experience increasingly heightened controversy, uneven outcomes and, possibly, a decline in legitimacy. National and transnational NGOs that have developed and flourished around human rights claims in the past decades risk being caught in this double bind (Stoeckl and Medvedeva 2018), where positions that are not easily assimilable to one or the other strand of the double helix are prone to lose out against the trend to more polarization and where real debate and reciprocal learning become ever more difficult. For example, the anti-vaccination (anti-vax) movements that gained global momentum with the COVID-19 pandemic drew on frames like "my body, my choice," developed by women's movements, and co-opted references to the Holocaust remembrance (the victimization of Jewish, Roma, communist, and queer people) when challenging state public health initiatives around vaccine passes or social distancing (della Porta 2023). Interestingly, these groups, which count supporters among both far right and New Age milieus, have come to center issues like "children rights" and "individual freedom" with connections to the homeschooling, homeopathic, and ecological movements.

This does not necessarily mean that the double helix will exist in perpetual tension or have equal effects across states. Indeed, as the DNA metaphor suggests, if one of the strands weakens considerably, the model may break, and its relational effects will wane. This may be the case in certain regions or domestic contexts where the actors supporting one of the rival movements dominate, and domestic resonance of that same movement's goals has become high. In such a case, more of a boomerang or spiral can model can cascade across regions or subregions as originally theorized. It is, for example, unlikely that moral conservatives will gain much traction in the Netherlands. But this does not apply the world over. As noted by former US ambassador to the UN Samantha Power, "unfortunately, internationally, those trends [on SOGI rights] are not being paralleled in very large swaths of the world" (cited in Bruni 2015). In some cases, it has become very hard for the SOGI movement to gain any footing, and while not unchangeable, it may take decades. In a contested case like the United States, where both strands have strong movements and find resonance in varied sectors of the state and society, inevitability for one strand is not guaranteed. Clarence Thomas's 2022 decision overturning *Roe v. Wade* and his warning—saying the court could also reconsider the decriminalization of homosexuality and marriage equality—is an example of the fragility of rights in states where both movements are active and influential. In sum, the double helix model, which sees as less likely the development of an overarching, strong, and truly *international* norm in this domain, leaves room for different scenarios and outcomes to play out in different states.

In addition to the validity of the double helix model across various examples, we have asked of our readers to follow us through the warped moral conservative narrative in order to become aware of its binarism, blindspots and parochialism. The narrative holds sway—for its supporters—because it ignores complexity and engagement with counterevidence. Scholarship and activism can respond to such closure and parochialism with broad-mindedness and inclusiveness where possible, for example by engaging with liberal theologians and religious activists who may have the tools to speak to new audiences, by folding in complex intellectual and indigenous histories and working across academic disciplines. Progressives stand to gain from opening up discourses (to other echo chambers) toward greater inclusivity. Of course, that may also involve offering the generosity of patience with mistakes around the introduction of new forms of self-expression and terminologies where possible, or willingness to engage across disciplinary boundaries. Reifying these divides is not a suitable response to the epistemic challenge that moral conservatism poses, because it ignores the powerful and persuasive contradictory forces that circulate close by and that attract a relatively large audience. The value of occasionally moving beyond our epistemic and intellectual comfort zones is one lesson that can be drawn from our intellectual attempt at piecing together a complicated narrative.[9]

Indeed, many are doing the hard work of shining a light on the contradictions of the moral conservative narrative. Coalitions between LGBTIQ and religious groups lay bare its false dichotomies, as does even the Catholic Church in some countries (e.g., Germany) by pushing back against elements of the narrative. For example, the group Muslims for Progressive Values has been developing an LGBTI rights affirming theological language in the context of Islam since 2007 and continues to guide some institutions and civil society on the thoughtful promotion of

SOGI rights in relevant contexts. Many Orthodox Christians also continue to engage critically with the conservatism and excessive focus on SOGI rights resistance inside their own churches. A further strategy that SOGI civil society has used is to directly point out how the legal strategies, talking points, and the funding that upholds moral conservative organizing is the "Western imposition" they argue against.

The reconstruction of the moral conservative narrative in chapter 5 also demonstrated that actors frequently couch their resistance to SOGI rights in conspiracy narratives. The idea that SOGI rights are the fruits of a global conspiracy occupies an important role in transnational moral conservative mobilization. Some of the moral conservative actors we encountered during our research clearly drew their sense of mission and belonging from the conviction that they had "seen through" the alleged conspiracy of SOGI rights. According to their strategic deployment of the moral conservative narrative, SOGI rights activists are painted as all-powerful and as pulling the strings of global political and economic systems. Paradoxically, those who made such arguments most forcefully were frequently part of the governing political establishment in their respective home countries, like Russia, Hungary, or the United States during the Trump administration. From the perspective of SOGI rights activism, this is a flipped script surrounding the actual relations of power and victimhood. Emblematic of the utter stalemate that is created by the conspiratorial mindset of many moral conservative activists is a line captured in Masha Gessen's report from the World Congress of Families in Tbilisi, which ends with a clear "No" by Brian Brown to Gessen's question "Is there a way that my family and yours can live in peace in the same society?" (Gessen 2017). While SOGI rights advocates will never win over these leaders of moral conservative activism—the Brian Browns—many people in the conservative or neutral mainstream that may now be partly swayed by the moral conservative narrative remain far more movable.

Fieldwork with moral conservative actors also generated the insight that resistance to SOGI rights is frequently not the initial step in moral conservative norm mobilization, but it is what some conservative actors arrive at through a process of framing their personal issues of concern in a specific way. Some of the actors we met during fieldwork attached the highest value to issues like abortion or homeschooling without relating these to questions of SOGI rights. It was only by encountering the moral conservative narrative strategically deployed by transnational activist networks that they made the connection between their ethical choices and the conspiratorial worldview that positions them as both victims of a dominant secularist and liberal culture and as those chosen to resist the advancement of SOGI rights. For SOGI activism, this means that the engagement with topics more commonly associated with the conservative agenda—for example family—is indeed important, since it creates alternative frames that pluralize the public debate on topics hitherto occupied by politicized moral conservatives.

* * *

This book has analyzed the actors, claims, and venues of a global moral conservative program for which gender and sexuality have become lightning rod issues. The resistance to SOGI rights is not just an effect of such movements, nor is it necessarily their primary purpose, but it is a tool for constructing and galvanizing political opposition. Moral conservatives repurpose gender justice and SOGI rights to create global political division—mirroring (while simultaneously complicating) older dichotomies like capitalism versus communism, or East versus West. The repackaging of old fault lines in new ways creates challenges for gender justice and SOGI rights movements because it impedes them in forging a new political landscape on their own terms.

By addressing the SOGI rights responses and the complicated role of SOGI rights in Ukraine's struggle for a pro-European political identity in the final chapters of this book, we leave room to question binary assessments of SOGI resistances and SOGI achievements as one-way streets. States' policies and societal attitudes are not static and determined once and for all. Nor has the moral conservative right "won" the hearts of these societal majorities or "taken over" whole countries, as some recent scholarship and commentary would have us believe. Rather, we can discern a struggle that is far from settled in one direction or another. Indeed, many more people in the world support SOGI rights today than they did ten to twenty years ago; before the global moral conservative movement's preoccupation with SOGI rights. For example, while marriage equality is relatively taken for granted in the United States today (Bishin et al. 2021), this acceptance is quite new. We often forget that as recently as 2008, even California—widely considered a pioneeringly progressive US state—voted against marriage equality. In Poland, Rafał Trzaskowski, who garnered just under 50 percent of the votes in 2020, endorsed SOGI rights in his campaign in a manner unprecedented in mainstream Polish presidential politics.

To offer a final illustration, we return to the war in Ukraine that shaped this conclusion. In a conversation with the Council on Foreign Relations, US special envoy Jessica Stern (2022) highlighted a recent ripple of moral conservative backfire, pointing out how Putin's use of SOGI rights to justify war has in fact not resonated widely. The image of the Russian state—a core institutional actor and crutch supporting the resistance to SOGI rights—has been badly damaged. As such, its version of moral conservativism has not acquired the luster that Putin had hoped would garner value-based influence in world politics. This may be especially true in countries of Central and Eastern Europe, which have their own complicated relationship with SOGI rights denial. Emma Graham-Harrison's (2023) reporting buttresses Stern's notion, documenting an uptick in support for SOGI rights among both the Ukrainian society and state since the start of Russia's full-scale invasion. She spotlights the shifting positions of Andrii Kozhemiakin, a Ukrainian member of parliament who regularly touts his Christian and family values credentials. Yet, he supported a 2023 draft civil union bill that would give same-sex couples legal status, justifying it by saying, "Anything that our enemy hates . . . I will support. If it will never exist in Russia, it should exist and be supported here, to show them and signal to them that we are different. This law is like a smile towards Europe. . . . So I support it" (Graham-Harrison 2023, 1). Evidently there remain many pathways that lead to support for SOGI rights.

Last, while we engaged our subjects in their own chosen vocabulary by calling them *moral* conservative actors, the analysis itself leaves many—as one reader put it—wanting to rescue the term moral.[10] Indeed, the deployment of this term as a frame—like the United States' "Moral Majority"—emphasizes the bankruptcy of attempting to signal one group's exclusive pact with morality. (The same holds true for the attempted ownership of terms like the family and traditional values, which, as chapter 7 emphasized, SOGI rights movements have also worked to reclaim.) Moral conservatism and moral progressivism each produce the discursive contests that carry on in the double-helix nature of this struggle, but the strand that people come to view as moral—in the meaning of ethical or subjectively right—is open to change as well. In this moment of contestation, despite a formidable and underestimated resistance, the SOGI rights movement has agency, and their resolve is not diminished. The contestation we have identified between rival actors does dampen glowing optimism, yet it does not suggest SOGI movements are losing a battle. Indeed, their work often shows how movements can weather serious challenges to human rights.

ACKNOWLEDGMENTS

Our collaboration was hatched on a terrace overlooking Florence in Fiesole, Italy, in 2014. We both had fellowships at the European University Institute at the time, and we met at a fantastic talk by Anna Grzymała-Busse on the politicization of religion in Europe, where Phillip asked about the project's connection to LGBTI rights. The question dovetailed very well with Kristina's latest work on postsecular conflicts, and this sparked a wonderful intellectual exchange over the eight years that followed. We have been exploring ideas of politicized moral conservative (PMC) activism since then, writing grant applications, holding workshop meetings, and taking long hikes in the beautiful Austrian Alps or the hills of Griffith Park in Los Angeles. The fieldwork in between, though often troubling and sometimes disturbing, was also invigorating given the urgency we felt about the issues at hand. And during the last stretch, our joint writing—involving near-weekly emails or Zoom conferences—brought some warmth to the pandemic's isolation and gave us the solace with which to process the latest iterations of the Russo-Ukrainian war that have affected countless lives in Europe. Indeed, the most intense episode of that war broke out with Russia's 2022 invasion of Ukraine just as we started our final book workshop in Los Angeles in February of that year.

In this long period of time from the earliest grant applications in 2014 to the close of the project in 2022, we have been inspired and supported by so many of our colleagues. Roman Kuhar and David Paternotte's important book on anti-gender campaigns has been especially motivating, and we are grateful to Roman and David for encouragement and support along the way. Kristopher Velasco, whose work brings the highest sophistication and nuance to these important questions of our times, has been a tremendous inspiration and will shape the field for the better in important ways. Peter Matjašič was an important source of support early on, inviting us to monitor some important events on SOGI responses.

276 | ACKNOWLEDGMENTS

Alongside those mentioned above, Cynthia Burack, Zoltán Búzás, Jennifer Dixon, Arturo Jimenez-Bacardi, Anna Korteweg, Violetta Zentai, Felipe Gonzalez Santos, Timo Koch, and Sahra Taylor read parts of the manuscript and offered fantastic feedback.

A successful European Research Council grant (2015–22) we wrote when we first met in Florence made much of this research possible. The numerous researchers and research assistants involved in the Postsecular Conflicts Research Project at the University of Innsbruck (POSEC, grant nr. ERC-STG-2015–676804) deserve thanks for their support and encouragement. Within the auspices of that project, we are particularly grateful to Julia Mourão Permoser and Dmitry Uzlaner for being companions in fieldwork and co-authors of other publications that help inform parts of our thinking in this study. Likewise, Caroline Hill, Olena Kostenko, Hannah Jordan, Kerstin Prohaska, and Vera Pozzi made valuable contributions to the broader project. Pasquale Annicchino, Regina Elsner, Brandon Gallaher, Susanna Mancini, Andrey Shishkov, Aristotle Papanikolaou, and Chrissy Stroop have helped us connect the dots across the fields of gender studies, sociology of religion, theology, legal studies, political science, and history.[1] Kristina Stoeckl is especially grateful to José Casanova and Georgetown University's Berkley Center for Religion, Peace and World Affairs, whose invitation to the "The Social Ethos of the Orthodox Church" conference in the spring of 2022 granted her precious extra writing time in Washington, DC, to work on our final draft. Phillip Ayoub is grateful to Alison Brysk and the Mellichamp Program at the University of California at Santa Barbara, whose regular invitations over the years (culminating with the Generating Human Rights workshop in 2023) offered such valuable direction. We also thank the John Hopkins School for Advanced International Studies and Nina Hall and Nina Reiners, who organized the Challenges and Opportunities in Global and Transnational Advocacy conference in May 2023, offering a final round of exceptional input, including from Daniel Bertram, Hannah Birkenkötter, Alexandra Budabin, Mette Eilstrup-Sangiovanni, May Farid, Jessica Gover, Heidi Haddad, Alvina Hoffmann, Kseniya Oksamytna, Chris Pallas, Andrea Schapper, Hans Peter Schmitz, Alex Tokhi, Maria José Urzua, Lisbeth Zimmerman, and Kelebogile Zvobgo. We thank Eszter Polgári and Tamás

Dombos, and Katja Kahlina, Heta Rundgren, and Riikka Taavetti, for productive conversations at the Central European University and at Université Paris 8, respectively.

We are also immensely grateful to our colleagues and to Occidental College (and its Young Initiative) for hosting the closing book workshop in February of 2022. We were so fortunate to have Madeline Baer, Olga Brzezińska, Anthony Chase, Roman Kuhar, Sabine Lang, Igor Logvinenko, Gabriele Magni, and Jennifer Piscopo read our draft and gather with us in Los Angeles. Their detailed and richly constructive comments (e.g., Kuhar and Lang even sent us inline comments, page by page) helped us finalize the manuscript and move it into the review stage. Our students Lauren Bauman, Jaya Duckworth, and Oli Vorster offered us valuable feedback and advice as research assistants at various stages of the project between 2015 and 2022. Kathleen Kearns and John Harbord have been tremendous sources of editorial support in bringing our prose together and preparing the book for a wide audience. Nicola Righetti created the visualizations of the network in chapter 3 and helped us improve them with his thoughtful comments and suggestions.

At NYU Press, we have been incredibly fortunate to work with Ilene Kalish and Yasemin Torfilli and benefit from their enthusiastic support and encouragement. Our series editors, Susan Burgess and Heath Fogg Davis, gave the project their initial stamp of approval. Indeed, we chose to submit our manuscript first and exclusively to NYU Press because of the LGBTQ Politics series they have pioneered. Book series that are specifically devoted to LGBTQ people are very rare in the discipline of political science, and NYU Press's concerted efforts to institutionalize a space for such work was a major appeal for us in selecting a home for this work.

We acknowledge publisher's permissions to include segments of previously published material in significantly expanded and reworked form in this book. This pertains to limited parts of the analysis contained in chapters 2 and 3, including figure 3.2, which have previously been published in a book chapter entitled "Transnational Illiberal Networks" in *The Oxford Handbook of Illiberalism*, edited by Marlene Laruelle (2023), as well as some segments of chapter 1, which have been previously published in Ayoub's book, *When States Come Out* (2016). Segments of the text have appeared in our article "The Double-Helix Entanglements of Transnational Advocacy: Moral Conservative Resistance to LGBTI Rights" (2024) published by the *Review of International Studies*. In an extension of this work, we have explored the use of the moral conservative narrative by authoritarian populist leaders, which appears in "The Global Resistance to LGBTIQ Rights", *Journal of Democracy* 35(1): 59–73, January 2024.

In our personal lives, several people kept us motivated and inspired with their presence as pillars of support during the lengthy period of our lives in which this book was developed and written. Phillip Ayoub is grateful for the unwavering support he has received from friends and family (many in Los Angeles and Berlin), including Reinhild Ayoub, Philip Claudy, Chris Zepeda-Millán, Steph Castro, Blanca Biosca Costa, Philipp Maximilian Ungeheuer, Jaimie Bleck, Janice Gallagher, Deondra Rose, Christoph Schippel, Björn Weiss, Nick Pope, Patrick Daniel Heck, Patrick Schramm, Manu Curiman, Patryk Majewski, Kosta Zarin, Anton Cobb, Tom Jäger, Felipe Neira, Sarah Kelly, Marina Henke, Monika Shankar, Mike Wang, Drew Strauss, Jason Michallef, Jamie Blasina, Ari Shaw, Miriam Ayoub, Darren Ayoub, Gabriele Gier, and Edith Gier. Kristina Stoeckl thanks family and friends who supported her by lending an ear, cheerleading for success, and granting time: Andrea and Theo, Hedi Stoeckl, Clara Brettfeld, Angela Ehrenreich, Mario Gallo and Mirella Costanzo, and the Austrian-Italian-French support network Paola di Lauro, Bettina Mahlert, Lisa Ariani, Michele Grazzini, Nathalie and Olivier Dobel-Ober, Sandra Gewinner, and Nicole and Peter Bendelow.

Finally, as co-authors we are grateful and indebted to each other for reciprocal encouragement, inspiration, and perseverance, without which this book would not have been possible. From Kristina Stoeckl: Phillip Ayoub bore the brunt of the work giving structure, direction, and shape to the manuscript, and deserves praise for taking his co-author by the hand and leading her into a new field. From Phillip Ayoub: Since working on grant proposals in 2014, Kristina Stoeckl's intricate knowledge of the actors that makeup the politized moral conservative movement opened wonderful interdisciplinary worlds for her co-author and for the LGBTIQ politics literature he was rooted in—to get a glimpse at different sides of contestation that scholars of sexuality rarely get to observe firsthand.

Ayoub dedicates this book to the memory of his great-aunt Anneliese Dörr (March 3, 1931–February 18, 2018), a tremendous intellectual inspiration and role model for him. She was a Catholic and Badenerin, who, deeply affected by war and reconstruction in Germany, drew on her personal experience of struggle in a forward-thinking way that always centered the inclusion of others. Endlessly curious, she felt it imperative to think deeply and critically about understanding difference and imparted that drive to all those fortunate enough to have known her.

APPENDIX

NETWORK ANALYSIS IN CHAPTER 3

The graphs were created with the R language and environment for statistical computing and graphics version 4.1.1 (R Core Team 2021). The code was written in the RStudio development environment, Ghost Orchid version (RStudio Team 2021). A number of packages were used: tidyverse (Wickham et al. 2019), igraph (Csardi and Nepusz 2006), ggmap (Kahle and Wickham 2013), ggraph (Pedersen 2021), and rnaturalearth (South 2017).

The latitude and longitude of congressional cities and participant states were found by querying the Google Geocoding API through ggmap's geocode function (Kahle and Wickham 2013). Triangles representing states are typically geolocated at the center of a state. In some cases, namely Spain, Italy, and Russia, they have been slightly shifted to avoid overlap or improve visualization clarity. The Spanish coordinates were placed near Madrid by the Google Geocoding API, overlapping with the conference held there. Those of Italy straddled those of the Vatican. To avoid excessive overlap, the locations of these states were slightly displaced. Russia was situated away from other European countries. To prevent overdispersion on the European close-up map, the triangle representing Russia was placed near Moscow.

The diagrams representing the congressional attendance of individuals and organizations are created using the ggplot function with the geom_tile option (Wickham et al. 2019). A darker color and lower position on the chart indicate more participation by a person or participants in a given organization, respectively. The blocks represent participation in a particular conference.

Finally, in order to get a better understanding of which countries are represented and how their composition varies at the WCF, we calculated the presence of speakers' countries over time. A simple comparison in percent shows that the WCF has diversified in recent years, in particular since 2014. Considering the overall composition of active participants at all the congresses after the Moscow WCF (2014), participation from countries of the European Union and former Soviet Union has increased. If we look only at the European Union, (EU-27) participation rose from 25 percent to 36 percent of the total participants. This corresponds to a 44 percent increase compared to the pre-Moscow phase. If one considers the geographical Europe (51 countries), the increase is from 32 percent to 50 percent, which corresponds to a 56 percent increase compared to the congresses before Moscow. However, the distributions of European participations over the congresses are skewed, with a high range of values, with certain congresses featuring a more- or less-high proportion of European participants. Therefore, these statistics represent a rough estimate of the trend in participation. Hence, in order to obtain a more reliable interpretation, we compared the frequency distributions of European participants up to the congress in Moscow of 2014, and after 2014, with a one-tailed Mann-Whitney test. The Mann-Whitney test is a nonparametric statistical test that can be used to ascertain if two distributions of values are equal or if one includes values that are systematically higher (or lower) than the other. In this case, the two distributions we compared are represented by the proportions of European participants to the World Congresses of Families up to and including the meeting in 2014 and the proportions after. The test was performed both on participants from European Union countries (EU-27) and from geographical Europe (fifty-one nations). Results show that the difference in participation from EU-27 countries has not significantly changed from before ($N = 5$, $Mdn = 0.21$) and after 2014 ($N = 5$, $Mdn = 0.20$) ($W = 16$, $p = 0.27$). Instead, the difference in participation from geographical Europe has significantly changed from before ($N = 8$, $Mdn = 0.27$) and after 2014 ($N = 5$, $Mdn = 0.54$) ($W = 33$, $p < 0.05$).

TRADITIONAL/FAMILY VALUES DISCOURSE
ANALYSIS IN CHAPTER 7

Coding and Data

Several different types of organization documents were coded, including annual reports, organization newsletters (*Euro-Letter*), and the annual conference delegate packets made available to us.

1. Annual Reports: a comprehensive report on ILGA-Europe's activities and events, finances and fundraising, board membership/staff, and important developments over the course of a year. Years made available and coded: 1998–2015.
2. Euro-Letter: a political and legal news bulletin put together by ILGA-Europe and partners (depending on the year), which highlights European news on LGBTI issues and ILGA-Europe organizational updates. Years made available and coded: 2000–2016.
3. Delegate Packet: conference information provided to the attendees/delegates of the annual ILGA-Europe conference, which includes conference schedules, panel/event details, and brief updates/information on ILGA-Europe and their priorities. We chose not to code conference reports, since they were not consistently published over the years and had greater fluctuations in page length. Years made available and coded: 2004–2016.

While we collected and coded these same three document types over the years, inconsistencies in the layout and length of these documents due to the organizations' decisions impact our research. Listed below are some particular concerns with the documents, coded as they relate to changing layouts and how this affects the interpretation of the coding.

1. Annual Reports
   a. On length—the length of each report is highly variable, with the shortest report at 10 pages (2012) and the longest at 72 pages (2010). Significant changes in length include:
      i. From 30 pages in 2006 to 52 in 2007
      ii. From 56 pages in 2011 to 10 pages in 2012
      iii. From 13 pages in 2014 to 25 pages in 2015
   b. On shifts in layout—
      i. From 1999 to 2000: move to more comprehensive coverage of regional activities and developments on LGBTI issues and coverage of thematic issues (e.g., immigration, HIV/AIDS, and the like)
      ii. From 2003 to 2004: move to reports according to strategic objectives rather than issue areas

284 | APPENDIX

       iii. From 2011 to 2012: move to a much more condensed update on yearly activities/provision of broad-level snapshots of a few completed activities; not based on strategic objectives or thematic issues; and does not include specific information on finances, board membership, or staff

       iv. From 2012 to 2013: a still-briefer update, but a return to framing the report around strategic objectives

2. *Euro-Letter*

   a. On length—the length of each newsletter changes from issue to issue, ranging from 3 to 35 pages, dependent on news and developments in LGBTI issues in Europe

       i. From 8 pages in November 2005 to 26 pages in December 2005

       ii. From 27 pages in June 2010 to 3 pages in July 2010

   b. On publication consistency—depending on year, the newsletter did not run consistently every month. To account for the inconsistency in publishing, we coded only six *Euro-Letter* newsletters (every other month, when possible).

   c. On shifts in layout—

       i. From November 2005 to December 2005: includes more updates on ILGA-Europe, funding opportunities, and more comprehensive reporting on LGBTI issues across Europe

       ii. From January 2006 to February 2006: new newsletter design, new cover image, longer table of contents, and provides more space for news stories

       iii. From June 2010 to July 2010: organization making the shift from designed PDF attachment to an HTML format—during the transition the *Euro-Letter* was an email summary of recent stories/ILGA-Europe news (moved to only three pages)

       iv. From April 2015 to May 2015: shifts to a webpage format—this increases the number of pages, even though the amount of content is similar

3. Delegate Packet

   a. On length—the overall trend was to become longer over time. The shortest packet is 21 pages (2007) and the longest is

88 pages (2016). Many of the additional pages that are added, though, do not add any new substantive information. We will break this down further under the "shifts in layout" section, but some examples include: new additions over the years, such as nicely designed front and back cover pages, longer introductions from the host, photos and bios of conference presenters and ILGA-Europe staff, list of participants, and the like. Some of these additions pack in many extra pages but should not impact the analysis or final raw counts. Over the years, the annual conference itself got bigger, meaning there were more workshops and other sessions. For example, the number of workshops starts at around 28, but slowly increases to 46 over time. This could have an impact on the end analysis.

    b. On significant shifts in layout

        i. 2004—includes a guide to the EU, CoE, and OSCE in relation to LGBT rights; also includes staff information (staff information stops after 2004 for several years)

        ii. Starting in 2005—includes more information on ILGA-Europe's strategies, accomplishments, and goals

        iii. 2007, 2008, 2012—does not include front or back cover pages

        iv. Starting in 2011—includes speakers' biographies

        v. Starting in 2012—longer sponsor/contributing organization pages, includes list of participants

Coding of Family Issues Category in Table 7.2:

    1. <u>Immigration</u>: text was coded as under the immigration subcategory when the document discussed immigration, asylum, refugee status, family reunification, or freedom of movement in relation to LGBTI families

        a. Example: "The full recognition of the diversity of families, and of same-sex partnerships and those involving a partner of transgendered status, in the Draft on the right of citizens of the Union and their family members to move and reside freely within the territory of the Member States" (Annual Report 2002–2003, 6)

b. Example: "[The workshop] will examine the case-law of the European Court of Human Rights on various aspects of family rights, including . . . freedom of movement and others" (Delegate Packet 2016, 42)

2. Children: text was coded as under the children subcategory when the document discussed children or guardianship of an LGBTI child, parenting as an LGBTI individual, adoption, and/or rights of parents and children of LGBTI families

   a. Example: "We will start from the methodology presented in the capacity building workshops on framing and values and apply them specifically to the issue of LGBTI parenting" (Delegate Packet 2015, 36)

   b. Example: "In this workshop participants will be given the opportunity to reflect on how rainbow families raising children are arguably a powerful instrument for changing society. . . . The workshop will also address the ways in which the reality of parenting in a rainbow family context has the potential to forge new alliances for the LGBT movement" (Delegate Packet 2014, 14)

3. Partnership: text was coded as under the partnership subcategory when the document discussed legal recognition of marriage, registered partnership, or cohabitation rights of LGBTI people

   a. Example: "This workshop shall shed light on the progress that has been achieved at the national level with regard to the legal recognition of LGBT families—whether through marriage, registered partnership or cohabitation rights" (Delegate Packet 2008, 9)

   b. Example: "ILGA-Europe argues for the inclusion of sexual orientation and gender identity in the non-discrimination clause, and for the clause on the right to marry and to found a family to adopt language recognizing the diversity of relationships in contemporary Europe" (Annual Report 1999–2000, 10)

Not all family issues neatly fit into these categories, but these were the main issues that came up across the ILGA-Europe documents. Text coded as family issues could be coded in only the parent node (family issues), the parent node and one child node/subcategory, or, when applicable, the parent node and multiple child nodes.

NOTES

INTRODUCTION

1 For more on resistance in Colombia, see the work of Emilio Lehouq (2021). He traces a history of moral conservative legal mobilization back to the 1990s in Colombia, though with increasing focus on so-called gender ideology, and LGBTI people—also seeking out new venues in the form of the courts—after 2007. Additionally, chapter 9 of Javier Corrales (2021) is a productive overview of the post-2010 backlash in Latin America more broadly, as is the collection by Leigh Payne, Julia Zulver, and Simón Escoffier (2023), which includes an LGBTIQ-focused chapter by Sam Ritholtz and Miguel Mesquita (2023).

2 Unless we are speaking of specific activists who identify themselves as lesbian, gay, bisexual, transgender, intersex, or queer actors or of research that uses that terminology, we typically opt to use the abbreviation SOGI in the body of this book. Given the global scope of our project, SOGI's more general meaning may be more inclusive and travel further than identities developed in the West (though scholars have demonstrated that the SOGI acronym is also not wholly satisfactory; see Waites 2009), even if marketing teams worried about the reach and understandability of that acronym in a book title. That does not diminish the fact that the SOGI movement itself represents multiple groups, takes on varied names, and has diverse sets of goals across different national contexts. Until recently, the movement often sidelined issues of gender identity and expression, which received less space and attention in organizing. When we use the SOGI shorthand, we aim to be as broad and universal as possible and to encompass communities marginalized by their sexual orientation, gender identity and expression, and sex characteristics (sometimes abbreviated as SOGIESC).

3 This sequential narrative of SOGI rights proliferation, which typically has partnership rights as following much after decriminalization (Waaldijk 2000), has occurred more rapidly in some states in recent years.

4 In response, European leaders had an unusually confrontational exchange at the June 2021 summit of the EU Council. Belgium's prime minister Alexander De Croo said he had never before seen such a dispute at an EU summit (Eydlin 2021).

5 Mashrou' Leila is a popular Lebanese rock band with an openly gay lead singer, Hamed Sinno. Aside from the arrests at their 2017 concert in Egypt, they have been banned from performing on various occasions, including in Jordan and

Lebanon. In the latter case, right-wing Christian groups organized to oppose their presence at the Byblos Festival concert via a homophobic online campaign that targeted their music for "promoting blasphemy and homosexuality."

6 Only recently, especially in roughly the last six years, has a flourishing literature, which we engage throughout, come to chart these developments (e.g., Corredor 2019; Cupać and Ebetürk 2020, 2021; Datta 2018a; Garbagnoli 2016; Graff and Korolczuk 2022; Kahlina 2022; Kuhar and Paternotte 2017; Möser, Ramme, and Takács 2022, Sanders 2018; Sanders and Jenkins 2022; Sauer 2020; Verloo 2018; Velasco 2023a, 2023b).

7 On occasion, moral conservative movements also invoke a rhetoric of what they call gender equality, but only insofar as gender roles remain intact—for example, an equal division of labor between men and women, with men as breadwinners and women doing domestic labor. We would also add that "nativist" panic in Europe and North America is often intertwined with Islamophobia and fears of "replacement" (Bracke and Hernández Aguilar 2020).

8 While these phobias are bundled together by moral conservatives, we must acknowledge that moral conservatives have galvanized around trans rights, specifically the idea of gender fluidity, with increasing pace, especially in many contexts where gay and lesbian rights have become more accepted. We thank Anna Korteweg for this comment (see also Bassi and LaFleur 2022).

9 When Slovenia adopted same-sex marriage (before a referendum), for example, Catholic, Protestant, and Muslim religious leaders issued a joint statement of opposition. Their collaboration was a historic first. Activists noted the irony that SOGI rights could bring such disparate figures together. We thank Roman Kuhar for this illustration. In early articulations, Bob (2012) called such collaborations the "Baptist-Burqa coalition" and Cupać and Ebetürk (2020) used the term "unholy alliance."

10 Building on the findings by Velasco and others that both networks exist and operate globally.

11 While Chetaille (2015) speaks mainly of mirroring movement frames, we use the term mirroring more expansively here. We set out to study the movement as increasingly global: consisting of powerful states, international organizations (IOs), and international nongovernmental organizations (INGOs) that work together across borders. (See also Ann-Kathrin Rothermel [2020] on anti-gender actors' appropriation of feminist discourse and knowledge production.) Furthermore, Armstrong and Bernstein (2008) emphasize that such mirroring may be influenced by institutional environments. This may be partly deliberative, but the commonalities may also reflect the fact that they both exist within the same institutional environment of a human rights regime, IOs, states, etc (cf. Velasco 2023a). So, while some decisions may be agentic choices, the institutional environment constrains the choice options.

12 And are possibly compelled to borrow due to their operation in similar institutional environments (Armstrong and Bernstein 2008).

13 While the politicized nature of these PMCs is central to the definition, for stylistic reasons we often use the shorthand "moral conservative" when we refer to actors, ideas, and narratives.

14 There had also been some more minimal movement forward on SOGI rights during the earlier Clinton administration (Burack 2018). The Trump administration exhibited confusion around its posture toward SOGI rights, as it attacked some of these rights (particularly those of trans Americans) at home, while simultaneously pandering to a small conservative wing of the SOGI movement with a global initiative to decriminalize homosexuality. The initiative, spearheaded by Ric Grenell, the US ambassador to Germany, earned minimal support from activists due to its homonationalist framework (often used to vilify Muslim countries like Iran) and bore little fruit (Ayoub 2019b). In many other respects the US State Department also encouraged and supported actors and policies seeking to challenge SOGI rights.

15 We rely on Cas Mudde's (2004) commonly employed definition of populism as "a thin-centered ideology that considers society to be ultimately separated into two homogeneous and antagonistic groups, 'the pure people' versus 'the corrupt elite,' and which argues that politics should be an expression of the volonté générale (general will) of the people" (543).

16 Take, for example, this excerpt from a 2021 speech by Russian president Vladimir Putin: "The destruction of age-old values, religion and relations between people, up to and including the total rejection of family (we had that, too), encouragement to inform on loved ones—all this was proclaimed progress and, by the way, was widely supported around the world back then and was quite fashionable, same as today. By the way, the Bolsheviks were absolutely intolerant of opinions other than theirs" (Putin 2021).

17 They consciously place their microscope over the Catholic Church and the national manifestation of transnational mobilizations in varied European country case studies.

18 In this formulation of "genderism," Legutko invokes "gender mainstreaming" policy in the EU. Moral conservative resistances in Europe emphasize what they see as the top-down insertion of gender equality advocacy by the public servants (often pointing to the EU's research framework Horizon Europe, which introduced gender-mainstreaming policies). The success of gender mainstreaming policies (and its felt top-down aspect) has offered opportunities for the contemporary moral conservative countermovement.

19 Kuhar and Paternotte (2017) give voice to the inner workings and perceptions of the anti-gender movement. Several other important recent works have added to our understanding of these phenomena. All acknowledge the cross-border and transnational processes that dislodge anti-gender movements from the confines of the state (Case 2016; Datta 2018a; Garbagnoli 2016; Graff and Korolczuk 2022; Kováts and Põim 2015; Sauer 2020; Verloo 2018; Möser, Ramme, and Takács 2022; Velasco 2023a, 2023b).

290 | NOTES

20 By contrast, SOGI rights activists have a community that coalesced transnationally (going back to the 1800s; Kollman and Waites 2009) around a set of issues pertaining to their own recognition.

21 In chapter 2 we develop this distinction using the *kintsugi* metaphor.

22 There is of course variation across domestic contexts, but such welfare subsides for certain kinds of families have also captured the imagination of conservatives, including figures like Tucker Carlson, who traveled to Central and Eastern European to learn how these programs bolster conservatism there.

23 Other scholars working in this domain (e.g., Graff and Korolczuk 2022, who provided an important statement and overview of the debates surrounding the political economy of anti-gender movements) have used concepts like neoliberalism more loosely, deploying it in ways that range from its economic definition to its understanding as an ethos. We think more specificity is essential here, also as it pertains to other concepts that are often deployed broadly and interchangeably in the study of this movement, including: right populist, right-wing, ultraconservative, far-right, conservative, and reactionary movements.

24 As Kuhar and Paternotte (2017) so clearly explain, "anti-gender movements are not necessarily direct reactions to massive or influential campaigns, but can be unleashed as a prophylaxis, a preventive means to impede the development of special claims" (254).

25 The same contradiction holds for states that have resisted SOGI rights, which house some of the most emboldened and organized LGBTI-movements (e.g., the Polish SOGI rights movement) (O'Dwyer 2018).

26 Future research on Europe will also place its telescope more on groups like One of Us, FAFCE, and the European Christian Political Movement. Others will investigate CPAC and its new interstate and diplomatic initiatives on issues like abortion or religious freedom more deeply. We thank David Paternotte for several suggestions to extensions of our work that shaped this paragraph.

27 Following dozens of cases before the court to limit trans rights, Justice Clarence Thomas used his concurring opinion on *Roe v. Wade* to link the uprooting of precedent in that decision to reconsidering rights for same-sex intimacy and same-sex partnership (directly referencing the landmark *Lawrence v. Texas* and *Obergefell v. Hodges* cases).

28 Colleagues are also doing exceptional work that focuses on the international level (see Velasco 2023a).

CHAPTER 1. ACHIEVEMENTS

1 These included Australia's Gay Liberation Sydney/Victorian Homosexual Law Reform Coalition; Denmark's Landsforeningen for Bøsser og Lesbiske/Forbundet af 1948 (LBL F-48, Danish National Association of Gays and Lesbians/The Association of 1948); Great Britain's CHE; France's Commission interaméricaine des droits de l'homme (CIDH, Inter-American Commission on Human Rights);

Northern Ireland Gay Rights Association (NIGRA); Republic of Ireland's National Gay Federation; Italy's FUORI! (OUT!); the Netherlands' Cultuur en Ontspanningscentrum, (COC, Center for Culture and Leisure); Scottish Homosexual Rights Group (SHRG); and the United States' National LGBTQ Task Force (NGTF).

Other groups would join in the near future: Spain's Front d'alliberament gai de Catalunya (FAGC, Catalan Front for Gay Liberation); the Netherlands' Federation of Working Groups on Homosexuality (FWH); Sweden's Riksförbundet för sexuellt likaberättigande (RFSL, Swedish National Organization for Sexual Equality); Canadian Lesbian and Gay Rights Coalition (CLGRC); and the United States' North American Man/Boy Love Association (NAMBLA) (Paternotte 2014).

2 Current as of August 16, 2023. ILGA World, 2023, ILGA World is a Worldwide Federation, accessed August 16, 2023, https://ilga.org/.

3 While there were some forms of unregistered partnerships before, Denmark was the first state to introduce same-sex registered partnership rights in 1989. The Netherlands was the first to introduce full marriage equality in 2001 (Kollman 2013).

4 For example, Hillary Clinton referred to LGBT people as "an invisible minority" in her Human Rights Day speech delivered December 6, 2011, at the United Nations in Geneva. Hillary Clinton, 2011, "Hillary Clinton On Gay Rights Abroad: Secretary Of State Delivers Historic LGBT Speech in Geneva," *Huffington Post*, December 6, 2011, www.huffingtonpost.com.

5 Thus, brokers are not only the umbrella organizations that connect disparate actors (Thoreson 2014); domestic LGBTIQ groups and rooted cosmopolitans also frame and graft international scripts to make them fit specific domestic contexts. The concept places emphasis on their local knowledge and the subsequent ability to translate the international to the local and vice versa.

6 This broad definition of learning draws upon a vast literature on processes of learning, both individual and collective (Deutsch 1963; Haas 1991) and both complex and simple (Checkel 2005; Zito 2009).

7 For a history of US-based homophile organizing, including groups like the Mattachine Society and the Daughters of Bilitis, see Cervini (2020).

8 Burack and Voss have explicitly examined norm contestation and SOGI at the UN Human Rights Council (Burack 2018; Voss 2018).

9 A/HRC/38/43, para. 38, and A/74/181, para. 34. See also Committee, UN General Assembly 3rd. 2021. Promotion and Protection of Human Rights: Human Rights Questions, Including Alternative Approaches for Improving the Effective Enjoyment of Human Rights and Fundamental Freedoms. UN, January 2, 2023, https://digitallibrary.un.org/record/3950709.

10 As Wilkinson states, citing the Checkprivilege.tumblr.com blog, "assimilationism means the gay quarterback gets to be home-coming king, but the freshman who likes make-up and listening to showtunes is still a f-g-t."

292 | NOTES

11 As Puar's work exemplifies, the queer theory and LGBTIQ politics literature has always included deeply self-reflective and critical strands geared to thinking of marginalization intersectionally and as part of a broader struggle for liberation.

12 DNA is also a dynamic and adaptable molecule, prone to changes in code and mutation.

CHAPTER 2. RESISTANCES

1 This dovetails more closely with Edenborg's (2023) discourse coalition concept described in the introduction.

2 Moral conservative civil society organizations in the United States had already existed in the eighteenth century—for example, the Temperance Movement promoting alcohol abstinence—and their spread reflects civic associationism as a key characteristic of American society (Gamm and Putnam 1999).

3 A caveat: In this book, we are not concerned with testing the empirical reality of the culture war divide, nor are we interested in exploring whether large parts of the American population belong (and vote) within one or the other camp. Hunter's subsequent work focused precisely on that (Hunter, Bowman, and Puetz 2020; Hunter 2016; Hunter and Wolfe 2006).

4 The case of *Romer v. Evans*, 1996, on protected status helped pave the way for *Lawrence v. Texas*, 2003, which decriminalized consensual adult homosexual relations.

5 This would change in the next decade, as from the beginning of the 1990s, Europe became a leader in terms of SOGI rights. By that time, decriminalization and more encompassing equal SOGI rights were already a reality in many European states (Ayoub and Paternotte 2014). In Europe, the norm that LGBTI people are entitled to fundamental human rights, deserving of state recognition and protection, was first articulated in the 1993 Copenhagen Criteria and the 2000 Employment Anti-Discrimination Directive (see chapter 1), and from there, it diffused into European national legislations.

6 In East Germany the Protestant Church sheltered various dissident groups in the 1980s, including some gay and lesbian activists (Hillhouse 1990).

7 The *Fristenlösung* regulation includes the nonpunishable termination of pregnancy during the first three months of pregnancy while upholding a general ban on abortions.

8 In *The Moralist International*, Stoeckl and Uzlaner (2022) offer a detailed analysis of the influence of the American Christian Right on the Russian Orthodox Church. (See also chapter 3 of this book.)

9 *Acquis communautaire* is the accumulated body of legislation, legal acts, and court decisions that constitute European Union law.

10 The term *aggiornamento*, which refers to the opening of the doors of the church, was central to the program the Catholic Church's Second Vatican Council developed to open a dialogue with the modern world. Generally, the term implies a process of gradual modernization and liberalization. Conservative *aggiornamento*

highlights the fact that modernization of church teachings and strategies can also take place in a conservative and illiberal key.

11 This initial process is different from the emergence of transnational advocacy around SOGI rights, where—even if they did want to see international pressure lead to domestic policy change—early activists had a deeply held ethos of solidarity with "like" people in other contexts. They even mobilized in countries that were not their own after winning certain rights at home (Paternotte 2012; Ayoub and Paternotte 2016).

12 Judith Butler has been personally attacked by moral conservative activists on several occasions (Jaschik 2017).

CHAPTER 3. TRANSNATIONAL ADVOCACY NETWORKS

1 The website Diskursatlas Antifeminismus (Kemper 2023) is a useful resource for researchers, since its authors have retrieved many documents related to anti-SOGI-rights mobilization through way-back internet searches.

2 In our research, partly because of the wide-tent constituencies present, we had not seen race thematized among moral conservatives in the same way that gender and SOGI rights have been. There is no narrative around race equivalent to those around gender and SOGI rights, though some references to anti-Semitism (especially evident in a preoccupation with and discourse around George Soros) or Islamophobia do appear. That said, with the emergence of critical race theory contests in broader and adjacent right-wing populism, which has already reached Europe (at this writing, ahead of the 2022 French presidential elections) and may trickle into moral conservative discourse.

3 We are grateful to Madeline Baer for drawing our attention to the importance of the functions of these organizations.

4 Many scholars who study transnational moral conservative norm mobilization have written about the World Congress of Families. One of us (Stoeckl 2020a) has reconstructed in detail the Russian founding moment of the WCF in 1995 and its development inside Russia since then. In addition, a consistent body of scholarship, taken together, provides a rather complete picture of the organization (Kane 2009; Blue 2013; Trimble 2014; Levintova 2014; Southern Poverty Law Center 2015; Stroop 2016; Moss 2017; Kováts and Pető 2017; Gessen 2017; Kalm and Meeuwisse 2020).

5 Clifford Bob quotes extensively from the proceedings of the 1999 conference in *The Global Right Wing*, highlighting the central role of American actors in initiating the creation of a Pro-Family Bloc at the United Nations (Bob 2012, 37). The Geneva meeting also figures prominently in Doris Buss and Didi Herman's *Globalizing Family Values* (Buss and Herman 2003) and in Jennifer Butler's first groundbreaking account of Christian Right activism at the UN (Butler 2000).

6 Kristopher Velasco and Jeffrey Swindle are working on an exciting new data collection project that also analyzes participants at the regional congresses. Their preliminary analyses support many of the findings in this chapter and it will be worth reading their important work in conjunction with this chapter.

7 The reasons for the split between the Rockford Institute and the Howard Center were considered at the time as lying "in the split between paleoconservatism and neoconservatism" (Frum 1989). It was, in any case, not the last institutional renewal. The creation of the IOF in 2016 represents the latest stage of institutional development.

8 The documents include information around the organization of the World Congress of Families Madrid in 2012 and the reorganization of the WCF into the IOF in 2016. CitizenGo reacted with a protest petition against WikiLeaks and the involved media partners, which was published on all of CitizenGo's websites.

9 The action described by the interviewee took place in March 2017. American media reported about it and identified the National Organization for Marriage, the International Organization for the Family, and CitizenGo as organizers (Simpson 2017).

10 The global summit planned in the Philippines in 2020 was canceled due to the COVID-19 pandemic.

11 Alicja Curanović has analyzed its global strategy in detail (Curanović 2021; EFP 2021).

12 The Bogota summit was attended by Alvaro Uribe, the former president of Colombia, who was the leader of the "No" camp in the failed peace referendum (see introduction).

13 Logarithmic transformation reduces data skew and we employ it to improve visual clarity. This was necessary to prevent disproportionately large and small data points. For instance, using the original values, the triangle showing participation from the United States would have been 137 times bigger than that representing a country with just one participation, like Zambia. In contrast, in the logarithmic scale, the difference between these nations is represented by scale of about 1 to 7.

14 In the case of three cities, their geographic location was moved slightly to make them legible on the map. Please see the appendix for further detail.

15 Most Christian Churches consider the LDS Church a different religion, whereas the LDS Church usually self-identifies as Christian (WWC 2015).

16 The Global Philanthropy (2021) report estimates the following: for the LGBTI movement, $643 million of the $1.2 billion originate in North America. For the PMC movement, $3.1 billion of the $3.7 billion originate in North America. Greater funding data transparency in North America may, however, bias some research findings in this area, underestimating the ample financial contributions flowing from European sources (Datta 2021). We thank David Paternotte for pointing out this possibility. Indeed, the common perception in Europe that moral conservative money is coming "from somewhere else" is naïve given the active involvement of the region (alongside others) in this movement. In an exciting new research endeavor, Kristopher Velasco is collecting data on anti-SOGI funding flows that will hopefully provide sharper answers in the future.

17 This explains our finding that the websites of the organizations we analyzed in the Russian context were all strikingly similar.

18 Elena Mizulina is the mother of Ekaterina Mizulina, director of the League for Safe Internet.

19 In its CitizenGo exposé, WikiLeaks revealed that Yakunina was the only participant at the Madrid WCF who received "super-VIP" treatment at the hotel (WikiLeaks 2021).

20 The court case has been appealed and is now awaiting its second and third degree of trial.

21 President Peña Nieto of Mexico signed an initiative to amend the Mexican constitution in May of that year. It sought to legalize same-sex marriage at the federal level, though its legal status still varies state by state in Mexico.

CHAPTER 4. STATES AND INTERNATIONAL ORGANIZATIONS

1 Indeed, sometimes this symbolic gesture can be hollow and counterproductive (Thiel 2020, 202).

2 Technically, the Vatican is a state. In terms of activism, however, the Holy See, which holds consultative status at the UN, functions more like an IO. We also treat the Russian Orthodox Church (ROC) as an IO case study even though it is, strictly speaking, a national organization. Its conspicuous portfolio of international activities justifies considering it as parallel to the Vatican for the purpose of the analysis here. The IOs and states this chapter considers are all implicated in what Daniel Philpott identified as the process of "unravelling the Westphalian state" (Philpott 2004).

3 The eight-stripe rainbow flag—designed by activist Gilbert Baker and others to reflect nature and unify a community in pride—first flew in San Francisco, California, in 1978 and is now widely recognized the world over. There are now also more inclusive variations of the Pride flag that, for example, make explicit statements on trans rights and racial justice.

4 Cooper-Cunningham (2021) refers to a state's use of traditional values arguments—which he links directly to political homophobia—in foreign policy or international political projects as *heteronormative internationalism*. He traces the concept to Russia, which he argues has used heteronormative internationalism to position itself against a "West" that it portrays as space of moral decay and sexual decadence.

5 The ruling (with respect to Article 11 of the European Convention of Human Rights) followed Warsaw's ban of an Equality March (similar to a Pride march) in 2005. The court has heard similar cases and issued near-identical rulings levied at Russia.

6 It is important to note that SOGI-rights-affirmative theology does exist inside Orthodoxy (see Papanikolaou 2017). Even inside the Russian Orthodox Church,

the range of attitudes to homosexuality is more varied than the official line (see Hill 2019).

7 The Social Doctrine ends its discussion of sexuality and gender identity with medical detail concerning intersex people: "Transsexuality should be distinguished from the wrong identification of the sex in one's infancy as a result of doctors' mistake caused by a pathological development of sexual characteristics. The surgical correction in this case is not a change of sex" (Social Doctrine 2000).

8 The Catholic, Protestant, and Orthodox Churches, as a rule, recognize baptisms conducted inside the other denomination and do not demand that an adult who is converting get baptized in the chosen creed once again.

9 This assessment is based on the fieldnotes of personal interaction between Stoeckl and representatives of the Department of External Church Relations of the Moscow Patriarchate. It is confirmed by programs, available on the internet, of seminars the ECLJ held with Russian participation (ECLJ 2018, 2012).

CHAPTER 5. STRATEGIES AND CLAIMS

1 The outcome is somewhat ironic given that colonial powers were often responsible for exporting the sodomy laws that criminalized homosexuality in the first place (Han and O'Mahoney 2014), an inconvenient truth ignored by moral conservatives. That history is not widely internalized, however—at least not to the degree that it has dissuaded moral conservative activists from accusing SOGI rights activists of colonizing traditionalist contexts with decadent progressive ideas (Waites 2019).

2 In the Russian document, the authority of the source was explained on the very first page, which described the World Congress of Families as "the most representative international association of supporters of family values, including hundreds of organizations from 80 countries" (FamilyPolicy.ru 2019).

3 The centrality of demography in the WCF's moral conservative narrative is made evident by the fact that several national organizations that spring from the WCF are built around this theme: the Russian Demographic Society, founded by the WCF's co-founder Anatoly Antonov; the Georgian Demographic Society, founded by Levan Vazadse, a Georgian businessman and host of the WCF Congress in Tbilisi; and the French Demographic Society, founded by the French WCF attendee Fabrice Sorlin.

4 Pro-natalism among right-wing political parties is one way to articulate an anti-immigration platform, with the explicitly voiced demand that autochthonous populations—not immigrant families—should be having children.

5 Masha Gessen gives a good account of the dynamics created at such congresses in their report from the WCF summit in Tbilisi in 2017 (Gessen 2017).

6 While the issue of race is often center stage in the United States—for example, in conservative debates about Black Lives Matter protests or those that consider critical race theory Marxist—the moral conservatives we observed put race very

much in the background at transnational meetings, which may be significant, tactical, or both.

7 This part of the narrative is reconstructed from fieldnotes taken during the World Congress of Families in Tbilisi (2016), a published source in Russian (AVA 2014), and the document "Religious Persecution in Russia by Soviet Marxists of the 20th Century and by Liberal LGBT Activists of the 21st Century," authored by Komov and included in the material from CitizenGo archives that WikiLeaks revealed under the title "The Intolerance Network" in 2021 (Komov 2015).

8 The rehabilitation of Stalin as a savior of the Russian people is commonplace among Russian conservatives. It derives not only from the fact that Stalin's Soviet Union defeated Nazi Germany, but also that Stalin, in 1941, revoked the extreme anti-religious policies of the 1920s and 1930s and permitted the election of a new patriarch and the reopening of churches, albeit under the strict control of the state and secret services (Roccucci 2011).

CHAPTER 6. VENUES

1 We pointed out the complexity inherent in these divisions in the Introduction and Chapter 3, in that PMC actors opposing SOGI rights span all these regions.

2 In chapter 5, we explained the thinking behind this extended agenda embedded in the moral conservative narrative.

3 All the resolutions are accessible through the United Nations Official Document System (UN ODS 2023).

4 Because the list of topics moral conservative actors draw from to frame their resistance to SOGI rights is so wide, we offer only exemplary anti-SOGI resolutions in that domain.

5 The contextualist approach to human rights was corroborated with the creation of regional rights catalogues, such as the African Charter on Human and Peoples' Rights (1981); the Universal Islamic Declaration of Human Rights, adopted by the Islamic Council of Europe in 1981; the Cairo Declaration of Human Rights in Islam adopted 1990 by the Organization of Islamic Cooperation (OIC); and the Arab Charter on Human Rights, adopted in 1994.

6 It is also common for pro-SOGI resolutions to be written primarily by one country (e.g., France) and brought forward by others (e.g., Argentina and Brazil) to create optics that dislodge the charge that SOGI rights are Western rights.

7 The ADF calls those cases it has won legacy cases. Had they won *Ladele v. United Kingdom*, it would have become model litigation for them.

8 The SOGI movement also uses strategic litigation. During our observations at ILGA Europe annual meetings (especially in the Hague in 2010), we observed panels on a comprehensive strategy at the European level to promote LGBTI cases at the ECtHR and at the European Court of Justice (cf. ILGA Europe n.d.). Indeed, in some instances, ILGA is keen on supporting cases in countries where they are unlikely to succeed in order to bring the case to the higher, European

298 | NOTES

level. This strategy has a successful history, for example the decriminalization of homosexuality in twenty-three jurisdictions in just over twenty years (chapter 1).

9 Interestingly, such strategies have also been used by trans-exclusionary radical feminists who may not identify with the moral conservative movement otherwise.

10 Ghiletchi has been identified as involved in Agenda Europe (Datta 2018b) (see chapter 3).

11 Also inherent in the text of this quote is the diplomatic language that is more common at the Council of Europe institutions, compared to the more polarized, zero-sum language of the UN.

12 The section on internet governance in PACE is reproduced from Stoeckl and Uzlaner (2022).

13 In 2019, Shlegel reportedly left Russia and took German citizenship (Meduza 2019).

14 The ongoing corruption case against Volontè, which is currently in the appeal phase, dates back to his work as a member of the European People's Party Group. The court found that he accepted bribes from the government of Azerbaijan (La Repubblica 2021; ESI 2012).

15 This list is compiled from the official member page of Luca Volontè at the Council of Europe PACE website (PACE Members 2023).

CHAPTER 7. MOVEMENT INTERACTION

1 It should be emphasized that this does not suggest strategies and instruments are identical. For example, moral conservative pro-life extremists in the United States have been more prone to use radical and violent tactics—such as assault, arson, and murders at abortion clinics—than their pro-choice rivals. We thank Sabine Lang for suggesting this clarification. Perception is another matter, however, and moral conservative groups like HazteOír have also described SOGI activists' tactics as amounting to violence—for example, the vandalism of an anti-trans bus. We thank David Paternotte for emphasizing this complexity.

2 We are grateful to David Paternotte for pointing this out.

3 Fundraising, which included private campaigns for charitable giving and international funding from the Open Society Foundations, was coordinated by KPH, Wiara i Tęcza and the Tolerado Association.

4 The conference also informed much of the qualitative analysis in this section.

5 This is our general, summarized retelling of the most-agreed-upon features of these debates.

6 In this case, the activist's use of "pink-washing" refers to governments that want to use SOGI rights as a way to signal modernity to their international communities.

7 An interesting case of the power of such frames, as well as the power of their reversal, plays out in the story of an individual Californian family, the Montgomerys. Wendy Montgomery, who mobilized to canvass in support of Proposition 8 (meaning she opposed same-sex marriage), said she was motivated by the family values frame: "One of the core tenets we believe in as Mormons is that

the *family is eternal in nature.* Our *family units are really strong*" (Donaldson James 2013). Yet when her own son later came out as gay, she both reconsidered her position and accepted her son, a shift she justified using the same language that "families are forever." That phrase also became the title of a film in which she appeared as an advocate for gay people, again centered on the importance of the family, but in a wholly new way.

8 *United States v. Windsor* determined Section 3 of the Defense of Marriage Act to be unconstitutional, paving the way for *Obergefell v. Hodges*, which two years later struck down all remaining state bans on marriage equality.

9 According to the logic of the *Advocate*, "One thing we know from 2013 is that no matter the dedication of our activists, in the end we are often faced with a straight person who decides our fate. Will the nine straight people seated on the Supreme Court—six of whom who are Roman Catholic—ever cast a far-reaching ruling that makes marriage equality legal in all 50 states?" (Grindley 2013).

10 We wish to highlight, however, the similar contested debates around the use of the family narrative in feminist organizing. For example, the critique of policies of joint taxation (like "*Ehegattensplitting*" in Germany) that discriminate against the women in the heterosexual families.

11 There are also comparatively better data given the organization's higher level of funding and large staff, for example, when compared to its ILGA parent organization based in Geneva.

12 The first occurrences were in 2002, both of which were reporting on the governments of Poland and Austria reinforcing "family dignity" and "family in the traditional sense" as in contrast to LGBTI lifestyles.

13 Since the *Euro-Letter* is a newsletter focused on reporting important issues related to ILGA-Europe members, and the European SOGI rights community more broadly, most coded texts are discussing national and transnational policy developments. This would help explain the higher proportion of reactionary references overall, since the core purpose of the *Euro-Letter* is to report on events, not to add ILGA-Europe commentary (though certainly some commentary is included).

CONCLUSION

1 It is noteworthy that, in years past, Kirill also blamed the rise of ISIS in the Middle East on Pride parades and the increasing global acceptance of gay and lesbian people (Hall 2016).

2 This position has resonated. When a BBC reporter asked a Russian citizen on her views about the war ("Defend it from what? From whom?") she replied: "Russia's being attacked on all fronts, including with LGBT propaganda. They're trying to force this upon us. We reject these alien ideas. We embrace Russian values. It's hard for me to explain this in words. I just feel it" (Rosenberg 2022).

3 IR-scholar Dan Nexon (2021) summarized the same concern in his tweets: "I don't think the IR community really groks the degree that LGBTQ+ rights are implicated in contestation over 'liberal international order.'"

4 The prose in the next two paragraphs is adapted from Ayoub (2018).

5 Ghana may take a different course on decriminalization, with some members of parliament having proposed the "Promotion of Proper Human Sexual Rights and Ghanaian Family Values" Bill in 2021, which would extend colonial-era laws by proscribing and criminalizing any advocacy of LGBT identity (Reid 2021).

6 Prime Minister Lee later said, "Let me reassure everyone that in handling the issue, the government will continue to uphold families as the basic building blocks of society. We will keep our policies on family and marriage unchanged and maintain the prevailing norms and social values of our society" (Paddock 2022).

7 We are grateful to Jennifer Dixon and Zoltán Búzás for wise council on this paragraph.

8 Even if it may affirm the power of human rights norms, given that both movement strands of the helix take the time to engage with them (cf. Sikkink 2018).

9 We say this reflecting on our own positionality as authors, and the challenges we sometimes faced in this project, to try and articulate a conservative narrative that we felt wholly at odds with personally.

10 We thank Sabine Lang for pointing this out.

ACKNOWLEDGMENTS

1 For more information on the Postsecular Conflicts Research Project (grant nr. ERC-STG-2015–676804), see POSEC 2022.

REFERENCES

Acharya, Amitav. 2004. "How Ideas Spread: Whose Norms Matter? Norm Localization and Institutional Change in Asian Regionalism." *International Organization* 58 (2): 239–75.

Adamczyk, Amy. 2017. *Cross-National Public Opinion about Homosexuality: Examining Attitudes across the Globe*. Berkeley: University of California Press.

Adamiak, Elżbieta. 2021. "Imaginations about Gender and LGBTI and Their Function in Ideological Discourses in Poland Today." Zentrum Für Osteuropa- Und Internationale Studien, accessed August 14, 2022. www.zois-berlin.de.

ADF International. 2019. "German Homeschoolers Appeal to Top European Court." *ADF International*, April 8, 2019. https://adfinternational.org.

———. 2022a. "Finnish MP Wins on All Charges in Major Free Speech Trial." *ADF International*, March 30, 2022. https://adfinternational.org.

———. 2022b. "Our Legacy Cases." *ADF International*, accessed April 16, 2022. https://adfinternational.org.

Agenda Europe Network. 2018. "Agenda Europe Position Regarding EPFPD Book on Agenda Europe." Accessed November 10, 2021. www.agendaeurope.org.

Allen, J. 1996. *Growing Up Gay: New Zealand Men Tell Their Stories*. Auckland: Godwit Publishing.

Allport, Gordon W. 1954. *The Nature of Prejudice*. Reading, MA: Addison-Wesley.

Alrababa'h, Ala', William Marble, Salma Mousa, and Alexandra A. Siegel. 2021. "Can Exposure to Celebrities Reduce Prejudice? The Effect of Mohamed Salah on Islamophobic Behaviors and Attitudes." *American Political Science Review* 115 (4): 1111–28.

Alston, Philip, and Ryan Goodman. 2012. *International Human Rights*. Oxford: Oxford University Press.

Altman, Dennis. 2017. "Conservatives Prevail to Hold Back the Tide on Same-Sex Marriage." *Conversation*, August 7, 2017. https://theconversation.com.

Anderson, Benedict. 1983. *Imagined Communities: Reflections on the Origin and Speed of Nationalism*. Brooklyn, NY: Verso.

Anderson, John. 2015. *Conservative Christian Politics in Russia and the United States: Dreaming of Christian Nations*. London: Routledge.

Annicchino, Pasquale. 2011. "Winning the Battle by Losing the War: The *Lautsi* case and the Holy Alliance between American Conservative Evangelicals, the Russian Orthodox Church, and the Vatican to Reshape European Identity." *Religion and Human Rights* (6): 213–19.

———. 2018a. "The Geopolitics of Transnational Law and Religion." In *The Conscience Wars: Rethinking the Balance between Religion and Equality*, edited by Susanna Mancini and Michel Rosenfeld, 258–74. Cambridge: Cambridge University Press.

———. 2018b. "Sovranismo religioso." *Il Foglio*, September 17, 2017. www.ilfoglio.it.

Armstrong, Elizabeth, and Mary Bernstein. 2008. "Culture, Power, and Institutions: A Multi-Institutional Politics Approach to Social Movements." Sociological Theory 26 (1): 74–99.

AVA. 2014. "Aleksej Komov v Kishinyove: Pora postavit' poslednuyu tochku v otnoshenii k kommunizmu" *AVA News Portal Moldova*, April 12, 2014. https://ava.md.

Ayoub, Phillip M. 2013. "Cooperative Transnationalism in Contemporary Europe: Europeanization and Political Opportunities for LGBT Mobilization in the European Union." *European Political Science Review* 5 (2): 279–310.

———. 2014. "With Arms Wide Shut: Threat Perception, Norm Reception, and Mobilized Resistance to LGBT Rights." *Journal of Human Rights* 13 (3): 337–62.

———. 2016. *When States Come Out: Europe's Sexual Minorities and the Politics of Visibility*. Cambridge: Cambridge University Press.

———. 2018. "Protean Power in Movement: Navigating Uncertainty in the LGBT Rights Revolution." In *Power in Uncertainty: Exploring the Unexpected in World Politics*, edited by Peter J. Katzenstein and Lucia Seybert. Cambridge: Cambridge University Press.

———. 2019a. "Intersectional and Transnational Coalitions during Times of Crisis: The European LGBTI Movement." *Social Politics: International Studies in Gender, State & Society* 26 (1): 1–29.

———. 2019b. "The Trump Administration Will Push to Decriminalize Homosexuality Worldwide. Surprised? Here's Why." *Washington Post*, February 27, 2019. www.washingtonpost.com.

Ayoub, Phillip M., and Olga Brzezińska. 2015. "Caught in a Web?: The Internet and the Deterritorialization of LGBT Activism." In *The Ashgate Research Companion to Lesbian and Gay Activism*, edited by David Paternotte and Manon Tremblay, 225–43. Farnham, UK: Ashgate.

Ayoub, Phillip M., and Agnès Chetaille. 2020. "Movement/Countermovement Interaction and Instrumental Framing in a Multi-Level World: Rooting Polish Lesbian and Gay Activism." *Social Movement Studies* 19 (1): 21–37.

Ayoub, Phillip M., and Jeremiah Garretson. 2017. "Getting the Message Out: Media Context and Global Changes in Attitudes Toward Homosexuality." *Comparative Political Studies* 50 (8): 1055–85.

Ayoub, Phillip M., and Douglas Page. 2019. "When Do Opponents of Gay Rights Mobilize? Explaining Political Participation in Times of Backlash against Liberalism." *Political Research Quarterly* 73 (3): 696–713.

Ayoub, Phillip M., and David Paternotte. 2016. "L'International Lesbian and Gay Association (ILGA) et l'expansion du militantisme LGBT dans une Europe unifiée." *Critique internationale* (70): 55–70.

———. 2019. "Europe and LGBT Rights: A Conflicted Relationship." In *The Oxford Handbook of Global LGBT and Sexual Diversity Politics*, edited by Michael J. Bosia, Sandra M. McEvoy, and Momin Rahman, 153–67. Oxford: Oxford University Press.

Ayoub, Phillip M., and David Paternotte, eds. 2014. *LGBT Activism and the Making of Europe*. London: Palgrave Macmillan.

Bahgat, Farah. 2021. "German Catholic Churches to Bless Same-Sex Couples." *Deutsche Welle*, May 9, 2021. www.dw.com.

Balzer, Carsten, and Jan Simon Hutta. 2014. "Trans Networking in the European Vortex: Between Advocacy and Grassroots Politics." In *LGBT Activism and the Making of Europe: A Rainbow Europe?*, edited by Phillip M. Ayoub and David Paternotte, 171–92. Basingstoke, UK: Palgrave.

Banaszak, Lee Ann. 2009. *The Women's Movement Inside and Outside the State*. Illustrated edition. Cambridge: Cambridge University Press.

Bandy, Joe, and Jackie Smith, eds. 2004. *Coalitions across Borders: Transnational Protest and the Neoliberal Order*. Lanham, MD: Rowman and Littlefield.

Barthélemy, Hélène. 2018. "How the World Congress of Families Serves Russian Orthodox Political Interests." *Southern Poverty Law Center*, May 16, 2018. www.splcenter.org.

Bassi, Serena, and Greta LaFleur, eds. 2022. "Trans-Exclusionary Feminisims and the Global New Right." Special issue, *TSQ: Transgender Studies Quarterly* 9 (3).

Bateson, Ian. 2016. "The 'New Ukraine' Is Failing Us, LGBT Activists Say." *Guardian*, March 31, 2016. www.theguardian.com.

BBC News. 2013. "Russian Duma Backs Adoption Ban on Foreign Gay Couples." June 18, 2013. www.bbc.com/.

———. 2015. "Ukraine Passes Anti-Discrimination Law." November 12, 2015. www.bbc.com.

Beachy, Robert. 2014. *Gay Berlin: Birthplace of a Modern Identity*. New York: Knopf Doubleday.

Belarus. 2015. "Group of Friends of the Family." *United Nations Department of Economic and Social Affairs*, February 18, 2015. https://sdgs.un.org.

Beltrán, William, and Sian Creely. 2018. "Pentecostals, Gender Ideology and the Peace Plebiscite: Colombia 2016." *Religions* 9 (12): 418.

Benford, Robert D. 1997. "An Insider's Critique of the Social Movement Framing Perspective." *Sociological Inquiry* 67 (4): 409–30.

Benford, Robert D., and David A. Snow. 1999. "Alternative Types of Cross-National Diffusion in the Social Movement Arena." In *Social Movements in a Globalizing World*, edited by Donatella della Porta, Hanspeter Kriesi, and Dieter Rucht, 23–29. New York: St. Martin's Press.

———. 2000. "Framing Processes and Social Movements: An Overview and Assessment." *Annual Review of Sociology* 26: 611–39.

Benne, Robert. 2015. "How a Decadent Culture Makes Me Think Like Sorokin." *First Things* January 19, 2015. www.firstthings.com.

Beger, Nico J. 2004. *Tensions in the Struggle for Sexual Minority Rights in Europe: Que(e)rying Political Practices*. Manchester, UK: Manchester University Press.

Berman, Morris. 2012. "Pitirim Sorokin." *Dark Ages America* (blog), April 28, 2012. http://morrisberman.blogspot.co.at.

Bettiza, Gregorio. 2019. *Finding Faith in Foreign Policy: Religion and American Diplomacy in a Postsecular World*. New York: Oxford University Press.

Bettiza, Gregorio, and David Lewis. 2020. "Authoritarian Powers and Norm Contestation in the Liberal International Order: Theorizing the Power Politics of Ideas and Identity." *Journal of Global Security Studies* 5 (4): 559–77.

Biebricher, Thomas. 2018. *Geistig-moralische Wende: Die Erschöpfung des deutschen Konservatismus*. Berlin: Matthes and Seitz.

Binnie, Jon. 2004. *The Globalization of Sexuality*. London: Sage.

Bishin, Benjamin G., Justin Freebourn, and Paul Teten. 2020. "The Power of Equality? Polarization and Collective Mis-Representation on Gay Rights in Congress, 1989–2019." *Political Research Quarterly* 62 (2): 355–65.

Bishin, Benjamin, Thomas J. Hayes, Matthew B. Incantalupo, and Charles Anthony Smith. 2021. *Elite-Led Mobilization and Gay Rights: Dispelling the Myth of Mass Opinion Backlash*. Ann Arbor: University of Michigan Press.

Blackmore, Elena, and Bec Sanderson. 2017. "The Framing Equality Toolkit." ILGA-Europe and PIRC. www.ilga-europe.org/files/uploads/2022/06/Framing-Equality-Toolkit-1.pdf.

Bloomfield, Alan and Shirley Scott, eds. 2017. Norm Antipreneurs and the Politics of Resistance to Global Normative Change, London: Routledge Press.

Blue, Miranda. 2013. "Globalizing Homophobia, Part 4: The World Congress of Families and Russia's 'Christian Saviors.'" *RightWingWatch*, October 4, 2013. www.rightwingwatch.org.

Blumenfeld, Warren J., and Diane Christine Raymond. 1988. *Looking at Gay and Lesbian Life*. Boston: Beacon Press.

Bob, Clifford. 2012. *The Global Right Wing and the Clash of World Politics*. Cambridge: Cambridge University Press.

———. 2019. *Rights as Weapons: Instruments of Conflict, Tools of Power*. Princeton: Princeton University Press.

Bourne, Lisa. 2017. "Pope Francis Guts Vatican Pro-life Academy of Members Chosen by St. John Paul II." *Life Site News*, June 15, 2017. www.lifesitenews.com.

Bracke, Sarah. 2012. "From 'Saving Women' to 'Saving Gays': Rescue Narratives and Their Dis/Continuities." *European Journal of Women's Studies* 19 (2): 237–52.

Bracke, Sarah, and Luis Manuel Hernández Aguilar. 2020. "'They Love Death as We Love Life': The 'Muslim Question' and the Biopolitics of Replacement." *British Journal of Sociology* 71 (4): 680–701.

Brooks, Stephen G., and William Curti Wohlforth. 2008. *World Out of Balance*. Princeton, NJ: Princeton University Press.

Brown, Harold O. J. 1996. *The Sensate Culture*. Dallas, TX: Word Pub.

Brown, Wendy. 2019. *In the Ruins of Neoliberalism: The Rise of Antidemocratic Politics in the West*. New York: Columbia University Press.

Bruce, Steven. 2002. *God is Dead*. Oxford: Blackwell.

Bruni, Frank. 2015. "Gay and Marked for Death." *New York Times*, August 22, 2015. www.nytimes.com.

Brumby, Edward. 1999. "What Is in a Name: Why the European Same-Sex Partnership Acts Create a Valid Marital Relationship." *Georgia Journal of International and Comparative Law* (28): 145–69.

Brunstetter, Daniel, and Arturo Jimenez-Bacardi. 2015. "Clashing Over Drones: The Legal and Normative Gap Between the United States and the Human Rights Community." *International Journal of Human Rights* 19 (2): 176–98.

Burack, Cynthia. 2008. *Sin, Sex, and Democracy: Antigay Rhetoric and the Christian Right*. Albany, NY: SUNY Press.

———. 2014. *Tough Love: Sexuality, Compassion, and the Christian Right*. Albany, NY: SUNY Press.

———. 2017. "Top Down, Bottom Up, or Meeting in the Middle? The U.S. Government in International LGBTQ Human Rights Advocacy." In *LGBTQ Politics: A Critical Reader*, edited by Marla Brettschneider, Susan Burgess, and Christine Keating, 477–92. New York: New York University Press.

———. 2018. *Because We Are Human: Contesting US Support for Gender and Sexuality Human Rights Abroad*. Albany, NY: SUNY Press.

———. 2022. *How Trump and the Christian Right Saved LGBTI Human Rights*. Albany, NY: SUNY Press.

Burgess, John P. 2017. *Holy Rus': The Rebirth of Orthodoxy in the New Russia*. New Haven, CT: Yale University Press.

Buss, Doris E. 1998. "Robes, Relics and Rights: The Vatican and the Beijing Conference on Women." *Social & Legal Studies* 7 (3): 339–63.

Buss, Doris, and Didi Herman. 2003. *Globalizing Family Values: The Christian Right in International Politics*. Minneapolis: University of Minnesota Press.

Butler, Jennifer. 2000. "For Faith and Family: Christian Right Advocacy at the United Nations." *Public Eye* 9 (2/3). www.politicalresearch.org.

Butler, Judith. 2021. "Why Is the Idea of 'Gender' Provoking Backlash the World Over?" *Guardian*, October 23, 2021. www.theguardian.com.

Buyantueva, Radzhana. 2018. "LGBT Rights Activism and Homophobia in Russia." *Journal of Homosexuality* 65 (4): 456–83.

Búzás, Zoltán I. 2021. "Racism and Antiracism in the Liberal International Order." *International Organization* 75 (2): 440–63.

Buzogány, Aron, and Mihai Varga. 2018. "The Ideational Foundations of the Illiberal Backlash in Central and Eastern Europe: The Case of Hungary." *Review of International Political Economy* 25 (6): 811–28.

Byrnes, Timothy A., and Peter J. Katzenstein. 2006. *Religion in an Expanding Europe*. Cambridge: Cambridge University Press.

C-Fam. 2015. "Submission to the Office of the High Commissioner for Human Rights from the Center for Family and Human Rights (C-Fam)." *Office of the High Commissioner of Human Rights*, October 28, 2015. www.ohchr.org.

Calvinist International. 2013. "An Interview with Allan C. Carlson." *Calvinist International*, May 29, 2013. https://calvinistinternational.com.

Carlson, Allan. 1990. *The Swedish Experiment in Family Politics: The Myrdals and the Interwar Population Crisis*. New Brunswick, NJ: Transaction Publishers.

———. 1993. *From Cottage to Work Station: The Family's Search for Social Harmony in the Industrial Age*. San Francisco: Ignatius Press.

———. 2000. *The New Agrarian Mind: The Movement toward Decentralist Thought in Twentieth-Century America*. New Brunswick, NJ: Transaction Publishers.

———. 2005. "Sweden and the Failure of European Family Policy." *Society* 42 (6): 41–46.

———. 2007. "Deconstruction of Marriage: The Swedish Case." *San Diego Law Review* 44 (1): 153–72.

———. 2015. "As Goes Sweden." *Touchstone: A Journal of Mere Christianity* (March/April 2015). www.touchstonemag.com.

Carlson, Allan C., and Paul T. Mero. 2005. *The Natural Family: A Manifesto*. Rockford, IL: The Howard Center for Family, Religion and Society and the Sutherland Institute.

Carlson-Rainer, Elise. 2021. *From Pariah to Priority: How LGBTI Rights Became a Pillar of American and Swedish Foreign Policy*. Albany, NY: SUNY Press.

Carlson-Rainer, Elise, and Jacqueline Dufalla. 2016. "The Foreign Policy of LGBT Rights: Russia's Reaction and Resistance to US Policy." *Global Studies Journal* 9 (4): 9–17.

Carnac, Romain. 2020. "Imaginary Enemy, Real Wounds: Counter-Movements, 'Gender Theory,' and the French Catholic Church." *Social Movement Studies* 19 (1): 63–81.

Case, Mary Anne. 2016. "The Role of the Popes in the Invention of Complementarity and the Vatican's Anathematization of Gender." *Religion and Gender* 6 (March 2016): 155.

Cervini, Eric. 2020. *The Deviant's War: The Homosexual vs. the United States of America*. Illustrated edition. New York: Farrar Strauss and Giroux.

Chase, Anthony. 2016. "Human Rights Contestations: Sexual Orientation and Gender Identity." *International Journal of Human Rights* 20 (6): 703–23.

Chappel, James. 2018. *Catholic Modern: The Challenge of Totalitarianism and the Remaking of the Church*. Cambridge MA: Harvard University Press.

Chappel, Louise. 2006. "Contesting Women's Rights: Charting the Emergence of a Transnational Conservative Counter-network." *Global Society* 20 (4): 491–520.

Checkel, Jeffrey T. 2005. "International Institutions and Socialization in Europe: Introduction and Framework." *International Organization* 59 (4): 801–26.

Chetaille, Agnès. 2011. "Poland: Sovereignty and Sexuality in Post-Socialist Times." In *The Lesbian and Gay Movement and the State*, edited by Manon Tremblay, David Paternotte, and Carol Johnson, 119–34. Surrey, UK: Ashgate.

———. 2013. "Une 'autre Europe' homophobe ? L'Union Européenne, le nationalisme polonais et la sexualisation de la 'division Est/Ouest." *Raisons Politiques* 49(1): 119–140.

———. 2015. "The Paradoxes of a History without Transition: between the West and the Nation, Gay and Lesbian Mobilizations in Poland (1980–2010)." PhD diss., École des Hautes Études en Sciences Sociales.

Christian News Wire. 2014. "Planning for World Congress of Families VIII Suspended." Christian News Wire, March 25, 2014. www.christiannewswire.com.

Chryssavgis, John. "Do the Gospels Really Worry about Supporting the Nuclear Family?" *Public Orthodoxy*, August 12, 2022. https://publicorthodoxy.org.

CitizenGo. 2015. "Podderzhivayem Gruppu druzey sem'i v OON!" [We support the UN Family Friends Group!]. CitizenGo Russia, March 14, 2015. www.citizengo.org.

———. 2021. CitizenGo Campaigning Platform. CitizenGo Germany, accessed November 6, 2021. www.citizengo.org.

———. 2022a. "About Us." CitizenGo. www.citizengo.org.

———. 2022b. "Statement on the Fake News about CitizenGO, Russia, and the Invasion of Ukraine." CitizenGo. www.citizengo.org.

Clark, Amanda. 2023. "Uganda's Anti-Homosexuality Act Isn't Just a Human Rights Crisis—It's a Public Health Crisis. Wilson Center Africa Program, May 3, 2023. www.wilsoncenter.org.

Cloutier, David. 2019. "Catholic Clericalism as Patronage Network. Berkley Center for Religion, Peace and World Affairs Forum, September 25, 2019. https://berkleycenter.georgetown.edu.

Coffin, Alice, Evelyne Paradis, Gordan Bosanac, Gráinne Healy, Julia Ehrt, Matthew Hart, Nicky McIntyre, et al. 2017. "Using Family as a Frame in Social Justice Activism: A Guide for Activists and Funders in Europe." *Creative Commons*, accessed January 1, 2022. www.reclaimingfamilyvalues.eu.

Cohn, Carol. 2018. "The Perils of Mixing Masculinity and Missiles." *New York Times*, January 5, 2018. www.nytimes.com.

Congregation for the Doctrine of Faith. 1975. "Persona Humana. Declaration on Certain Questions Concerning Sexual Ethics." Accessed April 5, 2022. www.vatican.va.

———. 1986. "Letter to the Bishops of the Catholic Church on the Pastoral Care of Homosexual Persons." Accessed April 5, 2022. www.vatican.va.

———. 2003. "Considerations Regarding Proposals to Give Legal Recognition to Unions Between Homosexual Persons." Accessed January 21, 2022. www.vatican.va.

Cooley, Alexander, and Daniel Nexon. 2020. *Exit from Hegemony: The Unraveling of the American Global Order*. New York: Oxford University Press.

Cooper, Alex. 2022. "Pride Parades Caused Russia-Ukraine War, Says Russian Church Leader." *Advocate*, March 7, 2022. www.advocate.com.

Cooper, Melinda. 2017. *Family Values: Between Neoliberalism and the New Social Conservatism*. New York: Zone Books.

Cooper-Cunningham, Dean. 2021. "The International Politics of Sex: Visual Activism in Response to Russian State Homophobia." PhD diss., the University of Copenhagen.

Corrales, Javier. 2021. *The Politics of LGBTQ Rights Expansion in Latin America and the Caribbean*. Elements in Politics and Society in Latin America. Cambridge: Cambridge University Press.

Corrêa, Sonia, ed. 2020. Anti-Gender Politics in Latin America. Rio de Janeiro: Associação Brasileira Interdisciplinas de Aids [ABIA], 1–184.

Corrêa, Sonia, David Paternotte, and Roman Kuhar. 2018. "The Globalisation of Anti-Gender Campaigns." *Democracy and Society*, May 31, 2018. www.ips-journal.eu.

Corredor, Elizabeth S. 2019. Unpacking "Gender Ideology" and the Global Right's Anti-Gender Countermovement. Signs 44 (3): 613–38.

Council of Europe. 2014. *Sexual Orientation and Gender Identity Unit.* Accessed March 17, 2023. www.coe.int.

———. 2021a. "LGBTI Persons' Rights. Thematic Factsheet." *Department for the Execution of Judgments of the European Court of Human Rights.* September 2021. www.coe.int.

———. 2021b. "Council of Europe Body Concerned by the Non-implementation by Russia of its Priority Recommendations on Abolishing the So-Called 'Gay Propaganda' Legislation." *Council of Europe SOGI Newsroom*, October 5, 2021. www.coe.int.

CPAC Hungary. 2023. "United We Stand." www.cpachungary.com.

Crisp, Richard J., and Rhiannon N. Turner. 2009. "Can Imagined Interactions Produce Positive Perceptions?: Reducing Prejudice through Simulated Social Contact." *American Psychologist* 64 (4): 231–40.

Crossley, Nick. 2016. "Networks, Interaction, and Conflict: A Relational Sociology of Social Movements and Protest." In *Social Theory and Social Movements: Mutual Inspirations*, edited by Jochen Roose and Hella Dietz, 155–73. Wiesbaden: Springer Fachmedien.

Csardi, G., and T. Nepusz. 2006. "The Igraph Software Package for Complex Network Research." *InterJournal*, Complex Systems, 2006. https://igraph.org.

Cupać, Jelena, and Irem Ebetürk. 2020. "The Personal is Global Political: The Antifeminist Backlash in the United Nations. *British Journal of Politics and International Relations* 22 (4): 702–14.

———. 2022. "Competitive Mimicry: The Socialization of Antifeminist NGOs into the United Nations." Global Constitutionalism 11 (3): 379–400.

Curanović, Alicja. 2012. *The Religious Factor in Russia's Foreign Policy.* London: Routledge.

———. 2021. "The International Activity of Ordo Iuris: The Central European Actor and the Global Christian Right." *Religions* 12 (12): 1038.

Currier, Ashley. 2010. "Political Homophobia in Postcolonial Namibia." *Gender & Society* 24 (1): 110–129.

———. 2012. "The Aftermath of Decolonization: Gender and Sexual Dissidence in Postindependence Namibia." *Signs: Journal of Women in Culture and Society* 37 (2): 441–67.

Datta, Neil. 2018a. "Modern-Day Crusaders in Europe. Tradition, Family and Property: Analysis of a Transnational, Ultra-Conservative, Catholic-Inspired Influence Network." *Političke Perspektive: Časopis Za Istraživanje Politike* 8 (3): 69–105.

———. 2018b. "Restoring the Natural Order: The Religious Extremists' Vision to Mobilize European Societies against Human Rights on Sexuality and Reproduction." *EPFweb*, April 2018. www.epfweb.org/sites/default/files/2021-03/rtno__EN_epf_online_2021.pdf.

———. 2020. "Modern-day Crusaders in Europe. Tradition, Family and Property: Analysis of Transnational, Ultra-conservative, Catholic-inspired Influence Network." *EPFweb*, June 2020. www.epfweb.org/sites/default/files/2021-01/EPF%20TFP_EN_Oct30_0.pdf.

———. 2021. "Tip of the Iceberg: Religious Extremist Funders against Human Rights for Sexuality and Reproductive Health in Europe 2009–2018." *EPFweb*, June 2021. www.epfweb.org/sites/default/files/2021-08/Tip%20of%20the%20Iceberg%20August%202021%20Final.pdf.

Davie, Grace. 2002. *Europe—The Exceptional Case: Parameters of Faith in the Modern World*. London: Darton, Longmann and Todd.

de Búrca, Gráinne and Katharine Young. 2023. "The (mis)appropriation of human rights by the new global right: An introduction to the Symposium." International Journal of Constitutional Law 21 (1): 205–23.

Deitelhoff, Nicole and Lisbeth Zimmermann. 2019. "Norms under Challenge: Unpacking the Dynamics of Norm Robustness." *Journal of Global Security Studies*, 4 (1): 2–17.

Della Porta, Donatella. 2023. *Regressive Movements in Times of Emergency: The Protests Against Anti-Contagion Measures and Vaccination During the Covid-19 Pandemic*. Oxford, UK: Oxford University Press.

Den Dulk, Kevin R. 2006. "In Legal Culture, but Not of It: The Role of Cause Lawyers in Evangelical Legal Mobilization." In *Cause Lawyers and Social Movements*, edited by Austin Sarat and Stuart A. Scheingold, 197–219. Stanford: Stanford University Press.

Deneen, Patrick J. 2018. *Why Liberalism Failed*. New Haven, CT: Yale University Press.

Deutsch, Karl W. 1963. *The Nerves of Government: Models of Political Communication and Control*. New York: Free Press.

Diani, Mario, and Ann Mische. 2015. "Network Approaches and Social Movements." In *The Oxford Handbook of Social Movements*, edited by Donatella della Porta and Mario Diani. Oxford: Oxford University Press.

Dick, Hannah. 2021. "Advocating for the Right: Alliance Defending Freedom and the Rhetoric of Christian Persecution." *Feminist Legal Studies* 29 (3): 375–97.

Dixon, Jennifer. 2017. "Rhetorical Adaptation and Resistance to International Norms," Perspectives on Politics 15 (1): 83–99.

DoC Research Institute. 2021. "Christine de Marcellus Vollmer." *DoC Research Institute*, accessed November 10, 2021. https://doc-research.org.

Doerr, Nicole. 2017. "Bridging Language Barriers, Bonding against Immigrants: A Visual Case Study of Transnational Network Publics Created by Far-Right Activists in Europe." *Discourse & Society* 28 (1): 3–23.

Donadio, Rachel. 2013. "On Gay Priests, Pope Francis asks, 'Who am I to judge?'" *New York Times*, July 29, 2013. www.nytimes.com.

Donaldson James, Susan. 2013. "Mormon Mom Who Fought for Prop 8, Now Fights for Gay Son." *ABC News*, June 20, 2013. https://abcnews.go.com.

Dorf, Michael C., and Sidney Tarrow. 2014. "Strange Bedfellows: How an Anticipatory Countermovement Brought Same-Sex Marriage Into the Public Arena." *Law & Society Review* 39 (2): 449–73.

Dornblüth, Gesine. 2019. "Religiöse Recht in Russland un den USA." *Deutschlandfunk,* November 19, 2019. www.deutschlandfunk.de.

Douglas, Karen M., Joseph E. Uscinski, Robbie M. Sutton, Aleksandra Cichocka, Turkay Nefes, Chee Siang Ang, and Farzin Deravi. 2019. "Understanding Conspiracy Theories." *Political Psychology* 40 (1): 3–35.

Dowland, Seth. 2015. *Family Values and the Rise of the Christian Right.* Philadelphia: University of Pennsylvania Press.

Dreher, Rod. 2013. "Sorokin & Twilight of the Sensate." *American Conservative,* August 14, 2013. www.theamericanconservative.com.

———. 2015. "Terrorism & This Religious Century." *American Conservative,* November 18, 2015. www.theamericanconservative.com.

———. 2017. *The Benedict Option: A Strategy for Christians in a Post-Christian Nation.* New York: Sentinel.

———. 2020. *Live Not by Lies: A Manual for Christian Dissidents.* New York: Penguin Random House.

———. 2021. "Orban Protects Euro Christianity Better than the Pope." *American Conservative,* June 4, 2021. www.theamericanconservative.com.

———. 2022a. "Hungary & American Conservatives." *American Conservative,* February 3, 2022. www.theamericanconservative.com.

———. 2022b. "Pope Francis is Queering the Catholic Church." *American Conservative,* January 6, 2022. www.theamericanconservative.com.

———. 2022c. "War & Culture War: Kirill & LGBT." *American Conservative,* March 8, 2022. www.theamericanconservative.com.

Driessen, Michael Daniel. 2020. "The Surprisingly Catholic Roots of the European Union." *America Magazine,* April 23, 2020. www.americamagazine.org.

Dunne, Peter. 2020. "Transgender Rights in Europe: EU and Council of Europe Movements Towards Gender Identity Equality." In *Research Handbook on Gender, Sexuality and the Law,* edited by Chris Ashford and Alexander Maine, 134–47. Cheltenham: Edward Elgar.

Dwyer, James, and Shawn Peters. 2019. *Homeschooling: The History and Philosophy of a Controversial Practice.* Chicago: University of Chicago Press.

ECLJ. 2012. "Seminar on the Autonomy of the Church in the Recent Case-Law of the European Court of Human Rights and of the USA Supreme Court." European Center for Law and Justice, June 7, 2012. https://eclj.org.

———. 2016. "Side-Event: The Rights of Parents and Children Belonging to Religious Minorities." European Center for Law and Justice, January 26, 2016. https://eclj.org.

———. 2018. "New Challenges to the Freedom of Religion in Europe in the Light of the Recent Judgments of the ECHR." European Center for Law and Justice, December 13, 2018. https://eclj.org.

ECtHR. 2019. "Case of Wunderlich v. Germany (Application no. 18925/15)." European Court of Human Rights, Strasbourg, January 10, 2019.

Edenborg, Emil. 2022. "Putin's Anti-Gay War on Ukraine." *Boston Review,* March 14, 2022. https://bostonreview.net.

————. 2023. "Anti-Gender Politics as Discourse Coalitions: Russia's Domestic and International Promotion of 'Traditional Values.'" *Problems of Post-Communism* 70 (2): 175–84.

EFP. 2021. "Foundation Ordo Iuris Institute for Legal Culture." *Intelligence Briefing of the European Parliamentary Forum for Sexual & Reproductive Rights*, March 24, 2021. www.epfweb.org/sites/default/files/2021-03/EPF%20Ordo%20Iuris%20-%20EPF%20Intelligence%20brief.pdf.

Elie, Paul. 2020. "Pope Francis Supports Same-Sex Civil Unions, but the Church Must Do More." *New Yorker*, October 25, 2020. www.newyorker.com.

Elsner, Regina. 2021. "Orthodoxy, Gender, and the Istanbul Convention: Mapping the Discourse in Ukraine." ZOiS Report 2/2021, March 18, 2021. www.zois-berlin.de.

Encarnación, Omar G. 2016. *Out in the Periphery: Latin America's Gay Rights Revolution*. Oxford: Oxford University Press.

Engeli, Isabelle. 2020. "Gender and Sexuality Research in the Age of Populism: Lessons for Political Science." *European Political Science* 19 (2): 226–35.

Engeli, Isabelle, Christoffer Green-Pedersen, and Lars Thorup Larsen. 2012. *Morality Politics in Western Europe: Parties, Agendas, and Policy Choices*. Basingstoke, UK: Palgrave.

Enloe, Cynthia. 2007. *Globalization and Militarism: Feminists Make the Link*. 2nd ed. Lanham, MD: Rowman and Littlefield.

EPP. 2017. "2nd Transatlantic Summit: Political Network for Values Brings Together Key Political Players and Civil Society Leaders in the European Parliament." Group of the European People's Party, April 27, 2017. www.eppgroup.eu.

Ergas, Yasmine, Jazgul Kochkorova, Andrea Petö, and Natalia Tujillo. 2022. "Disputing 'Gender' in Academia: Illiberalism and the Politics of Knowledge." *Politics and Governance* 10 (4): 121–31.

ESI. 2012. "Caviar Diplomacy–How Azerbaidjan silenced the Council of Europe." *European Stability Initiative*, May 24, 2012 www.esiweb.org.

Eslen-Ziya, Hande, and Alberta Giorgi, eds. 2022. *Populism and Science in Europe*. London: Palgrave Macmillan.

Esping-Andersen, Gøsta. 1990. *The Three Worlds of Welfare Capitalism*. Princeton, NJ: Princeton University Press.

Essig, Laurie. 2014. "'Bury Their Hearts': Some Thoughts on the Specter of Homosexuality Haunting Russia." *QED: A Journal in GLBTQ Worldmaking* 1 (3): 39–58.

European Parliament. 2022. "Russia's War on Ukraine: Russia Ceases to Be a Member of the Council of Europe." *At a Glance News Service of the European Parliament*, March 8, 2022. www.europarl.europa.eu/RegData/etudes/ATAG/2022/729296/EPRS_ATA(2022)729296_EN.pdf.

EUvsDisinfo. 2022. "Kremlin Evokes Satan in support of the war." *EU vs Disinformation European External Action Service*, March 12, 2022. https://euvsdisinfo.eu.

Eydlin, Alexander. 2021. "EU-Gipfel: Ungarns LGBT-politik sorgt für streit in Brüssel." *Die Zeit*, June 25, 2021. www.zeit.de.

Faludi, Susan. 2006. *Backlash: The Undeclared War Against American Women*. Anniversary edition. New York: Crown.

Faludi, Susan, Shauna Shames, Jennifer M. Piscopo, and Denise M. Walsh. 2020. "A Conversation with Susan Faludi on Backlash, Trumpism, and #MeToo." *Signs: Journal of Women in Culture and Society* 45 (2): 336–45.

FamilyPolicy.ru. 2019. "Pravovoi Analiz Proekta Federal'nogo Zakona 'O Profilaktike Semeino-Bytovogo Nasiliia V Rossiiskoi Federatsii'" ["Legal Analysis of the Draft of the Federal Law 'On the Prevention of Domestic Violence in the Russian Federation'"]. Accessed February 18, 2020. http://www.familypolicy.ru/rep/rf-19-051-01.pdf.

Farris, Sara R. 2017. *In the Name of Women's Rights: The Rise of Femonationalism*. Durham, NC: Duke University Press.

Fassin, Éric. 2016. "Gender and the Problem of Universals: Catholic Mobilizations and Sexual Democracy in France." *Religion and Gender* 6 (2): 173–86.

Feder, J. Lester. 2017. "A Leading US Social Conservative Just Launched a Mission to Moscow for the Trump Era." *BuzzFeed*, February 7, 2017. www.buzzfeednews.com.

Fetner, Tina. 2008. *How the Religious Right Shaped Lesbian and Gay Activism*. Minneapolis: University of Minnesota Press.

Feyh, Kathleen E. 2015. "LGBTQ Oppression and Activism in Russia: An Interview with Igor Iasine." *QED: A Journal in GLBTQ Worldmaking* 2 (1): 100–108.

Fieschi, Catherine. 2019. "America's Europe delusions." *Chatham House*, July 26, 2019. www.chathamhouse.org.

Finnemore, Martha, and Kathryn Sikkink. 1998. "International Norm Dynamics and Political Change." *International Organization* 52 (4): 887–917.

———. 2001. "Taking Stock: The Constructivist Research Program in International Relations and Comparative Politics." *Annual Review of Political Science* (4): 391–416.

FitzGerald, Thomas E. 2004. *The Ecumenical Movement: An Introductory History*. Westport, CT: Praeger.

Flores, Andrew R., and Scott Barclay. 2016. "Backlash, Consensus, Legitimacy, or Polarization: The Effect of Same-Sex Marriage Policy on Mass Attitudes." *Political Research Quarterly* 69 (1): 43–56.

Fodor, Eva. 2021. *The Gender Regime of Anti-Liberal Hungary*. Cham, Switzerland: Palgrave Pivot.

Fokas, Effie. 2018. "Religious American and Secular European Courts?: A Study of Institutional Cross-Pollination." In *Peter L. Berger and the Sociology of Religion: 50 Years after The Sacred Canopy*, edited by Titus Hjelm, 135–55. London: Bloomsbury Academic.

Fokas, Effie, and Dia Anagnostou. 2019. "The 'Radiating Effects' of the ECtHR on Social Mobilizations around Religion and Education in Europe: An Analytical Frame." Supplement, *Politics and Religion* 12 (S1): S9–30.

Forest, Maxime. 2018. "Europeanizing vs. Nationalizing the Issue of Same-Sex Marriage in Central Europe: A Comparative Analysis of Framing Processes in Croatia, Hungary, Slovakia, and Slovenia." In *Global Perspectives on Same-Sex Marriage: A Neo-Institutional Approach*, edited by Bronwyn Winter, Maxime Forest and Réjane Sénac, 127–48. Cham, Switzerland: Springer.

Frank, David John, Bayliss J. Camp, and Steven A. Boutcher. 2010. "Worldwide Trends in the Criminal Regulation of Sex, 1945 to 2005." *American Sociological Review* 75 (6): 867–93.

Friedman, Elisabeth Jay. 2012. "Constructing 'The Same Rights with the Same Names': The Impact of Spanish Norm Diffusion on Marriage Equality in Argentina." *Latin American Politics and Society* 54 (4): 29–59.

Froese, Paul. 2008. *The Plot to Kill God: Findings from the Soviet Experiment in Secularization*. Berkeley: University of California Press.

Frum, David. 1989. "Cultural Clash on the Right." *Wall Street Journal*, June 2, 1989.

Furedi, Frank. 2018. *Populism and the European Culture Wars: The Conflict of Values Between Hungary and the EU*. London: Routledge.

Gaither, Milton. 2008a. *Homeschool: An American History*. New York: Palgrave Macmillan.

———. 2008b. "Why Homeschooling Happened." *Educational Horizons* 86 (4): 226–37.

Gallaher, Brandon. 2018. "Tangling with Orthodox Tradition in the Modern West: Natural Law, Homosexuality, and Living Tradition." *Wheel* (13/14): 50–63.

Gamm, Gerald, and Robert D. Putnam. 1999. "The Growth of Voluntary Associations in America, 1840–1940." *Journal of Interdisciplinary History*, 29 (4): 511–57.

Garbagnoli, Sara. 2016. "Against the Heresy of Immanence: Vatican's 'Gender' as a New Rhetorical Device Against the Denaturalization of the Sexual Order." *Religion and Gender* 6 (2): 187–204.

Garner, Ian (@irgarner). 2022. "Thread: While you were laughing at Putin for his JK Rowling schtick yesterday, he wasn't trolling you or trying to distract us with cancel culture arguments. He was laying out visions of a West trying to destroy history & Russia itself. Here's what he said - and why it matters," Twitter/X, March 6, 2022, 1:05pm, https://x.com/irgarner/status/1507705315084615684?s=20.

Garretson, Jeremiah J. 2015. "Exposure to the Lives of Lesbians and Gays and the Origin of Young People's Greater Support for Gay Rights." *International Journal of Public Opinion Research* 27 (2): 277–88.

———. 2018. *The Path to Gay Rights: How Activism and Coming Out Changed Public Opinion*. New York: New York University Press.

Gartrell, Nanette, Henny Bos, and Audrey Koh. 2018. "National Longitudinal Lesbian Family Study—Mental Health of Adult Offspring." *New England Journal of Medicine* 379 (3): 297–99.

Gessen, Masha. 2017. "Family Values. Mapping the Spread of Antigay Ideology." *Harper's Magazine*, February 20, 2017. https://harpers.org/.

Geva, Dorit. 2019. "*Non au gender*: Moral epistemics and French conservative strategies of distinction," *European Journal of Cultural and Political Sociology* 6 (4): 393–420.

Geva, Dorit, and Felipe G. Santos. 2021. "Europe's Far-Right Educational Projects and Their Vision for the International Order." *International Affairs* 97 (5): 1395–414.

GHEX. 2012. "Berlin Declaration." Global Home Education Exchange, accessed April 16, 2019. https://ghex.world/wp-content/uploads/2018/05/Berlin-Declaration-English.pdf.

———. 2016. "Rio Principles, Declared in Rio de Janeiro, March 2016." Global Home Education Exchange, accessed April 16, 2019. https://ghex.world.

———. 2018. "Global Home Education Conference 2018. St. Petersburg and Moscow, Russia." Global Home Education Exchange, accessed April 16, 2019. https://ghex.world.

———. 2019. "About the African Home Education Indaba." Global Home Education Exchange, accessed February 28, 2020. https://ghex.africa.

Glanzer, Perry L. 2002. *The Quest for Russia's Soul: Evangelicals and Moral Education in Post-Communist Russia.* Waco, TX: Baylor University Press.

Global Philanthropy Project. 2021. "Meet the Moment: A Call for Progressive Philanthropic Response to the Anti-Gender Movement." Global Philanthropy Project, accessed 22 May 2022. https://globalphilanthropyproject.org.

Gorski, Philip S., and Samuel L. Perry. 2022. *The Flag and the Cross. White Christian Nationalism and the Threat to American Democracy.* Oxford: Oxford University Press.

Graff, Agnieszka, and Elżbieta Korolczuk. 2022. *Anti-Gender Politics in the Populist Moment.* Abingdon, UK: Routledge.

Graham, Billy. 1965. *World Aflame.* Garden City, NY: Doubleday.

Graham, Erin, Charles Shipan, and Craig Volden. 2013. "The Diffusion of Policy Diffusion Research in Political Science." *British Journal of Political Science* 43 (3): 673–701.

Graham-Harrison, Emma. 2023. "War Brings Urgency to the Fight for LGBT Rights in Ukraine." *Guardian*, June 5, 2023. www.theguardian.com.

Graubart, Jonathan, and Arturo Jimenez-Bacardi. 2016. "David in Goliath's Citadel: Mobilizing the Security Council's Normative Power for Palestine." *European Journal of International Relations* 22 (1): 24–48.

Greeley, Andrew. 2002. *Religion in Europe at the End of the Second Millennium: A Sociological Profile.* New Brunswick, NJ: Transaction.

Greif, Tatjana. 2005. "The Social Status of Lesbian Women in Slovenia in the 1990s." In *Sexuality and Gender in Postcommunist Eastern Europe and Russia*, edited by Aleksandar Štulhofer, 149–69. New York: Haworth.

Griffiths, Craig. 2021. *The Ambivalence of Gay Liberation: Male Homosexual Politics in 1970s West Germany.* Oxford: Oxford University Press.

Grindley, Lucas. 2013. "*The Advocate*'s Person of the Year: Pope Francis," December 16, 2013. http://www.advocate.com.

Groves, Rory. 2020. "The New Agrarian: An interview with Allan C. Carlson." *The Grovestead*, December, 18 2020. https://thegrovestead.com/the-new-agrarian-an-interview-with-allan-c-carlson/.

Grzebalska, Weronika, Eszter Kováts, and Andrea Pető. 2017. "Gender as Symbolic Glue: How 'Gender' Became an Umbrella Term for the Rejection of the (Neo)Liberal Order." Hal-03232926. https://hal.archives-ouvertes.fr/hal-03232926.

Grzymała-Busse, Anna Maria. 2015. *Nations under God: How Churches Use Moral Authority to Influence Policy*. Princeton, NJ: Princeton University Press, 2015.

Guardian. 2022. "Putin says West Treating Russian Culture Like 'Cancelled' JK Rowling." March 25, 2022. www.theguardian.com.

———. 2023. "Vladimir Putin signs law banning gender changes in Russia." July 24, 2023. www.theguardian.com.

Guasti, Petra, and Lenka Bustikova. 2020. "In Europe's Closet: The Rights of Sexual Minorities in the Czech Republic and Slovakia." *East European Politics* 36 (2): 226–46.

Haas, Ernst. 1991. *When Knowledge Is Power: Three Models of Change in International Organizations*. Berkeley: University of California Press.

Hadler, Markus. 2012. "The Influence of World Societal Forces on Social Tolerance: A Time Comparative Study of Prejudices in 32 Countries." *Sociological Quarterly* 53 (2): 211–37.

Hadler, Markus, and Jonathan Symons. 2018. "World Society Divided: Divergent Trends in State Responses to Sexual Minorities and Their Reflection in Public Attitudes." *Social Forces* 96 (4): 1721–56.

Hafner-Burton, Emilie. 2013. *Making Human Rights a Reality*. Princeton, NJ: Princeton University Press.

Hajer, Maarten. 2006. "Doing Discourse Analysis: Coalitions, Practices, Meanings." In *Words Matter in Policy and Planning: Discourse Theory and Method in the Social Sciences*, edited by Margo Van Den Brink and Tamara Metze, 65–74. Utrecht: Netherlands Graduate School of Urban and Regional Research.

Hall, John. 2016. "The Head of the Russian Church Has Blamed the Rise of ISIS on 'Acceptance of Homosexuality.'" *Independent*, January 18, 2016. www.independent.co.uk/.

Hall, Nina. 2022. *Transnational Advocacy in the Digital Era: Think Global, Act Local*. Oxford: Oxford University Press.

Han, Enze, and Joseph O'Mahoney. 2014. "British Colonialism and the Criminalization of Homosexuality." *Cambridge Review of International Affairs* 27 (2): 268–88.

Hark, Sabine, and Paula-Irene Villa, eds. 2015. *Anti-Genderismus. Sexualität und Geschlecht als Schauplätze aktueller politischer Auseinandersetzungen*. Bielefeld, Germany: Transcript.

Harris, Adam. 2021. "The GOP's 'Critical Race Theory' Obsession." *Atlantic*, May 7, 2021. www.theatlantic.com.

Harrison, Brian F., and Melissa R. Michelson. 2017. *Listen, We Need to Talk: How to Change Attitudes about LGBT Rights*. New York: Oxford University Press.

Hayes, Jarrod. 2000. *Queer Nations: Marginal Sexualities in the Maghreb*. Chicago: University of Chicago Press.

Healey, Dan. 2017. *Russian Homophobia from Stalin to Sochi*. London: Bloomsbury.

Herman, Didi. 1996. "(Il)legitimate Minorities: The American Christian Right's Anti-Gay-Rights Discourse." *Journal of Law and Society* 23 (3): 346–63.

Hill, Caroline. 2016. "Framing 'Gay Propaganda': The Orthodox Church and Morality Politics in Russia." MA thesis, Uppsala University.

————. 2019. "Framing 'Gay Propaganda': Morality Policy Arguments and the Russian Orthodox Church." In *Contemporary Russian Conservatism: Problems, Paradoxes and Dangers*, edited by Mikhail Suslov and Dmitry Uzlaner, 379–97. Leiden: Brill.

Hillhouse, Raelynn. 1990. "Out of the Closet behind the Wall: Sexual Politics and Social Change in the GDR." *Slavic Review* 49 (4): 585–96.

Hodzic, Amir, and Natasa Bijelic. 2014. *Neo-Conservative Threats to Sexual and Reproductive Health & Rights in the European Union*. Zagreb: CESI.

Höhne, Florian, and Torsten Meireis. 2020. *Religion and Neo-Nationalism in Europe*. Baden-Baden: Nomos.

Holt, John, and Pat Farenga. 2003. *Teach Your Own: The John Holt Book of Homeschooling*. New York: Perseus Publishing.

Holzhacker, Ronald. 2012. "National and Transnational Strategies of LGBT Civil Society Organizations in Different Political Environments." *Comparative European Politics* 10(1): 23–47.

Horowitz, Jason. 2021. "Pope Sends More Mixed Messages on LGBTQ Rights." *New York Times*, July 6, 2021. www.nytimes.com.

Horsfjord, Vebjørn. 2017. "Negotiating Traditional Values: The Russian Orthodox Church at the United Nations Human Rights Council (UNHCR)." In *Religion, State and the United Nations*, edited by Anne Stensvold, 62–78. London: Routledge.

HSLDA. 2018. "Recordsetting Event Promotes Homeschooling in Russia and the World." Home School Legal Defense Association, May 30, 2018. https://hslda.org.

Htun, Mala, and S. Laurel Weldon. 2018. *The Logics of Gender Justice: State Action on Women's Rights around the World*. Cambridge: Cambridge University Press.

Huckerby, Jayne, and Sarah Knuckey. 2023. "Appropriation and the Rewriting of Rights." *International Journal of Constitutional Law* 21 (1): 243–65.

Hull, Kathleen, and Timothy Ortyl. 2019. "Conventional and Cutting-Edge: Definitions of Family in LGBT Communities." *Sexuality Research and Social Policy* 16 (1): 31–43.

Human Rights Watch. 2018. "No Support: Russia's 'Gay Propaganda' Law Imperils LGBT Youth." Human Rights Watch. www.hrw.org.

Hunter, James Davison. 1991. *Culture Wars: The Struggle to Define America*. New York: Basic Books.

————. 2016. "The Enduring Culture War." In *Is There a Culture War? A Dialogue on Values and American Public Life*, edited by James Davison Hunter and Alan Wolfe, 10–40. Washington, DC: Pew Research Center, Brookings Institution Press.

Hunter, James Davison, Carl Desportes Bowman, and Kyle Puetz. 2020. *Democracy in Dark Times: The 2020 IASC Survey of American Political Culture*. New York: Finstock and Tew.

Hunter, James Davison, and Alan Wolfe. 2006. *Is There a Culture War? A Dialogue on Values and American Public Life*. Washington, DC: Pew Research Center, Brookings Institution Press.

Iannacone, Laurenc R. 1994. "Why Strict Churches are Stronger." *American Journal of Sociology* 99 (5): 1180–211.

iFamNews. 2020. "Brian Brown: Brand New Website." *International Family News*, September 3, 2020. https://mailchi.mp.

ILGA. 2019. *Rainbow Europe*, accessed November 3, 2019. https://rainbow-europe.org.

ILGA Europe. n.d. "Strategic Litigation." ILGA Europe, accessed May 15, 2022. www .ilga-europe.org .

———. 2021. "How the EU Strategy on the Rights of the Child Will Protect LGBTI Kids." March 26, 2021. www.ilga-europe.org.

Ingebritsen, Christine. 2002. "Norm Entrepreneurs: Scandinavia's Role in World Politics." *Cooperation and Conflict* 37 (1): 11–23.

Inglehart, Ronald, and Pippa Norris. 2003. *Rising Tide*. Cambridge: Cambridge University Press.

Inkpen, Andrew C., and Eric W. K. Tsang. 2005. "Social Capital, Networks, and Knowledge Transfer." *Academy of Management Review* 30 (1): 146–65.

Interights. n.d. "Vejdeland and Others v. Sweden. Application no. 1813/07. Third-Party Intervention by the International Commission of Jurists and Interights." ILGA Europe, accessed May 15, 2022. www.ilga-europe.org/sites/default/files/Attachments /vejdeland_v_sweden_third_party_intervention.pdf.

IOF. 2017. "Prime Minister Viktor Orbán's Opening Speech at the World Congress of Families IX Budapest Family Summit, Hungary." International Organization for the Family, October 4, 2017. https://profam.org.

———. 2020. "How to organize a World Congress of Families Regional Event, Regional Conference, or Summit." International Organization for the Family, September 21, 2020. https://profam.org.

———. 2022. "Article 16 Initiative." International Organization for the Family, accessed April 20, 2022. https://profam.org.

Irvine, Jill A., Sabine Lang, and Celeste Montoya, eds. 2019. *Gendered Mobilizations and Intersectional Challenges: Contemporary Social Movements in Europe and North America*. London: ECPR Press.

Jackson, Julian. 2015. "The Homophile Movement." In *The Ashgate Research Companion to Lesbian and Gay Activism*, edited by David Paternotte and Manon Tremblay, 31–45. Farnham, UK: Ashgate.

Jacobs, Larry D. 2017. "Making Families Great Again—Natural Family, Humanity and Virtue in the Post-Modern World." *Hungarian Review* 8 (3): 17–28.

Jaschik, Scott. 2017. "Judith Butler on Being Attacked in Brazil." *Inside Higher Ed*, November 13, 2017. www.insidehighered.com.

Jensen, Erik. 2002. The Pink Triangle and Political Consciousness: Gays, Lesbians, and the Memory of Nazi Persecution. *Journal of the History of Sexuality*, 11 (1/2): 319–49.

Jensen, Steven L. B. 2017. *The Making of International Human Rights: The 1960s, Decolonization, and the Reconstruction of Global Values*. Cambridge: Cambridge University Press.

Joachim, Jutta, and Birgit Locher. 2008. *Transnational Activism in the UN and the EU: A Comparative Study*. New York: Routledge.

Johnson, Paul. 2013. *Homosexuality and the European Court of Human Rights*. London: Routledge.

———. 2022. "LGBT Rights at the Council of Europe and the European Court of Human Rights." In *Personal Identity and the European Court of Human Rights*, edited by Jill Marshall, 1–32. London: Routledge.

Johnson, Steven Ross. 2022. "Gay, Lesbian Adults Have Higher COVID Vaccination Rates." *US News & World Report*, February 3, 2022. www.usnews.com.

Jordaan, Eduard. 2016. "The African Group on the United Nations Human Rights Council: Shifting Geopolitics and the Liberal International Order." *African Affairs* 115 (460): 490–515.

Juhász, Borbála, and Andrea Pető. 2021. "'Kulturkampf' in Hungary about Reproductive Rights: Actors and Agenda." *Journal for Human Rights / Zeitschrift für Menschenrechte* 15 (1): 168–88.

Juroš, Tanja Vučković, Ivana Dobrotić, and Sunčica Flego. 2020. "The Rise of the Anti-Gender Movement in Croatia and the 2013 Marriage Referendum." *Europe-Asia Studies* 72 (9): 1523–53.

Kahle, D., and H. Wickham. 2013. "Ggmap: Spatial Visualization with Ggplot2." *R Journal*, 5 (1): 144–61. http://journal.r-project.org/archive/2013-1/kahle-wickham.pdf.

Kahlina, Katja. 2022. "Learning from "The East": Transnational Anti-Gender Mobilization and the West/East Divide." Culture Wars Papers, 21 (1): 1–5.

Kalm, Sara, and Anna Meeuwisse. 2020. "For Love and for Life: Emotional Dynamics at the World Congress of Families." *Global Discourse* 10 (2): 303–20.

Kane, Gillian. 2009. "Exporting 'Traditional Values'; The World Congress of Families." *Public Eye* 24 (1): 3–4. http://www.publiceye.org.

Kaoma, Kapya J. 2013. "The Marriage of Convenience. The U.S. Christian Right, African Christianity, and Postcolonial Politics of Sexual Identity." In *Global Homophobia: States, Movements, and the Politics of Oppression*, edited by Meredith L. Weiss and Michael J. Bosia, 75–102. Urbana: University of Illinois Press.

Katzenstein, Peter J. 1996a. "Introduction: Alternative Perspectives on National Security." In *The Culture of National Security: Norms and Identity in World Politics*, 1–32. New York: Columbia University Press.

———. 1996b. *The Culture of National Security*. New York: Columbia University Press.

Kaufmann, Eric. 2011. *Shall the Religious Inherit the Earth*. London: Profile Books.

Keck, Margaret, and Kathryn Sikkink. 1998. *Activists beyond Borders: Advocacy Networks in International Politics*. Ithaca, NY: Cornell University Press.

Kelaidis, Katherine. 2017. "Why is the Church Silent about Anti-LGBT+ Violence in Russia?" *Public Orthodoxy*, January 9, 2017. https://publicorthodoxy.org.

Kelleher, Patrick. 2021. "Kathleen Stock Helps Launch New So-Called University with 'Forbidden Courses' but No Actual Degrees." *Pink News*, November 8, 2021. www.thepinknews.com.

Kemper, Andreas. 2015. "Christlicher Fundamentalismus und neoliberal-nationalkonservative Ideologie am Beispiel der 'Alternative für Deutschland.'" In

Unheilige Allianz. Das Geflecht von christlichen Fundamentalisten und politischen Rechten am Beispiel des Widerstands gegen den Bildungsplan in Baden-Württemberg, edited by Lucie Billmann. Berlin: Rosa Luxemburg Stiftung.

———, ed. 2023. *Diskursatlas Antifeminismus*, accessed March 25, 2023. www.diskursatlas.de.

Kenarov, Dimiter. 2015. "Dashed Hopes in Gay Ukraine." *Foreign Policy*, January 19, 2015. http://foreignpolicy.com.

Khagram, Sanjeev, James Riker, and Kathryn Sikkink. 2002. *Restructuring World Politics: Transnational Social Movements, Networks, and Norms*. Minneapolis: University of Minnesota Press.

Kiel, Christina, and Jamie Campbell. 2019. "Intergovernmental Organizations and LGBT Issues." *Oxford Research Encyclopedia of Politics*, June 2019. www.academia.edu.

Klotz, Audie. 1995. *Norms in International Relations: The Struggle against Apartheid*. Ithaca, NY: Cornell University Press.

Knorre, Boris, and Alexandra Zasyad'ko. 2021. "Orthodox Anti-Ecumenism as an Element of the Mobilization Model of Society: Political Aspects of Religious Fundamentalism." *State, Religion and Church* 8 (2): 69–98.

Kollek, Talia, and Yaroslaw Rasputin. 2023. "'So-Called Gender Freedoms': What Are the Origins of Russian Transphobia?" *Russia.Post*, July 21, 2023. www.russiapost.info.

Kollman, Kelly. 2009. "European Institutions, Transnational Networks and National Same-Sex Unions Policy: When Soft Law Hits Harder." *Contemporary Politics* 15 (1): 37–53.

———. 2013. *The Same-Sex Unions Revolution in Western Democracies: International Norms and Domestic Policy Change*. Manchester, UK: Manchester University Press.

———. 2017. "Pioneering Marriage for Same-Sex Couples in the Netherlands." *Journal of European Public Policy* 24 (1): 100–118.

Kollman, Kelly, and Matthew Waites. 2009. "The Global Politics of Lesbian, Gay, Bisexual and Transgender Human Rights: An Introduction." *Contemporary Politics* 15 (1): 1–37.

Komov, Alexey. 2015. "Religious Persecutions in Russia by Soviet Marxists of the 20th Century and by Liberal LGBT Activists of the 21st Century." Presentation in Madrid, Spain, December 22, 2015. Material revealed by WikiLeaks under the heading "The Intolerance Network." https://wikileaks.org.

———. 2017. "Uroki standartizatsii." *Pravoslavie.ru*, December 26, 2017. https://pravoslavie.ru.

Komov, Alexey, and Dmitry Smirnov. 2017. "Beseda s Alekseem Komovym. Temy: Domashnee Obrazovanie. Uroki Bol'shevistskogo Perevorota." [Conversation with Alexey Komov. Topic: Homeschooling. Lessons of the Bolshevik revolution.] Dmitry Smirnov (blog), December 26, 2017. www.dimitrysmirnov.ru.

Korolczuk, Elżbieta. 2020. "Counteracting Challenges to Gender Equality in the Era of Anti-Gender Campaigns: Competing Gender Knowledges and Affective Solidarity," *Social Politics* 27 (4): 694–717.

Korolczuk, Elżbieta, and Agnieszka Graff. 2018. "Gender as 'Ebola from Brussels': The Anticolonial Frame and the Rise of Illiberal Populism." *Signs: Journal of Women in Culture and Society* 43 (4): 797–821.

Kováts, Eszter. 2020. "Post-Socialist Conditions and the Orbán Government's Gender Politics between 2010 and 2019 in Hungary." In *Right-Wing Populism and Gender*, edited by Gabriele Dietze and Julia Roth, 75–100. Bielefeld, Germany: Transcript.

Kováts, Eszter, and Andrea Petö. 2017. "Anti-gender Discourse in Hungary: A Discourse Without a Movement?" In *Anti-Gender Campaigns in Europe: Mobilizing Against Equality*, edited by Roman Kuhar and David Paternotte, 117–31. Lanham, MD: Rowman and Littlefield.

Kováts, Eszter, and Maari Põim, eds. 2015. *Gender as Symbolic Glue: The Position and Role of Conservative and Far-Right Parties in the Anti-Gender Mobilizations in Europe*. Brussels: Foundation for European Progressive Studies in cooperation with the Friedrich-Ebert-Stiftung.

Krizsán, Andrea, and Conny Roggeband. 2021. "Opposing the Istanbul Convention: Actors, Strategies and Frames." In *Politicizing Gender and Democracy in the Context of the Istanbul Convention*, edited by Andrea Krizsán and Conny Roggeband, 55–119. Gender and Politics. Cham, Switzerland: Springer International Publishing.

Kuby, Gabriele. 2012. *Die globale sexuelle revolution*. Kissleg, Germany: Fe-Medienverlag.

———. 2018. "Gender-Programmierung durch Sexualerziehung—Zugriff der UN auf die Jugend der Welt." Gabriele Kuby (blog), December 14, 2018. www.gabriele-kuby.de.

Kuhar, Roman. 2011. "Use of the Europeanization Frame in Same Sex Partnership Issues across Europe." In *The Europeanization of Gender Equality Policies: A Discursive Sociological Approach*, by E. Lombardo and M. Forest, 168–91. Basingstoke, UK: Palgrave Macmillan.

Kuhar, Roman, and David Paternotte, eds. 2017. *Anti-Gender Campaigns in Europe: Mobilizing against Equality*. London: Rowman and Littlefield.

Kuhar, Roman and Metka Mencin Čeplak. 2016. "Same-Sex Partnership Debate inSlovenia: Between Declarative Support and Lack of Political Will." In *The EU Enlargementand Gay Politics: The Impact of Eastern Enlargement on Rights, Activism and Prejudice*, edited by Koen Slootmaeckers, Heleen Touquet, and Peter Vermeersch, 147–172. London: Palgrave.

Kurimay, Anita, and Judit Takács. 2016. "Emergence of the Hungarian Homosexual Movement in Late Refrigerator Socialism." *Sexualities* 20 (5–6): 585–603.

Lamb, Christopher. 2023. "'It Is Not a Crime'—The Pope's Approach to Gay Catholics." *Tablet: International Catholic News Weekly*, January 26, 2023. www.thetablet.co.uk.

Landolt, Laura. 2004. "(Mis)Constructing the Third World? Constructivist Analysis of Norm Diffusion." *Third World Quarterly* 25 (3): 579–91.

Lang, Sabine. 1997. "The NGOization of Feminism. Institutionalization and Institution Building within the German Women's Movement" In *Transitions, Environments, Translations: Feminisms in International Politics*, edited by Joan Scott, Cora Kaplan and Debra Keats, 101–20. New York: Routledge.

———.2013. *NGOs, Civil Society, and the Public Sphere*. Cambridge: Cambridge University Press.

———. 2014. "Women's Advocacy Networks: The European Union, Women's NGOs, and the Velvet Triangle." In *Theorizing NGOs: States, Feminism, and Neoliberalism*, 266–84. Durham, NC: Duke University Press.

Langlois, Anthony J. 2015. "Human Rights, LGBT Rights, and International Theory." In *Sexualities in World Politics: How LGBTQ Claims Shape International Relations*, edited by Manuela Lavinas Picq and Markus Thiel, 23–37. New York: Routledge.

———. 2020. "Making LGBT Rights into Human Rights." In *The Oxford Handbook of Global LGBT and Sexual Diversity Politics*, edited by Michael J. Bosia, Sandra M. McEvoy, and Momin Rahman, 75–88. Oxford: Oxford University Press.

La Repubblica. 2021. "Tangenti dall'Azerbaijan, quattro anni all'ex deputato UdC Volontè." *La Repubblica*, January 11, 2021. https://milano.repubblica.it.

Laruelle, Marlene. 2017. "Putin's Regime and the Ideological Market: A Difficult Balancing Game." *Carnegie Endowment for International Peace*, March 16, 2017. https://carnegieendowment.org.

———. 2020. "The Kremlin's Conservative Playbook." Culture Wars Today (blog). Berkley Center for Religion, Peace and World Affairs, January 2, 2020. https://berkleycenter.georgetown.edu.

———. 2022. "Illiberalism: a conceptual introduction." *East European Politics* 38 (2): 303–27.

———. 2023. "A Grassroots Conservatism? Taking a Fine-Grained View of Conservative Attitudes among Russians." *East European Politics* 39 (2): 173–93.

Laruelle, Marlene, and Kevin Limonier. 2021. "Beyond 'Hybrid Warfare': A Digital Exploration of Russia's Entrepreneurs of Influence." *Post-Soviet Affairs* 37 (4): 318–35.

Lassiter, Matthew D. 2008. "Inventing Family Values." In *Rightward Bound: Making America Conservative in the 1970s*, edited by Bruce J. Schulman and Julian E. Zelizer, 13–28. Cambridge, MA: Harvard University Press.

La Stampa. 2017. "Il Cardinale Parolin in viaggio per la prima volta in Moldvavia." *La Stampa*. September 15, 2017. www.lastampa.it.

Lega Salvini Premier Channel. 2013. "Congresso Federale Lega Nord 2013—Ambasciatore Russo Nazioni Unite Alexey Komov." Congress of the Lega Nord. Turin, Italy, December 18th, 2013. Accessed October 21, 2019. YouTube video, www.youtube.com/watch?v=DsgJtcNZZwQ.

Legro, Jeffrey W. 1997. "Which Norms Matter? Revisiting the 'Failure' of Internationalism." *International Organization* 51 (1): 31–63.

Lehoucq, Emilio. 2021. "Legal Threats and the Emergence of Legal Mobilization: Conservative Mobilization in Colombia." *Law & Social Inquiry* 46 (2): 299–330.

Lenzerini, Federico. 2014. *The Culturalization of Human Rights*. Oxford: Oxford University Press.

Lepore, Francesco. 2018. "Pro Vita e Generazione Famiglia lanciano la campagna choc #Stoputeroinaffitto: questa volta sotto attacco le coppie omogenitoriali di papà." *Gaynews*, 15 October 2018. www.gaynews.it.

Levenson, Michael. 2022. "Zelensky Says Ukraine's Government May Allow Civil Partnerships for Same-Sex Couples." *New York Times*, August 2, 2022. www.nytimes.com.

Levintova, Hannah. 2014. "How US Evangelicals Helped Create Russia's Anti-gay Movement." Mother Jones, February 21, 2014. www.motherjones.com.

Lewis, Andrew R. 2017. *The Rights Turn in Conservative Christian Politics: How Abortion Transformed the Culture Wars*. Cambridge, UK: Cambridge University Press.

Lilla, Mark. 2018. "Two Roads for the New French Right." *New York Review*, December 20, 2018. www.nybooks.com.

Linden, Markus. 2020. "Das Scharnier—Neuer Konservatismus und neue Rechte." *Merkur* 74 (855): 86–94.

Logvinenko, Igor, and Michael Dichio. 2021. "Authoritarian Populism, Courts and Democratic Erosion." *Just Security* (February 2021). www.justsecurity.org.

Lynch, John. 2005. "Institution and Imprimatur: Institutional Rhetoric and the Failure of the Catholic Church's Pastoral Letter on Homosexuality." *Rhetoric and Public Affairs* 8 (3): 383–403.

Magister, Sandro. 2010. "A Holy Alliance between Rome and Moscow is Born." *Chiesa Espresso*, May 24, 2010. http://chiesa.espresso.repubblica.it.

Magni, Gabriele, and Andrew Reynolds. 2020. "Voter Preferences and the Political Underrepresentation of Minority Groups: Lesbian, Gay, and Transgender Candidates in Advanced Democracies." *Journal of Politics* 84 (4): 1199–215.

Major Oreja, Jaime. 2017. "The Necessary Strengthening of Truth." *Hungarian Review* 8 (3): 6–10.

Mälksoo, Lauri, and Wolfgang Benedek, eds. 2017. *Russia and the European Court of Human Rights: The Strasbourg Effect, European Inter-University Centre for Human Rights and Democratisation*. Cambridge: Cambridge University Press.

Mancini, Susanna, and Kristina Stoeckl. 2018. "Transatlantic Conversations: The Emergence of Society-Protective Anti-abortion Arguments in the United States, Europe and Russia." In *The Conscience Wars: Rethinking the Balance between Religion and Equality*, edited by Susanna Mancini and Michel Rosenfeld, 220–57. Cambridge: Cambridge University Press.

Manhattan Declaration. 2009. "Manhattan Declaration: A Call of Christian Conscience." Manhattan Declaration, November 20 2009. www.manhattandeclaration.org.

Manners, Ian. 2002. "Normative Power Europe: A Contradiction in Terms?" *Journal of Common Market Studies* 40(2): 235–258.

Mannheim, Karl. 1995. *Ideologie und Utopie*. 8th ed. Frankfurt am Main, Germany: Klostermann.

Marks, Andrea. 2021. "What Provincetown's Gay Community Can Teach Us About Containing Covid." *Rolling Stone*, August 24, 2021. www.rollingstone.com.

Marschütz, Gerhard. 2014. "Wachstumspotenzial für die eigene Lehre. Zur Kritik an der vermeintlichen Gender-Ideologie." *Herder Korrespondenz* 68 (9): 457–62.

Marshall, Katherine. 2017. "Religious Voices at the United Nations: American Faith Perspectives as an Example." In *Religion, State and the United Nations*, edited by Anne Stensvold, 127–36. London: Routledge.

Marzouki, Nadia, Duncan McDonnell, and Olivier Roy, eds. 2015. *Saving the People: How Populists Hijack Religion*. London: Hurst.

Mason, Bekah. 2021. "Side B Christians Like Me Are an Asset Not a Threat." *Christianity Today*, December 3, 2021. www.christianitytoday.com/.

Mayer, Stefanie, and Birgit Sauer. 2017. "'Gender Ideology' in Austria: Coalitions around an Empty Signifier." In *Anti-Gender Campaigns in Europe: Mobilizing Against Equality*, edited by Roman Kuhar and David Paternotte, 23–40. Lanham, MD: Rowan and Littlefield.

Mazzei, Patricia. 2022. "DeSantis Signs Florida Bill That Opponents Call 'Don't Say Gay.'" *New York Times*, March 28, 2022. www.nytimes.com.

McAdam, Doug, Sidney Tarrow, and Charles Tilly. 2001. *Dynamics of Contention*. Cambridge: Cambridge University Press.

McCaffrey, Dawn, and Jennifer Keys. 2000. "Competitive Framing Processes in the Abortion Debate: Polarization-Vilification, Frame Saving, and Frame Debunking." *Sociological Quarterly* 41 (1): 41–61.

MCC International Guests. 2023. "International Guests." *Mathias Corvinus Collegium*, Budapest. www.mcc.hu.

MCC Press. 2023. "Könyvek." *MCC Press*, Budapest. www.mccpress.hu.

McCrudden, Christopher. 2014. "Human Rights, Southern Voices, and 'Traditional Values' at the United Nations." University of Michigan Public Law Research Paper no. 419, August 29, 2014. https://papers.ssrn.com.

———. 2015. "Transnational Culture Wars." University of Michigan Public Law Research Paper no. 447, April 5, 2015. https://papers.ssrn.com.

MCC Vision. 2023. "Vision." *Mathias Corvinus Collegium*, Budapest. www.mcc.hu.

McGoldrick, Dominic. 2016. "The Development and Status of Sexual Orientation Discrimination under International Human Rights Law." *Human Rights Law Review* 16 (4): 613–68.

McIntosh, C. Alison, and Jason L. Finkle. 1995. "The Cairo Conference on Population and Development: A New Paradigm?" *Population and Development Review* 21 (2): 223–60.

McKinley, Jesse, and Kirk Johnson. 2008. "Mormons Tipped Scale in Ban on Gay Marriage." *New York Times*, November 15, 2008. www.nytimes.com.

McTeirnan, Anthea. 2015. "Grandparents on Yes Equality Bus Take Message to Country." *Irish Times*, April 22, 2015. www.irishtimes.com.

Meduza. 2019. "'I Try Not to Exaggerate My Own Significance' Ex-lawmaker and Former Pro-Kremlin Youth Activist Robert Schlegel Explains Why He Left Russia to Raise His Kids in Germany." *Meduza News Portal*, December 3, 2019. https://meduza.io.

Mehta, Gautema. 2020. "Anti-abortion Activists Launch Publication to Counter the Drudge Report's 'Leftward Tilt.'" *Codastory*, September 4, 2020. www.codastory.com.

Mepschen, Paul, Jan Willem Duyvendak, and Evelien H. Tonkens. 2010. "Sexual Politics, Orientalism and Multicultural Citizenship in the Netherlands." *Sociology* 44 (5): 962–79.

324 | REFERENCES

Mero, Paul. 2017. "The True Relationship between LDS and Conservatism, a Response to Taylor Petrey." *Deseret News*, May 11, 2017. www.deseret.com.

Meyer, David, and Suzanne Staggenborg. 1996. "Movements, Countermovements, and the Structure of Political Opportunity." *American Journal of Sociology* 101 (6): 1628–60.

Meyer, John, John Boli, George Thomas, and Francisco Ramirez. 1997. "World Society and the Nation-State." *American Journal of Sociology* 103 (1): 144–81.

Minkenberg, Michael. 2003. "The Policy-Impact of Church-State Relations: Family Policy and Abortion in Britain, France and Germany." In *Church and State in Contemporary Europe*, edited by John T. S. Madeley and Zsolt Enyedi, 195–217. London: Frank Cass.

Mohler, Albert. 2004. "The Case against Homosexual Marriage." Albert Mohler January 15, 2004. www.albertmohler.com.

———. 2005. "The Age of Polymorphous Perversity, Part Four." Albert Mohler September 22, 2005. www.albertmohler.com.

———. 2015. *We Cannot Be Silent: Speaking Truth to a Culture Redefining Sex, Marriage, and the Very Meaning of Right and Wrong*. Nashville, TN: Thomas Nelson.

Monaghan, Jennifer. 2015. "United Russia to Unveil 'Straight Flag' in Honor of Traditional Family." *Moscow Times*, July 8, 2015. www.themoscowtimes.com.

Monro, Surya. 2015. *Bisexuality: Identities, Politics, and Theories*. Basingstoke, UK: Palgrave Macmillan.

Morello, Carol. 2019. "Some U.S. Embassies Still Hoist Rainbow Flags, Despite Advisory from Washington." *Washington Post*, June 8, 2019. www.washingtonpost.com.

Moreton, Bethany. 2010. *To Serve God and Wal-Mart*. Harvard: Harvard University Press.

Mos, Martijn. 2014. "Of Gay Rights and Christmas Ornaments: The Political History of Sexual Orientation Non-Discrimination in the Treaty of Amsterdam." *JCMS: Journal of Common Market Studies* 52 (3): 632–49.

Moscow Times. 2020. "Putin Mocks U.S. Embassy Rainbow Flag." *Moscow Times* July 3, 2020. www.themoscowtimes.com.

———. 2022a. "Russian Church Leader Appears to Blame Gay Pride Parades for Ukraine War." *Moscow Times*, March 7, 2022. www.themoscowtimes.com.

———. 2022b. "Russia Quits Europe's Rule of Law Body, Sparking Questions Over Death Penalty." *Moscow Times*, March 10, 2022. www.themoscowtimes.com.

Möser, Cornelia, Jennifer Ramme, and Judit Takács. 2022. *Paradoxical Right-Wing Sexual Politics in Europe*. Basingstoke, UK: Palgrave Macmillan.

Moss, Kevin. 2017. "Russia as the Savior of European Civilization: Gender and the Geopolitics of Traditional Values." In *Anti-Gender Campaigns in Europe: Mobilizing against Equality*, edited by Roman Kuhar and David Paternotte, 195–214. Lanham, MD: Rowman and Littlefield.

Mourão Permoser, Julia, and Kristina Stoeckl. 2020. "Advocating Illiberal Human Rights: The Global Network of Moral Conservative Homeschooling Activists." *Global Networks: A Journal of Transnational Affairs* 21 (4): 681–702.

Moyn, Samuel. 2015. *Christian Human Rights*. Philadelphia: University of Pennsylvania Press.

Moynihan, Robert. 2010. "Rome-Moscow Relations Begin New Era." *Zenit*, December 14, 2009. https://zenit.org.

Mudde, Cas. 2004. "The Populist Zeitgeist." *Government and Opposition* 39 (4): 541–63.

———. 2019. *The Far Right Today*. Cambridge, UK: Polity.

Murib, Zein. 2015. "Transgender: Examining an Emerging Political Identity Using Three Political Processes." *Politics, Groups, and Identities* 3 (3): 381–97.

———. 2017. "Rethinking GLBT as a Political Category in U.S. Politics." In *LGBTQ Politics: A Critical Reader*, edited by Marla Brettschneider, Susan Burgess, and Christine Keating, 14–34. New York: New York University Press.

Murray, Melissa. 2009. "Marriage Rights and Parental Rights: Parents, the State, and Proposition 8." *Stanford Journal of Civil Rights & Civil Liberties* 5 (2): 357–408.

Murtagh, Peter. 2015. "Couple denounces use of their image on No campaign posters." *Irish Times*, May 7, 2015. www.irishtimes.com.

NeJaime, Douglas, and Reva Siegel. 2015. "Conscience Wars: Complicity-Based Conscience Claims in Religion and Politics." *Yale Law Journal* 124: 2516–91.

———. 2018. "Conscience Wars in Transnational Perspective." In *The Conscience Wars: Rethinking the Balance between Religion and Equality*, edited by Susanna Mancini and Michel Rosenfeld, 187–219. Cambridge: Cambridge University Press.

NELFA. 2022. "Resources." Network of European LGBTIQ* Families Associations, accessed February 28, 2023. http://nelfa.org.

Nexon, Dan (@dhnexon). 2021. "I don't think the IR community really groks the degree that LGBTQ+ rights are implicated in contestation over 'liberal international order.'" Twitter/X, July 5, 2021.

Norocel, Ov Cristian, and Ionela Băluță. 2021. "Retrogressive Mobilization in the 2018 'Referendum for Family' in Romania." *Problems of Post-Communism* 0 (0): 1–10.

Norris, Pippa. 2021. "Cancel Culture: Myth or Reality?" *Political Studies*. August 2021.

Novak, Katalin. 2017. "A Strong Nation is Built on Intact and Happy Families—A Demographic Snapshot." *Hungarian Review* 8 (3): 29–38.

Nuñez-Mietz, Fernando G. 2019. "Resisting human rights through securitization: Russia and Hungary against LGBT rights." *Journal of Human Rights* 18 (5): 543–63.

Nuñez-Mietz, Fernando G., and Lucrecia García Iommi. 2017. "Can Transnational Norm Advocacy Undermine Internalization? Explaining Immunization against LGBT Rights in Uganda." *International Studies Quarterly* 61 (1): 196–209.

O'Connell, Gerard. 2021. "Pope Francis encourages Jesuit Father James Martin in his LGBT ministry." *American Magazine*, June 27, 2021. www.americamagazine.org.

O'Dwyer, Conor. 2012. "Does the EU Help or Hinder Gay-Rights Movements in Post-Communist Europe? The Case of Poland." *East European Politics* 28 (4): 332–52.

———. 2018. *Coming Out of Communism: The Emergence of LGBT Activism in Eastern Europe*. New York: New York University Press.

O'Dwyer, Conor, and Dong-Joon Jung. 2018. "Demographic Threat and Public Attitudes toward Homosexuality: A Comparison of Postcommunist and Western Europe." Paper presented at the European Politics Working Group, Department of Political Science, University of California, Berkeley, April 19, 2018.

Olavarria, Marian. 2018. "ATW assisting the Hungarian Family Protection Policy." *Alive to the World Organization*, March 12, 2018. alivetotheworld.org.

Oppenheimer, Mark. 2012. "Sociologist's Paper Raises Ruestions on Role of Faith in Scholarship." *New York Times*, October 12, 2012. www.nytimes.com.

Orbán, Viktor. 2021. "Samizdat No. 11." Prime Minister of Hungary, accessed January 30, 2022. https://miniszterelnok.hu.

O'Riordan, Seán. 1992. "Towards a New Evangelization of Europe? Reflections on the Special Synod of Bishops 1991." *Furrow* 43 (3): 131–38.

Owczarzak, Jill. 2009. "Defining Democracy and the Terms of Engagement with the Postsocialist State: Insights from HIV/AIDS." *East European Politics and Societies* 23 (3): 421–45.

Outreach. 2023. "Pope Francis Clarifies Comments on Homosexuality." *Outreach: An LGBTQ Catholic Resource*, January 27, 2023: https://outreach.faith.

Ozzano, Luca, and Alberta Giorgi. 2015. *European Culture Wars and the Italian Case: Which Side Are You On?* London: Routledge.

PACE. 2012. "Motion for a Recommendation Tabled by Mr. Robert Shlegel and Other Members of the Assembly: Coordinated Ftrategies for Effective Internet Governance." *Parliamentary Assembly of the Council of Europe* no. Doc. 13280, July 8, 2013.

———. 2013. "Motion for a Resolution 13333: The Protection of the Rights of Parents and Children Belonging to Religious Minorities." *Parliamentary Assembly of the Council of Europe*, October 10, 2013. https://pace.coe.int.

———. 2014. "Activities of the Assembly's Bureau and Standing Committee (5 October 2013–26 January 2014)." *Parliamentary Assembly of the Council of Europe* no. Doc. 13374, January 24, 2014. http://assembly.coe.int.

———. 2015. "Motion for a Resolution 13777: The Over-Sexualization of Children." *Parliamentary Assembly of the Council of Europe*, April 30, 2015. https://pace.coe.int.

———. 2016. "Report 14080: The Over-Sexualization of Children." *Parliamentary Assembly of the Council of Europe*, June 6, 2016. https://pace.coe.int.

———. 2017. "Resolution 2163: The Protection of the Rights of Parents and Children Belonging to Religious Minorities." *Parliamentary Assembly of the Council of Europe*, April 27, 2017. https://pace.coe.int.

———. 2019a. "Internet Governance and Human Rights." *Parliamentary Assembly of the Council of Europe* no. Doc. 14789, January 4, 2019. http://assembly.coe.int.

———. 2019b. "Resolution Nr. 2256 'Internet Governance and Human Rights.'" *Parliamentary Assembly of the Council of Europe*, January 23, 2019. http://assembly.coe.int.

———. 2022. "Compendium of Written Amendments 15425 Combating Rising Hate Against LGBT People in Europe." *Parliamentary Assembly of the Council of Europe*, January 24, 2022. https://pace.coe.int/.

PACE Members. 2023. "Representatives and SUBSTITUTES (A-Z since 1994): Mr Luca VOLONTÈ (Italy, EPP/CD)." *Website of the Composition of the Parliamentary Assembly of the Council of Europe*, www.pace.coe.int.

Paddock, Richard C. 2022. "Singapore to Repeal Ban on Sex Between Consenting Men." *New York Times*, August 21, 2022. www.nytimes.com.

Pakhnyuk, Lucy. 2019. "Foreign Agents and Gay Propaganda: Russian LGBT Rights Activism under Pressure." *Demokratizatsiya* 27 (4): 479–46.

Papanikolaou, Aristotle. 2017. "Whose Public? Which Ecclesiology?" In *Political Theologies in Orthodox Christianity: Common Challenges—Divergent Positions*, edited by Kristina Stoeckl, Ingeborg Gabriel, and Aristotle Papanikolaou, 229–42. London: Bloomsbury.

Paternotte, David. 2012. "Back into the Future: ILGA-Europe before 1996." *Destination Equality: Magazine of ILGA-Europe* 11 (1): 5–8.

———. 2014. "The International (Lesbian and) Gay Association and the Question of Pedophilia: Tracking the Demise of Gay Liberation Ideals." *Sexualities* 17 (1–2): 121–38.

———. 2015. "Global Times, Global Debates? Same-Sex Marriage Worldwide." *Social Politics* 22 (4): 653–74.

———. 2020. "Backlash: A Misleading Narrative." Engenderings (blog), March 30, 2020. https://blogs.lse.ac.uk.

Paternotte, David, Mary Anne Case, and Sarah Bracke. 2016. "The Sin of Turning Away from Reality: An Interview with Father Krzysztof Charamsa." *Religion and Gender* 6 (2): 226–246.

Paternotte, David, and Kelly Kollman. 2013. "Regulating Intimate Relationships in the European Polity: Same-Sex Unions and Policy Convergence." *Social Politics: International Studies in Gender, State & Society* 20 (4): 510–33.

Paternotte, David, and Mieke Verloo. 2021. "De-democratization and the Politics of Knowledge: Unpacking the Cultural Marxism Narrative." *Social Politics: International Studies in Gender, State & Society* 28 (3): 556–78.

Patriarchal Commission for Family Affairs. 2019. "Ob otnoshenii Patriarshei Komissii po voprosam sem'i, zashchity materinstva i detstva k semeinomu obrazovaniiu i programme 'Klassicheskie besedy'" ["Relation of the Patriarchal Commission for the Family, Motherhood, and Childhood to Homeschooling and the 'Classical Conversations' Program"]. Patriarchal Commission for Family Affairs, December 4, 2019. http://pk-semya.ru.

Payne, Leigh A., Julia Zulver, and Simón Escoffier. 2023. *The Right Against Rights in Latin America*. Oxford: Oxford University Press.

Pedersen, Thomas L. 2021. ggraph: An Implementation of Grammar of Graphics for Graphs and Networks. R package version 2.0.5. https://CRAN.R-project.org.

Pence, Mike. 2006. "Rep. Pence calls for Marriage Protection Amendment." *VoteSmart*, July 18, 2006. https://votesmart.org.

Perintfalvi, Rita. 2020. "Der Kampf um Geschlechtergerechtigkeit als ein Kampf um Demokratie." In *Anti-Genderismus in Europa. Allianzen von Rechtspopulismus und religiösem Fundamentalismus. Mobilisierung Vernetzung Transformation*, edited by Sonja A. Strube, Rita Perintfalvi, Raphaela Hemet, Miriam Metze and Cicek Sahbaz, 173–186. Bielefeld, Germany: Transcript.

Perreau, Bruno. 2016. *Queer Theory: The French Response*. Stanford, CA: Stanford University Press.

Perversion. 1965. "Perversion for Profit." Eastmancolor film first released in 1963, produced by Charleas Keating, distributed by Citizens for Decent Literature, narrated by George Putnam. YouTube video, 31 min., https://www.youtube.com/watch?v=pciD9gd3myo&t=252s.

Petö, Andrea. 2020. "Academic Freedom and Gender Studies: An Alliance Forged in Fire." *Gender and Sexuality* 15: 9–24.

Pettigrew, Thomas, and Linda Tropp. 2006. "A Meta-Analytic Test of Intergroup Contact Theory." *Journal of Personality and Social Psychology* 90 (5): 751–83.

Pew Research Center. 2017. "Religious Belief and National Belonging in Central and Eastern Europe." Pew Research Center, May 10, 2017. www.pewforum.org.

———. 2020. "The Global Divide on Homosexuality Persists." Pew Research Center, June 25, 2020. www.pewresearch.org.

Philpott, Daniel. 2004. "Religious Freedom and the Undoing of the Westphalian State." *Michigan Journal of International Law* 25 (4): 981–98.

Piscopo, Jennifer M., and Denise M. Walsch. 2020. "Introduction: Backlash and the Future of Feminism." *Signs: Journal of Women and Culture in Society* 45 (2): 265–78.

PNV. 2014. "Transatlantic Summit I: New York. Strengthening the Family for Sustainable Development." Political Network for Values, December 5, 2014. https://politicalnetworkforvalues.org.

———. 2019a. "Transatlantic Summit III: Bogota. Facing the Upsurge of the Global Crisis. Solid Principles for a Better Future." Political Network for Values, April 4–5, 2019. https://politicalnetworkforvalues.org.

———. 2019b. "Who We Are." Political Network for Values, accessed January 28, 2022. https://politicalnetworkforvalues.org.

———. 2022. "Transatlantic Summit IV: Budapest. Freedom at stake." Political Network for Values, May 26–27, 2022. https://politicalnetworkforvalues.org.

Ponkin, Igor V., Mikhail N. Kuznetsov, and Natalya A. Mikhailova. 2011. "DOKLAD O prave na kriticheskuyu otsenku gomoseksualizma i o zakonnykh ogranicheniyakh navyazyvaniya gomoseksualizma." Gosudastvo i Religiya, accessed January 21, 2022. www.state-religion.ru.

POSEC. 2022. Postsecular Conflicts Research Group. University of Innsbruck: https://www.uibk.ac.at/projects/postsecular-conflicts/.

Prearo, Massimo. 2020. *L'ipotesi neocattolica. Politologia dei movimenti anti-gender*. Milano: Mimesis.

Pro Vita & Famiglia. 2021. "Chi siamo." Pro Vita & Famiglia, accessed June 22, 2021. www.provitaefamiglia.it.

Przekażmy Sobie Znak Pokoju. 2016. "'Let us Give Each Other a Sign of Peace' Campaign." Accessed December 30, 2020. https://znakpokoju.com.

Puar, Jasbir K. 2007. *Terrorist Assemblages: Homonationalism in Queer Times.* Durham, NC: Duke University Press.

Putin, Vladimir. 2021. "Valdai Discussion Club Meeting." Presented at the Valdai Discussion Club meeting, Sochi, Russia, October 21, 2021. http://en.kremlin.ru.

R Core Team. 2021. "R: A Language and Environment for Statistical Computing." R Foundation for Statistical Computing, Vienna, Austria. www.R-project.org/.

Radnitz, Scott. 2021. *Revealing Schemes: The Politics of Conspiracy in Russia and the Post-Soviet Region.* Oxford: Oxford University Press.

Ramet, Sabrina P. 1998. *Nihil Obstat: Religion, Politics, and Social Change in East-Central Europe and Russia.* Durham, NC: Duke University Press.

———. 2006. "The Way We Were—and Should Be Again? European Orthodox Churches and the 'Idyllic Past.'" In *Religion in an Expanding Europe*, edited by Timothy A. Byrnes and Peter J. Katzenstein, 148–75. Cambridge: Cambridge University Press.

Rao, Rahul. 2020. *Out of Time: The Queer Politics of Postcoloniality.* New York, NY: Oxford University Press.

Read, Barbara. 2018. "Truth, Masculinity and the Anti-Elitist Backlash against the University in the Age of Trump." *Teaching in Higher Education* 23 (5): 593–605.

Reclaiming Family Values. 2017. "Webinar." http://www.reclaimingfamilyvalues.eu.

Reid, Graham. 2021. "Homophobic Ghanaian 'Family Values' Bill Is Odious and Beggars Belief." *Human Rights Watch*, August 10, 2021. www.hrw.org/.

Regnerus, Mark. 2012. "How Different Are the Adult Children of Parents Who Have Same-Sex Relationships? Findings from the New Family Structure Study." *Social Science Research* 41 (4): 752–70.

Regnum. 2016. "PATsE poruchila estontsu zavershit' rossijskij raport ob opasnostyakh interneta." *Regnum.ru*, June 27, 2016. https://regnum.ru.

Renkin, Hadley Z. 2007. "Predecessors and Pilgrims: Lesbian History-Making and Velonging in Post-socialist Hungary." In *Beyond the Pink Curtain: Everyday Life of LGBT People in Eastern Europe*, edited by Judit Takács and Roman Kuhar, 269–86. Ljubljana: Politike Symposium.

Riabov, Oleg, and Tatiana Riabova. 2014. "The Decline of Gayropa?—How Russia Intends to Save the World." *Eurozine*, February 5, 2014. www.eurozine.com.

Riccardi-Swartz, Sarah. 2021. "American Conservatives and the Allure of Post-Soviet Russian Orthodoxy." *Religions* 12 (12): 1036.

———. 2022. "In His "Forgiveness Day' Sermon—a Slightly More Sophisticated 'Globo-homo' Rant—Kirill Lays Out an Authoritarian Vision in Which His Version of God Might Dominate and Rule the Human Race." *Religiondispatches*, March 7, 2022. https://religiondispatches.org.

Riigikogu. 2016. "Herkel Will Take Over the Report of Russia's PACE member" Press release, Riigikogu Press Service, June 22, 2016. https://m.riigikogu.ee.

Rimestad, Sebastian. 2015. "The Interaction between the Moscow Patriarchate and the European Court of Human Rights." *Review of Central and East European Law* 40 (1): 31–55.

330 | REFERENCES

Rimmerman, Craig A. 2014. *The Lesbian and Gay Movements: Assimilation or Liberation?* 2nd ed. Boulder, CO: Westview Press.

Risse, Thomas, Stephen Ropp, and Kathryn Sikkink, eds. 2013. *The Persistent Power of Human Rights: From Commitment to Compliance.* New York: Cambridge University Press.

Risse, Thomas, and Kathryn Sikkink. 1999. "The Socialization of International Human Rights Norms into Domestic Practices: Introduction." In *The Power of Human Rights,* edited by Thomas Risse, Stephen Ropp, and Kathryn Sikkink, 1–38. Cambridge: Cambridge University Press.

Ritholtz, Samuel and Miguel Mesquita. 2023. "The Transnational Force Anti-LGBTIQ Politics in Latin America." In *The Right Against Rights in Latin America,* edited by Leigh Payne, Julia Zulver, and Simón Escoffier, 98–111. Oxford: Oxford University Press.

Roccucci, Adriano. 2011. *Stalin e il Patriarca. La chiesa ortodossa e il potere sovietico 1917–1958.* Torino, Italy: Einaudi.

Roggeband, Conny. 2010. "Transnational Networks and Institutions." In *The Diffusion of Social Movements,* edited by Rebecca Kolins Givan, Kenneth M. Roberts, and Sarah A. Soule, 19–33. Cambridge: Cambridge University Press.

Rosenberg, Steve. 2022. "Ice Soldiers Mark Russia's Very Patriotic Christmas." *BBC News,* January 2, 2023. www.bbc.com.

Rothermel, Ann-Kathrin. 2020. "'The Other Side': Assessing the Polarization of Gender Knowledge Through a Feminist Analysis of the Affective-Discursive in Anti-Feminist Online Communities." *Social Politics: International Studies in Gender, State and Society* 27 (4): 718–741.

RStudio Team. 2020. "RStudio: Integrated Development for R. RStudio," PBC, Boston, MA. www.rstudio.com/.

Rupp, Leila J. 2014. "The European Origins of Transnational Organizing: The International Committee for Sexual Equality." In *LGBT Activism and the Making of Europe: A Rainbow Europe?,* edited by Phillip M. Ayoub and David Paternotte, 29–49. Basingstoke, UK: Palgrave.

Ruskline. 2018. "V PSTGU s lektsiyami o khristianskom brake vystupil amerikanskij sotsiolog Mark Regnerus" ["American sociologist Mark Regnerus gives lecture on Christian marriage at RSTGU"]. *Russkaya Narodnaya Liniya,* May 25, 2018. https://ruskline.ru.

Russian Federation. 2013. "Federal Law of the Russian Federation from 29 June 2013 No. 135-FZ on Including Changes to Article 5 of the Federal Law; on Protection of Children from Information Harmful to Their Health and Development; and Separate Legislative Acts of the Russian Federation with the Goal of Protection of Children from Information Propagandizing Rejection of Traditional Family Values." Adopted by the State Duma 11 June 2013, approved by the Federation Council 26 June 2013, published 2 July 2013. www.rg.ru.

Russian Orthodox Church. 2010. "Postoyannij predstavitel' Rossijskoj Federatsii pri otdelenii Organizatsii Ob" edinennykh Natsii i drugikh mezhdunardonykh organizatsiyakh v Zheneve udosten vysokoj tserkovnoj nagrady." Press Release of the Department of External Relations of the Moscow Patriarchate, October 5, 2010. www.mospat.ru.

Ryabykh, Igumen Filip. 2010. "V Sovete OON po pravam cheloveka proshel seminar posvyashchennyj pravam cheloveka i traditsionnym tsennostyam." Representation of the Russian Orthodox Church in Strasbourg, October 8, 2010. www.strasbourg-reor.org.

Ryabykh, Philip, and Igor Ponkin. 2012. "The Wearing of Christian Baptismal Crosses." *Stato, Chiese e pluralismo confessionale. Rivista telematica* 32, October 29, 2012. www.statoechiese.it.

Ryan, Erica. 2014. *Red War on the Family: Sex, Gender, and Americanism in the First Red Scare*. Philadelphia: Temple University Press.

Salzman, Todd A., and Michael G. Lawler. 2016. "'Amoris Laetitia' and Catholic Morals." *Furrow* 67 (12): 666–75.

Sandholtz, Wayne, and Adam Feldman. 2019. "The Trans-Regional Construction of Human Rights." *Contesting Human Rights*, January 25, 2019. www.elgaronline.com.

Sanders, Rebecca. 2018. "Norm Spoiling: Undermining the International Women's Rights Agenda." *International Affairs* 94 (2): 271–91.

Sanders, Rebecca, and Laura Dudley Jenkins. 2022. "Contemporary International Anti-Feminism." *Global Constitutionalism* 11 (3): 369–78.

———. 2023. "Patriarchal Populism: The Conservative Political Action Coalition (CPAC) and the Transnational Politics of Authoritarian Anti-Feminism." *International Spectator* 58 (3): 1–19.

Sauer, Birgit. 2020. "Authoritarian Right-Wing Populism as Masculinist Identity Politics. The Role of Affects." In *Right-Wing Populism and Gender: European Perspectives and Beyond*, edited by Gabriele Dietze and Julia Roth, 23–40. Bielefeld, Germany: Transcript.

Sauer, Pjotr. 2022. "Russia Passes Law Banning 'LGBT Propaganda' among Adults." *Guardian*, November 24, 2022. www.theguardian.com.

Schmidt, Rachel. 2020. "What Battles over 'Gender Ideology' Mean for Colombia's Women Human Rights Defenders." *Open Global Rights*, February 4, 2020. www.openglobalrights.org.

Schotel, Anne Louise, and Liza Mügge. 2021. "Towards Categorical Visibility? The Political Making of a Third Sex in Germany and the Netherlands." *Journal of Common Market Studies* 59 (4): 981–1024.

Schrad, Mark Lawrence. 2010. *The Political Power of Bad Ideas: Networks, Institutions, and the Global Prohibition Wave*. New York: Oxford University Press.

Schulman, Bruce, and Julian Zelizer, eds. 2008. *Rightward Bound: Making America Conservative in the 1970s*. Cambridge, MA: Harvard University Press.

Senèze, Nicolas. 2020. *Lo scisma americano. Come l'America vuole cambiare papa*. Milan: Mondadori.

Shahid, Ahmed, and Hilary Yerbury. 2014. "A Case Study of the Socialization of Human Rights Language and Norms in Maldives: Process, Impact and Challenges." *Journal of Human Rights Practice* 6 (2): 281–305.

Shevtsova, Maryna. 2020. "Fighting 'Gayropa': Europeanization and Instrumentalization of LGBTI Rights in Ukrainian Public Debate." *Problems of Post-Communism* 67 (6): 500–510.

Shishkov, Andrey. 2017. "Two Ecumenisms: Conservative Christian Alliances as a New Form of Ecumenical Cooperation." *State, Religion and Church* 4 (2): 58–87.

Siebold, Sabine. "It 'Is a Shame'–EU to Take Steps against Hungary over Anti-LGBT Bill." *Reuters*, June 23, 2021. www.reuters.com.

Siegel, Scott N., Stuart J. Turnbull-Dugarte, and Brian A. Olinger. 2022. "Where Is the Party? Explaining Positions on Same-Sex Marriage in Europe among Would-Be Members of Parliament." *European Journal of Politics and Gender* 5 (1): 83–108.

Sikkink, Kathryn. 2005. "Patterns of Dynamic Multilevel Governance and the Insider–Outsider Coalitions." In *Transnational Protest and Global Activism*, edited by Donatella della Porta and Sidney Tarrow, 151–174. New York: Rowman and Littlefield.

———. 2017. *Evidence for Hope*. Princeton, NJ: Princeton University Press.

Simpson, Hannah. 2017. "Commentary: Anti-Transgender Bus Invades New York City." *NBC News*, March 25, 2017. www.nbcnews.com.

Skocpol, Theda, and Alexander Hertel-Fernandez. 2016. "The Koch Network and Republican Party Extremism." *Perspectives on Politics* 14 (3): 681–99.

Sleptcov, Nikita. 2018. "Political Homophobia as a State Strategy in Russia." *Journal of Global Initiatives: Policy, Pedagogy, Perspective* 12 (1): 140–61. https://digitalcommons.kennesaw.edu.

Slootmaeckers, Koen. 2017. "The Litmus Test of Pride: Analysing the Emergence of the Belgrade 'Ghost' Pride in the Context of EU Accession." *East European Politics* 33 (4): 517–35.

Slootmaeckers, Koen, Heleen Touquet, and Peter Vermeersch, eds. 2017. *The EU Enlargement and Gay Politics*. Basingstoke, UK: Palgrave MacMillan.

Slootmaeckers, Koen, and Indraneel Sircar. 2018. "Marrying European and Domestic Politics? The Marriage Referendum in Croatia and Value-Based Euroscepticism." *Europe-Asia Studies* 70(3): 321–44. doi: 10.1080/09668136.2018.1457136.

Smith, Chris M., and Andrew V. Papachristos. 2016. "Trust Thy Crooked Neighbor: Multiplexity in Chicago Organized Crime Networks." *American Sociological Review* 81 (4): 644–67.

Snow, David A., and Robert D. Benford. 1992. *Master Frames and Cycles of Protest*. New Haven, CT: Yale University Press.

Snow, David A., and Sarah A. Soule. 2009. *A Primer on Social Movements*. New York: Norton.

Social Doctrine. 2000. "The Bases of the Social Concept of the Russian Orthodox Church." Official translation. Department for External Church Relations of the Moscow Patriarchate, August 16, 2000. www.mospat.ru.

Sorokin, Pitirim A. 1956. *The American Sex Revolution*. Boston: P. Sargent.

Soule, Sarah A. 2004. "Going to the Chapel? Same-Sex Marriage Bans in the United States, 1973–2000." *Social Problems* 51 (4): 453–77.

Soule, Sarah A., and Brayden G. King. 2006. "The Stages of the Policy Process and the Equal Rights Amendment, 1972–1982." *American Journal of Sociology* 111 (6): 1871–909.

Soule, Sarah A., and Susan Olzak. 2004. "When Do Movements Matter? The Politics of Contingency and the Equal Rights Amendment." *American Sociological Review* 69 (4): 473–97.

South, A. 2017. "Rnaturalearth: World Map Data from Natural Earth." R package version 0.1.0. https://CRAN.R-project.org.

Southern Poverty Law Center. 2015. "Everything you need to know about the anti-LGBTQ World Congress of Families (WCF)." Southern Poverty Law Center, accessed March 11, 2016. www.splcenter.org.

———. 2018. "How the World Congress of Families serves Russian Orthodox political interests." Southern Poverty Law Center, accessed October 4, 2018. www.splcenter .org.

———. 2021. "Scott Lively." Southern Poverty Law Center, accessed September 27, 2023. www.splcenter.org.

Spadaro, Antonio, and Marcelo Figueroa. 2017. "Evangelical Fundamentalism and Catholic Integralism: A Surprising Ecumenism." *La Civiltà Cattolica*, August 21, 2017. www.laciviltacattolica.it.

Sperling, Valerie. 2015. *Sex, Politics, and Putin: Political Legitimacy in Russia*. Oxford: Oxford University Press.

St. Petersburg Law. 2012. "Zakon Sankt-Peterburga O Vnesenii Izmeneniy v Zakon Sankt-Peterburga 'Ob Administrativnikh Pravonarusheniyakh v Sankt-Peterburge.'" ["On Amendments to the Law of St. Petersburg 'On Administrative Offenses in St. Petersburg'"]. Adopted by the Legislative Assembly of St. Petersburg on February 29, 2012, signed March 7, 2012. www.gov.spb.ru.

Stambolis-Ruhstorfer, Michael. 2020. "Producing Expert Capital: How Opposing Same-Sex Marriage Experts Dominate Fields in the United States and France." *Social Movement Studies* 19 (1): 38–62.

Stathi, Sofia, and Richard J. Crisp. 2008. "Imagining Intergroup Contact Promotes Projection to Outgroups." *Journal of Experimental Social Psychology* 44 (4): 943–57.

Stensvold, Anna. 2017. "Religion, State and Symbol Politic: The Catholic Church at the UN." In *Religion, State and the United Nations: Value Politics*, edited by Anna Stensvold, 95–110. London: Routledge.

Stern, Jessica. 2022. "A Conversation with U.S. Special Envoy Jessica Stern." Presented at the Council on Foreign Relations, July 21. www.cfr.org.

Stoeckl, Kristina. 2014. *The Russian Orthodox Church and Human Rights*. London: Routledge.

———. 2016. "The Russian Orthodox Church as Moral Norm Entrepreneur." *Religion, State and Society* 44 (2): 132–51.

———. 2020a. "The Rise of the Russian Christian Right: The Case of the World Congress of Families." *Religion, State and Society* 48 (4): 223–38.

——. 2020b. *Russian Orthodoxy and Secularism*. Brill Research Perspectives in Humanities and Social Sciences. Leiden: Brill.

——. 2022. "Russia's Spiritual Security Doctrine as a Challenge to European Comprehensive Security Approaches." *Review of Faith & International Affairs* 20 (4): 37–44.

Stoeckl, Kristina, and Kseniya Medvedeva. 2018. "Double Bind at the UN: Western Actors, Russia, and the Traditionalist Agenda." *Global Constitutionalism* 7(3): 383–421.

Stoeckl, Kristina, and Dmitry Uzlaner. 2022. *Moralist International: Russia in the Global Culture Wars*. Unpublished manuscript.

Strack, Christoph. 2021. "Katholische Gemeinden feiern die Segnung homosexueller Paare." *Deutsche Welle*, May 10, 2021. www.dw.com.

Strobl, Natascha. 2021. *Radikalisierter Konservatismus*. Berlin: Suhrkamp.

Stroop, Chrissy. 2016. "A Right-Wing International? Russian Social Conservatism, the World Congress of Families, and the Global Culture Wars in Historical Context." *Public Eye* (Winter): 4–10.

Strube, Sonja A., Rita Perintfalvi, Raphaela Hemet, Miriam Metze, and Cicek Sahbaz, eds. 2020. *Anti-Genderismus in Europa. Allianzen von Rechtspopulismus und religiösem Fundamentalismus. Mobilisierung—Vernetzung—Transformation*. Bielefeld, Germany: Transcript.

Studlar, Donley T. 2012. "The USA and Western Europa Compared: How the 'God Gar' Led the USA to Join the Religious World of Morality Politics." In *Morality Politics in Western Europe: Parties, Agendas and Policy Choices*, edited by Isabelle Engeli, Christoffer Green-Pederson, and Lars Thorup Larsen, 161–84. New York: Palgrave Macmillan.

Suslov, Mikhail, and Dmitry Uzlaner, eds. 2019. *Contemporary Russian Conservatism: Problems, Paradoxes and Dangers*. Leiden: Brill.

Swiebel, Joke. 2009. "Lesbian, Gay, Bisexual and Transgender Human Rights: The Search for an International Strategy." *Contemporary Politics* 15 (1): 19–35.

Swimelar, Safia. 2017. "The Journey of LGBT Rights: Norm Diffusion and Its Challenges in EU Seeking States: Bosnia and Serbia." *Human Rights Quarterly* 39 (4): 910–42.

Symons, Jonathan, and Dennis Altman. 2015. "International Norm Polarization: Sexuality as a Subject of Human Rights Protection." *International Theory* 7 (1): 61–95.

Szulc, Lukasz. 2017. *Transnational Homosexuals in Communist Poland: Cross-Border Flows in Gay and Lesbian Magazines*. Basingstoke, UK: Palgrave.

Tarrow, Sidney. 2005. *The New Transnational Activism*. Cambridge: Cambridge University Press.

——. 2013. *The Language of Contention: Revolutions in Words, 1688–2012*. Cambridge: Cambridge University Press.

Taub, Amanda. 2022. "Why Putin Name-Checked J.K. Rowling." *New York Times*, March 31, 2022. www.nytimes.com.

Taylor, Adam. 2015. "A New Swedish Message to Russian Submarines: 'This Way If You Are Gay.'" *Washington Post*, May 12, 2015. www.washingtonpost.com.

Tebano, Elena. 2023. "L'illusione ottica sulla maternità surrogata." *Corriere della Sera*, March 23, 2023. www.corriere.it.

Thiel, Markus. 2020. "The European Union's International Promotion of LGBTI Rights in Its Foreign Relations." *Oxford Research Encyclopedia of Politics*, August 27, 2020. https://oxfordre.com.

Thoreson, Ryan R. 2014. *Transnational LGBT Activism: Working for Sexual Rights Worldwide*. Minneapolis: University of Minnesota Press.

Tickner, J. Ann. 2014. "Hans Morgenthau's Principles of Political Realism: A Feminist Reformulation 1988." In *A Feminist Voyage through International Relations*. New York: Oxford University Press.

Tondo, Lorenzo. 2021. "'Disgraceful': Italy's senate votes down anti-homophobic violence bill." *Guardian*, October 27, 2021. www.theguardian.com.

Transparency International. 2022. "Hungary's Elections: Free but not Fair." *Transparency International*, April 4, 2022. www.transparency.org.

Trimble, Rita J. 2014. "Conceiving a 'Natural Family' Order: The World Congress of Families and Transnational Conservative Christian Politics." PhD diss., the Ohio State University.

Turnbull-Dugarte, Stuart J. 2020. "The European Lavender Vote: Sexuality, Ideology and Vote Choice in Western Europe." *European Journal of Political Research* 59 (3): 517–37.

TVSOYUZ. 2015. "Posol Vsemirnogo Kongressa Semey v OON Aleksey Komov." [Ambassador of the World Congress of Families to the UN Alexey Komov]. July 13, 2015. YouTube video, www.youtube.com/watch?v=XoO8zFHIXz4.

UN Affairs. 2022. "UN General Assembly votes to suspend Russia from the Human Rights Council." *United Nations News Service*, April 7, 2022. https://news.un.org.

UN ECOSOC. 2021. "List of Non-governmental Organizations in Consultative Status with the Economic and Social Council as at 1 September 2019." Economic and Social Council, United Nations, March 2, 2021. https://undocs.org.

UNHRC. 2012. "Preliminary Study on Promoting Human Rights and Fundamental Freedoms through a Better Understanding of Traditional Values of Humankind. Prepared by the Drafting Group of the Advisory Committee." *United Nations Human Rights Council* A/HRC/AC/9/2, June 1, 2012.

———. 2014. "Summary of the Human Rights Council Panel Discussion on the Protection of the Family." *United Nations Human Rights Council* no. A/HRC/RES/28/40.

UN ODS. 2023. Official Document System of the United Nations. https://documents.un.org/prod/ods.nsf/home.xsp.

Uzlaner, Dmitry. 2019. "Global Culture Wars from the Perspective of Russian and American Actors: Some Preliminary Conclusions." Culture Wars Today (blog), Berkley Center for Religion, Peace and World Affairs Forum, December 18, 2019. https://berkleycenter.georgetown.edu.

Uzlaner, Dmitry, and Kristina Stoeckl. 2017. "The Legacy of Pitirim Sorokin in the Transnational Alliances of Moral Conservatives." *Journal of Classical Sociology* 18 (2): 133–53.

van der Vleuten, Anna. 2014. "Transnational LGBTI Activism and the European Courts: Constructing the Idea of Europe." In *LGBT Activism and the Making of Europe: A Rainbow Europe?*, edited by Phillip M. Ayoub and David Paternott, 119–144e. Basingstoke, UK: Palgrave.

Velasco, Kristopher. 2018. "Human Rights INGOs, LGBT INGOs, and LGBT Policy Diffusion, 1991–2015." *Social Forces* 97 (1): 377–404.

———. 2023a. "Transnational Backlash and the Deinstitutionalization of Liberal Norms: LGBT+ Rights in a Contested World." *American Journal of Sociology* 128 (5): 1381–429.

———. 2023b. "Opposition Avoidance or Mutual Engagement? The Interdependent Dynamics Between Opposing Transnational LGBT+ Networks." *Social Forces* 101 (4): 2087–116.

Verloo, Mieke, ed. 2018. *Varieties of Opposition to Gender Equality in Europe*. New York: Routledge.

Verseck, Keno. 2021. "Hungary Approves Law Banning LGBTQ+ Content for Minors." *Deutsche Welle*, June 15, 2021. www.dw.com.

Vollmer, Christine. 2018. "More Proof that Francis' Pontificate Has Been 'Hijacked' by the 'Gay Lobby.'" *Life Site News*, January 12, 2018. www.lifesitenews.com.

Volontè Report. 2021a. "The Volontè Report." *International Family News*, accessed April 9, 2021. https://volontereport.com.

———. 2021b. International Organization for Family, accessed October 28, 2021. https://volontereport.com.

von Wahl, Angelika. 2019. "From Object to Subject: Intersex Activism and the Rise and Fall of the Gender Binary in Germany." *Social Politics: International Studies in Gender, State & Society* 28 (3): 755–77.

Voss, M. Joel. 2018. "Contesting Sexual Orientation and Gender Identity at the UN Human Rights Council." *Human Rights Review* 19: 1–22.

———. 2020. "Sexual Orientation and Gender Identity in International Institutions." *Oxford Research Encyclopedia of Politics*, February 28, 2020. https://oxfordre.com.

Waaldijk, Kees. 2000. "Civil Developments: Patterns of Reform in the Legal Position of Same-Sex Partners in Europe." *Canadian Journal of Family Law* 17 (1): 62–88.

Waites, Matthew. 2009. "Critique of 'Sexual Orientation' and 'Gender Identity' in Human Rights Discourse: Global Queer Politics beyond the Yogyakarta Principles." *Contemporary Politics* 15 (1): 137–56.

———. 2019. "Decolonizing the Boomerang Effect in global Queer Politics: A New Critical Framework for Sociological Analysis of Human Rights Contestation." *International Sociology* 34 (4): 382–401.

Wanner, Catherine. 2007. *Communities of the Converted: Ukrainians and Global Evangelicalism*. Ithaca, NY: Cornell University Press.

WCF. 1997. "A Declaration from the World Congress of Families to the Governments of the Globe Adopted by the Delegates to the World Congress of Families Prague, the Czech Republic." March 22, 1997. www.worldcongress.pl/docs/en/pdf/prague_declaration_1997.pdf.

WCF Chisinau. 2018. "Program of WCF XIII, Chisinau." Accessed May 20, 2021. http://worldcongress.md/wp-content/uploads/2018/09/Graficul_sesiunilor_eng .pdf.

WCF Geneva. 1999. "Program of WCF II, Geneva." Accessed May 20, 2021. https://web .archive.org/web/20010105073800/http://worldcongress.org:80/WCF2/wcf2_spkrs .htm.

WCF Madrid. 2012. "Program of WCF VI, Madrid." Accessed May 20, 2021. https: //web.archive.org/web/20120620231359/http://congresomundial.es/wcf-vi-madrid /program/.

WCF Mexico City. 2004. "Program of WCF III, Mexico City." Accessed May 20, 2021. https://web.archive.org/web/20090706053413/http://www.worldcongress.org:80 /WCF3/wcf3_spkrs.htm.

WCF Warsaw. 2007. "Program of WCF IV, Warsaw." Accessed May 20, 2021. www .worldcongress.pl/program.php?change_lang=en.

Weeks, Jeffrey. 2007. *The World We Have Won: The Remaking of Erotic and Intimate Life*. London: Routledge.

———. 2015. "Gay Liberation and Its Legacies." In *The Ashgate Research Companion to Lesbian and Gay Activism*, edited by David Paternotte and Manon Tremblay, 45–58. Farnham, UK: Ashgate.

Weiss, Meredith L. 2013. "Prejudice before Pride: Rise of an Anticipatory Counter-movement." In *Global Homophobia: States, Movements, and the Politics of Oppression*, edited by Meredith L. Weiss and Michael J. Bosia, 149–173. Urbana: University of Illinois Press.

Weiss, Meredith L., and Michael J. Bosia. 2013. *Global Homophobia: States, Movements, and the Politics of Oppression*. Urbana: University of Illinois Press.

Welch, Matt. 2022. "Victor Orbán flatters Republicans with the Lie that Progressive Liberals and Communists are 'the Same.'" *Reason Magazine*, May 8, 2022. https://reason.com.

Wendt, Alexander. 1999. *Social Theory of International Politics*. New York: Cambridge University Press.

Wesolowsky, Tony. 2021. "The Worrying Regression of LGBT Rights in Eastern Europe." *Radio Free Europe*, December 23, 2021. www.rferl.org.

Whitehead, Andrew L., and Samuel L. Perry. 2020. *Taking America Back for God: Christian Nationalism in the United States*. New York: Oxford University Press.

Whittier, Nancy. 2010. *Feminist Generations: The Persistence of the Radical Women's Movement*. Philadelphia: Temple University Press.

Wickham, Hadley, and Mara Averick, Jennifer Bryan, Winston Chang, Lucy d'Agostino Mc Gowan, Romain Francois, Garret Grolemund et al. 2019. "Welcome to the Tidy-verse." *Journal of Open Source Software* 4 (43): 1686.

WikiLeaks. 2021. "The Intolerance Network." WikiLeaks website, August 5, 2021. https://wikileaks.org/intolerancenetwork/press-release.

Wilcox, Clyde, and Carin Robinson. 2011. *Onward Christian Soldiers? The Religious Right in American Politics*. New York: Routledge.

Wilkinson, Cai. 2013. "Putting Traditional Values into Practice: Russia's Anti-gay Laws." *Russian Analytical Digest* (138): 5–7.

———. 2014. "Putting 'Traditional Values' into Practice: The Rise and Contestation of Anti-Homopropaganda Laws in Russia." *Journal of Human Rights* 13 (3): 363–79.

———. 2015. "LGBT Rights: The Perils of Becoming Mainstream." Duck of Minerva, July 8, 2019. https://duckofminerva.com.

Wilkinson, Cai, and Anthony J. Langlois. 2014. "Special Issue: Not Such an International Human Rights Norm? Local Resistance to Lesbian, Gay, Bisexual, and Transgender Rights—Preliminary Comments." *Journal of Human Rights* 13 (3): 249–55.

Wilson, Angelia. 2012. "Why Is Europe Lesbian and Gay Friendly?" *Perspectives on Europe* 42 (1): 57–63.

Wodak, Ruth. 2015. The Politics of Fear. *What Right-Wing Populist Discourse Means.* London: SAGE.

Wohlforth, William C., Benjamin de Carvalho, Halvard Leira, and Iver B. Neumann. 2018. "Moral Authority and Status in International Relations: Good States and the Social Dimension of Status Seeking." *Review of International Studies* 44 (3): 526–46. doi:10.1017/S0260210517000560.

Wojnicka, Katarzyna. 2022. "Theorising European Fathers' Rights Movements." Unpublished manuscript. Presented at the Council for European Studies Annual Meeting, Lisbon, Portugal, July 1, 2022.

Woods, Gregory. 2017. *Homintern: How Gay Culture Liberated the Modern World.* New Haven, CT: Yale University Press.

Woodward, Alison. 2004. "Building Velvet Triangles: Gender and Informal Governance." In *Informal Governance in the European Union*, edited by Thomas Christensen and Simona Paitonni, 76–93. Cheltenham, UK: Edward Elger.

Wuest, Joanna, and Briana Last. Forthcoming. "Church Against State: How Industry Groups Lead the Religious Liberty Assault on Civil Rights, Healthcare Policy, and the Administrative State." *Journal of Law, Medicine & Ethics*, December 22, 2022. https://ssrn.com.

WWC. 2015. "Inter-religious and Intra-Christian Dialogue in Ecumenical Conversation. A Practical Guide." *World Council of Churches*, November 19, 2015. www .oikoumene.org.

Yamin, Alicia Ely, Neil Datta, and Ximena Andión. 2018. "Behind the Drama: The Roles of Transnational Actors in Legal Mobilization over Sexual and Reproductive Rights." *Georgetown Journal of Gender and the Law* 19 (1): 533–69.

"Yogyakarta Principles." 2017. http://yogyakartaprinciples.org.

Zepeda-Millán, Chris. 2017. *Latino Mass Mobilization: Immigration, Racialization, and Activism.* New York: Cambridge University Press.

Zerofsky, Elisabeth. 2021. "How the American Right Fell in Love With Hungary." *New York Times*, October 19, 2021. www.nytimes.com.

Zito, Anthony R. 2009. "European Agencies as Agents of Governance and EU Learning." *Journal of European Public Policy* 16 (8): 1224–43.

Zorgdrager, Heleen. 2013. "Homosexuality and Hypermasculinity in the Public Discourse of the Russian Orthodox Church: An Affect Theoretical Approach." *International Journal of Philosophy and Theology* 74 (3): 214–39.

INTERVIEWS

Interview, Anonymous. 2017a. Interview conducted May 25, 2017, by Olena Kostenko in the context of the project Postsecular Conflicts with a participant from Africa at the World Congress of Families in Budapest (26 min.).

Interview, Anonymous. 2017b. Interview conducted May 25, 2017, by Olena Kostenko in the context of the project Postsecular Conflicts with an American participant at the World Congress of Families in Budapest (7 min.).

Interview, Anonymous. 2017c. Interview conducted February 23, 2017, by Ksenia Medvedeva in the context of the project Postsecular Conflicts with a member of the diplomatic corps to the UN of a post-Soviet country. The interview was conducted via Skype in Russian, and all quotes have been translated by April French (no. 23.02.2017).

Interview, Anonymous. 2017d. Interview conducted May 26, 2017, by Olena Kostenko in the context of the project Postsecular Conflicts with a participant connected to CitizenGo at the World Congress of Families in Budapest (12 min.).

Interview, Anonymous. 2017e. Interview conducted May 25, 2017, by Olena Kostenko in the context of the project Postsecular Conflicts with a Serbian participant at the World Congress of Families in Budapest (9 min.).

Interview, Anonymous. 2017f. Interview conducted May 27, 2017, by Olena Kostenko in the context of the project Postsecular Conflicts with a French participant at the World Congress of Families in Budapest (11 min.).

Interview, Anonymous. 2017g. Interview conducted on May 19, 2017, by Olena Kostenko with a participant at the Homeschooling Congress in Italy (Rome) in the context of the project Postsecular Conflicts (28 min.).

Interview, Anonymous. 2018a. Interview conducted February 23, 2018, by Kristina Stoeckl in the context of the project Postsecular Conflicts with an American stakeholder from the NGO sector. The interview was conducted in English (no. 23.02.2018.).

Interview, Anonymous. 2018b. Interview conducted September 15, 2018, by Caroline Hill in the context of the project Postsecular Conflicts with an American participant at the World Congress of Families in Chisinau, Moldova (43 min.).

Interview, Anonymous. 2018c. Interview conducted May 14, 2018, by Olena Kostenko in the context of the project Postsecular Conflicts with an American homeschooling curriculum provider at the Global Education Conference in St. Petersburg, Russia (11 min.).

Interview, Anonymous. 2018d. Interview conducted September 15, 2018, by Pasquale Annicchino in the context of the project Postsecular Conflicts with an Italian participant at the World Congress of Families in Chisinau, Moldova (25 min.).

Interview, Anonymous. 2018e. Interview conducted September 15, 2018, by Pasquale Annicchino in the context of the project Postsecular Conflicts with an American participant at the World Congress of Families in Chisinau, Moldova (18 min.).

Interview, Anonymous. 2018f. Interview conducted May 18, 2018, by Caroline Hill in the context of the project Postsecular Conflicts with an American participant at the Global Education Conference in St. Petersburg, Russia (16 min.).

Interview, Bielefeldt. 2017. Interview conducted by Kristina Stoeckl January 16, 2017, in the context of the project Postsecular Conflicts with Heiner Bielefeldt, former UN Ambassador for Religious Freedom. The interviewee agreed to waive anonymity. The interview was conducted via Skype in German.

Interview, Carlson. 2018. Interview conducted with Allan Carlson in Moscow on May 19, 2018, by Dmitry Uzlaner in the context of the project Postsecular Conflicts. The interview was conducted in English, and the interviewee agreed to waive anonymity (49 min.).

Interview, Carlson. 2019. Interview conducted with Allan Carlson in Verona on March 28, 2019, by Kristina Stoeckl in the context of the project Postsecular Conflicts. The interview was conducted in English, and the interviewee agreed to waive anonymity (49 min.).

Interview, Huebner. 2017. Interview conducted with Gerald Huebner on May 19, 2017, by Olena Kostenko at Homeschooling Congress in Italy (Rome) in the context of the project Postsecular Conflicts. The interview was conducted in English, and the interviewee agreed to waive anonymity (7 min.).

Interview, Komov. 2017. Interview with Alexey Komov conducted on January 31, 2017, by Kristina Stoeckl and Olena Kostenko in Moscow in the context of the project Postsecular Conflicts. The interview was conducted in Russian, and the interviewee agreed to waive anonymity (1 hr. 40 min.).

Interview, Vollmer. 2017. Interview conducted with Christine Vollmer on May 27, 2017, by Olena Kostenko at the World Congress of Families in Budapest, Hungary in the context of the project Postsecular Conflicts. The interview was conducted in English, and the interviewee agreed to waive anonymity (10 min.).

INDEX

Page numbers in italics indicate Figures and Tables

abortion, 185, 267; American Christian
Right on, 177; *Fristenlösung* regulation
regarding, 67, 292n7; pro-life arguments
against, 89; Russia and US conscientious objection initiative against, 188;
WCF Tbilisi themes against, 189; Western Europe decriminalization of, 67
academia, international, 205, 206, 229–30;
gender-critical academic literature,
225; MCC, 228; Regnerus influence on,
226–27; Sorokin influence on, 226
ACCEPT Association, 42, 43
Acquis communautaire, 292n9
activist families, Catholic, 121–24
ADF. *See* Alliance Defending Freedom
ADF International. *See* Alliance Defending Freedom International
Advocate, 244, 299n9
Africa, 160, 180; Ghana, 4, 300n5; Uganda,
179; WCF ties to, 115
Agenda Europe, 14, 15, 98, 131–32
aggiornamento, conservative, 81, 292n10
Alekseyev v. Russia, 156
Alfeyev, Grigory Valerievich, 155
Alive to the World curriculum, 122, 126
Alliance Defending Freedom (ADF), 30,
98, 216, 217, 297n7 (chap. 6)
Alliance Defending Freedom International
(ADF International), 72, 82, 122; *Lautsi
v. Italy* representation of, 216; WCF
involvement of, 109; *Wunderlich v. Ger-
many* legal representation of, 74

All-Out, 243
Allport, Gordon, 38
American Anthropological Association,
209
American Center for Law and Justice, 72
American Classical Conversations, 83
American Conservative Union, 148
American Conservative website, 229
American National Organization for Mar-
riage, 88, 100
The American Sex Revolution (Sorokin),
61–62, 226
amicus brief, 74
Amnesty International, 47, 146
Amsterdam, WCF in, 146
Amsterdam Treaty, 49, 72
Anagnostou, Dia, 75
Analytical Center for Family Policy Rus-
sia, 83
Andrikiene, Laima, 110
anti-communism, American, 60–61
Anti-Gender Campaigns in Europe (Kuhar
and Paternotte), 96, 157
Anti-Genderismus, 58. *See also* gender
ideology
Anti-Genderismus in Europa (Strube), 96,
157
anti-gender movements, 7, 19, 20, 289n19,
290n24
anti-hate-crimes law, Italy blocking, 182–83
Antiochian Orthodox Christian Archdio-
cese of North America, 95

342 | INDEX

anti-SOGI rights Transnational Advocacy Networks (anti-SOGI rights TANs), 8
anti-vaccination movements, 268
Antonov, Anatolij, 88
Argentina, 42
Arsuaga, Ignacio, 101, 109, 128, *129*
ARTE Television network, 131
Article 16 Initiative, 100
assimilationism, 291n10
Austin Institute for the Study of Family and Culture, 228
Australia, marriage equality in, 37
Austria, 299n12
Ayoub, Phillip M., 2

Bachman, Michele, 18
Bączkowski and Others v. Poland, 139
Baker, Gilbert, 295n3
Ban Ki-Moon, 51
baptisms, 296n8
Bases of the Social Concept of the Russian Orthodox Church. *See* Social Doctrine
bathroom cruising, 95
Beijing World Conference for Women, 17, 70, 157
Belarus, 167–68, 213
The Benedict Option (Dreher), 229
Berlin Wall, 80
Bill of Rights, US, 182
Billy Graham Evangelical Association, 144
birth control, Global South moral conservative actors against, 180
Blackmore, Elena, 237
Bob, Clifford, 293n5
Bolshevik revolution, 61, 201
Bolsonaro, Jair, 243
boomerang human rights model, 40, 56, 233, 266, 268
Bosia, Mike, 15, 142, 150
Boston Review, 262–63
Brandi, Antonio, 130
Brazil, UN resolution cosponsored by, 51

Brown, Brian, 88, 100, 109, 128, *129*; Gessen interview with, 270; Ukraine and Belarus toured by, 167–68
Budapest WFC summit, 126, 144, 145, 174, 178, 180, 182
Building our Collective Strength to Counter the Anti-gender Opposition ILGA World Conference workshop, 254
Burack, Cynthia, 13, 182
Butler, Jennifer, 57, 71
Butler, Judith, 19, 84, *85*, 293n12
Buzogány, Aron, 149
Byrnes, Timothy A., 79

Cairo, United Nations International Conference on Population and Development in, 17, 69–70, 157, 213
California, Proposition 8 in, 243, 271–72, 298n7
Campaign for Homosexuality Equality (CHE), 35
capitalism, 22, 195, 197
capitalism, cosmopolitan, 22–23, 195, 197–98
Carlson, Allan, 88, 123, 179; home economy agenda of, 195, 196; *The Natural Family* by, 118, 119, 192; on Orthodox Christian churches, 121; on Swedish welfare state model, 193–94; on WCF history, 99–100
Carlson, Tucker, 16, 228, 290n22
de Carvalho, Benjamin, 163
Catholic aristocrats, PMC TANs involvement of, 121–24
Catholic Church, 30, 72, 289n17; aggiornamento of, 292n10; under Francis, 121, 158, 159–60, 161, 164; German, 161; homosexuality and same-sex marriage, opposition to, 158; of John Paul II, 17, 69, 70, 76–77; on National Socialism, 66; Orthodox Christian church split from, 118; paternal Catholic modernism of, 69, 76–77,

157; in Poland, 79–80, 150; queering, 161; Russian Orthodox Church relations with, 137, 155–56, 159, 162; sexual abuse scandals in, 162; WCF presence of, 120

CEE. *See* Central and Eastern Europe

Center for Culture and Leisure *(Cultuur en Ontspanningscentrum)*, 46

Center for Family and Human Rights (C-Fam), 71, 212

Central and Eastern Europe (CEE), 189, 272; civil society organizing in, 68; Croatia, 159, 242; homosexuality in, 146; religious revival in, 76, 90; WCF attendees from, 191

Central European University, 149

C-Fam. *See* Center for Family and Human Rights

Chappel, James, 69

Charamsa, Krzysztof, 160–61

CHE. *See* Campaign for Homosexuality Equality

children: ILGA-Europe discussion of, 251; moral conservatism protection claim, 183–85; PACE resolutions on, 220–21, 222–23; in rainbow families, 239; rights of, 192, 220–21, 243

Chinese government, "sissy men" banned by, 262–63

Chisinau WCF, 167, 183–84, 197, 199, 202

Christian churches, 86, 153, 294n15; conservative ecumenism of, 119; in Europe, 72; Fidesz government role of, 150; Western, 154–55; Western Europe influence of, 67. *See also* Orthodox Christian churches

Christian Democrats, EU work of, 66

Christian faith, KPH frame embracing, 234

Christian Right, 89, 123; ADF International representing, 109; advocacy groups, 69, 90; human rights language used by, 60; Western, 78, 166–67

Christian Right, American, 30, 62, 63, 65, 68, 196, 292n8; on abortion, 177; advocacy of, 72–76; family values invention by, 64; homeschooling promoted by, 105; human rights language used by, 60; Hungary legislation praised by, 147; John Paul II influencing, 69; moral conservative litigation of, 215–16; moral conservative norm mobilization fueled by, 97; NGOs, 70, 71, 72, 90; religious revival regarding, 80; Russian Orthodox Church influenced by, 153–54; Vatican allied with, 70

Christmas Readings Pro-life Conference, 28

Church of Jesus Christ of Latter-day Saints. *See* Mormon Church

CitizenGo, 14–15, 30, 31, 98, 108, *129*, 294n8, 295n19; board members of, 128; coordinated actions of, 132; German, 102–3, *104*; HazteOir relationship with, 101; Malofeev support for, 120; NGO campaigns organized with, 103–4; Russian, 144; Spanish, 82

civic organizations, moral conservative actors creating, 63

civil rights movement, 62, 190

civil society actors, anti-SOGI rights, 57–58

civil society organizing, 68, 292n2

Civiltà Cattolica, 120

Classical Conversations, 107, 125

clientelism, 122–23

Clinton, Hillary, 150, 154, 291n4

CoE. *See* Council of Europe

Cold War, 60, 68; Carlson, Allan, on, 194; conspiracy theorists, 173; moral conservatism globalization impacted by, 69, 80; religious revival after, 76–80

Colombia, 2, 287n1, 294n12

colonization, 296n1

Coman, Adrian, 42–43

344 | INDEX

Combating rising hate against LGBT people in Europe PACE resolution amendment, 219–20

Commission for Family, Defense of Motherhood and Childhood, 186

Commonwealth of Orthodox Churches, 167

communism: American anti-communism, 60–61; cosmopolitan capitalism conflation with, 197–98; moral conservative narrative rejection of, 22, 191–95

communist bloc, former, 76, 78, 79

Communist Revolution, 61

communists, Orbán on, 19

Congregation of Faith, 158–59, 161

Connolly, Madeline, 243

conscientious objection, among taxpayers, 188

conservative ecumenism, 119

Conservative Political Action Conference, American (CPAC), 16, 19, 148, 290n26

Considerations Regarding Proposals to Give Legal Recognition to Unions Between Homosexual Persons, 158

conspiracy theories: conspiratorial mindset distinguished from, 175–76, 271; gay lobby in, 162, 175; "homintern," 173, 174; moral conservative narrative similarity with, 173, 177, 191, 203, 270

contact hypothesis, 38–39

content analysis, 27, 31, 247–49, 249, 250

conversion therapy, Russian support for, 261

Cooper, Melinda, 195

Cooper-Cunningham, Dean, 295n4

Coordinated strategies for effective Internet governance PACE recommendation, 221–22

Council of Europe (CoE), 20, 31, 49, 127, 205, 206, 214–19, 219, 220–24, 298n11; CHE group pressuring, 35; Russia in, 139, 140, 141, 156. *See also* European Court of Human Rights; Parliamentary Assembly of the Council of Europe

Countering Anti-gender Actors and Narratives workshop, 254

counterrevolutionaries, and revolutionaries, 200–204

court judgments, 73, 75

Court of Justice, EU, 42–43

Coventry, UK, 35

COVID-19 pandemic, 240–41, 268, 294n10

CPAC. *See* Conservative Political Action Conference, American

Crimea, Russia annexing, 112, 167

Croatia, 159, 242

cultural Marxism, liberalism equated with, 199

Culture Wars (Hunter), 62–63

culture wars, American, 62–63, 69, 70, 72, 75, 80, 86, 90, 117, 292n3

Cultuur en Ontspanningscentrum (Center for Culture and Leisure), 46

Curanović, Alicja, 294n11

Cyprus, Nicosia, 1, 234, 266

Datta, Neil, 120, 145, 220; on Agenda Europe, 131, 132; *Diskursatlas Antifeminismus* by, 96, 293n1; *Tip of the Iceberg* by, 124

Davis, Kim, 74

death penalty, in Russia, 141

Debra Bell Academy, 107

Declaration on Certain Questions Concerning Sexual Ethics, 157

delegate packets, ILGA-Europe, 250, 251, 252, 253

demography, 188–89, 296n3

Deneen, Patrick, 198–99

Denmark, 66

diplomacy, rainbow flag, 134, 147

discourse coalitions, 21

discrimination, 49, 174, 215, 260

disinformation experts, counter, 254
Diskursatlas Antifeminismus (Datta), 96, 293n1
Dmitry, Hieromonk, 150, 154
domestic violence legislation, 186
Donbas, Ukraine, 125, 257–58
Don't Say Gay Bill, 147, 184
double helix human rights model, 4, 23, 24, 30, 32, 44, 54, 117, 255; of anti-vaccination movements, 268; court system pattern in, 73; moral conservatism and moral progressivism dynamic in, 272–73; of moral conservatism networks, 56, 263–64; NGOs regarding, 71, 268; of PMC and SOGI rights TANs, 55; spiral human rights model compared to, 9, 10, 55, 266, 268; in US, 268–69; white nationalism applicability within, 266–67
Dreher, Rod, 147, 165–66, 228, 229
Drudge Report, 84
Duda, Andrei, 18–19
Dudgeon, Jeff, 47

Eastern Europe, 42–43, 78, 147, 159, 179, 241, 243–44, 288n9. *See also* Central and Eastern Europe
ECLJ. *See* European Center for Law and Justice
ECtHR. *See* European Court of Human Rights
Edenborg, Emil, 21, 258, 259, 262–63, 292n2
education, higher, 149
Egypt, 4, 212
embassies: British, 134, 147; protests at, 132–33; US, 134
employment discrimination, 49, 260. *See also* discrimination
Engels, Friedrich, 61
Equality March, 295n5
Equal Rights Amendment (1972), 63

ERC. *See* European Research Council
EU. *See* European Union
Euro-Letter newsletters, *251, 252,* 299n13
Europe, 292n5; Austria, 299n12; Christian churches in, 72; Eastern, 42–43, 78, 147, 159, 179, 241, 243–44, 288n9; Moldova, 167, 183–84, 197, 199, 202, 220; moral conservatism in, 60, 65–69; moral conservative advocacy networks in, 96; Muslim immigrant rejection in, 87; policy in, 66, 67; populist right parties in, 87; UK, 35, 47; Ukraine pro-European political identity, 271; US morality policy struggles compared to, 67–68; WCF organizing in, *113,* 117; Western, 67, 189
European Center for Law and Justice (ECLJ), 72–73, 74, 98, 109, 156, 217
European Commission, ILGA-Europe alliance with, 242
European Convention on Human Rights, 35, 139, 140, 295n5
European Court of Human Rights (ECtHR), 31, 47, 49, 72, 73, 188, 205, 206; *Bączkowski and Others v. Poland*, 139; German family homeschooling case brought to, 108; ILGA-Europe strategic litigation brought to, 297n8 (chap. 6); *Ladele v. United Kingdom*, 74, 75, 216, 297n7 (chap. 6); *Lautsi v. Italy*, 216; LGBTI anti-discrimination case law produced by, 215; Moscow Patriarchate involvement with, 156; rainbow family recognition by, 241; Russia under, 139, 140, 141; *Vejdeland and Others v. Sweden*, 217
European Forum of LGBT Christian Groups, 183
European Parliament, 42, 110
European Parliamentary Forum for Sexual and Reproductive Rights, 96
European People's Party, 110
European Research Council (ERC), 28

346 | INDEX

European Union (EU), 13, 31, 44, 50, 58, 117, 165, 181, 205, 214–15; accession requirements of, 148; Christian Democrats work on, 66; Council, 287n4; Court of Justice, 42–43; human rights recognition and protection in, 49, 72; Hungary response of, 15, 147; law, 292n9; as liberalization and democratization agent, 78; moral conservative narrative blaming, 199, 200

EU Strategy on the Rights of the Child, 242

Evangelicals, conservative, 105, 164

FACH. *See* Foundation for African Cultural Heritage

Faith and Rainbow (Wiara i Tęcza), 234

family: Catholic activist, 121–24; Croatia alliances of, 242; ECtHR case German homeschooling, 108; feminist organizing debates around, 299n10; Montgomery on, 298n7; moral conservatism protection claim, 187–88; No and Yes Campaigns use of, 246, *246*; pro-family UN block, 71, 82, 293n5; SOGI rights movement redefining, 239–46, *246*, *247*. *See also* rainbow families

family, heteronormative, 61, 64; Carlson, Allan, on, 99; Lassiter on, 62; natural family flag representing, 137, *138*; *The Natural Family* on, 118, 119, 192; Vatican on, 69; WCF pro-family agenda, 192–93

Family Day, in Georgia, 2, 266

family issues, 241–42, 248, *251*, *253*

family values, 1, 299n12, 300n6; content analysis of, 248, 249; ILGA-Europe organizing around, 249–50, *251*, *253*, 254; Lassiter on, 62, 64; love as, 243–44; SOGI responses, 249, *249*, 250, 252, 254; SOGI rights movement reclaiming, 238, 239; in Ukraine, 260; WCF attendee on, 81

FARC. *See* Fuerzas Armadas Revolucionarias de Colombia peace deal

fascism, 65–66

Federal National Security Strategy, of Russia, 259

feminism, 62, 299n10

Fetner, Tina, 8, 64–65

FHAR. *See* Front homosexuel d'action révolutionnaire

Fidesz government, 137, 148, 149, 150

Fighting the over-sexualization of children PACE resolution, 222–23

flag: natural family, 137, *138*; rainbow, 134, 137, 147, 202, 261, 295n3; red communist, 202

Florida, US, 147

Fokas, Effie, 75

Foundation for African Cultural Heritage (FACH), 115

France, marriage equality in, 244–45

Francis (Pope), 120, 122, 185; *Advocate* Person of the Year naming, 244; Catholic Church under, 121, 158, 159–60, 161, 164; gay lobby association accusation aimed at, 162; on homosexuality, 159–60

Franciscan Friars of the Renewal, 57

Frankfurt School, of Neo-Marxism, 201

Free Movement Directive, 250–51

Fristenlösung regulation, 67, 292n7

Front homosexuel d'action révolutionnaire (FHAR), 45

Fuerzas Armadas Revolucionarias de Colombia peace deal (FARC), 2, 3, 16, 96–97, 294n12

funding: for moral conservative actors, 124, 294n16; for NGOs, 126–27; for SOGI rights movement, 298n3

Gates, Bill, 201

Gates, Melinda, 201

Gay, Robert, 118–19

Gay Liberation Front (GLF), 45, 53

gay lobby, 162, 175

gender, 5, 259–63, 265; backlash, 58; equality, 288n7; policies mainstreaming, 289n18; studies, 149, 225, 227, 228

gender-critical academic literature, 225

gender ideology, 16, 51–52, 287n1; *Anti-Genderismus*, 58; FARC peace deal rhetoric about, 96–97; narrative, 18; symbolic glue, 21, 59; Vatican coining, 17

Georgia, 2, 118, 119, 185, 266. *See also* Tbilisi, WCF

Germany, 244, 292n6; *Anti-Genderismus* term in, 58; Catholic Church in, 161; ECtHR family homeschooling case from, 108; gay action groups in, 45; National Socialism in, 65–66; Polish LGBTIQ activists mobilizing in, 40; *Wunderlich v. Germany*, 74. *See also* CitizenGo, German

Gessen, Masha, 270, 296n5

Geva, Dorit, 228

Ghana, 4, 300n5

GHEX. *See* Global Home Education Exchange

Ghiletchi, Valeriu, 220–21, 222–23, 298n10

Ghudushauri-Shiolashvili, Irakli, 185

GLF. *See* Gay Liberation Front

Global Home Education Exchange (GHEX), 82, 98, 105, 108, *129*, 144; conferences, 28, 106; homeschooling curriculum providers at, 107; liberalism refutation at, 198; Universal Declaration of Human Rights article championed by, 130. *See also* Homeschool Legal Defense Association, US

Global Homeschooling Movement, 30

globalization: of American culture wars, 69, 70, 72, 75, 80, 86, 90, 117; of competing human rights framework, 74, 75–76; of moral conservatism, 69–76, 80

Global Philanthropy Project, 124, 294n16

The Global Right Wing (Bob), 293n5

The Global Sexual Revolution (Kuby), 183, 200, 229

Global South, 87, 96, 210; moral conservative actors, 180; UN blamed in, 200; WCF participation of, 115, 179. *See also* moral conservative actors, Global South

Graff, Agnieszka, 14, 197

Graham, Billy, 226

Graham-Harrison, Emma, 272

Gramsci, Antonio, 201

Grenell, Ric, 289n14

Guardian, 84

Gundyaev, Vladimir Mikhailovich, 155, 165, 166, 257–58, 299n1

Hamilton, Clai, 42–43

hate-groups, 141

HazteOir ("Make yourself heard"), 82, 101, 298n1

Helms, Jesse, 50

Helsinki Accords, 139

Herkel, Andres, 222

heteronormative internationalism, 295n4

Hirschfeld, Magnus, 45, 66

HIV/AIDS pandemic, 65, 68

Höhne, Florian, 96

Holocaust, 65–66, 268

Holy See, 70, 157, 295n2

home economy, 195, 196

homeschooling, 105, 107, 122, 126

Homeschool Legal Defense Association, US (HSLDA), 82, 105, 106. *See also* Global Home Education Exchange

homintern, 173, 174

homonationalism, 24, 54, 87, 289n14

homophile movement, 46

homophobia, 5, 15, 134, 142, 146–47, 150, 265, 295n4

The Homosexual is Not Perverse, but the Society in which He Lives (Nicht der Homosexuelle ist Pervers, sondern die Situation in der er lebt), 45

348 | INDEX

homosexuality: American Christian Right targeting, 64; Catholic Church opposition to, 158; in Central and Eastern Europe, 146; decriminalization of, 51, 266, 269, 287n3, 289n14, 290n27, 297n8 (chap. 6), 300n5; Francis on, 159–60; international conspiracy, 173; pedophilia conflated with, 146; in Russia, 139–40, 141–42, 143, 150; Social Doctrine denouncing, 152

Horizon Europe, 289n18

Horsfjord, Vebjørn, 212

Howard Center for Family, Religion, and Society, 82, 100, 207, 213, 294n7

"How to Organize a World Congress of Families Regional Event, Regional Conference, or Summit" (WCF), 177

HSLDA. *See* Homeschool Legal Defense Association, US

Huebner, Gerald, 106, 167–68

human rights, 36, 48, 73, 181, 297n5; boomerang model of, 40, 56, 233, 266, 268; EU recognition and protection of, 49, 72; language, 11, 12, 60; norms, 56, 130, 300n8; spiral model of, 4, 9, 10, 40, 55, 56, 233, 266, 268; universal human rights standards and human-rights-skeptical positions on, 209–10, 214. *See also* double helix human rights model; European Court of Human Rights; Universal Declaration of Human Rights

human rights, competing, 216; globalization of, 74, 75–76; protect women claim language of, 185; religious freedom framework of, 75–76, 182

Human Rights Council Advisory Committee, 211

Human Rights Day speech, by Clinton, 291n4

human rights diffusion, 32, 38–39, 43. *See also* boomerang human rights model; double helix human rights model; spiral human rights model

Human Rights Watch, 146

Hungarian Child Protection Act, 181

Hungarian Ministry for Family and Youth Affairs, 126

Hungary, 4, 30, 135; anti-gender mobilization of, 149–50; Christian turn in, 166; CPAC in, 16, 148; gender studies banned by, 149, 228; higher education attacked in, 149; Russia relations with, 136–37, 167; state-sponsored homophobic legislation of, 134, 146–47; traditional values agenda identity of, 164; US conservative politicians traveling to, 15–16, 166. *See also* Budapest WFC summit

Hunter, James D., 62–63

ICSE. *See* International Committee for Sexual Equality

IDAHOBIT. *See* International Day against Homo-, Bi-, and Transphobia

ideological entrepreneurs, 142–43

IGOs. *See* international governmental organization venues

ILGA. *See* International Lesbian, Gay, Bisexual, Trans and Intersex Association

ILGA-Europe. *See* International Lesbian, Gay, Bisexual, Trans and Intersex Association Europe

immigration, 250, *251*, 296n4. *See also* Muslim immigrants

INGOs. *See* international nongovernmental organizations

institutions, 47–49, 52; environments of, 288nn11–12; moral conservatives creating, 63; UN consultative status of, 50, 51, 53

Inter-American Commission on Human Rights, 50

Inter-American Court of Human Rights, 49–50

International Committee for Sexual Equality (ICSE), 46

International Day against Homo-, Bi-, and Transphobia (IDAHOBIT), 2
International Gay Association, 35
international governmental organization venues (IGOs), 135
International Lesbian, Gay, Bisexual, Trans and Intersex Association (ILGA), 35–36, 40, 45, 46–47, 52; Eastern European Pool of, 78; UN consultancy status of, 50, 51; World Conference, 254
International Lesbian, Gay, Bisexual, Trans and Intersex Association Europe (ILGA-Europe), 40, 43; content analysis of, 27, 31, 247–49, 249, 250; delegate packets, 250, 251, 252, 253; Euro-Letter newsletters within, 251, 252, 299n13; European Commission alliance with, 242; family issues organizing of, 248, 251, 253; family values SOGI rights organizing of, 249–50, 251, 253, 254; framework guide generated by, 237–38; results and discussion of, 250–51, 251, 252, 253, 254; strategic litigation used by, 297n8 (chap. 6)
international nongovernmental organizations (INGOs), 28, 42, 81–82, 96, 97, 238. See also World Congress of Families
International Organization for the Family (IOF), 14, 25, 30, 83–84, 100, 129. See also World Congress of Families
international organizations (IOs), 30, 31, 42, 47, 49–52, 134, 135, 136, 162–63; alliances of, 166–69; CHE group pressuring, 35; human rights recognition and protection of, 48; identities of, 164–66, 168–69; moral conservative narrative blaming, 199–200; rival TAN venue use of, 54
International Planned Parenthood Federation, 184, 199

international relations (IR), 9, 58, 135, 163, 164, 169, 260, 299n3
Interreligious Council of Russia, on ECtHR, 156
intersex persons, Social Doctrine on, 296n7
interviews, semistructured, 27, 28, 29
"The Intolerance Network" (WikiLeaks), 101, 297n7 (chap. 5)
"Inventing Family Values" (Lassiter), 62
IOF. See International Organization for the Family
IOs. See international organizations
IR. See international relations
Iraq, US invasion of, 181
Ireland, 1, 37, 238, 243, 245–46, 246
Ireland, Republic of, 47
Iron Curtain, 68, 77, 78
Islam, in Russia, 87. See also Muslim immigrants
Israel, 267
Istanbul Convention, 148
Italy, 243; anti-hate-crimes law blocked in, 182–83; family issues alliances in, 242; Lautsi v. Italy, 74, 216; protect children claim in, 184–85

John Paul II (Pope), 17, 69, 70, 76–77
The Joy of Love papal encyclical, 160

Katzenstein, Peter J., 79
Kaufmann, Eric, 123
"Kill the Gays" Bill, Ugandan, 179
King, Martin Luther, Jr., 190
kintsugi, 59, 290n21
Klassicheskie Besedy, 83
Komov, Alexey, 122, 125, 126, 128, 129, 143; conspiracy theory claimed by, 175; coordinated actions organized by, 132; moral conservative narrative promoted by, 200–202; on Ukraine, 168, 175; WCF involvement of, 207
Korolczuk, Elżbieta, 14, 197

350 | INDEX

Kováts, Eszter, 21, 58, 59, 149–50
Kowalczyk, Józef, 236
Kozhemiakin, Andrii, 272
KPH. *See* Polish Campaign against Homophobia
Der Kreis, 46
Kremlin, 126, 142; Moscow Patriarchate ideological arm of, 151; Russian Orthodox Church coordination with, 156–57; traditional values agenda of, 143, 144, 145, 163–64
Kuby, Gabriele, 122, 183, 200, 229
Kuhar, Roman, 26; *Anti-Gender Campaigns in Europe* by, 96, 157; on anti-gender movements, 290n24; on gender ideology, 16–17, 58

Ladele v. United Kingdom, 74, 75, 216, 297n7 (chap. 6)
La Manif pour tous (campaign), 16, 101, 159, 244–45
Lang, Sabine, 298n1
Laruelle, Marlene, 142–43
Lassiter, Matthew, 62, 64
Latin America, 49
Latin American Alliance for the Family, 122
Lautsi v. Italy, 74, 216
Law and Justice party, Polish (PIS), 18, 136
Lawrence v. Texas, 292n4
League for Safe Internet, 222, 295n18
learning, 41, 44, 291n6
left wing, global, 12
"Legal Analysis of the Draft Federal Law 'On the Prevention of Domestic Violence in the Russian Federation'" report (Russian Center for Family Policy), 186
legislative campaigns, 241
LEGO petition, on German CitizenGo, 103, *104*
Legutko, Ryszard, 18
Lehouq, Emilio, 287n1

Leira, Halvard, 163
lesbian, gay, bisexual, transgender, intersex, and queer (LGBTIQ), 1
Letter on the Pastoral Care of Homosexual Persons, 158
"Let us offer each other a sign of peace" (*Przekażmy Sobie Znak Pokoju*), 234, 235, 238
Lexicon (Pontifical Council for the Family), 159
LGBTIQ. *See* lesbian, gay, bisexual, transgender, intersex, and queer
LGBTIQ rights. *See specific topics*
liberalism refutation, of moral conservative narrative, 198–99
LifeSiteNews, 122
Lively, Scott, 179–80
Live Not by Lies (Dreher), 229
lobbyists, conservative, 57, 206
logarithmic transformation, 294n13
love, as family values, 243–44

Madrid WCF, 202, 294n8
Madrigal-Borloz, Victor, 51, 205
"Make yourself heard" (HazteOir), 82, 101, 298n1
Malofeev, Konstantin, 112, 120, 143; Russian Ukraine invasion support of, 125–26; Saint Basil the Great fund founded by, 125, 126, 222; traditional values represented by, 144, 145
Malta, 36, 244
Manhattan Declaration, 155
Marriage and Family Protection in Romania, constitutional revision referendum, 131
marriage equality, 53, 291n3; *Advocate on*, 299n9; in France, 244–45; in Ireland and Australia, 37; in Slovenia, 288n9; in US, 8, 243, 271–72. *See also* same-sex marriage
Marx, Karl, 61
Marxist spell, 194

Mashrou' Leila, 287n5

Masterpiece Cakeshop v. Colorado Human Rights Commission, 74, 75, 109

Mathias Corvinus Collegium (MCC), 228

McCarthyism, in US, 262

Medvedeva, Kseniya, 14

Meireis, Torsten, 96

Meloni, Giorgia, 184–85

men, 186, 262–63, 267

Merkel, Angela, 147

Mero, Paul, 118, 119, 192

method, 27–29

Metropolitan Hilarion. *See* Alfeyev, Grigory Valerievich

Mexico, same-sex marriage in, 295n21

mirroring frame, 288n11

misinformation, 267

Mizulina, Ekaterina, 222, 295n18

Mizulina, Elena, 126, 222, 295n18

Moldova, 167, 183–84, 197, 199, 202, 220

Montenegro, 241

Montgomery, Wendy, 298n7

moral conservatism, 177; American Christian Right advocacy influencing, 72–76; children protection claim of, 183–85; conspiratorial mindset of, 175–76, 271; in Europe, 60, 65–69; family protection claim of, 187–88; globalization of, 69–76, 80; *kintsugi* of, 59; moral progressivism double helix human rights model dynamic with, 272–73; nation protection claim of, 178–81; neoliberalism linked to, 195, 197; policy issue changes of, 88; religion protection claim of, 181–83; society protection claim of, 188–90; transnational philosophy of, 190, 191; in US, 60–65, 292n2; Vatican and UN impacting, 69–72; women protection claim of, 185–87

moral conservative actors, 5, 10–11, 12–16, 20, 30, 184, 185, 205, 289n13; civic organizations and institutions cre-

ated by, 63; conspiratorial framing of, 176; coordinated actions interaction between, 127, 132–33; ECtHR litigation of, 215–16; funding for, 124, 294n16; gender ideology perceived threat, 17; Global South, 180; INGOs created by, 81–82; movement initiatives of, 234; personal interaction between, 127–29, *129, 130*; programmatic interaction between, 127, 130–32; on race, 293n2, 296n6; rights issues rejected by, 192; traditionalist universalism of, 212; traditional values term used by, 137; against transgender rights, 288n8

moral conservative advocacy networks, 12, 28, 91; American Christian Right involvement with, 97; double helix human rights model of, 56, 263–64; in Europe, 96

moral conservative agendas, PACE role with, 224

moral conservative digital presence, Russian, 126

moral conservative movements, 19, 25–26, 264, 288n7

moral conservative narrative, 15, 16, 20, 23, 31, 174, 265, 269, 271; capitalism romanticized in, 22, 195; communism rejection, 22, 191–95; conspiracy theories similarity with, 173, 177, 191, 203, 270; global master frame, 21–22; human rights language borrowed by, 11; IOs blamed in, 199–200; Komov promoting, 200–202; liberalism refutation of, 198–99; nationalism and faith differences overcome with, 264; PACE influence from, 223; Putin rhetoric of, 258–59; strategic deployment of, 190–200; WCF perpetuating, 176–77, 203, 296n3

moral conservative worldview, 104, 176

The Moralist International (Stoeckl and Uzlaner), 292n8

moral progressivism, 272–73
Mormon Church, 118, 294n15, 298n7
Moscow, WCF congress in, 112, 114, 117
Moscow Patriarchate, 143, 144, 153, 167; "On Administrative Violations in St. Petersburg," law, involvement of, 150; Department of External Church Relations of, 296n9; domestic violence legislation condemned by, 186; ECtHR involvement of, 156; Kremlin ideological arm, 151; Traditional Values and Human Rights UNHRC workshop reported on by, 211; Universal Declaration of Human Rights interpretation by, 210; Western Christian churches ecumenical relations interrupted by, 154–55
Mudde, Cas, 289n15
Muslim immigrants: Europe rejection of, 87; Hungary nativist opposition to, 166; Orbán speech against, 181
Muslims for Progressive Values, 269–70
Myrdal, Anna, 193, 194
Myrdal, Gunnar, 193, 194

Nashi (Ours), 222
nationalism, 6, 82, 178; of Fidesz government, 149; homonationalism, 24, 54, 289n14; moral conservative narrative overcoming, 264; religion fusion with, 79–80; white, 266–67
National Socialism, 65–66
nation protection claim, 178–81
nativism, 6–7, 166, 288n7
The Natural Family (Mero and Carlson), 118, 119, 192
natural family flag, 137, *138*
Natural Family journal, 100
Nazism, 65–66
NELFA. *See* Network of European LGB-TIQ* Families Associations
neocolonialism, 26, 179
neoliberalism, 22–23, 195, 197, 290n23

Neo-Marxism, Frankfurt School of, 201
Netherlands, 46, 48, 163, 291n3
network analysis, 27, 30
networkers, key, 128, *129*
Network of European LGBTIQ* Families Associations (NELFA), 238–39
Neumann, Iver B., 163
New Family Structures Study, 227
Nexon, Dan, 299n3
NGOs. *See* nongovernmental organizations
Nicht der Homosexuelle ist Pervers, sondern die Situation in der er lebt (*The Homosexual is Not Perverse, but the Society in which He Lives*), 45
Nicosia, Cyprus, 1, 234, 266
No Campaign, 246, *246*
nongovernmental organizations (NGOs), 28, 84, 86, *129*, 207; American Christian Right, 70, 71, 72, 90; CitizenGo campaigns organized with, 103–4; double helix human rights model regarding, 71, 268; funding for, 126–27; PNV summit participation of, 110; rival global networks of, 14; Russian, 83, 142; transnationalization of, 82–83; UN pro-family, 71, 82; WCF associated with, 83, *114*
nonviolence, 190
Nordic states, 66
norm brokers, 40, 48, 291n5; ACCEPT Association, 42, 43; social movement organizations as, 44–47; in SOGI rights norm change model, 41, *42*, *43*
norm entrepreneurship, *116*, 127, 156–57, 211
norms: contending, 44; human rights, 56, 130, 300n8; international, 38; moral conservative mobilization of, 89, 90, 96, 97, 125; polarization of, 10, 262
norms, SOGI right, 48; change model of, 41–43, *43*, 44; diffusion of, 38–39, *43*; social movements spreading, 39–41; in world politics, 37–41

Norris, David, 47
Novak, Katalin, 145, 187–88

OAS. *See* Organization of American States
Obama, Barack, 134, 180, 243
Obamacare, 188
Obergefell v. Hodges, 8, 290n27, 299n8
Ohio University, 193
Okafor, Teresa, 87
oligarchs, Russian, 125, 143
"On Administrative Violations in St. Petersburg" law, 150
Open Society Foundations, 29, 149
Orbán, Victor, 16, 145, 184; communists and progressive liberals equated by, 19; Fidesz government under, 137, 148, 149; homosexuality and pedophilia conflated by, 146; Hungarian Child Protection Act employed by, 181
Ordo Iuris, 98, 109
Oreja, Jaime Major, 109–10, 182, 228
Organization of American States (OAS), 50
Orthodox Christian churches, 30, 77, 164, 270, 295n6; Carlson, Allan, on, 121; Catholic Church split from, 118; Georgian, 118, 119, 185. *See also* Russian Orthodox church
Ours (Nashi), 222
Outright International, 40

PACE. *See* Parliamentary Assembly of the Council of Europe
Palestine, 267
Parliamentary Assembly of the Council of Europe (PACE), 206, 215, 217, 298n12; amendments at, 218–20; resolutions at, 218–19, *219*, 220–23; Volontè declarations proposed at, 224
participant observation, 27, 29, 239
paternal Catholic modernism, 69, 76–77, 157

Paternotte, David, 26, 35, 229; *Anti-Gender Campaigns in Europe* by, 96, 157; on anti-gender movements, 290n24; on gender ideology, 16–17, 58
Patriarchal Commission for the Family, Protection of Motherhood and Childhood, 126, 154
Patriarch Ilia. *See* Ghudushauri-Shiolashvili, Irakli
Patriarch Kirill. *See* Gundyaev, Vladimir Mikhailovich
pedophilia, homosexuality conflated with, 146
Peña Nieto, Enrique, 295n21
Pence, Mike, 15, 166, 226
personal interaction, between moral conservative actors, 127–29, *129*, 130
Person of the Year, *Advocate*, 244
Perversion for Profit documentary, 226
Petö, Andrea, 149–50
pink-washing, 241, 298n6
PIRC. *See* Public Interest Research Center
PIS. *See* Law and Justice party, Polish
PMC. *See* politicized moral conservatism
PMC networks. *See* politicized moral conservative advocacy networks
PMCs. *See* politicized moral conservatives
PMC TANs. *See* politicized moral conservative Transnational Advocacy Networks
PNV. *See* Political Network for Values
Põim, Maari, 21, 58, 59
Poland, 40, 42, 136, 145, 184, 244, 299n12; *Bączkowski and Others v. Poland*, 139; Catholic Church in, 79–80, 150; faith-based campaign in, 245; KPH in, 234, 235, 236; *Solidarność* in, 68; Trzaskowski presidential campaign in, 272
policies: anti-SOGI rights TANs and SOGI rights TANs influencing, 8; COVID-19 pandemic, 240–41; in Europe, 66, 67; gender mainstreaming, 289n18; issues, 88; US, 13, 67–68

Polish Campaign against Homophobia (KPH), 234, *235*, 236

political homophobia, 15, 142, 150, 295n4

Political Network for Values (PNV), 30, 98, 109–10, 128, *129*, 145

politicized moral conservatism (PMC). *See* moral conservatism

politicized moral conservative advocacy networks (PMC networks). *See* moral conservative advocacy networks

politicized moral conservatives (PMCs). *See* moral conservative actors

politicized moral conservative Transnational Advocacy Networks (PMC TANs), 7, 25, 56, 133, 144, 265; business-politics-activism linkages, 124–27; Catholic aristocrats involvement with, 121–24; double helix human rights model of, *55*; INGOs, 96, 97; interdenominational characteristics of, 118–21; mobilization of, 80–84, *85*, 86–89; national and transnational, 81–84, *85*, 86; nodal organizations, 98–104, 105–12, *113*, 114, *114*, 115, *116*, 117; race regarding, 87. *See also* Alliance Defending Freedom International; CitizenGo; Global Home Education Exchange; Political Network for Values; World Congress of Families

Pontifical Academy of Life, 160

Pontifical Council for the Family, 120, 159

populism, 18, 87, 289n15

Power, Samantha, 268

von Praunheim, Rosa, 45

Presidential Young Artists, Putin speech to, 258

Pride parades, 2, 45, 257, 260

pro-choice activists, 298n1

programmatic interaction, between moral conservative actors, 127, 130–32

prohibition, 267

pro-life movement, 28, 63, 89, 298n1

Promotion and protection of human rights draft UNHRC resolution, 208, *208*

Promotion of Proper Human Sexual Rights and Ghanaian Family Values Bill, 300n5

pro-natalism, 296n4

propaganda: Russian anti-gay propaganda law, 139–40, 146, 184, 261; Russian Orthodox Church claims of, 152; of WCF, 100–101

Proposition 8, in California, 243, 271–72, 298n7

Protection of the Family UNHRC resolution, 212, 213

"The protection of the rights of parents and children belonging to religious minorities" (Ghiletchi), 220–21

Protestant Church, 66, 292n6

Pro Vita, 189

Pro Vita & Famiglia, 83

Pro Vita Generazione Familia, 184

Przekaźmy Sobie Znak Pokoju (Let us offer each other a sign of peace), 234, *235*, 238

Puar, Jasbir K., 292n11

Public Eye, 57

Public Interest Research Center (PIRC), 237–38

pundits, conservative, 229

Putin, Vladimir, 3, 142, 144, 146; moral conservative narrative rhetoric of, 258–59; Russian Ukraine invasion justifications of, 259, 272; on sanctions, 139; traditional values rhetoric of, 258, 261, 289n16; US embassy rainbow flag mocked by, 134; Valdai International Discussion Club speech of, 18

race, 87, 293n2, 296n6

racial equality, racism rival organizing against, 266–67

INDEX | 355

racism, 87, 266–67
rainbow families, 239, 245; alliances promoting, 241–42; COVID-19 pandemic policies overlooking, 240–41; Maltese campaign highlighting, 244
rainbow flag, 134, 137, 147, 202, 261, 295n3
Rao, Rahul, 115
Räsänen, Päivi, 217
Reclaiming Family Values Conference, 1, 29, 31, 234, 238, 266
red communist flag, 202
Red Scare, 60, 88
Red War on the Family (Ryan), 60–61
Regnerus, Mark, 226–27
religion, 79–80, 181–83
Religion and Neo-Nationalism in Europe (Höhne and Meireis), 96
Religion in an Expanding Europe (Byrnes and Katzenstein), 79
religious communities, 63, 183
religious freedom, 75–76, 103, 182
religious revival: American Christian Right regarding, 80; in Central and Eastern Europe, 76, 90; after Cold War, 76–80; in former communist bloc, 76, 78, 79; in Hungary, 166
religious traditionalists, 7
reproductive rights, 189, 199
"Restoring the Natural Order" manifesto (Agenda Europe), 131
revolutionaries, and counterrevolutionaries, 200–204
Revolutionary Armed Forces of Colombia peace deal. See *Fuerzas Armadas Revolucionarias de Colombia* (FARC)
Rights of the child UNHRC resolution amendments, 209
right wing, global, 12
rival transnational advocacy networks (rival TANs), 7, 8, 9, 10, 11, 29, 54, 55, 55, 56, 91, 233, 266. *See also* double helix human rights model

ROC. *See* Russian Orthodox Church
Rockford Institute, 100, 294n7
Roe v. Wade, 26, 268–69, 290n27
Romania, 42–43, 159
Romer v. Evans, 292n4
Roth, Claudia, 42
Rowling, J. K., 139, 258
Russia, 4, 13, 30, 58, 68, 72, 135, 180; academia in, 227; anti-abortion conscientious objection initiative in, 188; anti-gay propaganda law in, 139–40, 146, 184, 261; CitizenGo, 144; Communist Revolution in, 61; in Council of Europe, 139, 140, 141, 156; Crimea annexed by, 112, 167; Dreher on, 165–66; under ECtHR, 139, 140, 141; embassy protests in, 132–33; *Federal National Security Strategy* of, 259; GHEX conference in, 106–7; heteronormative internationalism in, 295n4; homosexuality in, 139–40, 141–42, 143, 150; Hungary relations with, 136–37, 167; internet governance and freedom of expression in, 222; Islam in, 87; missionaries in, 77; moral conservative digital presence in, 126; NGOs, 83, 142; oligarchs in, 125, 143; Orthodox Church, 118, 119; political homophobia of, 150; revolution in, 62; sanctions against, 139, 164; transgender rights crackdown of, 261; UN diplomats from, 211; UNHRC involvement of, 156–57, 206, 209, 210–11, 213–14; WCF in, 112, 114, 117, 293n4, 296n2; Western Christian Right identification with, 166–67; West split perception in, 179
Russian Center for Family Policy, 186
Russian Duma, 139–40, 142, 150
Russian Institute for Demographic Research, 83
Russian Olympics, in Sochi, 175

356 | INDEX

Russian Orthodox Church (ROC), 118, 119, 126, 136, 186–87, 213, 292n8, 295n2, 295n6; On Administrative Violations in St. Petersburg law support of, 150; alliance building of, 167; American Christian Right influencing, 153–54; Catholic Church relations with, 137, 155–56, 159, 162; norm entrepreneurship of, 156–57; Russian UN diplomats, cooperation with, 211; traditional values content provided by, 143, 261; Universal Declaration of Human Rights interpretation by, 210. *See also* Moscow Patriarchate; Social Doctrine

Russian Ukraine invasion, 32, 138–39, 163–64, 165, 209, 257–58, 299n2; Edenborg on, 262–63; Malofeev support of, 125–26; Putin justifications for, 259, 272

Ryan, Erica J., 60–61

Saint Andrew the First-Called Fund, 126

Saint Basil the Great fund, 125, 126, 222

Saints Peter and Fevronia Foundation for the Support of the Family and Demography, 83

Salaam, 183

same-sex marriage, 88, 260; American National Organization for Marriage mobilization against, 100; Catholic Church opposition to, 158; in Mexico, 295n21; Pence against, 226; referenda against, 159; in Ukraine, 261. *See also* marriage equality

same-sex partnership rights, 36, 290n27, 291n3

same-sex unions: Congregation of Faith response to, 161; ILGA-Europe discussion of, 251; Ukraine bill legalizing, 272

sanctions, 15, 48; against Hungary, 166; Putin on, 139; against Russia, 139, 164

Sanctity of Motherhood, 126, 189

Sanderson, Bec, 237

Saudi Arabia, UNHRC resolution no-action motion by, 212

Scientific Humanitarian Committee (Wissenschaftlich-humanitäres Komitee), 45

Selun, Bruno, 238

sensate culture, 226

sex, 183–84, 220

sexual abuse scandals, in Catholic Church, 162

sexual orientation and gender identity (SOGI), 3, 287n2. *See also* SOGI rights movement

sexual revolution, 61, 62, 68, 201

Shall the Religious Inherit the Earth (Kaufmann), 123

Shamolina, Irina, 122, 125

Shishkov, Andrey, 119

Shlegel, Robert, 221–22, 298n13

Singapore, 266

Sinno, Hamed, 287n5

Slavic Center for Law and Justice, 72

Slovakia, 159, 243–44

Slovenia, 159, 288n9

Smirnov, Dmitry, 126

Sochi, Russian Olympics in, 175

social capital, WCF personal interactions building, 129–30

Social Doctrine, 144, 151; homosexuality denounced in, 152; on intersex persons, 296n7; transgender identities condemned by, 153

social movements, 39–41, 44–47, 57–58

society moral conservatism protection claim, 188–90

SOGI. *See* sexual orientation and gender identity

SOGI rights. *See specific topics*

SOGI rights movement, 5, 7, 24, 28–29, 190, 255, 273; alliances, 241–42; family redefined by, 239–46, 246, 247; family values reclaimed by, 238, 239; funding for, 298n3; innovations, 237–42;

language adaptation of, 31; responses of, 234, 235, 236–37; strategic litigation used by, 297n8 (chap. 6)

SOGI rights Transnational Advocacy Networks (SOGI rights TANs), 5, 8, 55, 56, 254

Solidarność, 68

Sorokin, Pitirim, 61–62, 226

Soros, George, 107, 168, 181, 201, 293n2

Soule, Sarah A., 40, 63, 128, 190

Southern Poverty Law Center, 179–80

Soviet Union, former, 76, 77, 90, 117, 142; conspiracy theories in, 175; Russian Orthodox Church revival in, 151; Russian soft diplomacy in, 167; WCF attendees from, 191

Special Synod of Bishops, 69

spiral human rights model, 4, 9, 10, 40, 55, 56, 233, 266, 268

Stalin, Joseph, 201, 297n8

State Department, US, 134, 289n14

Stern, Jessica, 4, 272

Stoeckl, Kristina, 2, 14, 196, 292n8

Stonewall Inn riots, 45

St. Petersburg, 140, 144, 150, 181–82

Strasbourg effect, 139, 140

"A Strong Nation is Built on Intact and Happy Families" speech (Novak), 187–88

Strube, Sonja A., 96, 157

Supreme Court, US, 188; *Advocate* on, 299n9; *Masterpiece Cakeshop v. Colorado Human Rights Commission*, 74, 75, 109; *United States v. Windsor*, 244, 299n8

surrogacy, 175, 184

Sweden, 193–94, 217

Swedish Peace and Arbitration Society, 165

Swindle, Jeffrey, 293n6

symbolic glue, gender ideology, 21, 59

symbolism, 137

Synod on the Family, 158, 160–61

TANs. *See* Transnational Advocacy Networks

Tarrow, Sidney, 16, 39, 73, 80

Tbilisi, WCF, 2, 95, 118, 167, 174, 185–86, 297n7 (chap. 5); anti-abortion theme at, 189; Brandi speaking at, 130; Gessen report on, 270, 296n5; Vazadse claim of nation protection at, 179

TERFs. *See* trans-exclusionary radical feminists

Thiel, Markus, 14, 49, 295n1

Thomas, Clarence, 268–69, 290n27

Tip of the Iceberg (Datta), 124

traditionalist universalism, 212

traditional values, 137, 178; Hungary identity bolstered by, 164; ILGA-Europe references to, 253, 254; Kremlin agenda of, 143, 144, 145, 163–64; Putin rhetoric on, 258, 261, 289n16; Russia use of, 206, 261; UNHRC resolutions, 208, 209, 210, 211–12, 213

Traditional Values and Human Rights UNHCR workshop, 211

trans communities, retrenchment against, 264

trans-exclusionary radical feminists (TERFs), 185, 298n9

transgender identities, Social Doctrine condemning, 153

transgender rights: moral conservative actors against, 288n8; protect women claim used against, 185; Russian crackdown on, 261; Trenham talk on, 95; US debate around, 184

transhumanism, 201–2

Transnational Advocacy Networks (TANs), 4, 25, 30, 39, 43. *See also* double helix human rights model; International Lesbian, Gay, Bisexual, Trans and Intersex Association (ILGA) Europe; rival transnational advocacy networks

transphobia, 5, 15, 265

358 | INDEX

Trenham, Josiah, 95
Trotskyists, 201
Trump, Donald, 2, 134, 147
Trump administration, 182, 289n14
Trzaskowski, Rafał, 272
tsargard.tv, 125

Uganda, "Kill the Gays" Bill in, 179
UK. *See* United Kingdom
Ukraine: Crimea, 112, 167; Donbas, 125, 257–58; employment discrimination protections bill passed in, 260; Huebner and Brown touring, 167–68; Komov on, 168, 175; pro-European political identity of, 271; same-sex marriage in, 261; same-sex unions legalized in, 272. *See also* Russian Ukraine invasion
Ulrichs, Karl Heinrich, 45
ultraconservativism, 51
UN. *See* United Nations
UNHRC. *See* United Nations Human Rights Council
United Kingdom (UK), 35, 47, 134, 147
United Nations (UN), 90, 205, 206–8, *208*, 209–14, 268, 291n4; homosexuality decriminalization declaration by, 51; ICSE equal rights demand to, 46; institutional consultative status to, 50, 51, 53; moral conservatism globalization impacted by, 69–72; Preparatory Committee, 57; pro-family block accredited to, 71, 82, 293n5; Russian diplomats at, 211; WCF blaming, 199–200. *See also* Universal Declaration of Human Rights
United Nations Human Rights Council (UNHRC), 13, 14, 31, 144; Advisory Board, 211–12; resolutions, 187, 207–8, *208*, 209, 210, 211–12, 213; Russia involvement in, 156–57, 206, 209, 210–11, 213–14; SOGI expert position created for, 208; universal human rights

standards and human-rights-skeptical positions at, 209–10
United Nations International Conference on Population and Development, Cairo, 17, 69–70, 157, 213
United States (US), 135; American anti-communism in, 60–61; anti-abortion conscientious objection initiative in, 188; Bill of Rights, 182; CitizenGo NGO campaign in, 104; conservative politicians, 15–16, 50, 166; court system in, 73; Don't Say Gay Bill, 147, 184; double helix human rights model in, 268–69; HSLDA, 82, 105, 106; Iraq invasion by, 181; Israel and Palestine regarding, 267; marriage equality in, 8, 243, 271–72; McCarthyism in, 262; moral conservatism in, 60–65, 292n2; Obama administration, 180; policies, 13, 67–68; race in, 296n6; State Department guidelines, 134, 289n14. *See also* Christian Right, American; culture wars, American; Supreme Court, US
United States v. Windsor, 244, 299n8
Universal Declaration of Human Rights, 99; GHEX article championed from, 130; Russian Orthodox Church interpretation of, 210; Russia signatory of, 139; WCF pro-family reading of, 192, 207
University of Austin, 228
University of Los Andes, 2
UN Special General Assembly, 57
Uribe, Alvaro, 294n12
Using Family as a Frame in Social Justice Activism guide, 238
Uzlaner, Dmitry, 196, 292n8

Valdai International Discussion Club, 18
Varga, Mihai, 149
Vatican, 60, 136, 160–61, 164, 295n2; American Christian Right allied with, 70; Cairo United Nations Interna-

tional Conference on Population and Development response of, 69–70, 157, 213; Congregation of Faith influence on, 158–59; gay lobby accusation aimed at, 162; gender ideology term coined by, 17; Italy anti-hate-crimes law intervention of, 182; moral conservatism globalization impacted by, 69–72; paternal Catholic modernism of, 157; Regnerus influence on, 227; WCF presence of, 120

Vazadse, Levan, 179

Vejdeland and Others v. Sweden, 217

Velasco, Kristopher, 8, 96, 263, 293n6, 294n16

velvet triangle, 3, 36

Verloo, Mieke, 229

Verona, WCF, 83

Vollmer, Christine, 120, 121, 122, 146, 160, 161

Volontè, Luca, 84, 128, *129*, 228; corruption case against, 298n14; as moral conservative norm entrepreneur, 127; PACE declarations proposed by, 224

Volontè Report, 83, 84, *85*, 100

war. *See* Russian Ukraine invasion

Watchmen on the Walls, 179

WCF. *See* World Congress of Families

Weiss, Meredith, 15, 142, 150

welfare state, 193–94, 195

Weltliga für Sexualreform (World League for Sexual Reform), 45

West, 179, 201, 270

Western Europe, 67, 189

WFPC. *See* World Family Policy Center

white nationalism, 266–67

Wiara i Tęcza (Faith and Rainbow), 234, 236

WikiLeaks, 101, 120, 294n8, 295n19, 297n7 (chap. 5)

Wilkinson, Cai, 291n10

Windsor, Edie, 244

Wissenschaftlich-humanitäres Komitee (Scientific Humanitarian Committee), 45

Wohlforth, William C., 163

women moral conservative protection claim, 185–87

women's movements, 268

women's rights, 5, 181, 189, 192, 199, 206

Woodward, Alison, 40

World Aflame (Graham), 226

World Conference for Women, Beijing, 17, 70, 157

World Congress of Families (WCF), 2, 28, 30, 31, 71, 72, 81, 82, 88, 99, 108, 206; ADF International involvement with, 109; in Amsterdam, 146; in Budapest, 126, 144, 145, 174, 178, 180, 182; Catholic aristocrats participating in, 121–22; Catholic Church presence at, 120; Central and Eastern Europe attendees at, 191; in Chisinau, 167, 183–84, 197, 199, 202; CitizenGo influence from, 101; communism and capitalism conflation of, 197; demographic decline discussed at, 188–89; Eastern European partners with, 179; Europe organizing of, *113*, 117; GHEX connection to, 105; global anti-SOGI rights network role of, 98, 101, 111; government sponsorships of, 100; home economy theme at, 195; interdenominational characteristics of, 118–21; Komov involvement with, 207; in Madrid, 202, 294n8; members of, 114–15; moral conservative narrative perpetuated by, 176–77, 203, 296n3; moral conservative norm entrepreneurs attending, *116*; NGOs associated with, 83, *114*; Okafor attending, 87; personal interactions at, 128–29, *129*, 130; pro-family agenda of, 192–93; recruitment and propaganda of, 100–101; in Russia, 112, 114, 117, 293n4, 296n2; Sorokin influence on, 62;

360 | INDEX

World Congress of Families (WCF), (*cont.*) UN blamed by, 199–200; Universal Declaration of Human Rights pro-family reading by, 192, 207; in Verona, 83. *See also* International Organization for the Family; Komov, Alexey; Tbilisi; WCF

World Family Policy Center (WFPC), 71

World League for Sexual Reform (Welt-liga für Sexualreform), 45

World Summit in Defense of Persecuted Christians, 144

World War, Second, 65–66

Wunderlich v. Germany, 74

Yakunin, Vladimir, 125, 126, 143, 144

Yakunina, Elena, 126, 295n19

Yes Campaign, 1, 238, 243, 245–46, *246*

Yogyakarta Principles (YP), 48

Zelensky, Volodymyr, 261

ABOUT THE AUTHORS

PHILLIP M. AYOUB is Professor of International Relations in the Department of Political Science at University College London. His research bridges insights from international relations and comparative politics, engaging with literature on transnational politics, sexuality and gender, norm diffusion, and the study of social movements. He is the award-winning author of *When States Come Out: Europe's Sexual Minorities and the Politics of Visibility* and co-editor of *LGBT Activism and the Making of Europe: A Rainbow Europe?* with David Paternotte and *Leading from Behind: Gender Equality in Germany During the Merkel Era* with Petra Ahrens and Sabine Lang. He has also contributed to other journals and edited volumes.

KRISTINA STOECKL is Professor of Sociology in the Department of Political Science at LUISS, Rome. Her research fields are political sociology and sociology of religion with a special focus on Eastern Orthodox Christianity and Russia. She is the author of several books, including *The Moralist International: Russia in the Global Culture Wars* co-authored with Dmitry Uzlaner, and *The Russian Orthodox Church and Human Rights*.

Milton Keynes UK
Ingram Content Group UK Ltd.
UKHW021603250524
443121UK00001B/3